Books are to be returned on or before
the last date below.

2 7 NOV 2003

2 8 JAN 2004

LIBREX —

Temples of Mammon
The Architecture of Banking

No doubt, there are those who judge of a bank to a certain extent by its externals. A large and costly building is an assurance to some minds of corresponding wealth and stability within. A massive structure, bristling at all points with arrangements in iron, crowned with javelin tops, for the impalement as it might seem of would-be burglars, will appear to many persons a more secure place to deposit money, than a building ... of humbler pretensions; which was somebody else's shop and dwelling-house in the last generation, and would seem designed rather to invite burglarious attacks than to defy it.

George Rae (*The Country Banker* (London, 1885), p. 172)

Temples of Mammon
The Architecture of Banking

John Booker

Edinburgh University Press

© John Booker 1990

Edinburgh University Press
22 George Square, Edinburgh

Distributed in North America
by Columbia University Press
New York

Set in Linotron Ehrhardt by
Nene Phototypesetters Ltd, Northampton
and printed in Great Britain at
The University Press, Cambridge

British Library Cataloguing
    in Publication Data
Booker, John
    Temples of mammon; the
    architecture of banking.
    1. Great Britain. Banks.
    Architectural features, history
    I. Title
    725.24

    ISBN 0–7486–0198–8

Contents

Introduction

From the ranks of claimants to the title of the second-oldest profession in the world, bankers would not wish to be excluded. Classical Rome and even the early civilisations of Babylon and Nineveh have revealed evidence of a banking function, while the Chinese Ming Dynasty is credited with the invention of the banknote.

The architectural style of the period when the profession reached maturity was an inspiration for Victorian copyists. The date of this period has been variously interpreted. Sir Nikolaus Pevsner, for example, in his *History of Building Types*, pointed to the fourteenth and fifteenth centuries as the great eras of the Italian merchant bankers; this helps to explain the popularity of the Italian style for the premises of their nineteenth-century British successors. Gilbert Scott, on the other hand, had argued for the use of Gothic on grounds of the profession's medievalism. A third viewpoint was taken by the North Americans, who reckoned Greek temples were the earliest buildings associated with banking, the opisthodomos having been used as a repository for state money. This accounts for the neo-Greek tradition long popular with American bankers.

It is, of course, difficult to distinguish between designing by conscious association and designing in the wake of a general revivalist vogue. There are other complications as well. Similarity of style between buildings of a roughly comparable nature, such as the head offices of banks and insurance companies, may have been the result of a coincidence of views as to what was inherently suitable to express a broad concept of commercialism. Or perhaps it was just the favourite style of a shared architect. Undoubtedly, there is a case for a comparative study of commercial architecture in which the relationship between banking, insurance, and other broadly financial institutions, can be examined. But equally there are grounds for a study of banking architecture in its own right, for reasons stronger than the relative antiquity of the banker's profession.

More important to the architectural historian than the analysis of function, is the comparison of its exercise at the periphery of business. No insurance company, for instance, could or can match the bankers' network of provincial outlets in purpose-built premises. Today, the comparison is closer, in terms of offices, between banks and building societies, but the latter have nothing like the same historical depth or complexity of evolution. In some ways, a closer parallel is with brewing. Bankers and brewers have long competed for corner sites, and in both institutions the counter has been the basic element of interior division. It is interesting to read an article in the *Architects' Journal* of 1951 (Vol. 114, p. 487) comparing the *Festival* inn at Lambeth with a new Martin's Bank at Longton in Staffordshire: 'the bar appears to wish to be as respectable as a bank: the bank as hospitable as the bar.'

The similarity goes even deeper. The modern professions of banking and brewing are headed by a handful of corporations each resulting from decades of amalgamations, rooted in the nineteenth century. Once, every country town had its bank and its brewery — in some places, like Margate and Saffron Walden, controlled by the same family. Although in other and obvious respects the professions are different, an analysis of branch banks, *per se*, would be as valid and coherent as a study of local breweries.

The scope of the present book begins with the early eighteenth century when the London goldsmiths were evolving as private bankers. In country areas, private bankers often combined banking with some other trade or business, but later acquired distinct recognition and an unwritten code of conduct. From 1826 in England, but earlier in Scotland, bankers could form joint-stock companies. These were later to take over the private banks and establish branch networks, adding a new dimension to the techniques and traditions of the profession.

The very existence of a distinction between private and joint-stock banking suggests the possibility of differences between their places of business. Professor Reilly, for example, writing an article in the *Banker* in 1927, believed private bankers would have had more time for their premises and more interest in their design, 'a care and thought which the good architect only too eagerly reflected in his building' (Vol. 4, p. 166). The implication was that joint-stock bankers, on the other hand, built with inadequate emotion. There are also other areas of banking to suggest promising architectural distinctions. The Bank of England, having always enjoyed something of the prestige and authority of a Government department, is a case in point. Then there are the savings banks which had a quasi-philanthropic purpose to such a degree that the very name bank seems almost too liberal for their limited brief.

Because of these complexities, a study of bank buildings must be rooted in a knowledge of the development of banking. It is pointless to talk of a purpose-built bank without knowing the character of the institution which conceived it. Architectural history without an understanding of the client is like star-gazing without knowledge of the galaxies. At every stage, therefore, banks have been considered in this book against a background of professional development relevant to the age. Unfortunately, in the eighteenth century, no accurate picture can be formed of the full range of private banking. Early lists of banks, inconsistent in their initial selection of 'bankers', confounded partners with partnerships and branches with main offices. Furthermore, original banking records have suffered a colossal destruction through bankruptcy, mischance, neglect, and amalgamations. The deficiency is to some extent made up by a variety of extraneous material, mainly secondary, but not without calling into question the historical balance of the resulting picture. The banks whose premises are dealt with in the ensuing pages must be seen against the background of a vague but large number of firms who are little more than names in an appendix to the *Bankers' Almanac*.

Where documentation does exist, it is usually of no help in an architectural study. The consistent failure of nineteenth-century board and committee minutes to report discussion on the appearance of banks leads almost to the conclusion that joint-stock bankers were indifferent to their design. If this appears to support Reilly's assessment, mentioned above, it must be pointed out that records of private banking are no more helpful, particularly as, in the nature of things, they did not generally produce minutes at all. The absence in any surviving bank, except Lloyds, of records of a defined Premises Committee or Department before about 1920, necessarily transfers attention to the evidence of the architectural press. A possible lack of balance in this evidence is always in the researcher's mind. As for drawings, only the Midland, among the major clearing banks, has anything like a comprehensive series but these are not from in-house architects.

With these various points in mind, it has seemed sensible to undertake this book with three main objectives.

(1) To investigate bank design independently of any other commercial or financial institution.

(2) To see what differences existed between the styles of the various types of bank and the attitudes of the bankers, with particular reference

to the distinctions between the commercial banks and the savings banks.

(3) To assess the factors, arising both within and without the profession, which have influenced bank design.

It is implicit in such a wide brief that no systematic analysis of the design of British banks has ever been attempted. And yet the ubiquity of banks and their ability to enhance or mar the best urban positions suggest this analysis is overdue. The architectural historian has only to visit Leicester, with its remarkable assemblage of city centre banks, to appreciate the quality and attraction of styles which have at various times been thought appropriate. It is particularly important that planners and bank architects should have a datum from which the quality of uniqueness, or the virtue of rarity, can be understood or inferred. Too many good banks have been destroyed. It is also desirable that the enquiring mind of the layman, moved by such pathetic curiosities as a Victorian bank portal, tacked on to a supermarket in Romsey, Hampshire, should have somewhere to turn for satisfaction.

Acknowledgements

The origins of this book revert to 1979 when, as Archivist of Lloyds Bank, I mounted a public exhibition of premises' photographs, entitled 'The Face of Banking', to mark International Archives Week. Early ideas to capitalise on the success of the exhibition by a well-illustrated book came to nothing, but my enthusiasm was kept alive by a conviction that the subject, certainly unexplored, was also of some general appeal. With publication unrealised, my interest was channelled into research under the auspices of the Institute of Advanced Architectural Studies in the University of York, and the present book owes much to the thesis which resulted and the comments of the examiners.

In giving birth after this 10-year gestation, I could almost make a chapter of persons and institutions who gave antenatal support. Research has been mainly conducted at the Guildhall Library, the London Library, and the National Monuments Record, at all which institutions the staff have been unfailingly helpful. I would also like to thank county archivists, county librarians, and county and district planners throughout the country for considerable and sometimes most generous assistance. Branch managers of Trustee Savings Banks who, in the absence of a central archive, bore the brunt of historical requests, have also shown interest and patience and supplied valuable information unavailable elsewhere. I am much in their debt.

Certain individuals I would like to thank by name, at the risk of being uncharitable, by omission, to others. I am especially grateful to my supervisor at York, Dr Derek Linstrum, and to my colleagues, as follows, in clearing banks and other financial institutions: John Keyworth at the Bank of England; George Miles at Barclays Bank; Edwin Green (who features well in the Bibliography) at the Midland Bank; Richard Reed and Christopher Cove-Smith at the National Westminster Bank; Alan Cameron at the Bank of Scotland; and John

Orbell at Baring Brothers. Their assistance with documentary evidence and the provision of photographs is most warmly acknowledged. I would also like to mention valuable help from Angus Taylor of Doncaster over the Ulverston Savings Bank and from Ian Jackson of the Sydney Jones Library, Liverpool University, who supplied me with extracts from an early American periodical unavailable in London.

Two companies have been central to the realisation of this book. One is Trollope & Colls Management Limited who made a most generous grant which has been used to meet author's production costs. The other is my employer, Lloyds Bank Plc, in which I am particularly fortunate to have had the continued interest of the Chairman, Sir Jeremy Morse K.C.M.G., who opened the original exhibition in 1979. Among officers of the bank, my sincere thanks are due to the Company Secretary, Alastair Michie, for his characteristically supportive role before publication was secured; to Christopher Johnson, Economic Adviser, for the benefit of his advice and publishing experience; and to Iain Cheyne who, when General Manager of Corporate Communications Division, effected the happy introduction to Edinburgh University Press. No acknowledgement, however, should be construed to suggest that Lloyds Bank or any of its officers, or any other body or individual, is in any way responsible for any errors, opinions or failings in the present book: these lie at the door of the author.

Finally, the fact that the production of this book has been achieved alongside the proper distractions of a demanding job owes much to the efficiency and high standards of two most reliable helpers: Leo Maggs of Covent Garden who went to great pains with the artwork, and Mrs Barbara Chinnery of Maldon who typed an impeccable manuscript.

JOHN BOOKER
August 1989

Photographic Acknowledgements

Photographs are from the collections of Lloyds Bank, or the author, except the following, supplied by courtesy of:
Architectural Review: 70
Governor and Company of Bank of England: 1, 19
Bank of Scotland: 13
Barclays Bank: 7
Baring Brothers: 52
Birmingham Reference Library, Local Studies Department: 16

British Architectural Library, RIBA, London: 5, 38
British Library: extract from Parliamentary Papers; 26 (left)
Conway Library, Courtauld Institute of Art: 2
Midland Bank: 45 (upper)
National Westminster Bank: 34–37, 39, 40, 71
Royal Commission on the Historical Monuments of England: 27, 30
Trustees of Sir John Soane's Museum: 3
Trustee Savings Bank, High Wycombe: 32 ('before')
Williams & Glyn's Bank: 21, 44

List of Illustrations

Descent of Banks

The modern clearing banks have evolved from a complicated series of mergers which began in the middle of the last century. Their names have sometimes changed as a result of these mergers and continuity of identity can be elusive. References to banks in this book are by the name current at the time, with perhaps some slight rationalisation. To discover the evolution of any particular bank, the reader is referred to the relevant section at the back of any edition of the *Bankers' Almanac and Year Book*. It may, however, be helpful to give the following summary of the main avenues of descent of the largest English clearing banks:

Barclays
Incorporated in 1896 as Barclay & Co. Ltd from the merger of Barclay, Bevan, Tritton, Ransom, Bouverie & Co. of London with 19 other banks. Became Barclays Bank Ltd in 1917.

Lloyds
Established in 1765 as Taylors & Lloyds. Became Lloyds & Co., 1853; Lloyds Banking Co. Ltd, 1865; Lloyds, Barnetts & Bosanquets Bank Ltd, 1884; Lloyds Bank Ltd, 1889.

Midland
Began as Birmingham & Midland Bank, 1836. Became London & Midland Bank Ltd, 1891; London, City & Midland Bank Ltd, 1898; London Joint City & Midland Bank Ltd, 1918; Midland Bank Ltd, 1923.

National Westminster Bank
Three main roots:
   (1) National Provincial Bank of England Ltd, founded 1833.

Became National Provincial & Union Bank of England Ltd, 1918; National Provincial Bank Ltd, 1924.

(2) London & Westminster Bank, founded 1834. Became London, County & Westminster Bank Ltd, 1909; London, County, Westminster & Parr's Bank Ltd, 1918; Westminster Bank Ltd, 1923.

(3) Manchester & Liverpool District Banking Co. Ltd, founded 1829. Became District Bank Ltd, 1924.

The National Westminster Bank Ltd was registered in 1968 and operational from 1970.

The name of neither Lloyds Bank nor Barclays Bank carries an apostrophe in its strict (legal) spelling. In the case of Lloyds, evidence points to a plural form, there having been two founding partners of that surname. The form Lloyds' Banking Company appeared briefly in 1865 but the apostrophe has never reappeared. Today, mention of Lloyd's is taken in the City as a reference to (maritime) insurance, with which business the bank has no historical connection. In this book, neither Barclays nor Lloyds Bank, as joint-stock companies, is spelt with an apostrophe before the 's', although in the case of most private banks, bearing the surname of a founder, the apostrophe was traditional and has been used.

Chapter One

The Era of Private Banking

On 21 June 1773 Horace Walpole wrote to the Countess of Upper Ossory eulogising the nearby mansion of Osterley Park which Robert Adam was rebuilding for the owner, Francis Child. Walpole made a contrast between this 'palace of palaces' and the mere half acre of City land, meaning Child's Fleet Street bank, which had financed it. 'In short', he wrote, 'a shop is the Estate . . .', by which he meant the source of the wealth.

This brief and enigmatic extract holds two points of interest for the architectural historian. First, it shows concern for a fine house on the part of a professional banker — a concern which might have extended to his place of business — and, secondly, it introduces a particular definition of 'shop', part of the vocabulary of Georgian and Victorian banking.[1]

The word shop was originally a synonym for the bank itself, but it came to mean the banking-hall as opposed to the inner 'parlour' or interview room, which the *Illustrated London News*, in a flash of wit not unworthy of *Punch*, once described as a 'place to *take notes* in, and . . . a *drawing-room* to boot.'[2] Shop, parlour, and even the old term banking-house, a natural and accurate alternative to bank, are warnings that the modern concept of a purpose-built bank has no place in the domestic and commercial beginnings of the British profession.

The years before 1826, when legislation allowed the formation of joint-stock banking in England and Wales under certain conditions, are generally regarded as the era of private banking and this chapter considers banks conceived and, for the most part, executed to that date. In this period, virtually every bank was also a dwelling, usually for a partner and his family, perhaps for a manager, but sometimes also for clerks. The bank itself was usually no more than the ground floor. Having identified the kind of building which a banker felt appropriate for his place of business, the task is to trace the move to an architectural presentation: in other words, when the concept of a 'bank-like' façade, if not a bank-like building, superseded the original requirements of utility and domestic convenience.

Banking in Britain evolved and advanced in two different ways. In Restoration London it was the goldsmiths who developed procedures for deposit and lending, profiting by the windfall of Charles I's raid on the Tower of London in 1640. When this traditional repository for valuables became unavailable, the well-to-do relied increasingly on goldsmiths, *faute de mieux*. Although facilities for safe custody were sometimes little better than a stout iron safe, ingeniously lockable and much like a parish chest, goldsmiths enhanced banking technique by the conduct of 'running-cashes', roughly the equivalent of our current accounts, and by the issue of negotiable receipts against the deposit of plate and coin.

After the Great Fire, goldsmiths tended to settle in Lombard Street,[3] in houses erected with some grace and uniformity to the requirements of the Rebuilding Act. Pepys was well-enough impressed, recording a visit in March 1668 to Mr Colvill in Lombard Street 'where he is building a fine house . . . and it will be a very fine street.'[4] A later commentator, John Strype, was equally pleased: 'It is thoroughly graced with good and lofty Buildings, amongst which are many that surpass those in other Streets . . .'.[5] Private bankers had no need to move to another quarter. A house with a cellar below, a shop and parlour on the ground floor, and a sign outside, was as suitable for a self-styled banker as it had been for a goldsmith, particularly if he was one and the same man.

It will be seen later that banking in the country at large was far more a product of the Industrial Revolution. There are good reasons why the position in London should be considered before and apart from that elsewhere. First, the capital had a tradition of rudimentary banking a century before the rest of the land; secondly, it had the immediate influence and example of the Bank of England; and thirdly, the London bankers, by virtue of their long-standing influence and central position, had a wealth which might have been reflected in their premises.

The first purpose-built bank in Great Britain was erected by the Bank of England. Incorporated by charter under an Act of 1694, the Bank of England lent money to Government and developed a wider banking practice based on the elementary systems of credit exchange which had been developed by the goldsmiths. The early years of the bank were difficult and the ban on joint-stock banking partnerships, introduced in 1708,[6] was an attempt to increase its stability. But the bank, while lodging in Livery Companies' Halls, was in poor shape to fight off competitors for Government business like the South Sea Company, established in 1711.

When the 'bubble' burst and the bank's position became more secure, the directors decided to build. The chief office had to be in the City.[7] Land was purchased in Threadneedle Street in 1724 but because of the difficulty of determining leases, it was almost another 10 years before the new bank was erected. The design is credited to George Sampson, who, despite little experience, produced a façade 'which would not have disgraced any friend of Lord Burlington's.'[8]

In fact, this façade was on a building little more than a gatehouse leading towards the hall, accountants' office, and other buildings on a site nearly four times as long as it was wide (Plate 1). Sampson's achievement was to make the public elevation, only some 80 feet (24 metres) in frontage, suggest the dignity and aspirations of the bank as a whole. Belying its own narrowness, the gatehouse coupled elegance and symmetry with a sense of solidity imparted by the rusticated ground floor and the projection of the centre three bays. Through the rustication at keystone level, and continued at the same height through the entrance arches, ran a course of smooth stone. A feature of Italian Renaissance design, for instance on Palladio's Palazzo Thiene at Vicenza, the stone course on the Bank of England was designed by Sampson with a significant projection. The effect is that of a clamp constraining the stonework, adding an even greater feeling of security to the strength of the rustication. The first floor, believed to have been used as the bank's court room, retained with this function an importance befitting the *piano nobile* of an Italian *palazzo*.

The attribution of this stylish building to Sampson is not without its difficulties. The bank's court had appointed a building committee to choose from several plans submitted.[9] The committee reported back on 12 August 1731 that the plans of Mr Joynes and Mr Sampson were 'the most preferable' and the court appointed a further committee to make the final choice.[10] On 19 August members of this committee admitted that they could not agree and asked the full court itself to make the decision.[11]

The court decided two things: that there would 'be an Area to the Entrance into the House' and that Theodore Jacobsen should be thanked for his 'great pains and trouble'.[12] The court desired 'the Continuation of his Assistance'.[13] At no stage was Sampson officially announced as the architect and in no previous formal minute had

Plate 1. Sampson's Bank of England, Threadneedle Street, London, 1734.
Perspective.

Jacobsen been mentioned. However, the two names in the draft minute of 12 August 1731 had at first been written as 'Theodore Jacobsen and George Sampson' before the amendment to 'Mr. Joynes and Mr. Sampson.'[14] Clearly it had been a close thing, and Jacobsen's own unsuccessful design has survived.[15] The extent to which he modified Sampson's plan is unrecorded, but it was Sampson who was paid the 'surveying' fee in the end[16] and his name was apparently on the commemorative tablet.[17]

Sampson was succeeded as surveyor to the Bank of England by Sir Robert Taylor who, having first made his name as a sculptor in the City, established a clientele among merchants and financiers. It was a sign that the bank was in steady growth that Taylor was paid no fixed salary but allowed a commission of 2½ per cent on the value of property purchased for expansion and 5 per cent on the total of building costs.[18] Working in three distinct periods between 1765 and 1785, he built, among other additions, the 4 per cent reduced annuity office, rotunda, transfer office, and the quadrangle with the bank parlour. He also added wings, inspired by Bramante, either side of Sampson's façade. These were criticised by Malton[19] and later rebuilt by Soane, but Taylor's work as a whole impressed 'a foreigner of the first taste, M. de Colonne' who thought it 'with no exception but St. Paul's, to be the first architecture in London.'[20]

Building work at the Bank of England by Sampson and Taylor did not induce London's private bankers to follow suit. These men, at first opposed to the bank, set out on a road to development which tended to diverge from the path followed by the Bank of England. They accepted that they would lose their banknote issue, but there was ample room for the growth of other media of exchange and the development of customer and agency services. The Bank of England, on the other hand, was acquiring all the appearances of a department of state. The fine buildings probably had no greater influence on a private banker than to induce him to deposit some reserves there.

In the early eighteenth century the need was rather to establish a professional identity and develop an effective banking practice. As promissory notes became transferable to a third party,[21] as the legal rate for interest fell to 5 per cent,[22] and as paper money became widespread with the availability of Bank of England notes, so the private bankers created a framework of administration and procedure. Paperwork increased and was modified. A clientele had to be recognised, won over, and satisfied. The Earl of Lichfield preferred his 'old formes' to the new ones but Lady Carteret liked the idea of a pass-book.[23] In shaping his business, the London banker developed at the same time his personal characteristics, described by Daniel Hardcastle:

> . . . a man of serious manners, plain apparel, the steadiest conduct, and a rigid observer of formalities. As you looked in his face you could read . . . that the ruling maxim of his life . . . was, that he who would be trusted with the money of other men, should look as if he deserved the trust, and be an ostensible pattern to society of probity, exactness, frugality, and decorum. He lived — if not the whole of the year, at least the greater part of the year — at his banking-house; was punctual to the hours of business, and always to be found at his desk. The fashionable society at the west end of the town, and the amusements of high life, he never dreamed of enjoying; and would have deemed it . . . insanity to imagine . . . such an act . . . as that of a Banker's lounging for an evening in Fop's-alley at the Opera, or turning out for the Derby with four greys to his chariot, and a goodly hamper swung behind, and well stuffed with perigord-pies, spring chickens, and iced Champagne.[24]

Such a man would not have been ostentatious about his place of business.

The first new private banks in London were probably those erected in the 1750s. Sir Robert Taylor designed a banking-house at 70 Lombard Street for Sir Charles Asgill (Plate 2).[25] The son of a London merchant, Asgill had been a clerk in the bank of William Pepys & Co., and was taken into partnership by Joseph Vere in 1740.[26] He had been Master of the Skinners' Company in 1748 and was knighted during his shrievalty in 1752–3.[27] The building date was perhaps 1757 when Asgill was elected Lord Mayor for the ensuing year. Business considerations aside, a new bank would have been further publicity for the mayoralty which he marked by a particularly elaborate procession.[28]

Taylor had not yet begun work at the Bank of England but he was already wellknown in the City. He became a close friend of Asgill, designing his house at Richmond,[29] and his death in 1788 was the result of a cold caught at Asgill's funeral.[30] The banking-house passed to the brothers Nightingale when Asgill died, but they failed in 1796 and the building then passed to the Pelican Insurance Company.[31] It has since been demolished.

The ground floor façade of Taylor's bank was designed with a strength of classical features which contrasts with the restraint of the floors above. The Doric columns and entablature, with bulls' skulls and paterae in the metopes of the frieze, impart an elegance derived from Palladio. This attention to the ground floor was not unusual in

Plate 2. Robert Taylor's bank for Sir Charles Asgill, Lombard Street, London, c. 1757. Elevation.

the construction of substantial town houses and was displayed again by Taylor himself at Ely House, Dover Street. In the context of a private bank it had the useful effect of marking a division between place of business (ground floor) and dwelling-house (upper floors), in a sense isolating the practice of banking and restricting its commercial significance. This was to be the trend for most private banks in London and will be seen to be disappointing in relation to the rest of the country. Taylor himself appears to have made no other drawings for banks in the rest of his career.

The building of Asgill's banking-house confirmed the dissolution of his partnership with Joseph Vere. While Asgill stayed in Lombard Street, Vere joined with Glyn, Hallifax & Co., and moved a few yards away to 18 Birchin Lane, where new premises were apparently built in 1757.[32] A description of this bank, based on primary material, has survived, but no illustration. The architect is unrecorded. It was of four storeys, comprising shop, parlour and counting-house on the ground floor, kitchen on the first floor and Joseph Vere's dwelling-house, and lodgings for bank clerks, on the upper floors.[33] In other words, it was very much in the Lombard Street tradition.

Another bank of this decade was the one built by Messrs Drummond beside the newly aligned street at Charing Cross. It was designed in 1758, completed in 1760, and demolished in 1877.[34] A tradition in the bank that this building was designed by Robert and James Adam has been rejected by the bank's historians, who point out that James was then in Italy and Robert had only just come to London, and did not open an account with Drummonds & Co. until 1764.[35] Nevertheless, the building is of interest for being the first bank to run foul of a planning authority. The designs were unacceptable to the Westminster Bridge Commissioners because the proposed front was somehow 'different from the General Plan approved of . . .'.[36] The development of the site is a complicated story of acquisition and alteration, and there is better evidence of the Adam brothers' involvement in some reconstruction of 1777.[37] They certainly designed a ceiling, six mantelpieces, two chairs and two tables and, if their building work was not on the scale which certain drawings suggest it might have been, they were nevertheless paid £500 in 1781 'for alterations & repairs'.[38]

It is worth digressing here to mention another tradition associated with the Adam brothers — that they designed 59 The Strand for James Coutts in 1768. Bolton traced the story to Hilton Price, following Cunningham, and his own view was that the brothers did no more than 'alter and adapt' the older frontage to The Strand.[39] However, the bank's records reveal that the work was by James Paine, who was a friend and neighbour of James and Thomas Coutts and one of the executors of James's estate.[40]

For some 35 years after 1758 there appears to be no record of any wholly new banking-house in London. This may just be the result of a chance hiatus in the evidence; after all, it was the time when 'one begins to lose the impression of the City as a Philistine fort,'[41] when Acts were secured for a number of civic improvements, and when the Building Act,[42] in particular, gave bankers the chance to have what could have been, by definition, a first-rate building. But there were, in fact, good reasons for bankers not to build.

The banking-houses of the 1750s were exceptional: Asgill is shown to have been rather more flamboyant than his peers; Richard Glyn, in partnership with Joseph Vere, was wealthy and had been Asgill's fellow sheriff; and Messrs Drummonds had had a double incentive, being in competition with Coutts & Co. for royal business and being sited in a street which was realigned. The profession as a whole, however, was still innovating, consolidating, and developing new areas of business. The experimentation of the early eighteenth century had been superseded by attention to more sophisticated demands. For instance, it was the age of the Grand Tour. Travellers wanted letters of credit and when these were unsatisfactory a new means had to be found for drawing money abroad. The circular note — forerunner of the traveller's cheque — was developed by 1770[43] and correspondent relationships had to be negotiated with dozens of foreign banks in Europe and beyond. At home, in the Industrial Revolution, country banks were appearing quickly both ahead of and in the wake of economic expansion. These banks needed London correspondents to handle bills of exchange and supplies of gold and coin. The Bank of England, nicknamed by some the Bank of London,[44] took no interest in the country at large nor, for that matter, in the day-to-day work of the metropolitan private banks who set up their first clearing-house in the 1770s.

As business increased, the London bankers found a need to specialise, those in the West End continuing to serve royalty, aristocracy, and the landed classes, principally as banks of deposit and personal loan, while those in the City became increasingly banks of discount, serving merchants and shippers, and banks of agency, acting as the London correspondents of country colleagues. A little east of Temple Bar, a small but long-established enclave of banks was officially within the City but very much West End in outlook.

In administrative terms, the growth of business throughout London was overwhelming. Sites were outgrown and over-staffed. Banks which 50 years earlier had two or three principals and as many clerks, now had a payroll of perhaps 30. This phenomenon of growth, in the context of the Bank of England, has already been noticed: Sampson's buildings were adequate for 30 years, but then Taylor had to expand the site towards Lothbury and Princes Street, and further ground was added later by Soane until the bank covered 3 acres.

It is no more difficult to substantiate rapid growth in the realm of the private bankers. Coutts & Co. had reached 59 The Strand in 1739. No sooner, it seems, had Paine remodelled the bank in 1770–1 than it outgrew itself, and the partners were forced to lease property around William Street and John Street.[45] James Paine again made alterations in 1780–3[46] but within a few days another house had been added and two more were leased in 1799.[47] The early nineteenth century saw the addition of part of a Baptist chapel, an adjacent house (58 The Strand) and property at the west corner of John Street.[48] An even better example is Glyn's Bank. Within 30 years their new building in Birchin Lane, more a dwelling-house than a bank, was too small. Worse, they had lost their position in Lombard Street and it was expensive to attempt the return. In 1788 they moved across the road to 11 and 12 Birchin Lane, and merged the two buildings.[49] Other property nearby was leased in 1790 and thrown in with the rest in 1801.[50] In the next few years five more nearby houses were added and, at last, in 1821, they got back to Lombard Street, buying Nos. 66 and 67 which they rebuilt as one.[51] At Temple Bar, Child's Bank 'just grew . . . and, at various times, inns, alehouses and shops were drawn into the embrace . . . with programmes of alteration and rebuilding following in the wake of purchases.'[52] At nearby Gosling's Bank, adjoining houses both east and west of the main building were added in the eighteenth century.[53] Drummonds soon outgrew their new bank at 49 Charing Cross, taking No. 52 in 1766, other property in 1777, No. 50 in about 1825 and eventually Nos. 47 and 48.[54]

The apparent disinclination to build definitive premises was certainly not due to any lack of interest by private bankers as a whole in the merits of good architecture. Whatever the solemnity of the professional image, the evidence of association between bankers and fine buildings is almost overwhelming. It has already been seen that Child employed Adam at Osterley Park and Asgill employed Taylor for his house at Richmond. The Drummond family, as well as employing the brothers Adam, commissioned John Vardy and later William Chambers for work at Stanmore House.[55] Henry Drummond bought the famous Grange near Alresford in 1787 and owned it for 17 years.[56] Robert Drummond bought the manor of Cadland in Hampshire in 1772 and commissioned Henry Holland and Capability Brown for the mansion and gardens.[57] Colen Campbell designed Stourhead for Henry Hoare in 1722[58] and other members of the family had commissioned Edward Shepherd at New Hall near Chelmsford, Henry Flitcroft at Stourhead, and John Nash and Humphrey Repton at Luscombe Castle, near Dawlish.[59] James Paine did private work for James Coutts at Hampton in Middlesex.[60] George Basevi designed Bitton Grove, Teignmouth, for W. Mackworth Praed, while Basevi's master, Sir John Soane, created Tyringham Hall for William Praed.[61] The list could be extended.

The main reason, therefore, for the reluctance of bankers to build was the fact that growing demand for office accommodation made any one building too small in as little as 10 years. There is no evidence at all that bankers were prepared to surrender the living accommodation in banks for administrative purposes. And yet to the original shop and parlour they had to add perhaps a discount office, country office, stock office, town ledger office, transfer office and so on. A compromise solution was remodelling or refronting, perhaps disguising a medley of little offices behind a unifying façade. Even the benefit of this degree of expenditure could be short-lived, but many must have found it an acceptable gamble in an environment of increasing architectural awareness. Sir John Soane altered 56 Pall Mall for Ransom, Morland & Hammersley in 1791 and 62 Threadneedle Street for Grote, Prescott & Grote in 1818.[62] The elder Cockerell designed a bank parlour for Cocks, Biddulph & Co., at Charing Cross in about 1800.[63] The number of such alterations and refrontings which has passed unrecorded is probably large.

The answer of the later joint-stock banks to the problem of rapid growth was to build a head office of such monumental proportions that there was anticipated room for internal expansion over many years. Problems of capital and character aside, there were two powerful deterrents to building in this fashion in the late eighteenth and early nineteenth centuries. The first is that many sites were leasehold and the possibility of a 'bank-like' building in reversion may have suited neither landlord nor banker — particularly not the latter who would have been reluctant to spend too lavishly when he or his successors would eventually lose control of the investment.

The second deterrent was the ever-present risk of bankruptcy. An especially bad crash happened in 1772 when Neale & Co. went out of business. 'It is beyond the power of words' said the *Annual Register*, 'to describe the general consternation of the metropolis at this moment. No event for fifty years past has been remembered to have given so fatal a blow both to trade and public credit.'[64] The panic subsided, but not before false rumours of the imminent failure of Glyn's Bank, among others, had reached as far as Northumberland.[65] A wise banker did not lock up too many of his reserves in the bricks and mortar of his house of business.

Only in the last decade of the eighteenth century does this position appear to have changed. It was not a lessening of the problems of growth which brought this about but a complex business situation and a rather subtle change of attitude engendered by a wartime economy. The French Wars brought hectic and profitable business for the Bank of England (after the initial shock of the Suspension of Cash Payments[66]), but affected other London bankers inconsistently, less directly, and in ways they found difficult to predict. At first, increases in prices and rents, a rise in exports, and lack of restraint on the expansion of credit, combined to make good business. At Martin's Bank, for instance, overdrafts doubled and deposits rose by half.[67] But in 1803 the first major cycle of business was over and another boom, beginning in 1808, was short-lived.[68] West End bankers felt the loss of business with foreign correspondents as travel for pleasure and culture died away, and in the country generally the level of bank failures had never been higher.

In these heady and unstable years some bankers seem to have come to the view that a new building was more a show of stability than a squander of liquid assets. Soane's work at the Bank of England no doubt had a lot to do with this, influencing private bankers to an extent which Sampson and Taylor had never done. Succeeding Taylor in 1788, Soane virtually rebuilt the bank in three stages, extending the site to its present size, although very little remains of his work except the curtain wall.[69] It is interesting that despite the contemporary criticism of Soane's work in certain quarters,[70] the three private bank commissions recorded to his name[71] are more than the total for any other one architect before 1826. And yet the individuality of Soane's style, particularly the ornamentation later described by Cunningham as his 'besetting sin', [72] would seem at variance with the cautious and stolid character alleged to have been the hallmark of the London private banker.

Before more of Soane's work is considered, attention must be turned to the banking-house at 68 Lombard Street designed by George Dance, junior, for James Martin and built 1793–5,[73] a particularly bad period for the confidence of bankers. The number of differing illustrations of this building is such as to call into question not only the finer details of its style but also the numbers of bays and storeys.[74] It is clear, nevertheless, that this bank was in no sense an advancement on traditional designs and conformed with the Lombard Street pattern. That is to say, only the ground floor shop merited an architectural treatment and the division was thereby accentuated between place of business and residence — the two essential components of a banking-house.

The next new bank in Lombard Street was probably the one designed by Thomas Leverton.[75] His clients were Robarts, Curtis & Co. who had previously been at 35 Cornhill.[76] He exhibited the drawings at the Royal Academy in 1796 and described the building as 'then erecting'.[77] This was the first time a design for a private bank had been exhibited at the Royal Academy and it was not until 1838 that plans for an English bank were exhibited again.[78] For this reason alone, Leverton's building promises to have been important — perhaps the first unifying and 'business-like' treatment of the front elevation of a private bank. Two other facts suggest that this building was of more than usual interest: first, the position, 15 Lombard Street, was not a traditional banking site and it is likely, therefore, that Leverton had to design banking hall, offices, and rooms for safe custody; secondly, as he had already been responsible for offices for the Phoenix Fire Insurance Co.[79] and had designed their fire engine house in Cockspur Street (admired by Malton[80]), he no doubt had interesting ideas on what was necessary and acceptable generally for a commercial building. No illustration of the bank seems to have survived and its demolition was noted by *Building News* in 1861 without a murmur of regret.[81]

Away from Threadneedle Street, Soane's main contribution to the architecture of banking was the building designed for William Praed at 189 Fleet Street, in 1801[82] (Plate 3). Soane did what Taylor and Dance had not done, that is he extended an architectural treatment to the whole façade, masking the interior division between bank and living area by unifying external decoration and the use of round-headed windows in the shop, first floor, and attic. The panelled and fluted pilasters harked back to Soane's earlier work in the consols office and stock office of the Bank of England, while the fret-work frieze and decorative features of the cornice-balustrade found echoes in Soane's later rebuilding of the Bank of England's perimeter wall.

Praed called his new bank 'the most elegant and convenient' in the City,[83] and in this he was supported by the *Times*.[84] When Messrs Praed were later bought out, even hardened joint-stock bankers were in awe of the building,[85] although this did not prevent its later

Plate 3. John Soane's bank for Praeds & Co., Fleet Street, London, 1801. Elevation.

demolition. Praed came from a family of bankers with experience at
Exeter and Truro, but he was new to London and was not constrained
by the banker's image there. He needed the elegance of a good
building to catch the West End market, already well supplied with
banks, and he needed the convenience of Fleet Street to tap the traders
of Smithfield and compete with the City proper.

The bank was also convenient in another sense. The fact that the entrance was not in the middle meant that a customer, on entering the banking-hall, had his side and not his back to the window (ground plan, Plate 4). The counter in front of him could therefore be placed at right angles to the light. This allowed the clerks behind it a quality of vision which was not possible when they were sandwiched between the counter and the back wall,[86] although it will be shown later that working conditions in Soane's bank were far from ideal.

There is more evidence of the building and refronting of banking-houses in the 20 years after Soane's Fleet Street bank than in all the eighteenth century. Although it is tempting, therefore, to regard his work as a watershed, the incidence of information is so random and the state of banking in the early nineteenth century was so complex that unqualified conclusions are unwise. Furthermore, not all the new banks were built with Soane's flair. If Hilton Price is right, a banking-house at 60 West Smithfield was built for Messrs Pocklington & Lacy in 1808 and opened in the following year.[87] This owed nothing to Soane and there was little to distinguish it from neighbouring property; the bank of Young & Co. at 11 West Smithfield, founded in 1815, was no more exciting.

The most disappointing street, taken as a whole, was Lombard Street itself, where the lines of goldsmith-bankers' shops, fine by seventeenth and eighteenth century standards, were overtaken by civic improvements elsewhere in London and became a backwater of architectural restraint. When Malton paused in Poultry to describe the view to the east, he saw the Mansion House, the Bank of England and Cornhill but not Lombard Street.[88] When King William Street was built in 1830, slicing through the bottom of Lombard Street, the latter retreated still further to obscurity and was ignored by Tallis who preferred to draw Cornhill and Gracechurch Street.[89] By the middle of the nineteenth century Lombard Street 'had a most sober architectural aspect . . . dark and mysterious . . . .'[90] Perhaps Sir Robert Smirke's bank for Whitmore & Co., built in Lombard Street in about 1820, was more cheerful, but it was burnt out before 1867.[91]

Elsewhere in the City, and especially in the West End, the scene was a little brighter. In 1796–7 George Maddox was commissioned by Thomas Hammersley to make two inconvenient buildings into 'one large and substantial' banking-house at 69 Pall Mall.[92] The importance of this building is that Maddox made an entrance at each side, one door leading into the banking-hall, the other giving access to private accommodation above and behind. This was to become the usual arrangement for small banks later in the nineteenth century,

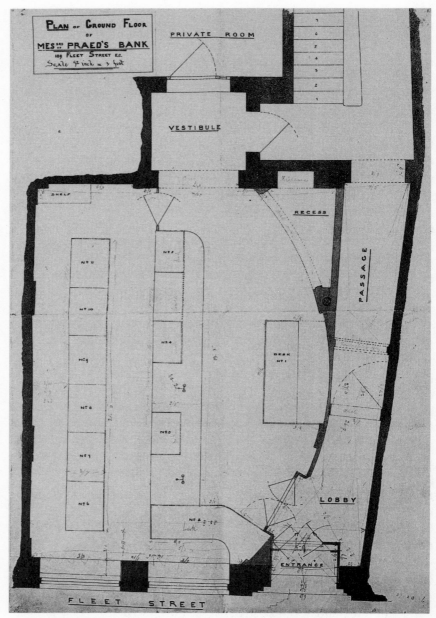

Plate 4. John Soane's bank for Praeds & Co., Fleet Street, London, 1801.
Ground plan (1877).

when one door often led to 'Bank Chambers'. In about 1808 Maddox rebuilt the front of Jones, Loyd & Co.'s Bank in Lothbury in a similar style pulling down the old town house, with its emphasis on the centre bay, and making what was probably a side entrance for the partner and his family.[93]

In another way, however, Maddox was traditional, perpetuating the obvious division between ground-floor bank and upstairs living quarters and making the bank like a shop in the most literal sense. The 10 or so years which separate his two banks brought no new ideas, learnt from Soane at Fleet Street, on the concept of a 'bank-like' building. And yet the fronts of Maddox's two banks and Soane's bank for William Praed were praised as one by 'Philalethes', a correspondent in the *Monthly Magazine* of 1817, who felt the virtues of smaller buildings were being neglected.[94]

The example set by Messrs Drummonds when they positioned themselves beside a road realignment in 1758, was followed by at least two other London banks in the early nineteenth century. The earlier was the bank of Hopkinson & Co. at 3 Regent Street, designed by G. S. Repton and built in 1819[95] (Plate 5); the other was the bank of Messrs Ransom at 1 Pall Mall East, designed by William Atkinson and opened in 1823.[96] That quite a wide feeling of the desirability of new premises had set in by the 1820s is shown by the decision of Messrs Greenwood & Cox to build a 'first-rate' bank with a 61-year building lease in Craig's Court (off Charing Cross), little more than a blind alley.[97] Even in the City, it seems, times were changing. Daniel Hardcastle described Messrs Fuller's new premises in Moorgate: '... one of the new Bank palaces ... shining with plate-glass, polished mahogany, brass railings, and bronze lamps, a glance at which would have half-driven its head and founder into Bedlam ...'.[98]

Whether or not this is just another instance of Hardcastle's purple prose, there seems no reason to view the post-Soane London banking-houses as anything more than disappointing, at least in the West End. Ransom's bank seems to have been a reversion to an eighteenth-century domestic façade and the appearance of Hopkinson's bank, in a particularly advantageous position by a newly built street, suggested nothing but respectability. In comparison with the unity and grandeur of composition achieved by the County Fire Office on the north side of Piccadilly Circus,[99] the bank was insignificant. It was a difference of ethics. West End banking was still an unobtrusive convenience for the upper classes, requiring in its execution a degree of restraint by which purveyors of fire and life cover were never

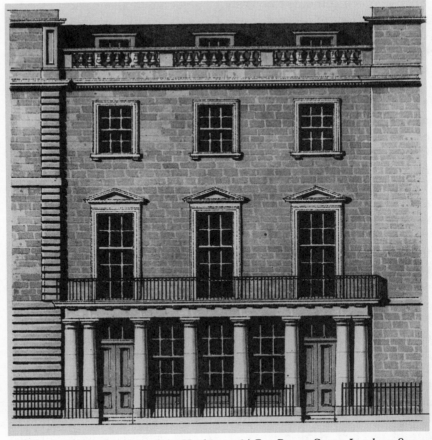

Plate 5. G.S. Repton's bank for Hopkinson & Co., Regent Street, London 1819.
Elevation.

inhibited. This state of affairs persisted well into the century. As late as
1854 one London commentator wrote that the West End private
bankers 'do not provide accommodation for the small shopkeepers
any more than they do for the working classes.'[100] The effect of this
was to make building for self-advertisement neither necessary nor
acceptable.

The least progressive of the London banks in the period to 1826
were the three near Temple Bar. 'Many of the old private banks . . .',
wrote the *Builder* in 1877, 'still carry on their business in the most
unpretending of houses; and perhaps the meanest is the dingy building
. . . occupied by the time-honoured bankers, Messrs Child and Co.'[101]

This was not the first attack on Child's Bank. Behind the weak disguise of 'Tellson's Bank' it had been described by Dickens in *A Tale of Two Cities* as 'very small, very dark, very ugly, very incommodious . . . the triumphant perfection of inconvenience.'[102] Any of the partners, he thought, would have disinherited his son on the question of rebuilding it. And yet this was the banking family who commissioned such fine work at Osterley Park.

Close to Child's Bank were the banks of Messrs Gosling (19 Fleet Street) and Messrs Hoare (37 Fleet Street). The latter, which had been on the same site since the late seventeenth century, survived through the first quarter of the nineteenth century, with a front which failed to distinguish it from the shops and houses on either side. Gosling's Bank had rather more pretensions but no particularly 'bank-like' qualities, with an emphasis on centrality which had become outmoded in the first decade of the nineteenth century. The irony is that in periods beyond the scope of this chapter all three banks erected impressive buildings. Hoare's new premises became the show-piece of private bank architecture as early as 1830, and Messrs Child commissioned a handsome new bank from John Gibson within a year of the above article in the *Builder*.[103]

It is appropriate now to consider the rest of the country where, as has been said above, banking sprouted and grew from a different root. Edmund Burke's contention that not a dozen bankers' shops existed in England in 1750 is thought to have been correct.[104] Perhaps only at Bristol were there early goldsmiths whose business diversified into banking.[105] More generally, banks were established in pace with the growth of the Industrial Revolution. The incentive came from two principal sources: on the one hand, from a new breed of industrialist needing money to pay workmen and buy raw materials, and also credit facilities beyond the basic arrangements which had existed since medieval days; on the other hand, from certain more passive and intermediary roles, such as those of receivers of taxes, lawyers, money scriveners, etc., who had natural facilities for the control or remittance of other people's money.[106] In other words, the impetus came both from the Industrial Revolution in its simplest form and more indirectly from the increased money which it generated in certain areas of society. Historians of banking place different emphasis on the role played by any of the basic divisions of industrialist, trader, merchant, remitter of money, or professional man. It would appear, however, that the drapery business, by which is understood the acquisition of wholesale yarn as well as retail selling, produced more bankers than any other one trade or calling — even more than brewing, perhaps the association which springs most readily to mind.[107]

A few examples will suffice to show the commencement of banking in relation to various commercial stimuli. At Halifax, Rawdon Briggs, well established as a merchant and manufacturer, called himself exclusively banker from 1807.[108] In the same town, however, the Rawson family continued as manufacturers after banking had commenced; their two concerns were kept distinct.[109] At Bradford, Messrs Peckover, Harris & Co. announced in 1803 that they would give up woolstapling and open a bank.[110] Also in Bradford, William Frobisher seems to have discontinued a ropery business when he turned to banking.[111] In Liverpool, William Clarke was known as a linen draper in 1766, a merchant and linen draper in 1769, and a banker and linen draper in 1774.[112] Three years later, there were directory entries for William Clarke & Son, bankers, and William Clarke, linen draper.[113] In 1816, Joseph Reynolds, a partner in the long-established Ketley Ironworks in Shropshire, gave up that business to concentrate full-time on the banking which he had practised as a side-line since 1805.[114]

Country banking has regional complications, of which two may be mentioned by way of example. In Lancashire, banks developed relatively late due to the general acceptance there of the bill of exchange, rather than the banknote, as a form of currency. Banks in agricultural districts tended to be centres of investment, taking savings from the lower middle classes and above, but those in industrial areas were mainly banks of loan. These facts, important in a study of the business aspects of banking, had little bearing in the matter of premises. Or rather, the overall level of evidence is too low to allow the effect of such fine considerations to be perceptible. However, three important points do emerge from this brief introductory discussion of country banking: first, there was no unity of architectural beginning, as there had been in the City of London, after the Great Fire; secondly, there was no common professional origin to suggest a like-minded attitude of restraint in questions of architectural presentation; thirdly, the country bankers had a wider clientele.

When a man considered that his banking activities were to become his whole career, or a very significant proportion of it, he had to decide whether his house, shop, office or manufactory was adequate. If it was not, he had the option of taking other premises on lease or building his own. The site of the bank was important. Whatever he did had to be attendant with some publicity. If he failed to attract enough custom at the outset, he might go out of business, or find himself straightening the bent nails in tea-chests to pass the time, like John Jones of Manchester, banker and tea-dealer.[115]

In the case of a partnership, the place of prospective business was often stated in the articles of agreement. For instance, at Bristol in 1750 partners agreed to purchase a 'convenient house' immediately,[116] and at Grantham in 1819 a firm decided to use the house of one of the partners.[117] Where a local newspaper had been established, a new bank was the occasion for an announcement, usually without reference to the precise nature of the premises. The community at large welcomed its first bank; an 'infinite Utility'[118] in business terms, it bolstered civic importance. The bank became a landmark. Following the establishment of the first bank in Manchester in 1771, the site was named Bank Street; the same happened in Bradford, Sheffield, Worcester, Ipswich and elsewhere. There are Lombard Streets in Newark and Portsmouth, for the same reason.[119] It is possible to conclude that a bank which was so much a part of the town would not have been insignificant in its appearance.

These considerations aside, noteworthy premises had a sound business advantage. An impressive building was a mark of solidity. The banker had to convince a prospective depositor that his service was better than the alternatives of hoarding plate or hiding coin. Few people would have entrusted money to a banker in a terrace cottage. As important as the place of business, was the evidence of personal prosperity. When a bank failed, the proprietor was liable for its debts and a country estate was visual evidence to an investor that, if the worst happened, there was a fund of money to be realised. The banker Viscount Stuckey agreed with a parliamentary committee in 1831 that when a banker had £6000 to £10000 a year in land, 'the farmers . . . and the persons who know that fact would prefer the paper of his Bank to all the Bank notes in the world.'[120] When Messrs Wentworth, Chaloner & Rishworth failed at Wakefield in 1825, creditors were comforted to know that Mr Rishworth had 'a nice old country house near Darton called Birthwaite Hall and . . . had built . . . Rishworth House in Wakefield as a residence for his eldest son, who was a partner in the firm.'[121] Wentworth, the senior partner, had extensive properties including 'the beautiful house and estate of Hickleton near Doncaster, the whole of which was of course brought into the market.'[122] Many other instances could be given. It is unlikely that a banker with an expensive private estate would have let himself down by doing business in poor urban surroundings.

Too much investment in property, however, for private or business ends, was injudicious. The banker had a dilemma: his real estate imparted confidence but it tied up capital and reserves which, in more liquid form, could save him from ruin in a panic 'run'. Perhaps Thomas Broadbent, a Sheffield merchant who turned banker in 1770, regretted the erection of Page Hall in 1773 when he became bankrupt in 1782.[123]

In brief, there are reasons for believing that most provincial bankers would have chosen to start business in good quality premises, probably purchased or leased rather than purpose-built, and in a central position. Examples are plentiful. Abel Smith, setting up first in Nottingham in 1754, bought two houses in the Market Place; for their Lincoln bank, begun in 1775, his firm rented and later bought the house of an alderman; at Hull, in 1784, another offshoot of Smith's firm probably traded from the Old Custom House in the High Street before moving to the well-known Wilberforce House.[124] Praed & Co. at Truro converted a school in 1774;[125] in Bristol, in the same year, Peach, Fowler & Co. opened in a former tavern.[126] A Palladian town house owned by one of the partners was chosen by Pitt, Bowly & Co. at Cirencester in about 1790.[127] At Manchester, Messrs Heywood took over the mansion of the Butterworth family in 1796;[128] and the Stockport & Cheshire Bank bought Underbank Hall, Stockport, in 1824.[129]

There is no doubt that a few country banks were purpose-built from the outset, but as the cost would have taken perhaps half of the capital at the disposal of a new partnership, the number was probably low. Nevertheless, there is a body of inconclusive evidence in that direction, frustrating in its inadequacy. At Tewkesbury and at Tavistock, late eighteenth century buildings survive which were apparently used as banks in that era.[130] Bankers at Sherborne illustrated their premises on a half-penny token issued in 1796.[131] Would they have been so proud of their building if they had not been responsible for its appearance? When the Allies reached Paris in 1814, would Messrs Bellair have flood-lit their bank in Leicester (on a site taken in 1807) if the façade was not something of interest?[132] Would the prosperous Gurney family have settled for less than a new building when moving to a new site in Norwich in 1779?[133]

The identity of the earliest purpose-built country banking-house will always be conjectural. One possibility is John Carr's house and warehouse in George Street, Halifax, designed for John Royds and dated 1766.[134] But there must be some doubt whether Royds was properly a banker. The formal practice of banking had not evolved by that date in the West Riding and Ling Roth has no record of any bank in Halifax before 1779. However, Royds's house was certainly used later as a bank by Messrs Rawson[135] and this may have given rise to the tradition that Royds himself had been a banker.

A more convincing candidate is the bank built in the Cathedral Yard at Exeter in 1769, in association with the hotel which became known as the *Royal Clarence*. These adjoining buildings still exist (Plate 6) and the hotel is dated 1769 in a panel above the cornice. The two buildings appear to have been a speculative venture on the part of Sir John Duntze and William Mackworth Praed, wealthy Exeter merchants with interest in textiles and, later, shipping.[136] Despite some later altera-tions, the main elevation of the bank retains a grandeur and harmony of design which shows that its appearance was not intended to be subordinate to that of the larger hotel. Indeed, the fact that the bank breaks forward, and has ground and first floors higher than the corresponding storeys in the hotel, points to a marketing flair which London bankers of that period would not have understood. In the light of this building, it is not difficult to see why William Praed (who was the son of William Mackworth Praed) felt able to depart from the traditional style of metropolitan banking-house when he commissioned Soane for the new premises in Fleet Street.

There is evidence of at least two new bank buildings in the next decade. At Sheffield in 1776, Samuel Shore conveyed to his son, John, two dwelling-houses. John 'forthwith erected . . . the first bank build-ing, pure and simple, that Sheffield had seen.'[137] In the same year, in Bristol, the proprietors of the Old Bank, founded in Broad Street in about 1750, intended to move on 1 May to 'the house erected for their business at the upper end of Clare Street . . .'.[138] In 1794 this bank moved again, to Corn Street.[139] By then another purpose-built bank had just been erected, at 35 Corn Street, by Tyndall, Elton, Edwards & Co. and much of the interior decoration has recently been found to be intact, although the building has been refronted.[140]

The pattern of an early change of premises after the first 10 or 12 years can be noticed frequently in provincial banking. But there is less evidence of the really serious problems of rapid growth which had troubled the London bankers from the mid-eighteenth century. There were two reasons for this: the first was that country bankers, by and large, felt it difficult or unnecessary to open branches in other towns and therefore the increase in their business was relatively slower than that of London bankers (who enjoyed a healthy growth, without branches, by virtue of the metropolitan position); the second was that

Plate 6. Former Exeter Bank premises, 1769 (i.e. 'Orchards', on right of photograph).

some of the business of the country banks was handled for them by the London banks. As a result, the country banks were unintentionally responsible for many of the problems of office accommodation which faced their London colleagues.

Two cases are known of businessmen erecting banks between their commercial premises and their dwelling-houses. The earlier example still exists, in King Street, Margate, and was apparently built in 1785 by Cobb & Co., brewers, when they added the business of bank-ing to brewing.[141] The other example was at Liverpool, where a bank was erected in 1807 between the house and warehouse of Thomas Leyland.[142] It is reasonable to suppose that other new bankers who entered the profession with good capital, spare land, and an established industrial or commercial concern would have done likewise.

The next developments in provincial bank premises were in the context of town centre reconstruction. At Ipswich, 'a spirit of improve-ment in building seems to have entered . . . in the year 1786, when the late C.A. Crickitt, esq., built the row of houses in Tavern Street called the Bank buildings . . .'.[143] Crickitt was a partner in the Ipswich Town & Country Bank which began business in that year. This appears to have been a commercial venture with the bank as the focal point and other property leased off as shops or offices. The term 'bank buildings' was not in itself a new one: it had been used to describe Sir Robert Taylor's building in London erected on land between Threadneedle Street and Cornhill. The name was also used later for the buildings designed by Sir John Soane on the south side of nearby Princes Street. But these were both speculative ventures by the Bank of England, the title implying no more than that the bank owned the freehold. Whether Ipswich was the first of the bank buildings actually to house a bank is unknown.

The earliest and best examples of contributions by banks to urban improvement were in the north of England. At Liverpool, Arthur Heywood changed from merchant to banker in 1773 and had premises in Castle Street by about 1776.[144] Ten years later the west side of the street was realigned and the houses rebuilt. Heywood & Co. took the central and outstanding property in the terrace. However, there was another very similar terrace built in Castle Street at the same time, and the building which served as a bank in one terrace had a counterpart of the same appearance in the other.[145] It seems improbable, therefore, that Messrs Heywood commissioned their own façade: the likelihood is that they took advantage of the best available position, close to their former premises, and the overall appearance was a matter for the corporation.

Heywood & Co. had outgrown this site by 1800 when they moved to purpose-built premises at the corner of Brunswick Street, which included a dwelling-house approached from Fenwick Street. The bank itself is now known as Barclays Bank (Heywood's Branch), 5 Brunswick Street, and the exterior has changed little[146] (Plate 7). The architect is unknown but this is nevertheless a most important building. The fact that the house was set back from, and at an angle to, the return wall of the bank, presumably emphasised that all three floors of the Brunswick Street building were used for banking. If so, then this fact, and the dimensions of the main building, bring to mind Sampson's Bank of England.

Stylistically, however, the two banks were quite different, having little more in common than the rusticated ground floor with string course — in the Liverpool case less obvious, but linking the entablature of the doorway with the bays at either side. What separates these banks, of course, is the absence at Liverpool of any applied Order on the upper floors. The tall sash windows of the first floor have plain architraves and the uncluttered ashlar wall surfaces contrast with the conventional fondness for column and pilaster. The result is a feeling of reserve and serenity, without losing the quality of strength. The return front has a strong vertical axis deriving from the central line of windows, blind in the upper floors, and chimney stack; but the disadvantage of this arrangement in a narrow frontage is offset by the house which, despite the altered building line, copies in its horizontal emphasis the architectural features of the bank. Also noticeable is the frieze formed between the string course, which terminates the rustication, and the sill band. This feature, balanced here by a broad course of stone beneath the cornice, became very popular with later bankers for carrying the name of the company in incised lettering.

It is possible to imagine a contemporary Liverpudlian looking at Heywood's Bank and finding it too grand for a shop or office, under-embellished for a public building, and in the wrong place for a town house. It would be nice to think that here, perhaps for the first time in Britain, the word bank came spontaneously to mind. Clearly, this was a bank and not a banking-house.

Another interesting bank in Liverpool in this period was that of Messrs Moss, Dale, Rogers & Co., originally timber merchants and general traders who had turned to banking in 1807. Completed in 1811, the square, robust building (Plate 8) was received enthusiastically

Plate 7. Heywood's Bank, Liverpool, c. 1800 (now branch of Barclays Bank).

by the press as 'A small but very fine specimen of Doric architecture ...'.[147] This compliment was reinforced by the newspaper with a reference to the bank's contribution to the wider cause of civic improvement: 'Such structures as these, in the middle of a great town, contribute greatly to the credit of, and of course to the benefit of, the place in which they are erected; whilst they reflect honour on the taste and spirit of their proprietors.'[148]

Moss's Bank, of which the architect is unknown, was reconstructed in 1864. In its unaltered state it might have had some influence on C.R. Cockerell in the design of his branch of the Bank of England in Castle Street, Liverpool, completed in 1848.[149] As well as the common feature of superimposed Doric and Ionic Orders, there is some similarity in treatment of the central upper floor windows.

A Doric bank earlier than Moss's was built at Chester for Williams, Hughes & Co., who were established in 1792. The date of this handsome bank at the corner of Foregate Street and St John's Street is given as c. 1815 in Broster[150] but can be brought forward from banking records[151] to 1802–3, when the capital of the bank was increasing rapidly, amassed from the industries of mining, copper smelting and

Plate 8. Moss, Dale, Rogers & Co.'s, Bank, Liverpool, 1811.

slate quarrying which the bank had been established to support. This was a bold departure from the black and white medievalism of central Chester. In view of the revised building date, it is likely that the architect was Benjamin Wyatt rather than Lewis William Wyatt to whom the building has been tentatively attributed.[152]

The grandest private banks of all in this early period were built at Manchester, although the town had been slower at first than Liverpool to develop buildings in keeping with its mercantile status. Perhaps encouraged by the purpose-built bank of Messrs Daintry & Ryle, erected in Norfolk Street in 1821,[153] Thomas Crewdson & Co. 'undertook the building of premises such as architecturally would have no rival among the Manchester banks.'[154] The site was in the new Market Street, being developed by Act of Parliament of 1821, and the bank was near the junction of Brown Street. Begun in 1824,[155] a year of good trading, the building was never occupied by Messrs Crewdson who went bankrupt in the sudden and widespread disaster of 1825–6. It was empty until 1829 when the Bank of Manchester took it over, and remained there until 1842.[156] The bank then became a shop[157] and was later demolished. There appears to be no surviving illustration and the architect is unrecorded.

The lack of illustration is the more disappointing as Grindon called the bank a 'pillared novelty'. In this respect, it probably influenced the premises of Cunliffe, Brooks & Co., built in 1827 to designs by Royle and Unwin[158] (Plate 9). This bank, too, has been long demolished, but clearly it was an impressive contribution to the townscape, much grander than the buildings on either side. The ground floor was unusually high, the four Doric columns suggesting the scale and extent of the banking-hall. The Ionic columns above, the same height as the Doric columns, were carried through two floors and there was a further attic storey above the cornice. It is probable that at least two of the floors above the banking-hall were residential, and that the bank also used the wings, above ground floor level, for business or private purposes. There seems little doubt, therefore, that this was one of the largest private banks in England at the time of its erection.

It is in the comparison of Cunliffe, Brooks's Bank in Market Street, Manchester, with Hopkinson's Bank in Regent Street, London, that the architectural precocity of the provincial bankers becomes really apparent. Both buildings were planned to occupy good positions in a major urban redevelopment. But whereas the London bank used the Greek Revival demurely, restricting it to the shop, the Manchester bank exploited it on the whole façade as a form of self-advertisement.

Plate 9. Brooks's Bank, Market Street, Manchester, 1827.

The fact that there was 8 years between them is of little significance. While the West End of London was still serving the personal needs of the upper classes, central Manchester was starting the aggressive search for new customers which was later to become a characteristic of the joint-stock banks. What London banker, moreover, would have flanked his bank by wings, let to shopkeepers?

Despite the sparse and random nature of surviving evidence, the overall picture is reasonably clear. No other provincial centre in England built banks like the ones at Liverpool and Manchester. The banker's desire to take advantage of an urban redevelopment was probably instinctive and common enough. At York, for instance, a bank was erected on the approach to the new Ouse Bridge, built 1810–20.[159] At Leeds, Thomas Taylor, enriching the urban scene with his schools and public buildings, built the Union Bank in Commercial Street in 1812–3.[160] Moxon's Bank in Silver Street, Hull, built before 1816, probably reflected the family's considerable status as merchants as well as the civic aspirations of the town.[161] Mansfield's Bank in Leicester, erected 'early in the 19th century', was later thought good enough to be a local branch of the Bank of England.[162] But these scattered examples are less than sufficient to prove that the attitudes of mind prevailing in Liverpool and Manchester were commonplace. In Birmingham, Bristol, Newcastle-upon-Tyne, Nottingham and Sheffield it was the next generation of bankers who erected the memorable buildings.

In Birmingham, and certain other towns, the Quaker influence may have had a restraining effect on bank buildings. Quaker bankers were in business against a background of growing interest in worldly considerations and it is possible that new premises were rejected for a long time on religious grounds. This would have been a spontaneous expression of principle rather than the result of a specific edict, although certain of the *Advices* issued by Yearly Meeting expressed a requirement for simplicity and economy in matters of trade.[163] It is particularly noticeable that the Quaker firm of Taylors & Lloyds (the root of the modern Lloyds Bank), established in Birmingham in 1765, had no change of premises for some 50 years, and even then the move was to nothing grander than a town house, later joined with a store and thrown into one behind a unifying façade.[164]

Throughout this early period the subject of building costs, interior decorations, furnishings and strong rooms is a vast, dark area barely penetrated by the light of surviving records. Even London is disappointingly obscure and the facts which are available show no pattern:

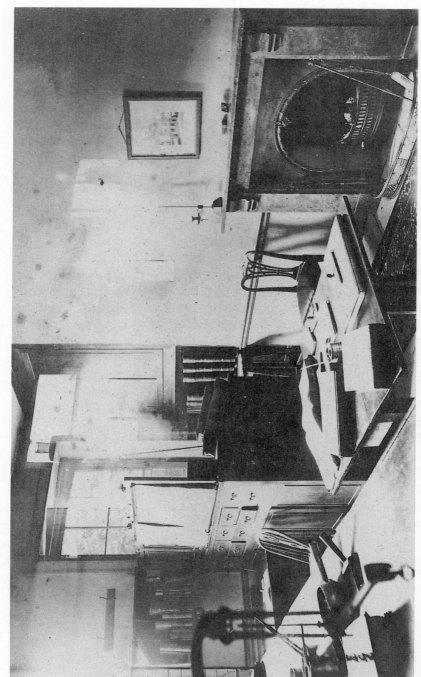

Plate 10. Newark Bank. Interior, c. 1880.

Sampson's Bank of England (1732–4) cost £13 153 7s. 9d.;[165] Dance's bank for Martin & Co. (1793–5) cost £8792;[166] the basic fabric of Greenwood & Cox's Bank in Craig's Court, Charing Cross (1820) was planned to be around £2500;[167] and Glyn's Bank in Lombard Street (completed 1824) cost £17692 6s. 9¼d. including furniture and fittings.[168]

As far as working conditions are concerned, the metaphor used above about dark areas barely penetrated by light acquires a new and literal significance. There is no doubt that the clerks' environment was appalling, particularly in winter and especially in London. Dickens's gloomy description of 'Tellson's Bank' has already been cited, and finds echoes in J.W. Gilbart's criticism of 'offices or rooms where twenty or thirty persons are breathing close together during the whole of the day, and gas lights are burning during the evening'.[169] Before gas was introduced, clerks who had to balance books by candlelight needed superhuman efforts to avoid error.

Despite a dearth of contemporary illustrations, the layout of the shop during the period of private banking can be deduced from a variety of later sources. An example of a rural bank, no doubt more scruffy than most, has survived in an early photograph from Newark (Plate 10). Here the air of informality must surely have led depositors to question the security of their money. It is hard to say which was the greater threat: fire from the open grate, or burglary through the unbarred window. By the 1840s most banks had metal shutters and cast iron slow combustion stoves.

Given that most bank interiors were more presentable than Newark, many of the fittings there were nevertheless typical. Pewter inkpots, brass balances and copper coin shovels have been part of the banker's stock-in-trade to well within living memory. Ledger shelves were also a universal feature and can be noticed again at the back of the shop in the illustration of Messrs Rogers's Lombard Street bank (Plate 11). The latter shows an interior more formalised than at Newark, and typical of London, or at least the City. It is not difficult to marry these dull surroundings with the unexciting image of the banker's character. Even if the décor of the banking-hall were more elaborate and attractive than that chosen by Messrs Rogers, a familiar feature of most London banks was the long mahogany counter, modestly relieved by vertical panels and topped at intervals by chest-high ledger rests.

The procedure was for the customer to transact day-to-day business in the shop, and to penetrate only into the parlour when there was some need for negotiation or advice, just as most transactions these

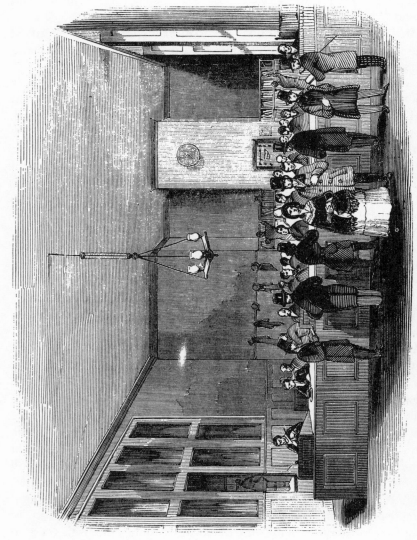

Plate 11. Rogers's Bank, Lombard Street, London. Interior, 1840s.

days are in the banking-hall but certain activities, like arranging an overdraft, are conducted in the manager's room. A customer depositing money would have given it to the counter clerk or teller who, having agreed the total, passed it to the ledger clerk alongside, who entered the sum in the 'waste book'.[170] Cheques for payment were passed by the teller to the clerk sitting behind him, who handed the money forward. It was for these practical reasons that the clerks were grouped so close together. It would seem that tellers and ledger clerks often worked without seats,[171] a tribulation made worse by inadequate three-burner gas lamps, as seen in the Rogers's Bank interior, and by heating contrivances which could never have affected them.

The layout of the shop in Soane's Fleet Street bank of 1801 can be deduced from the plan of 1877 (Plate 4): there is no reason to believe that any changes had occurred in the intervening years. The alternate placings for teller and ledger clerk can be clearly seen, the symbols like anemometers probably representing coin balances. Desk No. 1 would have been occupied by the chief clerk, and raised on a dais for the better surveillance of his juniors. The ledger shelf was at the far end of the working area, and the only source of heat was the fireplace in the arched recess on the other side of the room. Although the fire would have been an attractive feature for customers, it could have had no effect on the temperature prevailing in the banking-hall. Furthermore, clerks at desks Nos 5 and 11 were some 20 feet (6 metres) from natural light.

Despite these deficiencies, it is easy to imagine that Soane's banking-hall was pleasantly attractive, in contrast to the functionalism of Rogers's Bank. The ground plan hints at pilaster decoration, and shows a curved wall cradling the desk of the chief clerk, and arches into the vestibule and fireplace recess. It is reasonable to suppose that the nearer to the West End was the bank, the more costly and elaborate was the decoration. The brothers Adam, for instance, could hardly have failed to embellish the banking-hall and parlour of Drummond's Bank, for which they designed furniture.[172] But it is unlikely that any interior decorations were particularly 'bank-like' — that is to say, conceived to satisfy the requirements of banking rather than appeal to the sensibilities of the customers.

In this early period, the term strong room is something of a misnomer and many bankers must have resorted to cellars, protected by an unusually stout door, or simply strengthened existing rooms by linings of iron. There is no evidence in this early period of any architect-designed strong rooms and the patents of the security specialists, like Jeremiah and Charles Chubb, and Joseph Bramah, were concerned only with the construction of locks.[173]

The lack of information is disappointing because there is certainly reason to believe that bankers took security very seriously and there are interesting glimpses of problems and costs. From Newcastle, in 1788, a partner in a new banking venture was sent over to the Durham bank by his colleagues to inspect a kind of strong room, called the 'closet', as a possible model for their own.[174] At the Canterbury bank, the security fittings ('Iron Door, Iron Chest, Stone Closet, Stone Door Case') were valued at £60 in 1800.[175] It cost Herries, Farquhar & Co., in London, £760 to build two new strong rooms (and make certain other unspecified improvements) in 1807.[176] Seven years earlier, when Peacock & Co. were fitting out their Sleaford bank, they bought a pair of wrought iron folding doors 'in a frame with an exceeding good Lock to cover the door & false Lock [and] 2 brass handles' for £25.[177] They came from Larkins & Eade of Cheapside, London, and travelled by water.[178] In 1819 the Banbury bank bought an iron safe, also for £25, and a stone safe for rather more.[179]

The relatively high cost of installing security features and the impracticability of removing them thereafter must explain why banks so often kept to a traditional banking site, even in the inauspicious circumstance of an earlier bank having failed or given up there. There were instances of this at Manchester in 1788 and Sheffield in 1792.[180] In a sense it is material considerations of this kind as much as legislation which marks the end of the era of private banking. Soon a bank was to become a little fortress and the science of security was only one step behind the art of architectural presentation in the banker's table of priorities.

Chapter Two

From Fleet Street to Corn Street: The Impact of Joint-Stock Banking

A disappointing fact about the banks discussed in Chapter One is that so few of them remain. In fact, none of the private banks mentioned in London survived even to the last war. It is, therefore, pleasant to record that the two banks forming the *termini* of this chapter are not only standing, but still in use. The Fleet Street building, erected in 1829–30, is the oldest banking-house left in London. The Corn Street bank, built in 1854–7, is not the oldest surviving bank in Bristol but it is the best known. In the 25-odd years which separate these two buildings the architecture of banking made more advances than in all its previous history. One reason for this sudden progress was the advent of joint-stock banking.

The bank at 37 Fleet Street was built by Messrs Hoare, a private banking partnership established in the seventeenth century and continued in the best metropolitan tradition. The Corn Street bank was built by The West of England & South Wales District Bank, a joint-stock company incorporated in 1834 with unlimited liability.[1] Here, the capital was subscribed by shareholders (more usually known as proprietors) and the bank was managed by a board of directors.

As well as marking a constitutional difference in banking, the two buildings illustrate another dimension of change. From the late 1830s the Italianate style of architecture, rediscovered by Charles Barry for the Travellers' and Reform Clubs, was available and acceptable, allowing richness of detail without loss of propriety.[2] Buildings based on the Palazzo Farnese at Rome and the Palazzo Pandolfini at Florence become especially popular, later overtaken by those drawing from a wider Italian inspiration, particularly from Venice. Corn Street was the high-spot of derivative design before the eclecticism of the later Victorian era.

There are, then, two underlying and coincidental phenomena central to the investigation of this period. On the one hand, a new technique of banking; on the other hand, an opportunity to break with classical and Greek Revival styles and identify the *palazzo* image with the concept of joint-stock banking. However, it is difficult to establish that joint-stock bankers were aware from the beginning of the potential of Italianate as an expression of radical change.

In anticipation of what was to be, without doubt, a period of ill-tempered evolution, Hoare's Bank, designed by Charles Parker,[3] was a deliberate portrayal of elegance, calm and good manners[4] (Plate 12). It was a reassurance to customers that, whatever the meretricious appeal of the joint-stock revolutionaries, the established canons of reserve and solidity still held good with the London private bankers. Reputed to have cost £60000[5] (although the figure seems hardly possible), the bank 'while Georgian enough to suit the partners' conservative taste, struck the contemporary note of business-like Neo-Classical simplicity.'[6] But in any wider analysis it was already out of date. This was London catching up with Liverpool, a Heywood's Bank of 1800 translated to a London setting. 'The house is completely isolated,' marvelled the *Gentleman's Magazine*, 'its neighbours standing nearly a foot from its wide walls . . .',[7] but this was nothing new in the north of England. The entrances were at either side: but this had been the practice of Maddox and Soane, 20 and 30 years earlier. Within a short period of the building of Parker's bank, the concept and arrangement of bank premises were wholly to change, and for an understanding of the reasons for this a fuller explanation must be given of the character of the banking revolution.

Any discussion of the position in England must be prefaced by an explanation of the Scottish scene, and its evolution since the eighteenth century. There, the chartered Bank of Scotland surrendered its monopoly of joint-stock banking 21 years after its establishment in 1695. Two other chartered[8] banks had been founded — the Royal Bank of Scotland in 1727 and the British Linen Bank in 1746 — and 72 other banks were set up by 1815.[9] Most of these were joint-stock companies, but there were a few private banks in Edinburgh.[10] Inter-bank relations were generally good, and failures rare. Following the disasters among English bankers in 1825–6, it was to the 'Scotch system' that Parliament turned for inspiration. It is relevant here to outline the kind of premises in which this more stable regime had become established.

The design of the first purpose-built bank in Scotland had been prepared by William Adam in 1744 for the Royal Bank: these plans were executed with some revision by S. Neilson in 1750–4.[11] The site

Plate 12. Charles Parker's bank for Hoare & Co., 37 Fleet Street, London, 1829–30.

was Old Bank Close, High Street, Edinburgh. However, the existing town houses of Edinburgh were so good that most banks found purpose-building unnecessary. The Bank of Scotland occupied a Tudor building in Mauchan's Close, Edinburgh, throughout the eighteenth century; in 1802, new Palladian-style buildings were begun on the Mound to designs by Richard Crichton and Robert Reid[12] (Plate 13). These survived until 1870, when they were remodelled by David Bryce.[13] The third Scottish chartered bank, the British Linen Bank, took a lease of the Earl of Moray's Edinburgh mansion in 1753,

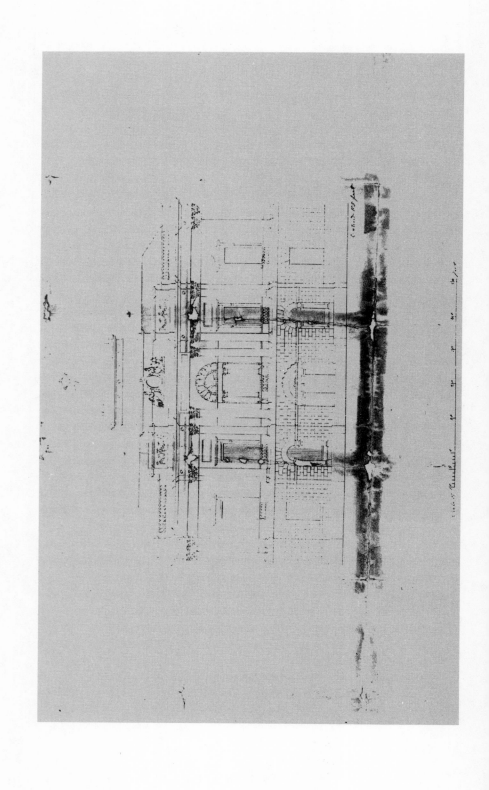

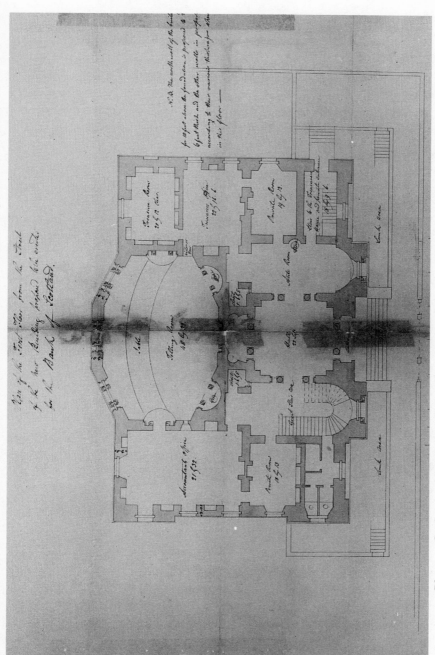

Plate 13. Crichton and Reid's Bank of Scotland, Edinburgh, 1802. Above: elevation. Below: first-floor plan.

Plate 14. Archibald Elliot's Royal Bank of Scotland, Glasgow office, 1827.

removing from there to the former family home of the Marquess of Tweeddale in 1790.[14] In 1808 they moved to the New Town, buying a mansion in St Andrew Square from the Dowager Countess of Dalhousie.[15] Alterations were made by Robert Reid.[16] The bank used this site as a nucleus around which to acquire other property, but no unifying reconstruction was made until 1851.[17] For the Commercial Bank, J.G. Graham altered a building in Picardy Place in 1810 and another in New Assembly Close, High Street, in 1813.[18]

Away from Edinburgh, the earliest purpose-built Scottish bank seems to have been at Perth. It cost around £1300 and was erected by 1791 for the Perth Banking Company.[19] As well as residential quarters, it had rooms to let commercially.[20] Other early purpose-built banks include the Leith Bank (1805–6), attributed to John Paterson;[21] the Union Bank in Dundee (1823); by William Burn;[22] the Commercial Bank in Stirling (1825), possibly by J.G. Graham;[23] and the Town & Country Bank in Aberdeen (1826), by Archibald Simpson.[24] It seems not to have been until 1827 that any purpose-built bank of significance was erected in Glasgow. This was the magnificent Greek Revival structure, with hexastyle Ionic portico, designed by Archibald Elliot for the Royal Bank of Scotland[25] (Plate 14). It is in the comparison of this building with Hoare's Bank in Fleet Street that the measure of difference is revealed between Scotland and England — or, rather, between Scotland and London. It was a difference not of wealth but of outlook and constitution.

The obstacle to joint-stock banking in England was the legal position of the Bank of England. Although the crisis of 1825–6 made it impossible for the bank not to accept a degree of change, its monopoly of joint-stock banking was not broken by the 1826 Act[26] except beyond 65 miles of London. Even then, the banks set up beyond that radius were allowed no establishment as bankers in London, although the Bank of England was empowered to open country branches as recompense for the partial loss of privilege. In 1833 amending legislation[27] allowed the foundation of joint-stock banks within the 65-mile limit. This, then, was the position at its simplest. In fact, it was an area of confused and contested law which cannot escape more detailed examination, even in such a context as buildings.

The legal basis of the Bank of England's monopoly lay in a prohibition, first stated in 1708[28] and repeated in subsequent Acts, against more than six persons uniting in partnership to issue bank-notes. However, with the increasing complexity of banking practice, note issue became no more than one role among many. From 1822, when Thomas Joplin of Newcastle-upon-Tyne began pamphleteering for reform, the view gained support that joint-stock banking might lawfully be conducted in England, even in London, for banks of deposit, as opposed to banks of issue. It was this argument, ignored in 1826, which was accepted in 1833, the Act of that year acknowledging in a recital that the title to the Bank of England's monopoly was not unassailable.

In the period between these Acts, banking in England appears immature, petty and acrimonious. Private bankers in London sided with the Bank of England in opposing the extension of joint-stock banking into the metropolitan area. With greater ferocity than their London colleagues, country bankers opposed both joint-stock banking and the Bank of England.[29] The fact that the new banks were likely to seek accounts from traders and other classes which the private banks neglected made no difference. Clearly, there were many accounts suited to more than one faction. In the face of entrenched opposition the new banking companies 'had to choose between making advances with caution, and getting very little business; and on the other hand, launching out liberally, and in this way attracting customers, but at risks far exceeding those which prudent banking would under any circumstances approve.'[30] With great suddenness, English banking, so long the scene of complacent privilege, was electric with a competition which could not fail to find expression in the choice of places of business.

In the capital, the first challenge to the Bank of England's supposed monopoly came from the London & Westminster Bank. Established in 1833, this bank had been planned even before the enabling legislation of that year was passed.[31] One of the first moves of the directorate was to instigate a Bill in the Commons to allow joint-stock banks within the 65-mile limit to sue or be sued in the name of a public official.[32] This very desirable provision had already been granted to joint-stock banks outside the 65-mile limit by the Act of 1826.[33] The Bill passed in the Commons but was rejected in the Lords, the Bank of England having arranged opposition, on the grounds that the Bill was an indirect threat to its privileged position. This point was not settled until legislation in 1844.[34] Hostility grew. The Bank of England refused to allow the London & Westminster Bank a drawing account and sued it for accepting bills of exchange at less than 6 months date.[35] At the same time, the London private banks refused all joint-stock banks permission to join the clearing house, a situation which was to last until 1854.[36]

It is necessary to understand this background to realise why, for some 30 years after the building of Hoare's Bank, the progress of banking architecture in London lacked the vigour and pace of advances elsewhere. It was not a complete stagnation. The private bankers, who had no quarrel with the Bank of England, maintained some kind of building programme. But Hoare's Bank did not inspire others to pre-empt or even match the grandeur of scale which became axiomatic of joint-stock building in the Midlands and north of England. Admittedly, the style was not always within the banker's control. Herries, Farquhar & Co., rebuilding in St James's Street in 1831, and Messrs Smith, Payne & Smith, resiting themselves in Lombard Street in 1836 beside the newly cut King William Street, had to conform with the requirements of the Crown Estate Commissioners and the Corporation of London, respectively.[37] In other areas of London, however, there is little evidence of advancement, beyond modernisation of established premises. Barnett, Hoares & Co. in Lombard Street used Samuel Kempthorne for a remodelling in 1838 and Coutts & Co. employed Thomas Hopper for a similar purpose at 59 The Strand in 1839.[38] Twining & Co., newcomers to banking, built themselves an elegant bank and tea warehouse at 215 The Strand in 1835–7,[39] but this was very much in the tradition of metropolitan banking-houses.

The London & Westminster Bank apart, the few joint-stock banks which were established in London within 10 years of the 1833 Act were generally content with purchased or leased premises for both their main office in the City and their branches in the West End. Besides the fact that brash new premises might have been considered provocative or aggressive by the other banking interests, there were more than enough suitable buildings for adaptation or conversion. If this were true of Edinburgh, then it were no less true of London. As late as 1856, one new joint-stock bank began in a mansion in Hanover Square: 'It has for many years past been appropriated as an aristocratic residence, and possesses all the space and convenience internally, as well as commanding exterior, to render it readily capable of conversion to the purposes of a banking-house suitable for the west of London . . .'.[40]

Some of the buildings available were former banks which had become vacant, normally through failure, and the lure of a ready-made strong room appears to have countered any misgivings from superstition. This phenomenon was noticed outside London in the last chapter as early as the 1790s. The London Joint-Stock Bank opened its western branch in the old premises of Wright's Bank in Henrietta Street, Covent Garden, in 1840, but moved to Hammersley's old premises in Pall Mall in 1841, releasing the Henrietta Street building for use by the Commercial Bank of London.[41] The London & County Bank took the old private bank premises of Lees, Brassey & Co. in Lombard Street.[42] The Union Bank of London even opened a branch in the Pall Mall premises of the Metropolitan Bank, a fellow joint-stock concern inauspiciously wound up in 1841 after only 2 years of business.[43]

Under the 1833 Act, the joint-stock banks of issue founded outside the 65-mile radius were still not allowed to have any London branch for banking purposes. Only the National Provincial Bank bothered to have any kind of non-banking metropolitan office. Some banks, like the North Wiltshire, probably had first-hand experience of how testy the Bank of England could be about the slightest trespass within the forbidden radius.[44] The National Provincial's office was no more than a co-ordinating centre at Salvador House, Bishopsgate, to which John Burges Watson added two Greek lodges.[45]

The exception to this wariness was the head office of the rebel London & Westminster Bank. Within 5 years of starting business, and 2 years after opening branches in Westminster, Bloomsbury, South-wark and St Marylebone, the bank's head office was opened in Lothbury in December 1838 (Plate 15). This was a magnificent building costing, together with the site, around £37000.[46] Further-more, it was directly opposite one side of the Bank of England, and the bank's architect, C.R. Cockerell, was responsible, with assistance from William Tite, for the design.[47] Although the choice of Cockerell as joint architect appears to have been the result of kinship with a London & Westminster Bank director[48] (and he was not, in any event, the unanimous choice of the building committee),[49] it is natural to view this building as a gesture of defiance both to the Bank of England and to the London private bankers for the miseries of the early years.

Although the façade of the London & Westminster Bank did not have the restraint of Parker's Fleet Street bank, it was no more affiliated to the style of Barry's clubhouses, nor did it anticipate any later style of banking.[50] This was a unique elevation for a banking company which was in an unprecedented situation, both constitutionally and on the ground. Having stood up to the Bank of England in a commercial sense, the company had now to achieve a building which would stand literally alongside that of its opponent. Although competition with the scale and grandeur of the Bank of England was clearly impossible, the need was for a building which would nevertheless hold its own — distinctive enough to show a spirit of independence and yet not so unharmonious with its mighty neighbour as to suggest the perpetuation of past differences. The result was an astylar frontage of classical symmetry, showing great originality and strength but sympathetic to Soane's perimeter wall of the Bank of England in the horizontal rustication of the stonework. At either side of the building, two boldly projecting piers, capped by statuary and linked by string course and cornice, defined the area of the banking-hall, which rose the full two storeys before the springing of the dome.

The importance of this building lies not so much in the merits of the façade in relation to the Bank of England but in a new attention to functionalism which dictated to some extent the exterior appearance. Clearly, the problem of light was uppermost in the architects' minds, and the central doorway, the bays of tall, tiered windows, and the domed banking-hall were working towards the same end.[51] The traditional banking-house had been two units: a bank on the ground floor and apartments on the floor or floors above, with their respective entrances at each side of the main elevation. But there came a stage when the banking-hall was so big that it covered a ground floor area too large to be lit satisfactorily from windows in the outside wall. Furthermore, joint-stock banks were, in the nature of things, more impersonally controlled and although a head office might well have rooms for residential use, it was essentially a bank and not a banking-house. There was, therefore, no objection to piercing through upper floors to bring in daylight from above. And once the dome had been introduced the main entrance could return to the centre of the front elevation, in grand manner. Another consequence of the dome was the introduction of interior columns, with opportunities for decoration and embellishment which the old banking 'shop' had never known.

Although the interior of the Cockerell-Tite bank did not show the lavishness of ornament by which later banking-halls were characterised, there was a pleasing attention to curved and rounded forms — perhaps another sign of Soaneic influence — which extended to the shape of the counter. Another feature to be noticed is the proliferation (and shape) of the gas lamps — all in all a contribution to working conditions which put Messrs Rogers's contemporary banking-hall (Plate 11) to shame.

Away from London, country bankers, unprotected by the Bank of England, were less complacent in their attitude to the new competition. Some, with small branch networks of their own, borrowed the joint-stock nomenclature. For instance, Foster & Co. preferred to call themselves the Cambridge & Cambridgeshire Bank, and Hughes, Lock & Co.

Plate 15. C.R. Cockerell and W. Tite's London & Westminster Bank, Lothbury, London, 1838. Below: interior.

adopted the name Devizes and Wiltshire Bank, in opposition to the North Wilts Banking Company founded at Melksham. There was also some spirited building in the 'safe' styles. Richard Roberts & Co. employed John Lloyd, Caernarvonshire County Surveyor, in 1830,[52] while Smith & Co., at Hull, took the pedimented central block of a terrace in Whitefriargate reminiscent of Liverpool in the 1780s.[53] The Devizes & Wiltshire Bank, and another at Bridport, settled for neo-Greek.[54] Undoubtedly there were many new premises of private banks which fell into the category of 'handsome and substantial', the near-contemporary description of premises erected by Nichols, Baker & Co. at Bewdley in 1832.[55]

For the new joint-stock bankers, legally positioned more than 65 miles from London, the choice of premises was of the first importance. The bank was a speculative venture — a product of the commercial aspirations of several hundred proprietors with no other common link between them. The readiest advertisement, the greatest cohesive factor, the most satisfactory source of corporate identity, was a purpose-built bank of some pretension. Publicity and self-confidence were at the heart of the joint-stock concept: banks were conceived at public meetings, born by printed prospectus and weaned on the frankness of open reporting. On the face of it, shortage of money was no obstacle to building. Subscribed capital averaged around £250000 in the 1830s, although the figure could vary from £15000 to as much as £5 million.[56] But whereas the partners of a private bank could spend money as they wished, there were curbs on the authority of joint-stock bankers which could make building a troublesome business.

In the absence of any statutory framework of practice, such as the Acts of 1826 and 1833 might have laid down, the activities of a joint-stock bank were controlled by its Deed of Settlement. Roughly comparable with the Memorandum and Articles of Association of a modern company, and far more complex than the articles of partnership of a private bank, an original Deed of Settlement bore the signatures and seals of all proprietors. Deeds were then published as a rule,[57] but without the appended names. There is usually a clue in opening clauses as to the site of premises hurriedly secured by the provisional committee for the commencement of business. For instance, the Liverpool Union Bank leased part of India Buildings; the Hampshire Banking Company bought an office in Southampton; and the Gloucester County & City Bank had premises in Gloucester's Westgate. Rarely, the minutes of a provisional or steering committee have survived, like those of the West of England & South Wales

District Bank, where the use is recorded of a room in Small Street, Bristol, formerly occupied by the Pitching and Paving Commissioners.[58]

The location of the permanent head office (or 'central bank', to use the earlier parliamentary term), could be a matter for considerable discussion. A joint-stock bank was sometimes the result of a voluntary merger between two or more private banks. The new company was therefore committed to business in several towns, all of which would be named in the Deed of Settlement. For instance, the Glamorganshire Bank had to open in Swansea and Neath, the Burton Union Bank in Burton and Uttoxeter, the Northamptonshire Bank in Northampton and Daventry, and so on. The Shropshire Banking Company, a union of private banks in Newport, Wellington, Coalbrookdale and Shifnal, was committed to business in all four towns. In 1837 Shifnal was chosen, for geographical reasons, as the 'central bank'.[59] But no new building was erected and in 1842 there was a move to take the role of head office to the other constituent towns by rota.[60] This was unworkable, and when a central bank was eventually built at Shifnal in 1845–7 it was predictably modest — very much a private bank by nature. A similar problem was solved by the County of Gloucester Bank, an amalgamation of three private banks, by the creation of simultaneous head offices at Gloucester, Cheltenham, Cirencester and, later, Stroud; minor branches such as Burford and Faringdon were attached to the nearest one.[61]

For the great majority of joint-stock banks, however, the problem was not the site of the head office but the timing of its construction. Despite the large sums of nominal capital, amounts actually paid up could be as little as one-fifth of the total.[62] Furthermore, the use of such money for building purposes could be subject to restrictions both specific and indirect imposed by the Deed of Settlement. The priority for prudent bankers was to build up a contingency fund from the first profits of business. The idea was to create a reservoir of ready capital, variously called the 'Guarantee Fund', 'Reserved Fund', or 'Reserved Surplus Fund', to meet what were called 'unforeseen problems or extraordinary demands'. More accurately, the money was to meet losses and prevent temporary reductions in dividend.[63] That the reservoir could save a bank from ruin was proved in the case of the Bank of Manchester, which came close to disaster in the difficult year of 1837.[64] Sometimes the fund was to be raised to a prescribed total, such as £20000 or £30000, at other times to such portion of net profits as the proprietors thought fit.

While this reserve money was being amassed, it was inevitable, unless the bank was unusually prosperous, that building programmes would be delayed. The Gloucestershire Banking Company, founded in 1831, assiduously built up a guarantee fund of over £20000 (supporting a paid-up capital of £100000) before appointing a subcommittee in September 1836 'to consider whether any alterations can be made in the buildings of the present Bank, or to prepare some other mode for providing better accommodation.'[65] In fact, this bank, although perhaps unrepresentative of the joint-stock scene as a whole, is an interesting example of how parsimonious management could be. The committee reported back with two proposals by S.W. Daukes. The more expensive (and yet no more than around £1000) was rejected and Daukes was told 'to direct his attention to the smaller alterations . . .'. However, by November 1836 the board felt they needed a different building altogether and Daukes had the opportunity to design new premises. The tenders came out at between £4922 and £5700, which was far more than the directors were prepared to pay, and the matter was 'adjourned for a larger attendance of the Board'. At this meeting, Daukes was asked to get £732 taken off the lowest tender. The directors then felt able to report to shareholders in August 1837 that the building was being erected with 'their especial attention to due economy'.

Specific control on expenditure for building was sometimes imposed in Deeds of Settlement, in the form of a clause requiring plans and specifications to be approved at special meetings of proprietors. If premises were to be purchased or leased, rather than built, this could be done by the board without higher authority. In all Deeds which have been examined, premises were to be regarded as personal estate — part of the joint-stock or capital of the bank and available to meet liabilities.

The question of building from new is further complicated by the growth of the branch network, a basic element in the philosophy of joint-stock banking. The speed with which branches were established varied enormously. A very few joint-stock banks had no branches at all,[66] while others established 10 or more within months of opening.[67] The siting of a branch or agency was often the result of specific proprietorial interests. The North Wilts Bank opened branches at Calne, Bradford-on-Avon and Marlborough for the convenience of its local directors.[68] At the first whisper of local encouragement the Devon & Cornwall Bank set up agencies or branches in Tavistock, Ashburton, St Austell, and elsewhere.[69] The Bristol-based West of

England and South Wales District Bank opened a branch at Exeter, 75 miles away, 'at the urgent request of numerous shareholders'.[70] Competition with other banks was itself a spur to branch expansion, directors being reluctant to allow rivals a monopoly of banking, however small the potential business. In the 1830s there were three banks with branches at Launceston in Cornwall, while Driffield, in the East Riding, with 2500 people and no trade outside the corn market, had two joint-stock and two private banks.[71]

The extent of branch expansion could be a further matter for regulation by the Deed of Settlement. The Glamorganshire Banking Company, for instance, could only open in the counties of Glamorgan and Carmarthen; Moore & Robinson's Nottinghamshire Banking Company could operate only within 40 miles of Nottingham; the Warwick & Leamington Bank could open anywhere in England, but the decision had to come from a board meeting attended by at least seven directors. Insistence on the board's unanimity was also not uncommon, as in the Burton Union Bank, while in the case of the Gloucester County & City Bank this unanimous resolution had to be approved by proprietors at two successive extraordinary meetings.

In no Deed of Settlement has it been possible to find a restriction on branch building, as opposed to branch opening, other than the controls which have been outlined above, in relation to overall powers of building. There is no doubt that some branch banks were purpose-built in the earliest years of joint-stock banking. The Manchester & Liverpool District Bank built a branch at Hanley in 1833 which will be discussed in a later chapter. The Gloucestershire Joint-Stock Bank erected premises at Stroud in 1834;[72] and the Lichfield & Tamworth Bank built a Birmingham branch in 1837 to designs by Messrs Bateman & Drury.[73]

Perhaps the best-received branch bank of this decade was at Burslem, in the Potteries: 'The most striking private building in the middle of the town, indeed almost the only one having the character of elegance, is the newly-erected house of business of the Commercial Bank of England, situate on the south side of the Market Place, erected in 1836, in the Italian style, fronted with free-stone with large Venetian windows on the ground floor, and the upper ones having ornamental balconies. This beautiful edifice, though for the use only of a branch bank, is, we believe the very *chef-d'oeuvre* of the Company's offices.'[74] The Commercial Bank of England suspended payment in 1840. None of the bank's records appear to have survived and it is impossible to know how far this style of building was typical of its other 17 branches which were in existence by 1836.[75]

Even when records do survive, no central policy can be traced on branch building. This is particularly disappointing in the case of the National Provincial Bank, which multiplied branches faster than any competitor: 53 in 1836; 76 in 1840; 94 in 1842.[76] Some of these were certainly purpose-built: Birmingham, for instance, was erected in 1840.[77] But there is nothing in the minutes of the Branches Committee to prove its involvement in purpose-building.[78] The earliest reference to the building of a branch seems to be in the Court Book of 1842; a local inspector was asked to furnish the board with plans of the proposed bank at Brecon, so that they could be submitted to an architect in London.[79] But this would suggest ratification for technical rather than stylistic purposes.

At national level, the end of the first era of branch banking came with the collapse of the Northern & Central Bank in 1836–7. Established at Manchester in 1834, this bank had opened about 40 branches 'solely with the view of disseminating the home-made notes.'[80] The network was far-flung and beyond effective central control. Warnings by more professional bankers of the dangers of branch proliferation had been unheeded.[81] A constitutionalist might have predicted the bank's failure from the weakness of its Deed of Settlement. The directors had power to purchase, lease, or build at will; the guarantee fund had no minimum target; and the board were not only allowed to open branches but positively instructed to do so. Whether, in the event, they had time to purpose-build is unclear, but certainly one critic referred to 'Luxurious accommodation' as a factor in the collapse.[82] Although a sharp lesson in prudential banking, the failure was no more than a temporary set-back to the practice of branch expansion. Within 20 years the *Bankers' Magazine* was bemoaning 'the street system, whereby miniature banks are put down at about a gun shot . . . from the principal office.'[83]

It is appropriate now to return to the subject of head offices. What has been said above about restrictions in Deeds of Settlement should not disguise the fact that a sufficiently determined group of directors found little impediment to building. One of the earlier and most noticed joint-stock banks was erected by the Manchester & Liverpool District Bank, which, established 30 April 1829, began building 20 June 1834.[84] This building was designed by T.W. Atkinson and sited in Spring Gardens.[85] It was an astylar Italianate bank which the *Builder* later considered as important in the architectural history of Manchester as the Travellers' Club was in London.[86] It was certainly a change from the Mancunian tradition of neo-Greek.[87]

In Birmingham, early purpose-built premises included those of the Birmingham Banking Company (also established in 1829), designed with portico and colonnade in the Corinthian Order by T. Rickman and H. Hutchinson.[88] Built in 1830, the bank still stands at the corner of Waterloo Street and Bennett's Hill as a branch of the Midland Bank. The main entrance was originally in Bennett's Hill itself, the present corner entrance having been designed by H. Yeoville Thomason in about 1868 to match that of the rebuilt National Provincial Bank across the road.[89] However, the most important bank architect in Birmingham in the 1830s was Charles Edge, who designed premises for the Bank of Birmingham in Bennett's Hill in 1832, and for the Birmingham & Midland Bank in Union Street in 1836[90] (Plate 16). The former had entrance porches of the Doric Order, with full entablature, at each side of the building; the latter had a central doorway with Ionic porch. Both designs show the residual influence of private banking.

Although some continuing Grecian element was usual enough in the early years of joint-stock banking, there was at first no common style appropriated to this particular commercial faction any more than there was to savings banks. There were advantages in variation, to safeguard commercial identity. The fact that different styles, the one with giant Corinthian Order, the other based on the Palazzo Pandolfini, were chosen by rival banks in Gloucester in 1838–9,[91] would not have been fortuitous. The influence of competition will be a recurrent theme in this chapter.

Goodhart-Rendel considered that 'Banking houses were Italian because bankers had seen and admired the palaces Barry had built either as residences or as club-houses for their more important depositors.'[92] This view can be broadened into the proposition that the *palazzo* style was middle-class and therefore representative of the market which bankers were trying to attract.[93] There were also two other factors to encourage Italianate building, in a wide interpretation of that term: one was political, the other suggested by association.

The political point was supported indirectly by Walter Bagehot, who regarded the City as Whig because the Bank of England had been founded by a Whig government.[94] Bagehot had not been thinking architecturally but if the basic Victorian division is accepted between Gothic (Tory) and Italianate (Whig) idealism, it can be argued that the latter style was uppermost in bankers' minds. More convincing,

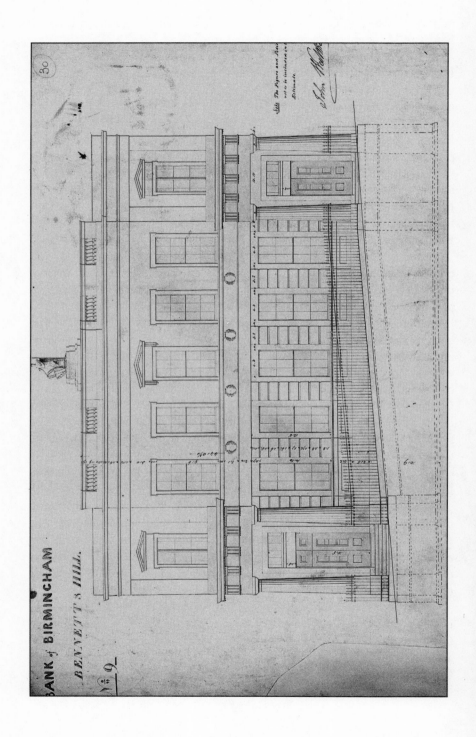

BANK of BIRMINGHAM

BENNETT's HILL.

N.º 9

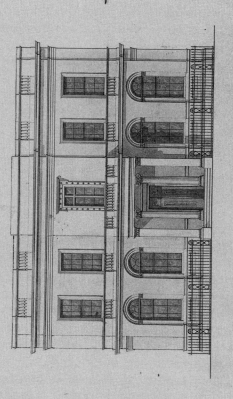

FRONT ELEVATION

BIRMINGHAM & MIDLAND BANK
UNION STREET

Nº 5

Plate 16. Above: Charles Edge's Bank of Birmingham, Bennett's Hill, Birmingham, 1832. Elevation. Below: Charles Edge's Birmingham & Midland Bank, Union Street, Birmingham, 1836. Elevation.

however, especially in respect of the provinces, is the case for Italianate by association. As banking gained something of its present form and practice from Florentine and other Italian bankers of the fifteenth century, so it was appropriate that Victorian bankers should borrow the style of their *palazzi*.[95]

In some towns, the bank was part of a wider scheme for civic improvement, and therefore its appearance might be outside bankers' control. The Derby & Derbyshire Bank, built in 1837–9 to designs by Robert Wallace, was part of a rebuilding plan for central Derby, including Post Office, Athenaeum and Royal Hotel, all in Greek Ionic.[96] The Manchester & Salford Bank, completed in 1838, had a pediment carried on Corinthian columns, but the architect R. Tattersall was also designing a warehouse with which the bank was integrated.[97] At Sheffield, the enormous bank opened in 1838 had to harmonise with the Cutlers' Hall, then recently rebuilt: Samuel Worth designed both buildings.[98] In the Lake District, attractive classical banks built at Whitehaven[99] and Kendal,[100] both in 1830s, appear to have resulted from the same desire for urban enhancement which had motivated certain private bankers in the eighteenth century. In these towns, and for that matter in Birmingham and Sheffield, joint-stock banks were among the first public or semi-public buildings of any consequence.

The closest association between bank premises and town planning took place at Newcastle-upon-Tyne. The particular importance of the Newcastle redevelopment is that it saw the first purpose-built branch of the Bank of England.[101] Enabled to set up country branches by the Act of 1826, the bank had first opened in Gloucester in 1827, and then at Manchester, Swansea and Birmingham all by the end of that year.[102] At three of these four centres they bought the premises of failed banks.[103] In the following year, branches were opened at Liverpool, Bristol, Leeds and Exeter, the premises at Bristol having been acquired by public advertisement.[104] The first Newcastle site followed in 1828 and then Hull and Norwich in 1829.[105]

There was much hostility from local private bankers, who were supported by the press and even by trading interests: '. . . of all men who are sinned against by this uncalled-for interference on the part of the Bank of England', complained an Exeter editorial, 'none are less deserving of it than the bankers of our own City.'[106] At Newcastle, the Chamber of Commerce petitioned the Bank of England to stay away, seeing 'no prospect whatever of good from such an establishment.'[107] A similar rebuff was sent by the mayor of Hull, who warned that if a branch were established it would neither be at the request of the inhabitants, nor for their accommodation.[108] Such bitterness was not lost on Bank of England staff. At Manchester, the clerks arrived 'with much the same sort of emotions that men would have today on being despatched to Kamchatka. After dark they used to get a watchman, one of the old Charleys, rattle in hand, to see them safe home.'[109]

At the request of the Navy, further branches were opened at Plymouth and Portsmouth in 1834, both in leased houses.[110] By then, Cockerell had already been appointed architect to the bank in succession to Sir John Soane.[111] Branches changed buildings in Leeds in 1835 and Birmingham in 1838, but not to purpose-built premises.[112] Cockerell designed a house for the Plymouth branch in 1835 but this may not have been built:[113] within a short time he was drawing up plans for the bank in Courtney Street opened in 1842.[114] The Bank of England's decision to build new branches as a matter of policy was probably the result of Cockerell's influence, but no abrupt change of thinking was ever minuted.[115]

As for Newcastle, it was decided that ground should be purchased and a branch erected in the 'new street' being planned by Richard Grainger.[116] The building which resulted (Plate 17), was opened in 1838 and has been attributed at various times since to Benjamin Green, Thomas Oliver, and Grainger himself.[117] In contrast with the scale and assertion of the giant Corinthian Order, the ground floor was restrained: horizontally rusticated piers were to be seen elsewhere in the street, and the bank had no grand entrance. Allowing for such aspects to have been influenced as much by the Newcastle urban plan as by the bank, it is nevertheless possible to see a judicious compromise between a desire to mark the authority of a central institution, and a reluctance to flaunt this authority in the face of the citizen on the pavement.

The Bank of England, so well placed in Newcastle, would have felt the mediocrity of certain other of their branches the more keenly. The very title 'Bank of England' had overtones of grandeur to find expression in the calibre of its buildings. Some fell rather short of it. 'I inquired for the edifice in which the branch . . . of the Bank of England is transacted . . .', wrote 'A Stranger' to Liverpool in 1841, 'naturally expecting an edifice worthy of this great establishment . . . and the spirit shown in so expensive a one in London. But what was my astonishment and disappointment on being shown a poor little paltry pitiable place, in Hanover Street, where there is neither beauty outside nor sufficient space in; some places dark and all botched, inconvenient

Plate 17. Bank of England, Newcastle-upon-Tyne branch, 1838.

and defective! Surely the Leviathan of Threadneedle Street will not be outdone by the pettiest banking-house in Liverpool.'[118]

It would have been better for the 'Stranger' if he had set the poor quality of the Bank of England's Liverpool branch not against the pettiest banking-house but rather the premises of some pretension which the joint-stock banks had been building there for several years. It was, after all, his own view that 'Few things more strike a stranger's notice, or give him a better idea of the wealth of this most wealthy town, than the number and excellence of the banking-houses'.[119] Perhaps the earliest of these new buildings was the Royal Bank in Dale Street, later the Queen Insurance Buildings, and now part of the Queen's Arcade. This bank was erected in 1837–8 to designs by Samuel Rowland.[120] Professor Reilly found the Greek detail 'coarse' and 'loose',[121] but Rowland was probably less interested in the grammar of his composition than its overall effect.

The academicism associated with neo-Greek no doubt contributed to the gradual adoption in its place of Italian styles by worldly joint-stock bankers, even if criticism were bound to follow. Edward Corbett of Manchester, having designed grand premises with Corinthian portico for the Liverpool head office of the North & South Wales Bank opened in 1841, did not mind too much if his temple-form building, with three stories in an Order, was 'an outrage on architectural propriety and taste'; or if his swelled frieze was 'a licentious practice, made use of in few buildings of importance, except the Temple of Bacchus, near Rome, the Basilica of Antoninus, and afterwards by Palladio, in the Rotunda of Capra, and a very few others.'[122] His eye was on the nearby Liverpool Union Bank for whom Messrs Cunningham & Holmes were designing a 'chaste' bank with Ionic portico.[123]

Corbett's responsibility, in effect, was to design premises for his client which would be no less impressive to a prospective customer than those of the opposition. Attention to classical authority was not a matter for bankers and therefore of subordinate concern to their architects. The directors of the Liverpool Union Bank gave no guidance to Cunningham beyond the knowledge that his revised plans 'gave much satisfaction'.[124] This was by no means a situation confined to Liverpool. It is in vain that the minutes of early joint-stock banks are combed for precise expressions of architectural preference on the part of the directorate. Certainly there were building committees to advise the main board; some even travelled to see other banks, like the

Plate 18. Cunningham & Holmes's Liverpool Union Bank, opened 1841.

committee of the Sheffield Banking Company who visited new premises at Huddersfield.[125] Plans could be criticised and styles compared;
specifications could be judged inadequate; the need could be stressed
for 'respectability'.[126] But no battle in the board room can be traced
between supporters of Italianate and those of neo-Greek. No doubt
some individual bankers had strong personal views; but the board's
selection of final design was within the range of styles which the
architect thought fit to produce.

The Union Bank in Liverpool, completed in 1841, was one of the
last neo-Greek banks built in an Order other than Corinthian (Plate
18). It cost less than £5000,[127] which was £1000 less than the site itself,
and in line with the cost of building at, for instance, Gloucester, in the
same period.[128] The Union Bank had no branches and as paid-up
capital was £171 750 within 6 months of the commencement of business
in 1835,[129] this does not seem an extravagant outlay on accommodation. But within a year of the opening there was a misfortune in
joint-stock banking which threatened to call even this degree of
expenditure into question. This misfortune befell the Yorkshire
Agricultural & Commercial Bank, founded in 1836 and based at York
and Whitby.

There was no lack of speculation on the cause of this collapse, which
brought ruin not only to customers but also to shareholders, who were
'mostly of the humble class.'[130] There was agreement that the
management had been generally feckless, and the *Times* blamed it in
addition for having taken business of the failed Northern & Central
Bank.[131] The *Bankers' Magazine* added other specific allegations, one
of them concerning premises. It is worth quoting at some length:

> In 1840–41, much to the surprise of that portion of the mercantile
> public, who know by experience the importance of not locking up in
> investments which are of highly unconvertible nature, the Directors
> expended £10,000 or £12,000 in the erection of magnificent premises at
> York and Whitby. At York, especially, the outlay was very large; ... if
> the erection of a splendid and spacious banking-house ... had been the
> object for which the company was formed, the shareholders would have
> had every reason to be satisfied. The York premises are now conspic-
> uous among the architectural beauties and the commercial follies of that
> great county ...[132]

It is the historian's misfortune that such a positive and authoritative
statement of date and costs should be thrown into confusion by
evidence from another quarter. But the fact is that in 1850, some 10
years after these premises were built and 8 years after the bank itself

had ceased to exist, the *Civil Engineer & Architect's Journal* published elevations, ground plans and full architectural description of both, as if they had just been erected.[133] For the journal to have published at that remove, and in contemporary terms, facts which must have revived in some people the most painful memories, was grotesque. It seems reasonable, however, to accept the descriptions as accurate for the earlier date. The architects of both buildings were J.B. & W. Atkinson who chose classical styles, Whitby recalling features of Hoare's bank in London while York was more specifically Italianate. Both buildings had counters at right angles to the light. The journal put total building costs at around £5600,[134] which weakens the charge of extravagance by the *Bankers' Magazine*, although the latter's figure might have included the purchase of sites. The Whitby building appears to have been demolished but the York premises have survived, outwardly intact and unremarkable, as the Nessgate branch of the Midland Bank. It seems difficult now to understand the intensity of the criticism.

The Atkinsons' choice of Italianate is of some interest. York, like other towns in the north of England, had been caught up in the competitive fervour of joint-stock banking. In 1837 the premises of both the York City & County Bank (established 1830) and the York Union Bank (established 1833) were opened on the south-west side of Parliament Street.[135] The former bank, with a rusticated base supporting Doric pilasters and entablature, was by Robinson & Andrews.[136] Enlarged in 1874,[137] it later became a branch of the Midland Bank and was demolished in 1971. The Union Bank building was pulled down earlier. It was evidently stone-faced and elegant[138] and would hardly have been less attractive than its rival a few yards away. It was while these banks were building that the Commercial & Agricultural Bank was formed, with its premises at the corner of High Ousegate and what was then called Castlegate. The choice of Italianate was no doubt a step to establish a distinct and positive identity.

It is possible that this disaster, attributed in no small degree by the banking *cognoscenti* to the perils of building, was responsible for the relative pause in construction work which seems to have occurred among joint-stock banks between 1842 and 1847. But there were perhaps other reasons as well: most of the early-established banks had already built their premises if they were going to build at all; and some bankers would have wanted to see the results of Parliamentary activity, which culminated in the Bank Charter Act of 1844,[139] before risking reserves on assets difficult to realise.

In this 'close' period, interest centres again on the Bank of England for whom Cockerell was designing his well-known branches at Bristol and Manchester (opened in 1847) and Liverpool (opened in 1848)[140] (Plate 19). Cockerell's recent biographer has traced the origins of this particular style to his Westminster Life Office in the Strand, of 1831.[141] In the realms of banking this individuality had a particular relevance. It has been suggested that Cockerell's bank was 'certainly quite consciously intended to overshadow other local banks as completely as the Bank of England ... overshadowed all British private bankers.'[142] While this is broadly true, in so far as the bank could no longer afford the kind of criticism of insignificance it had received at Liverpool, it misses the technical point that it was the joint-stock banks with which the Bank of England was basically in competition. The difficulty which Cockerell faced was that of designing a building which was no more than a branch bank in the scale of its business, but able to hold its own architecturally with the head offices of the banking corporations. He achieved this by building with a strength and monumental quality expressed through the Doric Order, which has won consistent admiration.[143]

While Cockerell was developing his own interpretation of neo-Greek, the joint-stock banks were moving towards Italianate, both in a modest way for smaller buildings and in a lavish *palazzo* manner for head offices. The latter style was particularly suited to the spirit of the age. It was the decade of railway mania, speculation and technological confidence, all resting on the bed-rock of dependable banking. Launched in 1844, the *Bankers' Magazine* began a monthly summary of the railway share market in its first volume. This soon developed into a detailed and analytical 'Railway Digest'. The philosophy of banking was moving away from the private bank virtues of solidity and reserve. These characteristics were not necessarily neglected but the trend was now towards competitiveness, growth, and ostentation. The architectural expression of this new vitality was embellishment, and one means of providing it was the introduction of allegorical statuary.

The first signs of such statuary were in the 1830s. The pediment of Smith & Co.'s bank at Hull had representations of sea and river gods, and various emblems of commerce.[144] Cockerell's London & Westminster bank was crowned by female figures representing the two cities — figures which were soon nicknamed Principal and Interest by City wags.[145] The Liverpool Union Bank of 1841 displayed 'very handsome illustrative carvings', and flowers and honeysuckle on the frieze.[146] E.F. Law's Northamptonshire Union Bank, also 1841, still an attractive building in The Drapery, Northampton, has a phoenix carved in

Plate 19. C.R. Cockerell's Bank of England branches. Above: Manchester, opened 1847. Below, left: Bristol, opened 1847. Below right: Liverpool, opened 1848.

Plate 20. David Rhind's Commercial Bank of Scotland, Edinburgh office, 1847.

the pediment above the Corinthian portico.[147] But it was again Scotland which had anticipated the English practice and it is necessary now to catch up with the developments there since the mid-1820s.

Joint-stock banks built a succession of fine buildings between 1833 and 1842 at Kirkcaldy, Stirling, Dingwall, Peterhead, Aberdeen, Banff, Greenock, Montrose and Dundee.[148] The most prolific bank architect in Scotland was William Burn, but Archibald Simpson and J.G. Graham were also in demand. During this period, however, there was little new building by Edinburgh bankers, still content for the most part with the legacy of *hôtels particuliers*. In 1825–8 Archibald Elliot remodelled a mansion in St Andrew Square, originally by Sir William Chambers, for the Royal Bank of Scotland.[149] The initiative in building had now passed to Glasgow, in step with its development as a great industrial city. The Greek Revival Royal Bank of Scotland, of 1827, has already been mentioned. The Glasgow Union Bank built a handsome classical building, 1836–8, which later became the premises of the City of Glasgow Bank.[150] The favoured architect in Glasgow was David Hamilton, who designed the Clydesdale Bank in Queen Street (1840), the Western Bank in Miller Street (1840), and the Italianate British Linen Bank in Queen Street (1840–1).[151]

The bank by Hamilton which had most influence was the Union Bank, designed originally for the Glasgow & Ship Bank and opened in 1842.[152] Hamilton's Doric portico faced Virginia Street, but a new façade, in the direction of Ingram Street, was built by John Burnet in 1876–9.[153] The entablature of Hamilton's bank was surmounted by statues symbolizing Britannia, Glasgow, Wealth, Justice, Peace and Industry.[154] The sculptor was John Mossman.[155] Hamilton's specific inspiration for the grand entrance appears to have been Palladio's Palazzo Chiericati at Vicenza, from which the main elements of the Glasgow design, including the statuary, are translated from colonnade to portico.

At Edinburgh, David Rhind's Commercial Bank in George Street, opened in 1847,[156] the first wholly purpose-built bank in that city for many years, carried a pediment busy with symbolism (Plate 20) and reminiscent of Tite's Royal Exchange in London, opened in 1844. It is interesting to compare Rhind's bank with Elliot's Royal Bank of Scotland in Glasgow of 1827 (Plate 14) and to note that a change to the Corinthian Order, and the introduction of statuary to the pediment, were the only significant differences between two temple-form buildings 20 years apart. Closer to Hamilton's form of statuary, but atop a building of quite different inspiration, were the six figures, 8 feet high,

Plate 21. J.E. Gregan's Heywood's Bank, Manchester, 1848.

crowning the British Linen Bank in Edinburgh, opened in 1851 to designs by Burn and Bryce.[157] These statues depicted Agriculture, Manufacture, Commerce, Science, Architecture and Navigation, another commendably broad vision by bankers of the extent of their influence or interest.

The style in England in the late 'forties was still relatively conservative. John Cunningham's Liverpool Commercial Bank, with a façade of Corinthian pilasters, had only 'enormous, ill-shaped vases' on the balustrade, and some ornamentation on the return front.[158] This bank was not completed until 1848, having been delayed in a strike.[159] Another bank of 1848 was the one designed by J.E. Gregan for Heywood & Co., of Manchester, sited on a corner of St Ann's Square.[160] Subsequently, it became the bank of Williams, Deacon & Co. Gregan's building consisted of a bank proper connected to chambers by an arched entrance (Plate 21). Reilly found the bank so satisfying that he would have wished the name, Gregan, to be a household word in Manchester.[161] 'If anyone wants to build a small three-storeyed structure for almost any domestic purpose in a town', he wrote, 'where could a better model (outside Italy) be found? . . . this bank group is a model of civic reserve and good manners combined with strength and character.'[162]

Although Gregan's bank was a free interpretation of Italian motifs, the scale, grouping, and particularly the articulation provided by the entrance placed to the side of the main building owed much to the Palazzo Pandolfini at Florence. This particular precedent, perhaps first used for a bank at Gloucester some 10 years ealier,[163] was better suited to private banks than to joint-stock companies. Not only was the scale too compact for a head office of even moderate size, but there was a quality of reserve, as Reilly noticed, and this did not fit the joint-stock bank mentality. It is, therefore, at this period (the late 1840s) that we see the break beginning away from the Barry-type clubhouse and towards a far more lavish style of building from a wider variety of Italian sources. Once again Scotland led the way and the influential bank of the 'new' style was John Gibson's National Bank of Scotland, opened in Queen Street, Glasgow, in 1849[164] (Plates 22 and 23).

Gibson had been a pupil of Barry, but his own Italianate was innovatory. The Glasgow bank, as well as being the first commission in banking to a man who was to become the most distinguished and prolific of Victorian architects in that field, is important also as a forerunner of the Venetian style, which was to become popular for banks in the 1850s. The National Bank was sumptuous. It was some

Plate 22. John Gibson's National Bank of Scotland, Glasgow office, 1849.

Plate 23. John Gibson's National Bank of Scotland, Glasgow office, 1849. Interior.

time since banks had been designed with superimposed Orders. Instead of Ionic on Doric, it was now Corinthian, with lavish entablature, on Ionic, both Orders applied. Coupled pilasters were used on the return fronts, and at the angles, but the pilasters between the first and second bays of the front elevation were single. This gave more emphasis to the third and central bay which broke forward with three-quarter columns and was crowned by the national Arms, flanked by statues of Peace and Commerce. These were by John Thomas, who also sculptured the vases placed on the cornice in logical determination of the pilasters, and the keystone heads on ground floor windows and doorway 'emblematic of the principal rivers of the United Kingdom'.[165]

The domed interior of the bank was no less stunning and revolutionary. Now, probably for the first time in a British bank, the eye met 'a gorgeous arrangement of sparkling colour' and a 'dazzling shower of coloured rays profusely shed through the deep-stained glass of the cupola'.[166] Apparently, much of the porphyry and marble were imitation, and there were features of this bank which had been rehearsed elsewhere: Gibson, for instance, had used a similar style of ground-floor window for his slightly earlier Imperial Assurance Office in London, and Edward Moxhay's Hall of Commerce in London, completed some 5 years before the National Bank, had anticipated much of the shape and magnificence of Gibson's 'Telling-Room' or banking-hall.[167] But in the realms of banking this was pioneering stuff, with the architect taking advice from Bogle & Co. of Glasgow in coloured and gilded decoration and from Ballantine & Allan of Edinburgh in stained glass.[168] The ensemble won the praise of Ralph Wornum, Government Inspector of the National Schools of Design.[169]

Whether or not Gibson's bank was particularly Venetian, it had a luxuriance quite alien to the Roman and Florentine precedents which bankers had traditionally followed. As Gibson would have designed the bank a little before Ruskin's influential patronage of all things Venetian, it is appropriate to ask whether the exuberance of Venice was seen as architecturally more appropriate for the philosophy of joint-stock banking, or whether the banking practice of Venice was realised as being professionally more in keeping with the new image. The former proposition is much more attractive than the latter. The history of Venetian banking is a catalogue of failures, particularly in the sixteenth century, and the city which gave us the word 'giro' had a conservative banking practice which made the transfer of money an oral rather than written procedure, even into the eighteenth century.[170]

Gibson had won the Glasgow contract in a competition which had opened in 1844. In most cases bankers probably selected their architect by direct commission, choosing a local man who was already respected for his public buildings. But a competition had a natural connotation of publicity which the more forward banks would have liked. Less welcome, of course, was the bad press which many competitions seemed to attract. Edward Corbett, architect of the North & South Wales Bank in Liverpool, was prepared to accept technical criticism of his design; but it was too much to have his alleged faults ascribed to 'the effects of modern competition; where the successful architect, having had his design accepted in consequence, it is said, of his private interest in the committee of management, has not only the advantage ... of examining those of his competitors ... but is permitted to expend about twice the amount to which they were ... limited, and this for the purpose of producing a building which is a perfect burlesque on all correct proportion.'[171] Attacks on the principle of competitions were renewed by the *Westminster Review*, who saw them as 'mere contests of intrigue to serve friends or favourites',[172] a sentiment echoed later by the *Quarterly Review*.[173] However, in the context of banking, the accusations were probably uncharitable. There is no reason to believe that the directors of early joint-stock banks, accountable to shareholders for a decent annual dividend, were collectively moved to further the career of an aspiring protégé. They had other matters to worry about.

Another feature of the 'forties, and one which had its own impact on the move to embellishment, was the rise of an informed and often critical architectural media. To the *Civil Engineer & Architect's Journal* was added the *Builder* and the *Illustrated London News*; the last-named was not, of course, specifically architectural in its outlook, but plates of new buildings, banks among them, were common enough, and the paper's coverage was national even from the beginning. Of the two newcomers, the *Builder* was naturally the more critical, but although it found fault stylistically with certain individual banks,[174] it had no suggestions of its own about the appearance and arrangement which bankers should adopt. And yet, one architect at least, exhibited a model 'Design for provincial bank' by 1846.[175] When the *Builder* did publish such matters, in 1849,[176] it was as a reprint from certain pages of Gilbart's *Practical Treatise on Banking*, the first vade-mecum of banking practice.

J.W. Gilbart (1794–1863) was a professional banker.[177] He began his career with a London private bank and later joined the Provincial

Bank of Ireland in a managerial position. He then moved to the London & Westminster Bank for whom he became the first general manager, 1833–59. As a result of the annual lecture in his name, Gilbart's fame as a joint-stock banker has endured; but his pioneering advice on the siting and appearance of banks has never been recognised in architectural circles. His *Practical Treatise* ... had first been published in 1827; the 1849 edition was the fifth, and the first to appear in two volumes. None of the earlier editions had dealt with matters architectural.

Gilbart's opening remarks, in the matter of premises, come as no surprise: 'The proper situation of a bank is a matter of some importance. It should be situated in what is deemed the most respectable part of town. If it be placed in an inferior locality, approachable only by narrow and disagreeable streets ... it is not likely to be so much frequented ...'.[178] Of more importance is his advice on a bank's appearance: 'Another point to be observed is, that the bank itself should be a handsome building. The necessary expenditure for this purpose is no sin against economy: it is an outlay of capital to be repaid by the profits of the business that will then be acquired.'[179] Although this was no licence to be profligate, it must nevertheless have been music to the ears of many bankers, who faced with ever-increasing competition, had also to justify their architect's expenditure at meetings of shareholders.

Less liberal than Gilbart was George Rae, general manager of the North and South Wales Bank.[180] Also in 1849, Rae had the *Bankers' Magazine* publish the letters of 'Thomas Bullion' to a 'Branch Manager', dealing *inter alia* with the quality of premises: '... your customers will care little whether they approach your counter through a plain street door, or from beneath a Grecian portico. A certain air of sobriety is what should pervade a banking establishment ... Flash and glitter, and ostentation, are the natural properties of your Colonial Emporiums, Cigar Divans, and Tailoring Marts.'[181]

As for bank interiors, Gilbart argued for space, light and ventilation: space for cashiers and clerks to work in some comfort; light to avoid errors and deter robbery; ventilation to safeguard the clerks' health in their gas-lit environment. He made no mention of heating, and by ventilation he meant fresh air. The following description of part of the Bank of England in 1837 crystallises the problem as Gilbart might have seen it: 'The very large room ... in which so many clerks sit, seems very highly heated, by the heat radiating from so many persons. The only fire heat in the room arises from a few open fireplaces, without which the want of ventilation would be dreadful: as it is, the clerks are under the necessity, from the defective ventilation, of reinhaling the vapours emitted by the lungs of themselves and their neighbours.'[182] Elsewhere in the Bank of England the problems of ventilation and heating had been linked, and allegedly solved, by the 'ingenious contraption' of a Mr Oldham, first tried at the Bank of Ireland, which forced external air 'through the interstices of iron cases filled with steam'.[183]

Gilbart's answer to the problem of light — a matter which had also troubled Cockerell[184] — has already been mentioned in this chapter and in Chapter One. It was shown that the practice which he recommended in 1849 had certainly been adopted by the end of the eighteenth century. His advice was 'that the entrance be placed at the right or left corner [of the front elevation], and the counter be made to run from the window to the opposite wall; the light will thus fall lengthways on the counter, and the space behind the counter will be occupied by the clerks'.[185] This was not, however, the style of his own bank in Lothbury, nor of most other head offices. It has already been shown that when the banking hall was lit from a cupola the special relationship ceased between the entrance and the siting of the counters.

The writings of Gilbart and Rae were only one aspect of a new professional cohesion and awareness taking place among bankers. Fostered by the forum of the *Bankers' Magazine*, first issued in 1844, and informed about colleagues by the *Bankers' Almanac* (from 1845), the profession formed a Banking Institute in 1851.[186] The inclination to discuss matters of functional as well as philosophical importance was encouraged by the coincidence of that most functional of all Victorian events — the Great Exhibition. In December 1850 a letter was published in the *Bankers' Magazine* from 'A General Manager' drawing attention to the relevance of the Exhibition to bankers and suggesting that the profession should institute an essay competition on the theme: 'In what way can any of the articles collected at the Industrial Exhibition of 1851, be rendered specially serviceable to the interest of practical banking?' In the next issue, Gilbart announced a prize of £100 for the best essay on that subject, a fact which suggests that he himself might have written the letter.[187] The prize was awarded to Granville Sharp, a 27-year-old clerk in the East of England Bank at Norwich, and his essay was published on its own, with illustrations, while a slightly abbreviated, and at times curiously paraphrased, text appeared in the *Bankers' Magazine*.[188]

The essayists' exact brief was to examine innovations in the following areas:[189]

> Architectural Models that may suggest improvements in the Bank House or Office
> Inventions by which Light, Heat, and Ventilation may be secured, so as to promote the health and comfort of Bank clerks
> Discoveries in the Fine Arts, by which the interior of the Bank may be decorated, or the Bank furniture rendered more commodious
> Improvements in Writing Paper . . .
> Improvements in Printing and Engraving . . .
> New inventions in the construction of locks, cash boxes, and safes . . .

Sharp thought that the architecture of a bank 'should be marked externally, internally, and everywhere, by *stability*, as its leading feature; which a builder of intelligence will not fail to combine with *taste*'.[190] He regretted that many banks fell short of this ideal, because 'to save perhaps 5% upon the outlay, an architect of inferior ability has been employed, and the whole building wants that grace and character which every structure should possess. It is quite possible to have something of ornament, without approaching to what would be called 'ornate'; and architectural beauty, symmetry and accordance may be perfectly compatible with the purposes and objects of the most substantial edifice.'[191]

It is clear from these remarks that Sharp found nothing in the Exhibition which was relevant to 'Architectural Models' in an aesthetic sense and his comments steer a compromising path between the positions of Gilbart and Rae. They must have been a real disappointment to the architectural profession, who read that the union of stability with taste was a matter for the builder, rather than the architect, and that the latter should be aware that his commission was perhaps aimed at undercutting the expense of a more capable colleague. If the words of Sharp, at his relatively young age, have any real significance, it is to point to a gulf existing between the professionals of banking and architecture, to the extent that the former had no understanding of the latter and certainly no interest in the architectural controversies of the day. This reinforces the conclusions already arrived at in this chapter, and is not contradicted by Sharp's feeble comments about 'Discoveries in the Fine Arts', which are restricted to admiration for carved oak figures of royalty and dignitaries — suitable also for the reproduction of bankers — and to the promotion of imitation marbles, painted on wood and slate, and patent earthenware as a substitute for plaster.[192]

In other respects, however, Sharp's essay is most interesting, revelatory of a growing anxiety for every aspect of security which the banking profession has never been able since to relax. It is difficult for us today, punch-drunk by the reporting of violent robbery, to realise that Britain of the 1840s was in the grip of a crime wave of unparalleled extent and sophistication. The *Bankers' Magazine* lamented that 'a large class exist by robbery'; that 'bank robberies of late years . . . have been planned with extraordinary sagacity'; that 'an unsuccessful attempt to rob a bank is seldom heard of'.[193] There were many ways to set about robbery, some depressingly similar to modern experience. Customers were attacked as they left the banking-hall, occupiers were won over or intimidated if there was accommodation above the bank, and bizarre tools like the 'Screw' for forcing shutters, or the 'Jack-in-the-Box' for tearing out the centre locks of iron doors, kept pace with the technology of security.[194] Most banks held firearms, some a whole armoury, and clerks were issued with 'life-preservers', which were a form of cosh.

In step with this situation arose a national obsession for locks, evoking controversy at the Great Exhibition, giving bankers a topic for discussion at the first meeting of their Institute, and provoking challenge and counter-challenge among manufacturers.[195] To the ranks of Bramah and Chubb came Edward and John Tann and Thomas and William Milner, broadening the battleground of patents from locks and latches into boxes, chests and safes.[196] Ingenuity was boundless. Messrs Chubb developed a well-safe, patented in 1839. This was an iron box which could be winched down a brick shaft at night from first-floor level to basement. Several firms designed safe custody boxes with outer cases, the space between box and case being filled with non-conducting material.[197] Perhaps the most curious example was designed by Thomas Milner & Son of Liverpool, whose case held 'a vegetable powder, and a number of metal tubes, filled with a strong alkaline solution. When the heat becomes very great, these tubes melt, and allow the liquid to saturate the powder, so that the power of resisting the action of the fire is very great'.[198]

In other ways, too, fire was seen as a problem second only to security. The fire-proof system of construction of Messrs Fox & Barratt was frequently referred to in the architectural press. Patented by Henry Hawes Fox, a country doctor in Gloucestershire, the system relied on layers of mortar, lime, road grit, coal ash, and cement, in varying proportions, forming a kind of barrier between combustible components of floor, ceiling and roof.[199] Fox stressed that his system involved no new fire-proofing principles but only an improved mode of execution.[200] The weight must have been colossal, and the new technique was only suited to the largest banks, of stone and iron framework. Because of these inherently fire-resisting materials, fires in banks were, in any case, said to be 'one of the rarest of accidents'.[201] For this reason the Provincial Fire Insurance Company, formed at Wrexham in 1852, offered bankers a much lower premium on basic cover.[202]

Perhaps the most successful speculation in this period of invention and innovation were the revolving iron shutters patented in 1836 by Joseph Bunnett, a window-blind maker of Newington Causeway, Southwark.[203] The shutters, coiled at the top of the window, were lowered by a crank-handle at waist height, which acted through bevel gearing to turn a vertical shaft or axle, ending at the roller wheel. The bank messenger charged with raising and lowering a full set of these blinds in the course of each day must have gone home an exhausted man. Bunnett was briefly in partnership with a Mr Corpe, at a time when his invention was, to all appearances, copied and marketed by one John Harcourt Quincey.[204] But Corpe and Quincey both gave up, while Bunnett himself, aided by three sons, went from strength to strength, with a factory at Deptford, an office in Lombard Street and depots at Birmingham, Liverpool, Manchester, Glasgow, Dublin and Belfast.[205] No new bank, it seems, was built without Bunnett's shutters, and a very few are still in place. Staff at Lloyds Bank in Boston (a building of 1864) recall that in recent renovation the contractor disturbed a rolled shutter, unseen and long forgotten behind a modern pelmet. It uncurled to the floor with the ferocity of a guillotine and the noise of a bomb.

Only towards the end of the 1840s does the term strong room acquire its modern sense of a reinforced, purpose-built chamber, resistant to fire and robbery, and designed as an integral feature of the building. Even then, the legacy of smaller banks in adequate surroundings was such that the greater interest of banker and manufacturer alike lay in free-standing safes of prodigious weight and strength, some large enough for clerks to walk into, like a modern shipping container, and many impossible to install in existing premises without partial demolition.[206] The *Bankers' Magazine* recommended that whenever possible the door of the strong room, or similar chamber, should be protected by an iron bolt, to pass through the ceiling and eventually to the bedside of the bank's resident official.[207] Such relics of industrial archaeology are still to be traced in some country branches.

In step with embellishment and technological progress, there arose a more sophisticated banking practice which led to the value of many premises being deliberately marked down. In this rare respect, the English practice appears to have been ahead of Scotland.[208] As early as 1839 the Gloucestershire Banking Co. wrote £1000 off the value of its new premises[209] and the collapse of the Yorkshire Agricultural & Commercial Bank must have induced many others to follow suit. The practice was common enough in the 1850s.[210] The idea was to reduce the book value of premises so that the asset would not appear to be more on paper than it would fetch if realised. The more 'bank-like' a building became, the less opportunity there would be to sell it quickly, if this should become necessary, at anything approaching the capital cost of construction. The principle was taken to extremes by the Bank of England, whose premises were marked down to nothing during the nineteenth century.[211]

The decade of the 1850s marks the cautious re-entry of London into the national panorama of banking. The disappointing record of the metropolis had not passed unnoticed. The Union Bank of London, near Regent Street, built in 1840 to designs by Newnham & Webb, had prompted the *Civil Engineer & Architect's Journal* to hope that the joint-stock banks, like the assurance offices, would give some employment to architects in the capital, as they had already done in the country.[212] 'Any thing in fact is worthy of encouragement which rises above the mere brickbat and whitewash style.'[213] But the promise came to nothing. The *Illustrated London News*, in 1855, remarked that 'Architectural Embellishment has received little encouragement at the hands of the banking interest south of the Tweed. Edinburgh and Glasgow can boast several magnificent structures devoted to banking; but London has yet to acquire the reputation of having contributed from the profits of business to the elevation of street architecture.'[214]

The immediate cause of that remark was yet another example of a London bank choosing to do business in second-hand premises.[215] But it was also an expression of deep-seated disappointment about an occurrence some 2 years earlier. The bank which had seemed likely to end the sterility of London was the new Bloomsbury branch of the London & Westminster Bank, in High Holborn, completed in 1853[216] (Plate 24). The architect had been chosen by a competition which was well received by the *Builder* although limited to the bank's customers.[217] The abortive plans of Messrs Smith & Thurston, one of the six competitors, were shown at the Royal Academy.[218] The commission was awarded to Henry Baker of Upper Gower Street, who, on the strength of this project, found later work in the City with

other bankers.[219] Baker's building was received by the *Illustrated London News* with a brave face. What a change, the paper thought, from the old branch, 'gas burning all day — dirt, darkness and discomfort everywhere — unfit even for the passing visit of a customer and most obnoxious to the health of the employés doomed to inhale the foetid atmosphere daily for 8 or 9 hours'.[220] Mentioning what it called

Plate 24. Henry Baker's London & Westminster Bank, Bloomsbury branch: 1853 elevation, and modern appearance as High Holborn branch of National Westminster Bank.

Gilbart's 'hints', the paper went on to praise the space, light and ventilation of the new building. There was heating by hot water; fittings were of oak and Spanish mahogany, materials which were later to become quite standard for bank interiors. The building still stands, as the Bloomsbury branch of the National Westminster Bank, and the main elevation has scarcely been altered.

Despite high praise for the comfort and fittings, the *Illustrated London News* could muster nothing more than 'satisfaction' for the Italianate appearance, and a recognition of the 'happy effect produced by good proportion and well-studied detail.'[221] The *Builder* omitted to comment stylistically on Baker's design, perhaps not wishing to be too critical about the first purpose-built branch of a joint-stock bank anywhere in London for more than a decade. But it had no such inhibitions about P.C. Hardwick's Bank of Australasia, opened in Threadneedle Street in 1855, and 'erected without any attempt at unity of style, or even an effort at picturesque relative arrangement.'[222] The nearby City Bank of 1856, by W. & A. Moseley,[223] was more successful. It was another mark of the interest which London banks were arousing that plans for both this building and Hardwick's were exhibited at the Royal Academy.[224] But in all the 1850s there was still no grand building in London by joint-stock bankers to match the achievements in Scotland. Even in relation to contemporary banks elsewhere in England, for example at Northampton, Preston and Bradford, London was noticeably backward.

It was not, then, in the capital that equality with the Scottish manner of building was first achieved. Neither was it, for that matter, in the Midlands or north of England. Rather it was at Bristol, a city which has scarcely been mentioned so far, outside the context of the Bank of England.

In 1854 the West of England & South Wales District Bank, always an adventurous company,[225] opened a competition for the design of their new head office, to be built on a site in Corn Street, Bristol.[226] Over 50 designs were submitted and unsuccessful contenders included E.M. Barry and John Gibson.[227] Both these architects were rewarded by 'premiums'.[228] The winning design, prepared jointly by W.B. Gingell of Bristol and T.R. Lysaght of London (Plate 25), was derived from Sansovino's Library of St Mark, in Venice, but with a freer interpretation of that exemplar than Sydney Smirke had allowed himself earlier for the Carlton Club.[229]

If the *Illustrated London News* had been lukewarm in Bloomsbury, it was enraptured in Bristol: 'the architects ... have succeeded in producing a façade that for architectural and sculptural beauty may fairly be said to have no rival out of Venice ...'.[230] The same source put the total cost, including land, at around £30000, but Latimer's figure of more than £40000 may be nearer the truth. Apparently, the assessment for poor rate, at £2000 per annum, was more than the figure for all other bank premises in Bristol put together.[231]

Although it is to some extent right to see Corn Street as a product of the 'enviable self-confidence' of nineteenth century Bristolians,[232] it is more accurately seen as an example of the effects of competition.

Plate 25. W.B. Gingell & T.R. Lysaght's West of England & South Wales District Bank, opened 1857, now the Corn Street, Bristol, branch of Lloyds Bank. The original building was of five bays with a central entrance. The left-hand entrance bay, added in the 1920s, can be detected as an addition by the arrangement of urns on the parapet.

Cockerell had built the branch Bank of England in Broad Street, and nearby Corn Street was developing into a banking enclave of some importance. In 1852, Stuckey's Banking Company, a prestigious joint-stock bank which had been founded in 1826 out of the Langport-based private bank of Stuckey & Co., opened its new premises at the junction of Corn Street and St Nicholas Street.[233] This was a handsome, late-classical bank, designed by a local man, R.S. Pope. In all probability, it was buildings like these (and not the neo-Greek premises next door) which Gingell & Lysaght had to beat. A building with Venetian richness of detail not only rang the changes but made it difficult for the opposition to go one stage better. In banking terms, however, the precedent was not particularly apt: if Sansovino was in

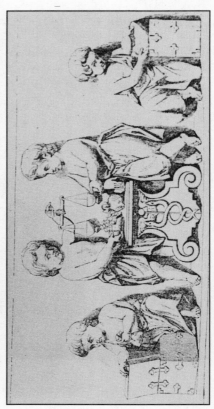
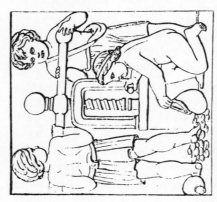
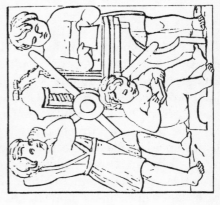

favour, then his Venetian waterside Zecca, or mint, around the corner from the library, gave an exemplar more appropriate for a repository of money. But it was in a style too severe for the mood of the day.

Luckily, this was not another 'York'. The bank had overspent, but survived another 20 years before coming near to disaster.[234] The professional, post-Gilbart opinion of the *Bankers' Magazine*, which had been so critical of the Yorkshire Agricutural & Commercial Bank, was never given. The magazine had certainly mellowed. Indeed, in 1857, the year when the Bristol bank opened, it felt able to note that 'The Ulster Banking Company is about to erect a splendid building for its purposes at Belfast'[235] — sentiments which it would never have expressed in the previous decade. The fact was that the magazine could no longer ignore or reject the rising appreciation which bankers, among others, were receiving for the quality of their buildings. The position had been summed up 3 years earlier by the *Quarterly Review*: 'At the present day far more attention is paid to architectural appearance than formerly. A numerous class of buildings — to wit, private banks, insurance and other offices, which used to make so little pretension to external character as to be scarcely distinguishable from the ordinary houses around them — now contribute to the adornment of our streets. Although not exactly public buildings, they shame several which are included in that prouder title ... they serve as landmarks ....'.[236] The Bristol bank was nothing if not a landmark. Today, a branch of Lloyds Bank, it carries an extra bay added earlier this century to move the doorway from the centre to the side.

By contrast, and no doubt to save expense, the interior of the Bristol bank was relatively plain. It was, however, very well proportioned, with a large rectangular ceiling light carried on vaulted ribs, rising from coupled Corinthian columns set on plinths. This arrangement was to become as influential on Gibson as Gibson had himself been influential in Bristol.

Also in 1857, another of the grand banks of Glasgow was completed: this was David Rhind's Commercial Bank of Scotland in Gordon Street,[237] popular later as 'a most successful Venetian design'[238] although the inspiration seems to have been more widely Italian. This bank had an interesting detail in common with the one by Gingell and Lysaght (Plate 26). At Glasgow, the rustication at ground-floor level,

Plate 26. Left, top and bottom: panels from David Rhind's Commercial Bank of Scotland, Glasgow office, opened 1857. Right, top and bottom: details of frieze from Gingell & Lysaght's West of England & South Wales District Bank, Bristol, opened 1857. Both sets of carvings by John Thomas of London.

on either side of the central block, had sculptured panels depicting *putti* pressing and coining;[239] the actual carving was by John Thomas of London, who had worked on Gibson's National Bank.[240] Now, at Bristol, Thomas was also employed[241] and similar carvings are represented on the frieze. It would be interesting to know how much freedom Thomas was allowed at Bristol, and if the repetition of motif was wholly by his own initiative.

The importance of Corn Street is that it marks the point when the premises of English joint-stock bankers reflected the level of professional self-confidence which had been achieved long before in the Scottish Lowlands. The hegemony of Scotland never quite returned, and soon London banks were at last to reflect the status of the capital as a centre of international business.

Before this change is considered, however, attention must dwell on savings banks, which have so far been neglected in these discussions. This neglect is in no sense a judgment on the historical or architectural importance of savings banks, but rather a deference to the status of these institutions as a self-contained unit of study.

Chapter Three

The Early Savings Banks

The range of customer services provided by the modern Trustee Savings Bank, in many respects competitive with those of the Big Four clearing banks, obscures the origin of its business in nineteenth century voluntary and charitable work, far removed from the world of commercial banking. These beginnings are so little remembered that, in modern classifications for architectural purposes, a bank is a bank. It is usual to include old savings banks under such headings as 'Commerce & Industry'.[1] Even the most conscientious of local historians can misunderstand them. E.L.S. Horsburgh, for instance, believed 'the primary purpose' of the Bromley savings bank 'was economic rather than social or philanthropic',[2] and it may be this uncertainty as to their role which has led to savings banks being a neglected field of study.[3]

The Victorians, of course, knew at first hand what purpose the savings banks were to serve and had no difficulty distinguishing them from other kinds of bank. For example, the city of Worcester in 1840, had 'the good fortune to possess five [banks], four of them being for the mercantile part of the community, one for the humble but ... thrifty artizan'.[4] A description of Stourport at the same date commented on the lack of a bank for 'the merchants, manufacturers, and tradesmen', but was thankful for a savings bank for the labouring poor.[5] That a distinction should sometimes have been made between the character of buildings for the reception, on the one hand, of the pennies of the working class, and for the loan, on the other hand, of money for speculative business and middle-class investment, is an obvious expectation of research.

One body of people who took a close, but not necessarily supportive, interest in savings banks, were professional bankers — that is to say, bankers associated with commercial banks, both private firms and joint-stock companies. This interest was expressed through the *Bankers' Magazine* which, in its second volume, carried an editorial comment so important to the architectural historian that it forms the backbone of this chapter:

> Complaints have frequently been made, that a large portion of the profits of Savings' Banks has, from time to time, been expended in the erection of houses and official residences, in a style, and of a character, utterly incompatible with the nature of such institutions, and in other than the localities where the humbler classes . . . usually reside . . . [6]

This statement was followed by a list of nine English savings banks which had each withdrawn over £3000 from its 'Separate Surplus Fund', a term which is at the heart of any investigation into extravagance. It will be helpful to examine what this surplus fund was, how it arose, and the uses to which it was put. Before this, however, savings banks must be put in some historical perspective.

The English banks evolved in the first decade of the nineteenth century from pioneering ventures at Wendover (1798) and Tottenham (1799). Although it was the bank founded by Dr Duncan at Ruthwell near Dumfries which was the first to anticipate the organisation later required by statute, Scotland was on a different monetary footing and was exempt from prevailing legislation until 1835.[7] In Scotland money could also be lodged with joint-stock banks which gave interest on deposits. In the rest of Great Britain, where joint-stock banks had not yet been authorised, the savings banks tried different ways, none wholly successful, to give security to depositors and an assured return on their investments.

In this situation, where 'the personal confidence entertained by the one party in the integrity of the other was the only security',[8] parliamentary control was inevitable. The first Act to standardise management procedure was passed in 1817.[9] Banks were to be run by honorary trustees and managers; money entrusted to them was to be paid into the Bank of England, to the account of the Commissioners for the Reduction of the National Debt, who would invest it in 3 per cent bank annuities. The Commissioners were to pay interest to trustees at the fixed rate of £4 11s. 2d. per cent. per annum.[10] The rate of interest paid to depositors varied from one bank to another.[11]

It was the lack of inter-relation between these three levels of payment which was fortuitously responsible for the erection of purpose-built savings banks. The yield which the Commissioners received was governed by fluctuations in the price of stock; the return paid by the Commissioners to trustees was fixed by statute; and the rate of interest paid by trustees to depositors was fixed in the published rules drawn up at the establishment of each bank. The inadequacy of the money which the Commissioners sometimes received from investments in stock was a matter for parliamentary alarm[12] but does not concern the subject of this chapter. What is important here is that the trustees received, in practice, more money from the Commissioners than they themselves paid to depositors. There therefore arose quickly, in all but the smallest banks, an unclaimed 'surplus fund', which seems not to have been envisaged in 1817.

Within a few years the amount of this surplus in the larger banks was such as to require legislation. By an Act of 1824 trustees were enabled, after 30 days' notice to the National Debt Office, to share out half their surplus fund among depositors.[13] The other half was to be retained to 'answer deficiencies'. The trustees of some savings banks no doubt felt that distribution was a gesture of reassurance to depositors following the collapse of many commercial banks in 1825–6. At Exeter, and perhaps elsewhere, distribution was necessary in any event under the bank's rules. There followed dozens of applications to the National Debt office; each one was referred to the Commissioners and is recorded in the minutes of their meetings.[14] It was this early element of supervision on the part of the Commissioners which led to them being treated by Parliament, and by the savings banks themselves, as something other than the disinterested bankers which the 1817 Act had intended.

In December 1824 the trustees of Redruth bank asked the Commissioners whether any part of their surplus fund 'can be appropriated to the building of Rooms for the accommodation of the Savings Bank'.[15] The Commissioners simply replied that the case did not come under their cognizance. But West Cornwall was still ambitious. In September 1826 the trustees of Truro savings bank made a similar request, and the Commissioners replied as before.[16] No doubt by then, with applications for the distribution of surplus money arising at every meeting, the Commissioners had real fears about the kind of minutiae of administration which seemed destined to come to them. They were seven men of importance: the Speaker, the Master of the Rolls, the Chief Baron of the Exchequer, the Chancellor of the Exchequer, the Accountant General of the Court of Chancery, and the Governor and Deputy Governor of the Bank of England.[17] Such men would not concern themselves with the merits of purpose-building in Redruth, especially as savings banks were only one aspect of their responsibilities.

Their secretariat was the National Debt Office whose principal, the Comptroller-General, attended Commissioners' meetings. In 1858, in evidence to a parliamentary committee, the Comptroller-General admitted that the Commissioners had taken little executive action. With only three as a quorum, their work had been 'entirely matters of routine; principally for the signature of accounts'.[18] Yet the problems of investment, return and surplus, in the field of savings bank finances, had become more complex by the year.

The attention of Parliament to the anomalies of the 1817 Act was called by Joseph Hume.[19] The burden of his speeches was directed at the disparity between the money received from investments by the Commissioners and that paid by them to trustees, and he referred only in passing to the other level of incongruity which had led to 'the great surplus which the managers always had in possession untouched'.[20] No overt allegation of extravagant expenditure was made but the very existence of a large and increasing fund, which arose only by the fortuitous difference between two rates of interest, was a matter for attention. To regulate the financial position, and more generally to consolidate a variety of minor legislation since 1817, an Act was passed in 1828.[21]

If the Commissioners had been worried earlier about their involvement in petty administration, the new legislation cast them deeper in gloom. Trustees, who had previously had the management of the surplus fund to themselves (subject only to the approval of the National Debt Office if they chose to distribute), were now compelled to release the surplus to the Commissioners, 'reserving such Portions as may appear necessary to meet current Expenses'. Once in the Commissioners' hands, the surplus was invested but not for the benefit of the banks. However, all or part of the capital sum could be reclaimed by trustees 'for the purposes of the Institution'. It now appeared that, as well as the duty of controlling further investment, the Commissioners would be asked to decide whether the withdrawal of money by a savings bank, on any given occasion, was for a legitimate purpose.

Fortunately for the Commissioners, the 1828 Act empowered them to appoint a full-time barrister to certify that the rules of new savings banks were framed according to law.[22] As this was hardly a daily task, it was probably accepted by Parliament that a barrister would be generally useful for the Commissioners to establish their *modus vivendi* with the trustees. The man appointed was John Tidd Pratt, then aged 30; when William Lewins wrote his *History of Savings Banks*, 36 years later, he did not conceal his admiration for Pratt, who was still in office.[23] The author of several books on savings banks, as well as other topics, Pratt emerges as a remote, unassailable and uncompromising figure, invested with wider responsibilities by successive Acts, and disliked by clergymen-trustees in rural towns who had more interest in the spirit of the law than its rigid interpretation.

From the date of this appointment the question of purpose-building was no longer a matter for the Commissioners. Pratt submitted to them a form of certificate[24] to enable trustees to draw upon their surplus funds and thereafter withdrawal for building purposes could be handled as a clerical matter by the staff of the National Debt Office. In other words it was Pratt who decided what 'purposes of the Institution' were acceptable as a matter of policy. The Commissioners, however, continued to discuss applications for withdrawal in matters of embezzlement or managerial incompetence.[25]

Only twice do the earlier minutes of the Commissioners' meetings record any transactions in the realm of premises. The first concerned Newark in 1833 and the second Manchester in 1840.[26] In both cases the Commissioners were asked to approve withdrawals for 'purchase' and no mention was made of demolition and rebuilding. Newark may have been discussed because it was the second withdrawal in 4 months; Manchester, because of the size of the sum. But more probably they slipped through to the agenda by an oversight.

There was no further legislation on savings banks until 1844[27] despite continued public attention. Several banks petitioned Parliament unsuccessfully in 1831 for an alteration to the clause in the 1828 Act which had limited the maximum investment by any one depositor.[28] There was another but abortive attempt by Joseph Hume for fresh legislation in 1838, when he returned to his earlier criticism of the inequality between receipts from the public funds and the interest paid to depositors.[29] In the following year the Chartists began their criticism of savings banks and in 1842 came the first of many unpleasant attacks in the *Times*.[30] Although there was undoubtedly a widespread feeling of dissatisfaction with many aspects of savings bank business, particularly in the area of annuities,[31] the allegation of 'frequent complaints' of reckless expenditure, made by the *Bankers' Magazine* seems exaggerated. There was no parliamentary criticism, and only one passing attack in a letter to the *Times* on 'handsome residences, which have sprung up in various parts, and which could never have been contemplated ... in ... 1817'.[32] The point was returned to, but not developed, by other correspondents.

What prompted the magazine's allegation was undoubtedly the publication by Parliament in 1844 of surplus fund statistics.[33] Unlike figures on this subject published earlier and later, the 1844 publication

A RETURN from each Savings Bank in the United Kingdom, of the House or Building in which the Business is transacted; whether it is the Property of the Trustees, or Hired or Lent gratuitously; if used for other and what Purpose than that of the Savings Bank; and whether Actuary, Secretary, or other Officer Resides therein, with Amount of Rent paid by him.—*continued.*

SAVINGS BANK.	Name of House or Building.	If the Property of the Trustees.	If Hired.	If Lent gratuitously.	If used for other, and what Purpose.	If Actuary, Secretary, or other Officer Resides therein, and Amount of Rent paid by him. — Officer.	Rent.	Number of Days the Bank was Open for the Receipt and Withdrawal of Deposits during the Year ending 20 November 1851.	Number of Days the Bank was Open for the Receipt and Money Withdrawn or Deposits in the Year ending 20 Nov. 1851, without a Trustee or Manager present.	By whose Signature the Entry made in Depositor's Book of Money Lodged or Money Withdrawn authenticated; if by that of a Trustee or Manager, or by that of a Paid Officer. — Trustee or Manager.	Paid Officer.
ENGLAND—*continued.*											
Fulham	- - In a house called Holcroft's Tower, situate in the High-street of Fulham town.	-	Yes	-	- - The only other public purpose for which it is used, is for the monthly transaction of business connected with the Fulham Friendly Society. At other times the rooms are used by the family who reside in the house.	No	-	52	On no day -	- - By the initials of a trustee or a manager; the former uniformly attending during one moiety of the year, and the latter during another, to assist the secretary, who lives in an adjoining house, and who keeps the account books.	
Gainsborough	- - In our office, situated in the Market-place.	-	Yes	-	No	No	-	104	Not one -	- - A trustee or manager.	
Glossop	-	- - Town-hall buildings, High-street.	-	Yes	No	No	-	52	14	The manager.	
Gloucester	- - In the house erected for that purpose in 1850.	Yes	-	-	- - The wife and family of the actuary reside in it.	The actuary	- - He does not pay rent, but pays all rates and taxes.	50	- - A trustee or manager was always present, and in general both.	- - The entries made in the depositors' books of all receipts and payments are signed either by the trustee or manager in attendance, and not by a salaried officer.	
Godalming	- - The secretary's residence.	-	Yes	-	Residence of secretary -	-	-	52	None -	- Entered by the secretary, and signed by a manager or trustee in attendance.	
Goole	- - In a room in Bank's Terrace.	-	-	Yes	- - For a private dwelling of one of the clerk's of the Aire and Calder Navigation Company, to whom the house belongs; the room in which the savings bank is held therein being unoccupied by him.	No -	-	52	11	- - A manager when present; if not, the treasurer.	

Extract from 'Return of Savings Banks' published in British Parliamentary Papers, 1852 (xxviii), pp. 757–817 (overall pagination).

gave the actual amount drawn by each savings bank up to the end of November 1843. The magazine felt able to imply that the largest withdrawals were made for building, while conceding with reluctance that 'the parliamentary papers ... afford no data upon which an exact opinion can be formed ...'.[34] It would be preferable, thought the magazine, for Parliament to vote an annual sum to each bank for the expenses of management, rather than meet them by a difference of interest.

If the assertion in the *Bankers' Magazine* of frequent complaints about trustees' expenditure cannot be substantiated, there may nevertheless have been some truth in the allegation itself. It was to be expected that the savings banks would react, and they defended their position in the next issue. The details of this defence will be explained later. To examine charge and refutal, it is fortunate that parliamentary papers, supported by other sources, allow a list of purpose-built savings banks in England[35] to be compiled with some confidence as far as the end of 1852. In the 8 years which followed the magazine's editorial, there is still no evidence of overt criticism of expenditure. However, many more bank buildings were erected, a situation which allows the basic elements of the 1844 controversy to be studied in a wider perspective.

The list of purpose-built English savings banks, by the end of 1852, forms Appendix One. Beyond the fact that it was the last year when trustees were allowed to include accommodation for their actuary, as distinct from a caretaker, in any new premises,[36] the year itself marks no change in the position of Parliament, or of the National Debt Office, in the realm of purpose-building. It is simply the latest possible date for a comprehensive appraisal.

The best single source for this is the published return to an address of the House of Commons, dated 26 April 1852.[37] On 25 June the Commons ordered the return to be printed. A sample page is reproduced here (opposite page). Why the questions should have been couched as they were, indeed why the return was needed at all, is not explained in the Commons *Journal*. There had been little build-up towards it, and the follow-up was insignificant. In February a motion had been made regretting the continued neglect of the Government to introduce a Bill for the regulation of savings banks, but the motion was withdrawn.[38] In the summer of 1853 such a Bill was introduced but the provisions narrowly failed to become law.[39] An Act amending savings bank legislation was passed in 1854 but mainly in relation to Ireland.[40] To a minor extent the questions about premises in the 1852 return can be seen to have influenced the 1853 Bill,[41] but no attempt was made in the latter to legislate on purpose-building. It is likely, nevertheless, that a questionnaire in which seven out of 11 headings were in some degree concerned with premises, was framed so as to provide a fund of statistics in an area where legislation might have been thought necessary. No other questionnaire, before or after 1852, probed for such information.

Paradoxically, the most useful heading in the questionnaire for the purposes of this chapter is probably the one by which Parliament set the least store.[42] 'Name of House or Building' is curiously vague. What answer did Parliament expect? Many trustees took the question at its simplest and answered 'The Savings Bank'. Others, particularly when the bank shared premises with a school or other institution, gave some account of joint tenure. But this kind of information was sought in column five. Fortunately, in 49 cases where the bank had been, or was in the process of being, purpose-built, trustees took the opportunity to declare it. Two other groups of trustees (Howden and Ormskirk) said their bank was new, without using the verbs 'build' or 'erect'. For the great majority of other banks, the information given is enough to rule out purpose-built premises without further enquiry. However, for some 70 banks the position is uncertain, particularly when the trustees' answer to question one was 'The Savings Bank', or simply an address, or when the answer to question two indicates the bank was their own property. In these cases, recourse must be made to other sources of which the most consistently useful have been parliamentary papers of another kind.

In 1838, 1844 and 1849 statistics were published showing the state of the surplus fund in each bank as at the end of November in the preceding year.[43] Allusion has already been made to the further information in the return of 1844. The 1838 and 1844 returns dealt with surplus funds alone, but the figures returned in 1849 formed only one part of a general questionnaire. On several other occasions, there were published statements of the combined total of all surplus funds without breakdown.[44] Except in the case of Manchester,[45] the resources of individual banks seemed of little interest to politicians, and no further detailed returns were published after 1849.

Given the fact that new premises were generally financed from the surplus fund, it will be clear that the three sets of statistics, with their 5-year spacing, provide a useful guide to the date when building took place. These statistics are given for each bank in Appendix One. For instance, as Malton had £700 in its surplus fund in 1843, and nothing in 1848, it is reasonable to assume building took place between those years. The extra information in the 1844 return (giving, as well as the state of each fund in November 1843, the total amount drawn at any time up to that date) is especially useful for the earlier purpose-built banks. At Windsor, for instance, the surplus fund stood at £443 in 1838, £605 in 1843, and £814 in 1848. But the bank had at some time withdrawn £1410. There are therefore grounds for believing that the purpose-built bank mentioned in the 1852 questionnaire was erected earlier than 1838, because the bank could not have amassed that amount of money between then and 1843. A date some years earlier than 1838 is also to be deduced, because the bank had had time by then to recreate a reasonable fund.

Important though they are, the surplus fund figures have two drawbacks. The first is that trustees could sometimes draw on their fund for purposes other than building, usually to make good losses by defalcation or embezzlement. Some of these sums were as large as those withdrawn for premises: Berwick-on-Tweed, for instance, withdrew its entire surplus fund of £896 to cover a managerial fraud.[46] The £2000 withdrawn by Hertford, leaving only £60 in the fund, was probably for the same purpose.[47] There is therefore no reason to believe that Burton-on-Trent, for example, built its own premises simply because it had withdrawn its entire surplus fund of £792 by 1843. The 1852 return makes it clear that the Burton savings bank was then in the secretary's private office which was part of his dwelling-house. Furthermore, there is no way of knowing whether a withdrawal for new premises was only to purchase existing property, without plans for demolition and rebuilding. Withdrawals to make good embezzlements and the like can be traced in the records of the National Debt Office, but no central check is possible of withdrawals for other purposes.

The second drawback is that some of the earlier savings banks were built from resources other than the surplus fund. The tiny savings bank at Whitchurch (Shropshire) erected in 1823 and perhaps the first purpose-built savings bank in England,[48] was financed by 'the balance of subscriptions'.[49] The banks at Stone and Ellesmere were both built in 1830 but no withdrawals were apparently made from their surplus funds.[50] In the same year the ambitious York savings bank was opened: the premises had cost around £5000 but it seems that only £300 had been withdrawn from their surplus fund between 1828 and 1843. When the trustees at Newcastle were planning their prestigious new building in 1828 they took £5000 from their 'reserve fund' and placed it with a local banker: soon afterwards they withdrew £1027 from their surplus fund to complete the building.[51] It is not clear how long these two funds were allowed to run in parallel.

The most interesting case of early expenditure concerns the St Martin's Place bank, in London. The Comptroller was asked by a parliamentary Select Committee in 1858, if the building had been financed by the surplus fund.[52] No, he replied: the bank had had its own fund, accumulated before the 1828 Act, which had been invested in stock.[53] The £1275 withdrawn from the surplus fund in 1834 was only to make good a banking deficiency.[54]

Unfortunately, the combined information of the 1852 questionnaire and the surplus fund statistics is still not quite enough, by itself, to furnish a reliable table of purpose-built banks. There are three distinct problems. The first is that some savings banks had ceased by 1852 and one or more might have built premises.[55] But only Rochdale, which collapsed after a spectacular fraud in 1849, seems at all likely and there is nothing to indicate that it did.[56] The second problem is that at least two savings banks, that is to say Whitchurch (Shropshire) and Alnwick, had early purpose-built premises which were not in use as late as 1852 and therefore not returned. Whitchurch built premises twice,[57] but Alnwick sold its first bank and did not build again.[58] There is not the slightest hint, in parliamentary papers, of the first Whitchurch bank. The early expenditure at Alnwick is picked up in surplus fund withdrawals but the 1852 return mentions only the bank's premises at that date, which had been purchased. The risk is that other banks may have been in the position of Whitchurch — Bakewell and Birmingham being the most likely.[59] It is not probable that there were others like Alnwick.

The third and most interesting problem concerns the late-built banks at Leek, Richmond (Yorkshire) and Warminster. The first was called 'intended' in an 1851 directory; the second is dated 1851 on the façade but was opened much later; and the third, on firm evidence, was in use during 1852. In each case the 1852 return appears to give misleading, if not deliberately false, information. It is as if the trustees, suspicious of the nature of the new questionnaire, wished their building projects not to be known. There is a slight possibility that other trustees made similarly equivocal statements which have not been noticed.

The deficiencies of the parliamentary material have been satisfactorily overcome by recourse to a wide variety of primary and secondary sources. The most reliable source of all, of course, is the records of the banks themselves. The policy of the modern Trustee Savings Bank is to deposit the old records of its constituent banks in public repositories. By historical accident, records of certain other of these defunct banks are held by the major clearing banks. Architects' drawings have been traced only for Birmingham, Sheffield and Ulverston.[60] Extracts from original minute books are sometimes quoted in publicity booklets, commissioned by the head offices of local Trustee Savings Banks before the recent centralisation of authority. A number of the older surviving banks published histories some 60 or more years ago as centenary souvenirs.[61] These were often prepared by trained historians, with access to full documentation, and the few which can be traced today are invaluable. Unfortunately, editions were very small and the histories which would be the most useful, like the one about Devonport, are untraceable.

Happily, the elements of philanthropy and beneficence inherent in the constitution and management of savings banks earned them an attention in contemporary directories, newspapers, periodicals and local histories which was not afforded to banks of a more commercial nature. The best directories in this respect are those with the fullest narrative description preceding the lists of professions, trades and addresses. Examples are Bagshaw's *Cheshire* (1850), and White's *Staffordshire* (1851). Almost any directory by White has a fund of factual comment plagiarised by later publishers. On the other hand Slater and Pigot are often disappointing and most directories by Kelly yield little until editions were enlarged in the 1870s. Generally, when information is found it appears not in any description of public buildings but in the list of quasi-charitable organisations, ranging from mechanics' institute to Dorcas society, which tend to follow churches and schools.

Newspapers are helpful in various ways. At Hull the trustees placed an advertisement inviting contractors to view building plans at the office of George Jackson, junior, their architect;[62] at Truro the local newspaper described the bank's elevation when still at planning stage;[63] at Doncaster and Rotherham there were reports of opening ceremonies.[64] But of more consistent use are the series of balance sheets which trustees tended to publish in newspapers after each annual meeting. They had no statutory duty to do so, and in the earlier years, when the statements would be most useful, they are sometimes absent.[65] But there was evidently a general feeling among trustees that they should account publicly for other people's money.

Balance sheets show the amount of the surplus fund, as well as money in hand for management expenses. When the fund drops sharply, in the case of a bank known to have erected premises, the date of building can be deduced. This acts both as a check on the parliamentary returns already mentioned, and as a further source of evidence for intervening years. In the case of a few banks, like Exeter and Manchester, the trustees accompanied the published balance sheet with a useful commentary on the year's business. Sometimes the paper itself drew attention to the accounts in an editorial in the same issue, but this was seldom more than a précis of the year's results. The position of the press is well summed up generally in the *Windsor & Eton Express* of the 1830s. The annual meetings of the Windsor Royal Dispensary, the National Schools Board, and the savings bank happened roughly together and the balance sheets appeared normally in the same issue: the editor sent his own reporter to the first meeting, carried a participant's report of the second, and had only three lines of general commendation on the good works of the last.[66] But at least he carried the balance sheet.

The value of the architectural journals in the field of savings banks is impaired by their relatively late beginnings. The earliest reference is in the short-lived *Architectural Magazine and Journal* of 1834, which mentions a new savings bank of the Ionic order, then being built at Wakefield from designs by Charles Mountain of Hull.[67] The *Civil Engineer and Architect's Journal* is more useful and carries illustrations and good architectural notes on savings banks at Finsbury and Chester.[68] The *Builder* has a note on the competition at Newbury, and details, illustration and ground plan of the bank at Gloucester.[69] The *Illustrated London News*, intending to show Lichfield corn exchange and market hall, has also a view of Lichfield savings bank which adjoined them.[70] The drawings of Bath, Bury St Edmunds and Newbury banks were exhibited at the Royal Academy.[71]

Local histories and guide books have proved quite profitable, for instance in revealing the Warminster Bank. However, many such published sources, including directories, have also been found inaccurate. Whittle's history of Bolton, published in 1855, states that the savings bank building was erected in 1817 (a year before the bank was established); it gives a cost and full description which fit exactly the premises erected more than 20 years later. Whellan's Durham directory of 1856 states that South Shields savings bank was erected in Barrington Street in 1824; the 1864 edition paraphrases the same information. The bank was in fact built about 1841.[72] Simpson's history of Lancaster, published in 1852, states that the savings bank was erected in New Street in 1823, but this was when the bank itself was established. Mannex's directory of 1881 correctly records the foundation as 1823, but dates the building to 1843. In fact, it was built in 1848.[73] The worry has been that this ratio of error might also exist undetected and the search for corroborating material has extended to the visual evidence of surviving buildings.

Books about architectural styles and periods tend to treat all banks together, and then only in passing. An exception was H.R. Hitchcock who drew attention to Bath savings bank (Plate 27) as an early copy of the Reform Club style, and Lichfield as a rare example of Elizabethan.[74] Only one savings bank building — Ulverston — seems to have been the subject of a published monograph.[75]

The last and best check, where a building is known or suspected to survive, is a visit to the site. Apart from the obvious advantage of seeing the façade at first hand (13 banks, for instance, carry building dates), it is helpful to see the environment. The 1852 return stated that Reading savings bank was No. 35, London Street. Today No. 35 is a listed building, architecturally plausible for a small bank, but looking rather late. When the street is examined as a whole, No. 72, across the road, appears as an earlier Italianate building with the words READING SAVINGS BANK engraved in masonry. The street was renumbered in the late nineteenth century. Confusion is usually greater in small towns and villages where streets were often not numbered at all. At Cainscross and Poulton-le-Fylde the savings banks appear to have had no addresses by street name which were ever recorded. At Tonbridge, Back Lane became Bank Street when the bank was erected there.[76] At Truro the bank had two addresses, River Street and Frances Street, because the boundary between them was never certain. High Wycombe savings bank was No. 15, Church Street, but the address in directories was usually Paul's Row.[77] Union Street, Horncastle, site of that town's savings bank, was renamed Queen Street between 1863 and 1868. Luckily, Victorian large-scale Ordnance Survey maps usually indicate the location of savings banks, even in towns.

It is then as a synthesis of a variety of primary and secondary material, with the 1852 questionnaire as a *point de départ*, that Appendix One is presented. It is the most likely situation, in respect of purpose-built savings banks, as at the end of that year, but it is no more than that. As Parliament never asked trustees 'Is your bank purpose-built?', no definitive statement can ever be made. Doubts remain, for instance, about the Quay parish bank in Ipswich which owned its premises and had withdrawn £1000 from its surplus fund by 1843. But there is no other evidence. There are suspicions, too, about Ashford,

Plate 27. George Alexander's Bath Savings Bank, 1842. Now Register Office.

Kent, where today No. 25, High Street, looks reasonably appropriate, and £560 had been withdrawn from surplus by the bank at that address. But there is a reason why it is not included.[78] A case could be made for Kidderminster, where the surplus fund fell to zero in 1853, and for Bishopsgate (London), Canterbury, Falmouth, Halifax and Knaresborough. Each has been examined but results are inconclusive. The Appendix includes only those banks where purpose-building is beyond doubt; if the total was, in reality, different, it was higher by no more than half a dozen — a figure which does not invalidate the Appendix nor materially affect the conclusions which will be drawn from it.

The next problem to be considered must be the definition of purpose-built. This is not, of course, a consideration restricted to savings banks but the 1852 return adds its own element of confusion which calls for study. It will be seen from the Appendix that the returns from Bedford, Biggleswade and Rugeley indicated specifically that each of those banks was purpose-built. The implication is that each building was a defined unit, determinable if not detached. But this was hardly the case. It is just possible that at Bedford a new bank was built in 1845 on the site of buildings adjoining the houses of the secretary and superintendent of the Bedford Rooms Company,[79] but the balance of probability is that the return was referring to the bank of 1836 — an annex to the rear of the Assembly Rooms paid for exclusively by the trustees, and provided with an independent entrance.[80] Should that fairly have been described as 'Buildings erected for the sole use of the savings bank'? Following their neighbours, the trustees at Biggleswade made a similar return. But their bank was recorded in 1850 as at the Town Hall.[81] This building still stands, now in commercial use; it was designed by J.T. Wing and opened in 1844.[82] The likelihood is that the Biggleswade bank, like the one at Bedford, was a suite of rooms designed for bank use within a new public building. No more reason can be found for the exaggeration in Bedfordshire than for the gamesmanship of a different kind, in Richmond and elsewhere, already mentioned. Both banks have been accepted as purpose-built.

The problem at Biggleswade leads on to that at Rugeley. Here the 'building erected for the purpose' was no more than an extension to the Town Hall made in 1844.[83] At Lichfield, a few years later, the savings bank was also built attached to a public building but there it was a corn exchange and market hall, and the whole complex was new.[84] More difficult is the case of Settle, where a large public building was erected of which the main components were market house, savings bank,

library, and newsroom.[85] If the bank had taken its part at rent, then it
would be wise to conclude that it was merely using a room, or rooms,
which might equally well have been let for other purposes. But the
1852 return makes it clear that Settle owned its premises and allowed
other institutions to use them. It can therefore be deduced that the
bank was involved at the design stage and paid its share of building
costs, and this has been the criterion of purpose-building for this study.
In all other cases of co-habitation, except at Howden, the principle has
worked to the exclusion of the bank from the Appendix. At Brigg, for
instance, the bank had a room in the corn exchange but the trustees
paid rent to the directors and had exclusive use only in banking
hours.[86] The position at Howden was that 'a public building' was
begun in the churchyard in August 1850, intended for a savings bank,
a mechanics' institute, and a magistrates' room.[87] The 1852 return,
referring to 'the new savings bank' makes it clear that the bank was the
owner.

A curious case is that of Clitheroe, a very late-established bank,
which was housed, according to the 1852 return, 'In a room erected for
the purpose'.[88] The meaning of that form of words has not been
discovered, and Clitheroe has been excluded from Figure 2 (see page
106).

In 1852 there were 449 savings banks in England of which 109 (24.2
per cent) are presented in Appendix One as purpose-built.[89] This was
not, however, the largest homogeneous unit. The biggest group of
banks (139, or nearly 31 per cent) formed part of private and domestic
premises, usually a room or rooms in the dwelling-house of the
actuary, or other principal officer. Some 40 (nearly 9 per cent) were in
premises owned by the banks but not purpose-built; 39 (8.6 per cent)
were attached to town halls, 34 (7.5 per cent) to schools, 25 (5.5 per
cent) to 'offices', 10 (2.2 per cent) to commercial banks, and 4 (0.9 per
cent) to churches. The remaining 11 per cent or so of savings banks
were in a variety of public, official and quasi-charitable buildings
including inns, poor law union offices, mechanics' institutes, literary
institutions, subscription rooms and even judges' lodgings.

The spatial distribution of the purpose-built banks is shown in Figure
1, the numbers thereon representing a particular bank as listed in the
alphabetical arrangement in the Appendix. An arbitrary division has
been made between north and south. Figure 1, used in conjunction
with Figure 2, helps also with the analysis of building costs. The
numbers within circles show the expensive banks, with a gross cost of
over £2500; the numbers within squares show moderately dear banks

costing between £1500 and £2500.[90] It is recognised that this evidence is not without its drawbacks: for one thing, the cost of many banks is not known; for another, the purchasing power of money changed between the 1820s and 1852, and varied between regions of England. Figure 2 adds the further dimension of dating.

It is clear from Figures 1 and 2 that most purpose-built savings banks were erected north of a line through Birmingham, particularly in Cheshire, Derbyshire, Lancashire, Shropshire, Staffordshire and Yorkshire. On the other hand, there were areas in the south quite bare of such banks. Herefordshire, Oxfordshire and Surrey had none at all;

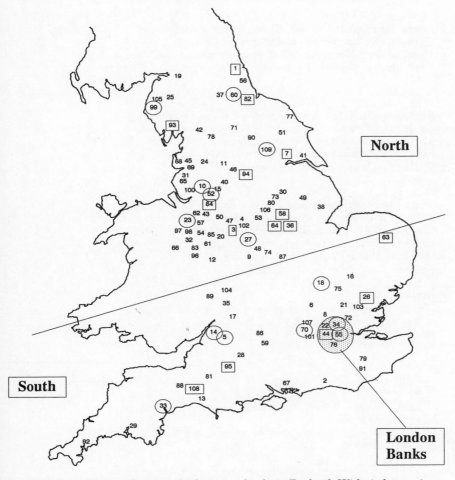

Fig. 1. Distribution of purpose-built savings banks in England. With circles: costing over £2500; with squares: costing £1500–£2500.

Note: banks in italics are regarded as in the South of England

Building dates	North	South	Total
By end of 1830: Devonport, Ellesmere, Hull, Morpeth, Oswestry, *St Martin's Place*, Scarborough, Stone, *Taunton*, Much Wenlock, Whitchurch (1), Worcester, York	10	3	13
1831–35 Alnwick, *Bristol*, Leeds, Newark, Newcastle-upon-Tyne, Settle, Sheffield, *Sherborne*, Wakefield, Whitehaven, *Windsor*	8	3	11
1836–40 *Bedford*, Bradford, Bridgnorth, *Chelsea*, Derby, *Exeter*, Finsbury, Hexham, Huddersfield, Knutsford, Lincoln, *Montague Street*, Northwich, Nottingham, *Portsmouth*, Poulton, South Shields, Shrewsbury, Ulverston, Wigan, *Yeovil*	14	7	21
	32	13	45
1841–5 Ashbourne, *Bath*, Beverley, *Biggleswade*, *Cainscross*, Carlisle, Cheadle, *Chelmsford*, *Colchester*, Doncaster, Grantham, Macclesfield, Manchester, Mansfield, *Norwich*, Preston, Rugeley, *Sevenoaks*, Stockport, Tamworth, Wirksworth, Workington, Worksop, *High Wycombe*	16	8	24
1846–59 *Arundel*, Bakewell, Birmingham, Bolton, *Bridport*, Bury, *Bury St Edmunds*, Cambridge, Cockermouth, *Devizes*, Eccleston, *Gloucester*, Horncastle, Kirkby Lonsdale, *Lambeth*, Lancaster, Lichfield, Malton, Market Drayton, Nantwich, *Newbury*, Ormskirk, *Reading*, *Romford*, *Saffron Walden*, Thirsk, *Tonbridge*, *Truro*, Whitchurch (2), *Witham*	16	14	30
1851–2 Chester, Howden, Leek, Newcastle-under-Lyme, Richmond (assuming begun 1851), Rotherham, *Swindon*, *Tewkesbury*, *Warminster*	6	3	9
	38	25	63
	70	38	108

Figures show:
Of total banks built before 1841, roughly 71 per cent in north, 29 per cent in south.
Of total banks built 1841–52, roughly 60 per cent in north, 40 per cent in south.

Fig. 2. Building dates of English savings banks.

Cornwall, Hampshire, Norfolk and Sussex had one each. And yet the overall distribution between north and south of savings banks, as institutions, was roughly equal. Not only did the north build more often, but it built earlier. Figure 2 shows that the number of purpose-built banks in the south was always lower but that the discrepancy was less noticeable after 1841. As for costs, however, Figure 1 suggests that banks in the south were relatively more expensive. Whether this amounted to extravagance will be considered later.

There is no obvious reason why the north was more forward in the matter of purpose-building. It was highly unusual for a town to have had more than one savings bank so there was no need to build to gain a competitive advantage.[91] Indeed, there was no need for communication at all between groups of trustees for business purposes: savings banks did not issue cheques or notes, or discount bills.[92] They were independent banks of deposit. It might be argued that the north was more populous than the south; that northern banks tended, therefore, to have more depositors; and that this led eventually to a bigger surplus fund. But building did not depend on the existence in the surplus fund of a certain minimum sum. Newcastle-upon-Tyne and Eccleston in the north, and Exeter and Cainscross in the south, are examples in each sector of banks which chose to build from the greatest and the slenderest of resources.[93] And Liverpool and Southampton, both very prosperous banks, did not build at all until the 1860s.[94]

The important question is not why the north built earlier and more often than the south, but why savings banks, open one or two mornings a week, needed purpose-built premises at all. Why did certain trustees, wherever they happened to be, decide to build when others did not? And why did some build in a grand manner? To answer these points, attention must be focused on the published riposte[95] (already briefly mentioned) to the criticisms of extravagance made by the professional bankers.

The protagonist for the savings banks called himself 'XY' and was probably an actuary of one of the larger banks. Two elements can be detected in the structure of his answer: the first, a defence for building at all; the second, an explanation for building well. As for building at all, he saw three justifications: the need to 'secure accommodation to the depositors'; the desirability of a safe place for books and papers; and the advantage of a residence for the 'responsible officer'. These must be dealt with first. The interests of customers was probably the reason to put to the National Debt Office and doubtless many banks were in substandard rooms, or thought their business could be better placed.

At Stockport, the inconvenience was bad enough to be remarked upon in the local paper.[96] At Stafford, it was thought the bank should be in a more central position;[97] at Taunton, in a more prestigious one.[98] At Tewkesbury a new building was simply felt 'desirable';[99] at Ulverston it was seen as a mark that the bank was well established.[100] The need to protect books and papers (why not money as well?) was also valid and it would have been difficult to adapt some buildings, particularly if timber-framed, to provide the standard of security prevalent among commercial banks.

The alleged need to provide on-site accommodation for the responsible officer is the most interesting justification. By the 1830s many savings banks were able to afford at least one salaried officer[101] and it was convenient, and a further security precaution, to keep him on the premises. The 1852 return shows 180 banks (not necessarily purpose-built) with family accommodation, above or adjacent to the place of business, for professional staff.[102] Usually the executive officer was called the actuary (118 cases), but also secretary (44), clerk (9), cashier (6), and treasurer (3). Another 24 banks had non-professional staff living in: at Workington the resident was called a caretaker, at High Wycombe an attendant. In the London area three banks called him a messenger, using a title borrowed from commercial banks. House-keepers resided at five banks and porters at 10. A total of 204 savings banks (about 45 per cent), therefore, had manned premises by 1852 — the one statistic which seems to have influenced the authorities. In 1853 the Solicitor General ruled that in future living accommodation attached to banks would be built only for non-professional staff.[103]

Among the purpose-built banks, however, it would appear that as many as 24 did *not* have on-site accommodation. The figure is misleading to some extent: Bedford, Biggleswade, Newcastle-upon-Tyne, Rugeley, Settle, and possibly Howden, did not need resident staff to maintain security as they were part of larger buildings. Saffron Walden let the accommodation area to professional, but non-banking, people.[104] Bridgnorth and Wirksworth let to an 'individual' and a 'tenant' respectively,[105] who were no doubt well vetted. That reduces the total to perhaps 15, a figure which does not significantly weaken XY's claim.

Before the question of building well is discussed it is necessary to consider again how new premises were financed. The trustees 'applied such sums', wrote XY, 'as had been originally raised by subscription on the formation of banks (and such sums were considerable) together with such profits as they had been enabled, by strict economy, to realise, to this purpose'.[106] The word 'profit', used also in the original allegations of extravagance, is misleading. XY no doubt meant it in the sense of return from investments of surplus funds made before the 1828 Act. These proceeds accounted, as has been shown, for such savings bank buildings as St Martin's Place and Newcastle-upon-Tyne. But after 1828, when trustees were obliged to send to the Commissioners for the Reduction of National Debt the total year's surplus (reserving only what they needed for annual expenses of management), the opportunity to invest on their own account was removed. The implication, in the magazine's attack, was that profits in the old sense were continuing and one would have expected XY to challenge this.[107]

It was only after he had mentioned subscriptions and profits that XY drew attention to the surplus fund *per se* which 'did not produce the trustees any interest whatever'. Apparently too embarrassed to put the main source of capital first, XY could also not bring himself to state that if the money were not spent on premises it would be wasted. The emphasis on subscriptions was also quite misleading. Although important for some banks in the early years (as has been shown), sums generally would have been small,[108] and the money collected in this way at the establishment of banks is unlikely to have lasted beyond about 1830, and the building of the banks at Stone and Ellesmere. Only one bank — Tonbridge — is stated in the 1852 returns to have been financed wholly by subscription, but this was exceptional in another sense, in that it was not established until 1845.[109] Another late-established bank, at Newcastle-under-Lyme, built its premises with half the surplus fund of Pirehill-Meaford bank (at Stone), of which it was an offshoot.[110] No form of finance could begin to match the one which XY pretended to find least significant — the surplus fund — and some banks stated openly in the 1852 questionnaire that costs had been met from that source.[111]

These, then, were the reasons why trustees built in the first place, and the resources from which their premises were financed. What must be considered now are XY's reasons for building so well. It was only at this stage that he was countering the allegations of extravagance. He had two explanations.[112] The first was that trustees were in many cases compelled to follow such elevations and plans as the freeholder chose, to improve or protect the value of his land. 'It must be borne in mind', wrote XY, 'that the trustees cannot hold freehold property'. The second reason was that buildings should be erected 'in accordance with the desire of the present day, for improving and embellishing every place of a public character, making them gratifying and pleasing to all'.

The first explanation raises obscure and complex issues. Although most banks probably had a medium-term lease, like the 99 years at Ellesmere,[113] there were definitely some with freehold estate. Romford, for instance, admitted this in the 1852 return, and trustees at Swindon and Tewkesbury both used the word 'conveyance' when referring to the 'purchase' of property.[114] Whether some other kind of title deed was, in fact, intended is not clear. The trustees at Preston, for example, referring to their intended 'purchase', asked their solicitor 'to prepare the draught [sic] of a conveyance for a long term of years'.[115] This was clearly not freehold tenure and the deed was legally a demise — perhaps for a period as long as the 999 years term at Whitchurch.[116] This gave the next best thing to a freehold estate, and if some banks held by lease-for-lives, which seems quite possible,[117] they had what was regarded in law as a freehold title. Within 10 years of XY's comment the prohibition seems to have become irrelevant or unworkable. The fact that the 1852 questionnaire distinguished between 'hired' and 'owned' seems almost an indication that freehold tenure existed. The final admission came in the abortive savings bank Bill of 1853, which sought to make it clear that any property, 'whether freehold, leasehold or copyhold' already purchased by trustees, or to be purchased thereafter with the consent of the National Debt Office, was held in trust for the bank itself.[118] This clause may have been another result of the statistics afforded by the 1852 questionnaire.

XY had another point about leases. As they 'fell in', he claimed trustees decided to erect their own offices to avoid the renewal of heavy rents.[119] This was certainly done at Swindon, where the trustees bought premises as a building plot to save themselves £20 a year.[120] But Swindon seems to have bought freehold property, which XY was claiming to be impossible. No doubt he was advocating ideally the use of a long-term demise, where there was a substantial initial payment followed by only a peppercorn rent, but he failed to recommend it specifically.

The most which can be said in this perplexing matter is that the expiry of short-term leases, often taken out in 1817–9, provided the *opportunity* to build. Sometimes the question was brought to a head before the lease was ended. At Lambeth, for instance, it was occasioned by an extension to a railway line;[121] at Sheffield, by the Cutlers company, who wanted to move their Hall, in which the bank was based.[122] Certainly there were building leases granted to savings bank trustees,[123] but there is insufficient evidence to confirm or refute XY's view that landlords wished new property to be of a certain grandeur. Perhaps XY was from the St Martin's Place bank, where the ground landlord was the Crown.

What remains to be discussed is XY's frank admission that savings banks were built to match the expansive spirit of the age. Where this could be done, 'it must form a subject more of praise than blame; assisting as it does the growing desire for comfort and taste . . .'.[124] But how general was this grandeur, and was it bought too dearly? Appendix One and Figure 1 show building costs which test, more objectively than XY's defence, whether savings banks were extravagantly built. Even in cases where a specific figure is not stated, costs can be largely deduced from the state of the surplus fund. This does not only apply to those cases where a definite sum had been withdrawn by 1843. It can be reckoned, for instance, that premises at Devizes cost no more than £900, but at Cockermouth over £1000. Sometimes the expense can be proved to match the surplus fund. Knutsford, Northwich and Preston cost almost exactly the sums withdrawn.

Despite this, the whole area of costs is difficult. It has already been shown that some of the earliest purpose-built premises were aided by subscriptions. These made little difference from about 1830 — any more than did other local benefits, like the existence of a 'Friends in Need' account for Tewkesbury bank[125] or the gift of some stones for the façade at Doncaster.[126] But other factors are more elusive. How far did trustees manipulate the element of surplus fund money which they could retain for expenses of management? At Swindon, £112 out of the total building costs of £628 came from what was called the 'Current Surplus Fund'.[127] That was more than could have accrued in 1 year. If these reserves existed on a widespread scale, they would undermine the value of the surplus fund withdrawal figures as a yardstick of costs. More important still, how far were matters like the purchase of the site, demolition of existing premises, architect's and solicitor's fees, and fitting out, represented in a bald statement of building costs?

It is this grey area of expenditure, outside the contractor's main tender, which must account for some of the alarming discrepancies between surplus fund withdrawals and building costs quoted in printed sources, usually directories.[128] At some places, the actual building expenses were small in relation to the costs of buying and preparing the right site. It would appear that Bury St Edmunds savings bank cost, in total, £2300, although building and fitting up amounted to only £1257.[129] The high cost of the site must explain why Chelmsford withdrew £2572, when the building tender itself was only £950;[130] why Macclesfield withdrew £4350 when the building cost £2583;[131] why Bristol withdrew £5200 when the building cost £3500;[132] and why Sheffield withdrew £2835 when the building cost £898.[133] Although the normal cost of a site was nearer the £350 paid at Tewkesbury[134] than the large sums quoted above, there is evidence that they cost £1500 at Norwich[135] and £2000 at Newcastle-upon-Tyne.[136] The most expensive site was probably the one at Manchester. No precise figure is known but the entire sum of £6916 was withdrawn from the surplus fund for expenses incurred before building began.[137] At least another £4000 was spent on the actual premises.[138]

Figure 1 shows, encircled, 14 banks which appear to have cost in total (i.e. including site, fitting up, etc.) more than £2500. It shows also, within squares, another 15 banks which are believed to have cost £1500–2500. In other words there were 80 banks (around 75 per cent) which appear to have cost less than £1500 and a fair number of those cost less than £1000. It is these figures which finally condemn the *Bankers' Magazine* article as mischievous. To have selected nine English banks which had each withdrawn over £3000 from their surplus fund, and to have made out from this a general case against ostentatious building, was deliberately to distort the evidence of the surplus fund statistics as a whole.

The best which can be said in the magazine's defence is that its appreciation of the importance to savings banks of their surplus fund, in the context of premises, was accurate. Architects were told by trustees to keep within the maximum sum which the state of the surplus fund allowed. At Ulverston, expenditure was to be no more than £1300.[139] At Tewkesbury, five tenders were sent in between £598 and £700, including one from the bank's builder-architect, Thomas Collins, for £599.[140] All the sums exceeded the surplus fund and Collins was told to prepare new plans for a building which would cost only £400.[141] At Bury St Edmunds, the architect N.J. Cottingham aroused anger among trustees when he was thought to be exceeding the budget.[142] At Finsbury, the ceiling for expenditure was so low 'that the architect chose to be at some part of the expense of the external decorations of it, rather than suffer it to undergo further mutilation'.[143]

Enough names of architects are given in Appendix One to allow some conclusions to be drawn about them. Of the 40-odd known, or believed to be known, only two — George Webster and John Dobson — are thought to have designed more than one savings bank. In most cases the architect was a local man of some repute with an established practice, like Charles Edge (Birmingham), Charles Dyer (Bristol), John Clark (Leeds), Richard Lane (Manchester), John Dobson (Newcastle), Thomas Owen (Portsmouth), John Latham (Preston), Robert Potter (Sheffield), and Philip Sambell (Truro). Some of these commissions, for instance of Lane, Latham, Sambell, and Dobson at Hexham, appear to be unrecorded elsewhere. Certainly in one case (Tewkesbury), probably in another (High Wycombe), and quite possibly in the majority of other cases where the architect is not known, the design was done by a local builder-architect. When this happened, it is likely that the trustees employed a building surveyor to draw up specifications for tender.[144] If the doubtful attributions in the Appendix are all correct, trustees employed two county surveyors (Carver at Taunton and Haycock at Shrewsbury), one city surveyor (Stannard at Norwich), and one surveyor to a local board of health (Fenton at Chelmsford).

Of the known commissions, only three were given to architects who were not local. The earliest of these was at Grantham, in 1841, where Anthony Salvin designed the savings bank in a style which harked back to nearby Harlaxton Manor, where he had been working in the 1830s. The trustees may have called him in because of his work at Harlaxton,[145] but in 1841 he had other business at Grantham in any case, designing the church of St John, Spittlegate.[146]

Next came the savings bank at Bury St Edmunds (Plate 28), 'a rather unfortunate effort'[147] of 1846 usually attributed to L.N. Cottingham but completed under the guidance of his son N.J. Cottingham, who was awarded a fee of £30, to include the five guineas originally voted to his father.[148] As the elder Cottingham was a sick man in 1846, it is very possible that his son was a major influence in the design from the beginning.[149] It was N.J. Cottingham who exhibited the savings bank drawings at the Royal Academy, 7 years later, as his own work.[150] The initial involvement of the elder Cottingham at Bury was certainly the result of his restoration of the adjacent Norman Tower; work on this, at its height in 1843, was not completed until 1852.[151]

The last of the three was the savings bank at Newbury designed by George Truefitt and probably completed during 1849.[152] Truefitt had been a pupil of the elder Cottingham but that probably had no bearing in this instance. Newbury was one of apparently only three cases where the architect for a savings bank was chosen by public competition — the other cases were Wakefield and Newcastle (1860).[153] Always a lover of competitions, [154] Truefitt was in any case a strong contender, having had his unsuccessful but attractive design for the Army & Navy

Plate 28. The Cottinghams' Bury St Edmunds Savings Bank, dated 1846.

Club published in the *Builder* in the previous year.[155] Later in life, Truefitt became a bank architect of some importance.[156]

It is interesting that Salvin, the Cottinghams and Truefitt each produced a bank in the style known in the 1840s as Elizabethan. All three buildings have survived: Salvin's style is 'a wayward Jacobean',[157] while the other two are more closely neo-Tudor, with less Renaissance detail. But all three were a clear departure from the classical, and in particular from the Italianate, style, more normal for banks in that decade. In these three cases the use of non-classical designs can be explained with some confidence. Salvin had already been working in the Elizabethan style, as has been said; Cottingham was an ecclesiastical architect and neo-Tudor was probably as close to church Gothic as he felt able to go; and Truefitt was smart enough to have done his homework. The patrons of Newbury savings bank were the Earls of Carnarvon, whose nearby seat, Highclere Castle, had been remodelled by Barry for the 3rd Earl in the Elizabethan style in 1839–42.[158] Truefitt, whose Army & Navy Club design had been Gothic, must have been confident of success. His elevation for Newbury, although some way removed from the style of Highclere, was perhaps the only non-classical design submitted.

It is this use of styles which is the most important revelation of Appendix One. Including the three above, no less than 18 savings banks (including Howden) are known to have been in some variant of the Elizabethan style by the end of 1852. As the designs of some dozen are unknown, the true figure is likely to have been higher. The earliest, and in a way the most Gothic, was William Smith's Alnwick savings bank which the trustees later abandoned as being too small. That was an exceptional style for 1835. While the Alnwick bank was being built, the trustees at Ulverston rejected an Elizabethan façade, offered to them by George Webster, in favour of the alternative Italian style.[159] It was not until the 1840s that Elizabethan became acceptable generally with savings bank trustees and it was rarely in favour with the commercial banks until the 1860s and later.

The use of Elizabethan for savings banks had nothing to do with any historical aspect of banking. It was a reflection of the position of savings banks in society. The style acceptable for national school, parsonage, or almshouse was not unacceptable for the premises of a philanthropic, non-profit-making institution managed largely by local clergymen. When a savings bank was built beside a Gothic schoolroom, as at Eccleston, Lancashire (Plate 29), the influence was particularly appropriate. Although the majority of trustees felt that their bank

Plate 29. Former Eccleston (Lancs.) Savings Bank, 1849. The building on the left was once a school, dated 1819.

image should be paramount, and approved a classical design, a significant number chose to emphasise, by the Elizabethan style, the basic constitutional and ideological differences which set the savings banks apart from the world of private and joint-stock banking. Cottage-like banks, at Much Wenlock, Poulton-le-Fylde and Tonbridge, were further acknowledgements of humble origin.

Nevertheless, other groups of trustees might have a different vision of propriety. XY was right to call it an age of improvement and embellishment. Public buildings — and a savings bank was as much a public building as an athenaeum, or a corn exchange — were the subject of comment and appraisal. Often this was vague and perfunctory. Bank after bank is described in the narrative part of directories and guide books as 'neat', or 'neat and commodious'. Some banks themselves preferred stronger sentiments: Exeter liked 'respectability' without 'ostentation';[160] Howden was 'ornamental and useful';[161] Doncaster's design was 'a monitor and incentive to the industrious and frugal passerby — a monitor to remind him that his savings may be lodged therein with perfect security, and an incentive to induce him to press perseveringly forward in the course of industry and frugality'.[162] It was a short step, if the surplus fund allowed, from a pleasing and practical design to one which was ebullient, an expression of civic pride and the architect's genius. Richard Lane's Manchester savings bank was reckoned his most successful work,[163] and the trustees thought it a model which others might like to copy.[164] At Newcastle-upon-Tyne, trustees planned unashamedly to build 'a handsome edifice . . . which would be an ornament to the Town . . .'.[165] At Sheffield, the savings bank was one of the first buildings in the town centre with any pretension of elegance.[166] At Truro, the local press, having examined the bank's building plans, looked forward to seeing 'in a town almost totally devoid of legitimate architectural ornament . . . an advance in the direction of good taste'.[167]

For trustees interested in urban embellishment, only a classical design was acceptable. Before the 1840s some element of neo-Greek, usually a Doric porch, as at Whitehaven, was popular, but no rigid delineation of styles, in relation to dates, is possible. While the 'disintegration' of the neo-Greek style was noticed in John Clark's Leeds savings bank of 1834,[168] Ellesmere, built 4 years earlier, was closely Italianate. The most Grecian of all savings banks — Macclesfield (Plate 30) — was as late as 1841–2. The Italianate style, in the sense of Barry's *palazzo* designs, found relatively little favour with trustees. George Alexander's Bath savings bank, of 1841 (Plate 27),

Plate 30. Former Macclesfield Savings Bank, c. 1842, photographed as a branch of Martin's Bank.

has been noticed as an early and important copy of the Reform Club. 'It was here in Bath . . .', wrote Henry-Russell Hitchcock, 'that Barry's paradigm for the Early Victorian clubhouse seems first to have been adapted to financial uses . . .'.[169] Certainly there were others too which showed Barry's influence, as at Ashbourne and Wirksworth, but they are not typical of savings bank premises. The *palazzo* was a style of commercial banking: it stood for opulence, not petty savings; it reflected worldliness, not beneficence. There was really no one style which the savings banks made their own. The appearance of any series of buildings to house institutions which had no competitive pressure, no shareholders to satisfy, thirsty for dividends, could reflect no more than the taste which any particular set of trustees thought appropriate. The result is a paradox: it is impossible to say that an average savings bank building exists, yet at the same time, given an English country town and a street known to contain the savings bank, it is often possible to select it intuitively.

Hitchcock noticed that at Bath the adaptation of Barry's style for banking purposes had been achieved 'by totally ignoring the symmetry of the exterior in the interior disposition'.[170] As only a handful of savings banks remain in bank use, and as those which do have been modernised within to present-day standards, it is difficult to judge how far banking-halls were designed and constructed in sympathy with the façade. One can speculate that in smaller and cheaper banks, like High Wycombe, the interior was featureless. On the other hand, it is possible that many of the Elizabethan-style banks carried neo-Tudor decoration into the public areas. This was certainly the case at Chester, where interior panelling was 'in happy unison' with the exterior.[171] The bigger and more expensive the bank, the more trouble was taken generally with accommodation. Facilities were as important as decoration. Exeter savings bank had a banking hall 60 feet (18 metres) long, 40–60 feet (12–18 metres) broad and very lofty.[172] At Gloucester, the only savings bank before 1852 of which the ground plan was published, the banking-hall was approached through a waiting room, itself entered by a lobby.[173] There was also a waiting room at Devizes.[174] Most banks, of course, had living accommodation and many of the larger ones had a board room which, when the trustees did not need it, was lent to other philanthropic or charitable organisations. At York, where the savings bank was founded by the Lord Mayor and Recorder, there was a room for public meetings, lectures and exhibitions.[175]

The most interesting interior was perhaps at Finsbury, a bank constructed on such a tight budget that, as has been said above, the architect paid for part of the external decoration himself. The facilities were certainly there: a public office 30 feet (9 metres) long; three private offices; a strong room; a depositors' waiting area 44 feet (13 metres) long; two entrance halls, each 11 feet 8 inches (3.3 metres) by 20 feet (6 metres); a board room 30 feet (9 metres) by 14 feet (4.2 metres); two staircases; and 13 domestic apartments.[176] But this was too much for the money available and the stylish Palladian façade masked an interior 'totally destitute of every description of decoration'.[177]

Although most surviving savings banks from before 1852 are listed buildings, the extension of this protection seems in many cases fortuitous. There appears to be no national and, in most cases, no local recognition or understanding of the place of the institution in the social and economic framework of the district. Also, the distinction between the year of the establishment of a savings bank and the date when its premises were built causes widespread confusion, not only among planners. The old bank building at Rochester is listed as an '1816 Savings Bank': that is, indeed, the approximate age of the building, but the bank, founded coincidentally in 1816, had nothing to do with that site until the 1840s.[178] Ellesmere savings bank is also listed as built in 1816, following similar reasoning. A recent survey of buildings in York dates the savings bank to 1819, 10 years too early, although the date of establishment is correctly given;[179] at Gainsborough, the bank chairman himself, opening a new branch in the 1950s, referred to the first savings bank in the town as erected in 1819.[180]

Confusion of this kind is natural enough. What is more disappointing is carelessness, and failure to take notice of visual evidence.[181] Newcastle-under-Lyme savings bank, built in 1852, is listed as *circa* 1800. Bath, of 1842, is listed as late eighteenth or early nineteenth century. Chester savings bank was by James Harrison, not Thomas. Beverley is of three bays, not five. Bury St Edmunds was a savings bank, not a penny bank. Newark bears a cast-iron plate stating that the first stone was laid by the mayor, 24 October 1831, but the building is listed vaguely as early nineteenth century. Tewkesbury and Lichfield, both now used as shops, still bear the name Savings Bank, but the official descriptions ignore this. In fact, it is doubtful whether Lichfield savings bank is even covered by the listing of the Corn Exchange, of which it forms an essential, and yet distinct, component. Derby and Cheadle savings banks, the former an attractive neo-Greek building, the latter an Elizabethan intrusion in a street of artisans' cottages, are certainly unlisted. So is Preston, now disguised as the Wesleyan Lecture Hall, but its erection by John Latham is well documented.[182]

Sixteen savings banks are listed, but without reference to their former use.[183] Admittedly, for some the previous use is not widely known: at Wirksworth and Witham, for instance, the attribution has only been confirmed by title deeds. But it is disappointing that no mention of banking origin is made at Bath, which Hithcock found so important stylistically; at Truro, where the Royal Institution of Cornwall are aware of their building's original use; at Wakefield, where No. 1 Burton Street is still called Bank House; and at Gloucester, for which the *Builder* carried description, elevation and ground plan.[184]

Figure 2 shows nine savings banks built in 1851–2, and on this basis it is likely that some 40 others were built in that decade. The years 1854–7 were difficult economically but the general state of the country had never had a direct effect on the banks' building programmes. Certainly, deposits fluctuated with changes in social conditions. Manchester trustees confessed publicly to local 'panic' in 1839,[185] but it did not deter them from building. In 1847 and 1848, with social distress and Chartism at its height, withdrawals throughout the country far exceeded deposits, and 1849 and 1850 were only slightly better. Yet, more savings banks were built in 1846–50 than in any earlier 5-year period. In one sense, this is further evidence of the extent to which the surplus fund was irrelevant to the operational stability of the banks. In most cases it was too small to act as a reservoir of reserve capital, against withdrawals, and building remained the only sensible outlay to absorb it. If any one factor did check building after 1852, it was the decision not to allow banks to build accommodation for their actuary as an integral part of new premises. Trustees at Portsmouth, Hereford and Marlborough all petitioned the National Debt Office in 1853 for withdrawals for this purpose and, when told of the new ruling, two of them at least did not pursue their intention.[186]

It is disappointing that no sources exist which would enable a checklist of purpose-built savings banks to be compiled 10 years later than the 1852 questionnaire. Some banks after 1852 have been revealed by chance reference, others are known because they still exist, but the overall positon is obscure and statements are unreliable. In their commemorative publication, the West Midland TSB knew nothing about the Leominster bank premises: after 1828 'information is unobtainable', they wrote, although research had 'followed every possible path, newspaper files were examined and libraries searched without success ...'.[187] Yet a savings bank was erected in Burgess Street in 1857 and an illustration was published.[188]

The seven other banks of this period undoubtedly built were at Banbury (1853), Worcester (1853), Brewood (c. 1854), Sandbach (1854), Gainsborough (1856), Leominster (1857), Sleaford (1857) and King's Lynn (1859).[189] It is interesting that five of the last six were neo-Tudor, if not Gothic, further evidence that the quasi-charitable function of savings banks had in no way been seen to have weakened.

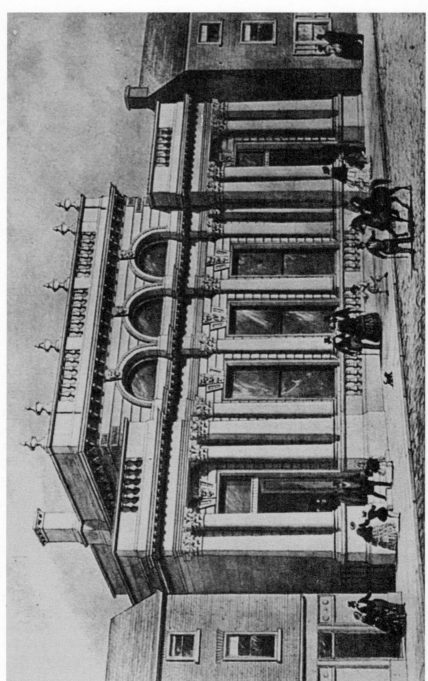

Plate 31. T.J. Flockton's Sheffield Savings Bank, 1860.

King's Lynn bank (dated in the Ministry List as 1885) is particularly important. Virtually the only Tudor–Gothic building in the town, it was designed by Medland and Maberley of London and Gloucester and built for £2000.[190] It was noticed in the *Builder*, which drew attention to exposed ceiling timbers and open fireplaces of Caen stone, elaborately carved.[191] The YMCA bought the premises in 1891 and their initials, confusingly, are on the exterior. The building, which recently escaped demolition, is now a clubhouse.

In 1860 another Elizabethan-style savings bank was built in Lincolnshire, this time at Louth. It was designed by James Fowler of that town, cost reputedly £600, and has since been demolished.[192] At Sheffield, in the same year, a savings bank was erected in classical style to designs by T.J. Flockton[193] (Plate 31). This superseded the earlier purpose-built bank in Sheffield designed by Robert Potter. Other banks of this decade, at Newcastle-upon-Tyne, Southampton and Liverpool, have been mentioned above. Undoubtedly there were many smaller savings banks also built in this period, like the little one at Faringdon dated 1863, but legislation was tending to discourage it.

In 1861 had been passed the Post Office Savings Bank Act[194] which broke the monopoly of the existing banks. Their decline was inevitable, but not immediate, and checked by the consolidating powers of the Trustee Savings Bank Act of 1863.[195] But business dwindled: 33 banks closed in 1864; 15 in 1865; 14 in 1866; 19 in 1867; 22 in 1868; 10 in 1869, and so on.[196] What was important now was that the savings banks were facing competition, and this had as profound an influence on their buildings as it did on their deposits. It was not only the post office savings banks which threatened them. More slowly, but with equal effect, the penny banks were eroding their position. From a humble origin at Greenock, in 1847, these little institutions spread to London, Hull and Selby in 1849.[197] The Birmingham penny bank, established in 1851, collected over £52 000 in 6 years, in amounts from one penny to one pound.[198] Faced with this competition, the large Birmingham savings bank, to the consternation of sister institutions, went out of business in 1864. Other penny banks had been set up at York (1854), Halifax (1856), Derby (1857), and Southampton and Plymouth (1858).[199] They were by then so well established that legislation to cover their management was passed in 1859.[200]

Planners and historians — epecially local and architectural historians — should be aware not only of the distinctive nature of savings banks but also of the basic elements of this distinction which set savings banks apart from the mainstream of banking history. Their

Plate 32. Former High Wycombe Savings Bank, 1842, before and after conversion to a jeweller's shop.

premises came about from circumstances quite unlike those which prompted building by commercial banks. The latter had depositors; the more depositors, the greater the fund of money available. Taking the gamble that all this money would not be withdrawn at once, the commercial banks used it to finance their buildings. The savings banks took in money as well, and most local histories took delight in pointing to the strength of a bank by quoting the balance of deposits. But these were not current accounts and as far as premises were concerned, the total of deposited money was irrelevant. The money was untouchable. The only fund available to the trustees for building purposes was the fortuitous surplus arising from the difference between rates of interest. No other class of semi-public buildings had such a casual origin and there is nothing to suggest that if the surplus fund had not existed, Government would have subsidised a building programme.

It may not be that, as a group, early savings banks are any more worthy of total preservation than, say, all purpose-built mechanics' institutes. But it is to be hoped that a better understanding of the nature of savings banks will prevent in the future misfortunes like the destruction of the small and dignified façade at High Wycombe (Plate 32).

Chapter Four

High Victorian Confidence and Experimentation

More than one reference has already been made in this work to the 'mainstream' of banking. In one sense the metaphor, until now, has been inexact. From the 1830s there were three parallel and independent streams, as different in strength as in source. Private and joint-stock banks were jealous of their distinctions and savings banks had been founded for philanthropic reasons under separate statutory control. If the mainstream of banking existed, then it was as an ill-defined, procedural area in which the broadest principles of banking were common to all types of establishment. It would be possible, for instance, to see the development of book-keeping techniques as a manifestation of the mainstream in a working sense, and also the provision by private and joint-stock bankers of banknotes, cheques, and letters of credit. Still more evidential of common thinking was the way in which Italianate styles came to dominate the appearance of banking premises, including those of the savings banks, in the late 1840s.

Twenty years later the mainstream was in full flow, quickened and swollen by the first of hundreds of mergers between the rising joint-stock companies and the dwindling pools of private banking. The effect of this was increasingly to identify the mainstream with the fortunes of the joint-stock companies. In relation to the monopoly of business which private bankers had enjoyed until 1826, it was a complete change of river-bed. The irony is that as banking became ever closer to its modern image, it lost the main visual expression of the mainstream — a near uniform presentation of banking architecture.

Much of this chapter will be concerned with the causes and consequences of the rejection of a standard image, and the starting point must be the changing character of bankers themselves. Despite a few major catastrophes, still occurring at roughly 10-year intervals, bankers were acquiring a professional self-confidence and sense of well-being which allowed them to add some spice to conventional tastes. There is clear evidence of this in their private architectural commissions, bankers being among the leading groups of builders of Victorian country houses.[1] Some of the earlier of these, for instance Abberley Hall for J.L. Moilliet (by Samuel Daukes) and Kiddington Hall for Mortimer Ricardo (by Sir Charles Barry), were Italianate, but the trend was towards neo-Tudor designs such as A.W. Pugin's Albury Park, for Henry Drummond (1846–52), or Gothic, like W.E. Nesfield's Cloverley Hall for J.P. Heywood (1864–70), or picturesque, like George Devey's Ascott for Lionel de Rothschild (1874–80s). Although one house might now be considered 'terrible'[2] and another 'depressing',[3] most showed a freshness of spirit, indicative of rising confidence.

In purely banking terms there was a reversion to the feeling of the 1830s that competitive advantage might lie not in uniformity of design but in calculated variation. Furthermore, now that the possibilities of orthodox Italianate had been realised, a rapid and unwelcomed debasement of that style was the only way forward, unless alternative designs were introduced. Of particular influence in bringing about this variation was the national background of movement in architectural taste, more particularly the increasing acceptance of Gothic for a variety of secular purposes. The role of this outside influence, coupled with certain other internal factors, like renewed branch expansion, will be examined in the course of this chapter.

The most radical and significant expression of the new temperament was the rebuilding of Lombard Street. In 1861 *Building News* looked forward to a street 'as different in its architecture from what it was a quarter of a century ago as it was then from the old thoroughfare which Stow described.'[4] Part of a wider impetus for the modernisation of many aspects of City building, the new banks were evidence of the rightful appropriation by the metropolis of its position as the centre of the banking world. Questions of style aside, they were triumphs of planning and negotiation. Lawyers faced leasehold tenure and a complexity of rights and easements; architects met narrow, crooked streets and awkward plots; both had the problem of ancient lights. The height of the banking-hall of the National Provincial Bank's head office was dictated by the sill of the lowest window in an adjacent property.[5] It took 2 years of legal negotiation before builders could begin there, while another company lost even more time, and considerable capital, buying freeholds of the minimum area required for expansion.[6]

The earliest of the new banks, and a definite trend-setter, was the

London & County Bank head office, completed in 1862, and designed by C.O. Parnell (Plate 33).[7] Only the roof, chimneys and quoins recalled the limited Italianate tradition to which banking was accustomed. The ground floor introduced three-quarter columns with rusticated bands and windows with rounded corners and carved lintels. The upper floors diminished progressively in decoration, the middle windows of the second and third floors repeating the style of the side windows below them. The emphasis on centrality which resulted was off-set by the doorway, placed to the side, but the building was characterised by its narrow, vertical axis, squeezing above the roof-lines of neighbours and capping its dominance with a handsome foliated frieze. Such intrusion by banks into the skyline was to become very common. Belying its appearance from Lombard Street, the bank had a return frontage in nearby Nicholas Lane. The building was, therefore, 'L'-shaped, and the first floor accommodated a board room, and rooms and offices for inspectors, other staff, committees, and the handling of transfers and dividends; the upper floors were the residence of a 'confidential clerk'.[8]

The bank was very well received, particularly by *Building News*: 'The Lombard-street front is beautifully proportioned; but it is largely indebted for its magnificence to the great care with which every detail has been studied, and to the absence of any weakness of design or trifling eccentricity. It is rich without being overladen with ornament . . . It is a design which we should hardly have expected to meet with out of Pall-mall.'[9] The last point was picked up elsewhere in the same commentary: 'the new premises of the London and County Bank exhibit the architectural magnificence which has hitherto been seen almost exclusively in the club-houses in Pall-mall.'

The *Builder*, although a little worried by the projection of cornices and decoration, found the building 'bank-like', borrowing from Hardwick's bank for Jones, Loyd & Co., at Lothbury, both the Roman Doric Order and the accentuation of the lower storey.[10] In approving the practice of laying emphasis on the ground floor, as if this were innovatory, the journal seems to have forgotten that this was a traditional feature of London private banks, and especially of Lombard Street. However, the *Builder* did make a good point about the escalation of property values and its effect: companies 'able to begin with expenditure of . . . this kind . . ., are not likely to think much of the slight additional cost of decoration, — the building being on their own ground. In short, having been under-valued or disregarded, decoration is now tending to excess . . .'.[11] Perhaps also bankers were tired of

Plate 33. C.O. Parnell's head office for the London & County Bank, Lombard Street, London, 1862.

being regarded, by all appearances, as poor relations to the insurance companies, whose buildings were 'invariably Italian, with something of the comfortable monumentality but none of the reserve of Barry's Pall Mall clubs.'[12]

Among other new Lombard Street buildings of the early to middle 'sixties were the three private banks of Messrs Robarts, Curtis & Lubbock, Messrs Barclay, Bevan & Co., and Messrs Alexanders, Cunliffes & Co. The first two were by P.C. Hardwick[13] and the last by Alfred Waterhouse.[14] There was also the London, Scottish & Australian Bank by Henry Baker,[15] and the Royal Insurance Company by John Belcher.[16] The only domestic joint-stock bank to rebuild in Lombard Street at that time was the London & County Bank, mentioned above. It must, therefore, be wondered whether the *Builder*'s memory was wholly correct when it stated, in 1877, that 'joint-stock Banks in London were among the first to erect grandiose buildings for their offices, and the example set by them, and followed by others, has helped to make some of the narrow streets of the City appear to be filled with palaces.'[17] The point is of little importance, however, because rebuilding was not confined to Lombard Street and, whoever was responsible for the initial burst of reconstruction, the practice spread quickly to Cornhill and Nicholas Lane, Finch Lane and Poultry. Building costs between £20000 and £40000 appear to have been normal.[18]

Undoubtedly, the influential architect in this period was P.C. Hardwick, whose position as architect to the Bank of England ensured continuing commissions.[19] Close to him in style was F.W. Porter who had a long association with banking developed through the Union Bank of London.[20] Two of his branches for this bank — one in Chancery Lane, the other in Spring Gardens, off Charing Cross — are still used by the National Westminster Bank. His main work, the Union Bank's head office opposite the Mansion House,[21] has been demolished. It was in the tradition of Hardwick and Porter that the typical London suburban bank, with corner entrance, was to develop.

The only bank building in London in the 1860s to break dramatically with this style — and it may be this bank which coloured the *Builder*'s later recollection — was John Gibson's head office for the National Provincial Bank at the junction of Bishopsgate and Threadneedle Street. This building, saved from demolition and restored, is now the National Westminster Hall. It was begun in October 1864, finished late in 1865, and opened in January 1866[22] (Plates 34–36).

Established in 1833 as a bank of issue, the National Provincial Bank

Plate 34. Above: John Gibson's head office for the National Provincial Bank, Bishopsgate, London, completed 1865. Two further bays were added to the main frontage in 1878. Below: same building, interior.

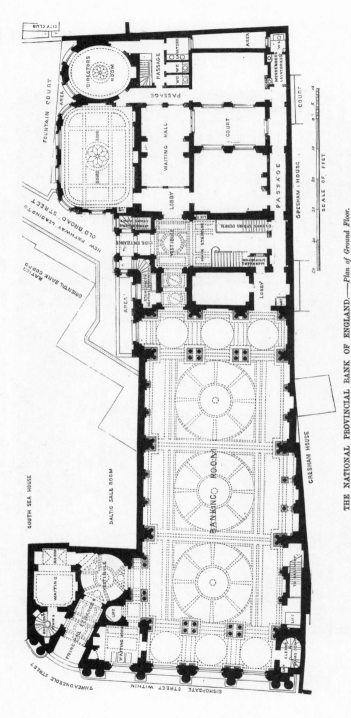

THE NATIONAL PROVINCIAL BANK OF ENGLAND.—*Plan of Ground Floor.*

Plate 35. Ground plan of Gibson's head office for the National Provincial Bank.

could have no London head office for public banking until it accepted Bank of England notes. When legislation, expected to end this problem, did not materialise, the bank withdrew its notes and decided to build in the City. It was fitting that a joint-stock bank of such relative antiquity, with some 120 outlets, should have outstanding premises but it was too late to jostle with established interests and buy up a site in Lombard Street. The bank, therefore, stayed more or less on the site of its existing administrative office.

Gibson's achievement was to bring Glasgow to London, as decisively as Gingell & Lysaght had brought it to Bristol. It was not the single Corinthian Order which was particularly Glaswegian: it was the confidence of the architect, the boldness, the mastery of decorative detail, features which made the Lombard Street *palazzi* seem fussy and debased. For the first time, a London bank had sculptured panels and allegorical statuary massive in scale, meaningful in concept, and rich in visual impact. Single figures were placed above single columns and groups above double columns, with representations (working from the back of the rounded entrance) of Manchester, England, Wales, Birmingham, the Potteries, Dover and London. These carvings were by Messrs Colley, who had also worked for Parnell in Lombard Street. The six panels were modelled by John Hancock, depicting the Arts, Commerce, Science, Manufactures, Agriculture and Navigation.[23]

The ground plan (Plate 35) reveals that the bank extended back to a depth which could hardly be imagined from the road. Although the adaptation of the bankers' requirements to the intricacies of the site was ingeniously conceived, the siting of the main entrance resulted more from a desire to have an address in Threadneedle Street (home of the Bank of England), than from the dictates of the layout. However, it gave Gibson the chance to produce a masterful solution to the problem of a doorway set at an angle to the street elevation. Instead of a splayed entrance, which would have broken the rhythm, he designed a rounded end which repeated the panels and double columns of the main façade, while breaking back the entablature.

Another significant achievement was the impression from the road that this was a monumental banking-hall, uncluttered with the offices and lodgings more generally associated with a major bank. In fact, this was *trompe l'œil*: not only did the bank embrace a board room, rooms for directors and managers, a strong room and several lavatories, but there was a vast basement beneath, dedicated to book rooms and a strong room, and there were living quarters at the back, on the first

*Plate 36. Statuary by Messrs Colley flanking the entrance bay of Gibson's head office
for the National Provincial Bank.*

floor. Separate staircases were provided between ground floor and
basement for managers, clerks and messengers.

In a wider context this was, of course, derivative building: the figures
on the cornice were reminiscent of Bryce and Hamilton, the ceiling of
the banking-hall had been rehearsed by Gibson himself for the
National Bank of Scotland, and *putti* in the interior frieze, pressing and
coining, reverted to Rhind, and to Gingell & Lysaght. Also reminiscent
of Corn Street were coupled interior columns supporting the dome.
The inspiration for this building dated back, therefore, to the 'fifties if
not beyond. Perhaps in more technological ways, Gibson was also
traditional. The main girders were of boxed plate-iron, whereas
Parnell had used girders of Sheffield steel for the upper floors of his
Lombard Street bank 'apparently deflected only one-inch each with
a distributed weight of 200 tons', and occupying half the depth
required by iron.[24] But it was still a building of power and distinction.
This was a quality of design which the capital had not seen since
Cockerell's London & Westminster Bank nearly 30 years earlier.

It has been mentioned above that one of the new buildings in
Lombard Street was the bank of Messrs Alexanders, Cunliffes & Co.,
designed by Alfred Waterhouse. This was a Gothic design. When the
Builder was reviewing construction work, only one storey had been
completed. 'The work is not sufficiently advanced to say more about it,

than that polished granite will be used for some of the shafts . . .'.[25] It seems remarkable, however, that the nature of the style was not visible behind the scaffolding or known by enquiry. And yet no occasion was taken here, either in this journal or in *Building News*,[26] to comment on the relevance or suitability of Gothic in such a position. This omission requires that the place of the Gothic style in banking, and the steps which were necessary to reach acceptability, must now be considered from the earliest examples of its use.

It was shown in Chapter Three that the quasi-charitable origins of the savings bank movement suggested the suitability of a neo-Tudor presentation among its buildings. It is in this style, too, that the origins of Gothic for commercial banking can be traced, but with no similar justification for its adoption. In the context of business premises, the precedents for building in a style other than some variety of classical were not extensive. The first recorded departure from what was incontestably safe, was John Shaw's office for the Law Life Assurance Society, erected in 1833,[27] which still survives in Fleet Street. The inspiration for this was Northumberland House, built near Charing Cross in 1603, and pulled down in 1876. Other contemporary buildings, more domestic in nature, followed the same design — 'the latest style of Old English domestic architecture . . . which seems to be increasing in favour.'[28] While often summarised as 'Elizabethan', the style allowed bay windows and was very much influenced by the English Renaissance. But the classical elements were apparently too weak for the style to win favour with the architects of banking.[29]

Contemporary with this building, and therefore a very brave venture indeed, was a branch built at Hanley, near Stoke-on-Trent, for the Manchester & Liverpool District Bank. In March 1833, the minutes of the bank's main board recorded that 'the erection of a Bank at Hanley was approved and committed to the Local Board there', who engaged T.W. Atkinson, then of London, as architect.[30] Why Atkinson, who at that time was designing the Italianate Manchester head office of the same bank, should have chosen neo-Tudor for this branch, is not explained. The boldness of style in terms of the Hanley environment, if not of the practice of banking, was noticed by the historian of the Potteries, writing soon after the bank's completion. He found it:

> spacious and elegant . . . built in the gabled or Tudor style of architecture, of pale brick, with ornamental door and window fronts and other members of stone. Its elevation rises above all the neighbouring houses, and makes it conspicuous at a considerable distance. We take

the liberty, however, of questioning the good taste of the architect, who fixed on a style of building of three centuries' date for a mansion like this in the centre of a modern town, which presents nothing at all similar to keep it in countenance.[31]

The bank was demolished around 1880 and replaced by another in similar but weaker style.

There appears to be no evidence for any other commercial bank of the 1830s in a style which was not classical, or neo-Greek, or Italianate, but the possibility of others in neo-Tudor style must always remain. Statements that the present-day Barclays Bank at Boston, a mildly Gothic building formerly a branch of the Stamford, Spalding & Boston Bank, was erected in 1835, seem based on a curious misunderstanding of the visual and published evidence.[32] The bank is no earlier than 1876, designed by Lockwood & Mawson,[33] the latter having been son-in-law of one of the bank's directors.[34] Neither the alleged early date, nor a specific attribution to H.F. Lockwood, seem explicable, particularly as the company had no earlier purpose-built bank at Boston which might have caused the confusion.

The next confirmed bank in this series is probably that at Gloucester opened by the National Provincial Bank in Westgate Street in 1844 and designed by S.W. Daukes (Plate 37). The style, with cusped tracery and perhaps ball-flower ornament below the lower sill band, was more Gothic than Atkinson's, and some reason must be found for it. Minute books of the bank's directors, although allowing the dates of construction and other details to be verified, provide no explanation of the appearance.[35]

A number of reasons can be proposed. First, Daukes had already designed at least one of the banks built in classical or Italianate style in Gloucester in the 1830s and may have felt the need for competitive distinction. But this was hardly enough to justify a change of style of such violence. Secondly, the bank appears, on the evidence of the illustration, to have accommodated also 'public rooms'. As Gothic or neo-Tudor was suitable for a free library, news room or public dispensary, it might also suit this evidence of philanthropy. But that would suggest the 'rooms' were more important than the bank. Thirdly, there was a connection with 'Jemmy' Wood, the eccentric proprietor of the oldest private bank in the district.[36] Although Wood's business passed to the Gloucestershire Banking Company, the site was bought by the National Provincial Bank and the well-known sixteenth century building which he had occupied was demolished. Was Gothic

Plate 37. *S.W. Daukes's Gloucester branch of the National Provincial Bank, with public rooms above, 1844.*

perhaps chosen as a mark of respect for this historical association of the site?

The fourth and last speculation rests on the involvement of Sir Matthew Wood (probably no relation of 'Jemmy'), who was certainly in correspondence with the London Board while the new bank was under discussion in 1843.[37] This is potentially the most interesting associational reason. A municipal and political reformer, Wood took a leading role in improving the City of London, but he lived and died at Matson House, near Gloucester.[38] This Tudor house, mullioned and gabled, was given sash windows 'with pretty cusped Gothic tracery, the result no doubt of two visits by Horace Walpole to George Selwyn.'[39] Whether or not Daukes was directly influenced by Wood, the combination of Wood's involvement and an unusual bank complimentary to the style of his house, cannot be seen as wholly coincidental.

If any new Gothic or neo-Tudor commercial banks were erected in the next 10 or so years, they appear not to have merited attention in the architectural journals. In 1857, however, perhaps in token recognition of increasing interest in the suitability of Gothic for secular purposes, *Building News* published a picture of a Gothic-style bank entrance in Leicester Square, designed by John Billing (Plate 38).[40] But the journal made no comment, aesthetic or ethical, and the significance of this design might have been overlooked, had it not received further attention from a correspondent to *Punch*, in September 1864: 'On Sunday', wrote one Little Ben, recounting a journey through London, 'I attempted to enter what I thought was a pretty little Gothic Chapel, not a hundred miles from Leicester Square. I was nearly taken up by a Policeman for attempting a burglary upon the London and Leicester Square Bank! There seems to be some want of originality in design among our architects. Let a Chapel be a Chapel, a Music Hall be a Music Hall, a Bank a Bank . . .'.[41]

This point was immediately taken up by the *Builder*, which felt that a bank in this style would 'express its purpose not anywhere in London'.[42] In the same issue, the editorial restated the question as to whether a bank-like version of Gothic should exist, but without expressing an opinion. Despite this disappointment, the Leicester Square episode can be appreciated as the only occasion when the merits of Gothic for bank architecture came in any way close to public discussion. The bank itself was, in business terms, obscure. Seale, Low & Co. (also calling themselves, according to *Punch*, the London & Leicester Square Bank) were first recorded in 1856, in Leicester Place; the following year, they moved nearby to No. 7, Leicester

Plate 38. John Billing's Leicester Square bank for Seale,
Low & Co., 1857, mentioned in Punch, *Sept. 1864.*

Square.[43] This was certainly the address at which Billing worked, because illustrations of the front of the premises are found, quite fortuitously, in prints of the fire and damage at nearby Saville House, in 1865.[44] Although there is some slight difficulty in matching these views exactly, it is quite clear that the Gothic motif extended to no more than the ground floor of No. 7, which retained, in upper storeys, the late Georgian features of its neighbours. As for Seale, Low & Co., they disappeared from directories in 1870 and no records are known to have survived.

The more widespread acceptability of Gothic among bankers was a phenomenon of the 1860s and it is unfortunate that the relatively trivial episode of the Leicester Square bank should have spoilt the opportunity for a deeper and more forceful discussion by the journals of the large Gothic banks designed by architects of national distinction. The two names which can be associated with Gothic acceptance in this context are Gilbert Scott and John Ruskin. Scott's abortive Gothic design in the competition for Government Offices in 1857 led to the well-publicised exchanges known as 'The Battle of the Styles', and banks headed the list of urban public buildings for which he advocated Italian Gothic.[45] Ruskin's influence was less direct, but equally pervasive. He brought the Gothic Revival away from the Roman Catholic church, where Pugin had placed it, and back to Protestantism. Once Gothic was reunited with the Establishment, it was possible to accept Gothic ornamentation, which to Ruskin was of basic importance, and also to use the Venetian style which he had praised in *The Stones of Venice*.[46] As the use of Venetian classical designs was already established for banks, the transition to Venetian Gothic was the more easy.

The availability of this style coincided with the first major change in joint-stock bank organisation since the 1830s. Symptomatic of this change was the extension of limited liability to banking in 1858.[47] Although opposed by some old-school bankers as lessening the commitment of the banker to his customer, limited liability nevertheless characterised and enhanced the sense of corporate identity at a time when joint-stock banks were beginning to grow by merger with competitors, and entering the second major phase of branch expansion. The proliferation of outlets led inevitably to the need for greater central control and consequent expansion of head office facilities: the 1860s witnessed, therefore, a burst of head office construction as widespread as at any time previously. Just as the scale of this rebuilding can be noticed in the architectural press, so the *Bankers' Magazine* reveals the growing vigour and complexity of professional expertise.

When the Gothic Revival is seen against this background of fundamental change in the structure and pace of banking, it may be wondered whether there was not a lost opportunity; whether the Gothic style might not have been adopted as an expression of a new direction in the mainstream of banking, in the way that Italianate had been characteristic of the old. Alternatively, this might have been seen as the occasion to create an entirely new style, a possibility which troubled Gilbert Scott: 'Are we, then, to invent, a spick-and-span new style to suit them?'[48] He was emphatically against it, arguing from lack of precedent. 'No age of the world has ever deliberately invented a new style, nor yet made use of a style for one class of buildings different from what it applies to others.'[49] Scott's belief was that a commercial system which originated in Europe in the Gothic Middle Ages should be visually sympathetic to that period rather than a plagiarism of

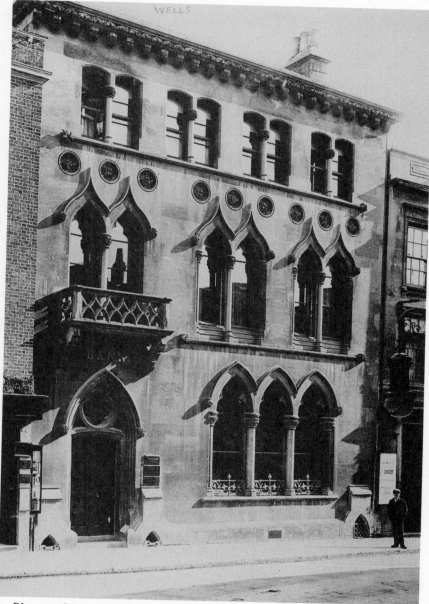

Plate 39. Stuckey's Bank in Wells, Somerset, opened in 1858, before removal of balcony and replacement of ground-floor windows.

Plate 40. George Gilbert Scott's bank for Beckett & Co., Leeds, 1863–7.

Ancient Rome 'with which these institutions have no historical association',[50] or of the works of Italian Renaissance copyists. The authority for change was strong, the business climate was suitable, but the break with classicism was never conclusive.

Elements of Venetian Gothic had reached banking before the Battle of the Styles had broken. Pevsner attributes a bank in this vein at Knutsford to 1856.[51] William White's Venetian-style bank was built at St Columb Major in Cornwall in 1857,[52] and Stuckey & Co.'s bank at Wells, opened early in 1858.[53] The Wells bank (Plate 39), by an unrecorded architect, was quite interesting. The first floor, emphatically defined by the string courses, appeared to aspire to Venice in the shape of the arches, which were surmounted by sunken quatrefoils, in the balcony, and more subtly in the asymmetry of the left-hand double casements. The ogee-headed drip-moulds complemented those above the three-light Gothic windows of the ground floor. By contrast, the second-floor windows were more reminiscent of French Gothic, although some degree of unity was given to the whole façade by the repetition at each level of foliated capitals. Dismally impracticable for banking, the ground-floor lancets were later replaced by two sets of windows, each of four main lights under low-arched heads. Unfortunately, this has led to removal of the balcony and the loss of the building's charm.

Also called 'Venetian Gothic' by the *Builder* was Paull & Ayliffe's Union Bank at Huddersfield of 1867,[54] but this building, and more particularly Hoskins's bank for Backhouse & Co., at Bishop Auckland, completed in 1873,[55] showed an influence more obviously French. It is, in fact, very difficult to establish clear precedents influencing the banks of this period and the categorisation so popular with the Victorians is invariably too dogmatic. Such descriptions as 'Early Geometrical, with a deal of Early French Gothic' and a 'free adaptation of Lombardic Gothic' point to an attention to the vocabulary of commercial architecture as close as it had been under Rickman in the religious context.

The better-known banks associated with the Gothic Revival were by G.G. Scott at Leeds (1863–7),[56] sadly now demolished, and by Alfred Waterhouse for the District Bank, Nantwich (1864–6), for Alexanders, Cunliffes & Co., Lombard Street, London (1865–6), for Bassett & Co. at Leighton Buzzard (1865–6) and for the head office of the Bradford Old Bank (opened 1867).[57] In none of these was the Gothic precedent straightforward and the influence of France and England was as marked as that of Italy. Scott's bank at Leeds for Beckett & Co. (Plate 40) was perhaps the most interesting of the group. The attention to symmetry seemed at odds with Gothic inspiration, but the bank made an important contribution to polychromy which would have been difficult to achieve if dressed in classical garb. Special red facing bricks were manufactured at Thirsk — smooth, thin, and laid in dark mortar. Relieving this intensity of colour were the stone shafts of the capitals, the string courses, and stone elements of the parapet. Although the overall style has proved difficult to characterise — the *Builder* called it 'Early English'[58] — there were interesting echoes of Venice in the corner colonnettes of the first floor, repeated on the entrance porch above impost level.

One of the best Gothic interiors to have survived is at Leicester on a corner site in Granby Street. Now a branch of the Midland Bank, the building was erected for the Leicestershire Banking Company in 1870 from designs by Joseph Goddard.[59] The red-brick exterior straggles in a confusing assemblage of angles and styles, part-native, part-French and part-Italian. All this is in massive contrast to the simplicity of the banking-hall. An arcade of square columns, with foliated capitals, separates a kind of aisle (giving access to interview rooms) from the banking-hall proper. The latter rises sheer, with the drama of a cathedral nave, to a wooden truss roof, above which a rectangular lantern is enlivened with Gothic arcading.[60]

It is interesting that an English style was used at Oxford and Cambridge where the architects F. & H. Francis, designing branches for the London & County Bank in the 'sixties, chose the Decorated or Middle Pointed period in deference, no doubt, to the Camden Society.[61] London was, despite Waterhouse's bank in Lombard Street, and the example of certain other commercial premises, such as the Crown Life Assurance Society building of 1858,[62] reluctant to use any manifestation of Gothic, or Ruskinian teaching, for banking purposes. Only in the north of England did Gothic have any real impact on head office building, and even here Newcastle and the biggest urban centres of Manchester and Liverpool remained largely faithful to classical styles until the 1880s.

Away from the Gothic arena, classical styles developed in many directions from the relatively restricted exemplars of 20 years before. Designs rooted in specific Renaissance precedents were rare, although Critchlow's Hampshire Bank at Southampton, of 1866, showed clear influence of the Palazzo Vendramin-Calergi in Venice, an association not without merit for a flourishing seaport.[63] Most architects borrowed from the Glasgow–Bristol school or from the Barry clubhouse tradition, staying one stage removed from original precedents. None of these styles showed anything other than a progressive mannerism and debasement, and there was an unfortunate trend in the larger urban centres for massive, florid and overworked designs deriving from the conventionalised metropolitan grandeur of Porter and Hardwick. The Alliance Bank in Liverpool was an example.[64] There was also some innovative interpretation of Italian Renaissance themes. It will be useful to look at some of these trends more closely.

The style which John Gibson had created in Glasgow for the National Bank (Plate 22) seems to have been the inspiration for such buildings as the new office of the Bury Banking Company, in Bury, Lancashire, and the head office of the Ulster Bank in Belfast. The Belfast bank was the earlier of the two, having been completed in 1860 to designs by James Hamilton of Glasgow[65] (Plate 41). It was the result of a well-publicised competition and 2 months' travel by two of the bank's executives, selecting the features of the Glasgow and Edinburgh *palazzi* which appealed to them most.[66] They particularly liked the appearance of Gibson's National Bank and Hamilton's interpretation of their choice took him to the same Venetian precedent as had appealed to Gingell and Lysaght at Bristol. Of seven bays and two storeys, the Ulster Bank was in marked contrast to Charles Lanyon's nearby head office of the Belfast Bank, completed in 1846, a little model of Italianate propriety in the Barry manner.[67]

The central three bays of the Ulster Bank broke forward into a portico, the coupled Doric columns of the ground floor resting on a base considerably raised from street level and approached by some dozen steps. This height was needed to clear the unusual raised basement, necessary for structural reasons,[68] but an awkward feature in a bank, where considerations of security kept sight of non-public areas to a minimum. A difference from the Bristol interpretation of Sansovino was the more traditional entablature of the first floor, with frieze of metopes and triglyphs, and the change from Ionic to Corinthian in the upper Order. Hamilton also dispensed with columns dividing the end bays of both floors. Very much in the Corn Street manner, however, was the upper frieze, with its *putti*, while the arms and statuary (Justice, Peace and Plenty) on the parapet harked back to Gibson at Glasgow. The clusters of three antique vases were as if to emphasise the extra degree of enrichment — Belfast going one better than Glasgow where three vases had been restricted to the corners of the main elevation.

The banking-hall, here called the cash office, was approached by

Plate 41. James Hamilton's Ulster Bank, Belfast, opened in 1860.

eight more steps leading from the vestibule. The dome was carried by four Corinthian columns of polished Aberdeen granite with marble plinths. Above allegorical figures in the glass of the dome were portraits of people with appropriate associations: for instance, William Brown of Liverpool was linked with commerce, Shakespeare with poetry, Wren with architecture, Cook with navigation, and Grote with banking.[69] All this was the work of Sipthorpe of Dublin, while a Belfast man, George Crowe, designed the rich decoration of the groined ceiling, busy with fruit, foliage, and mythological figures. Either side of the cash office were rooms for directors and officers of the bank, and apparently also for shareholders. The second floor was residential. Books, notes, bullion, etc., were kept in the semi-basement where the strong rooms were of solid masonry, entered through iron doors. The total cost of the bank was around £30000, and it apparently evoked the question whether 'a bank should be such a beautifully ornamented piece of lofty architecture, or merely a squat house of sufficient strength'.[70] The answer was dismissed to the domain of 'political economists' — who might not, perhaps, have introduced the necessary moral element to the debate.

At Bury, the bank was designed by Messrs Blackwell, Son, & Booth and completed in 1868[71] (Plate 42). In its proportions the building echoed Gibson's National Bank. Both were of five bays with the centre breaking slightly forward. At Bury, however, the relationship with classical precedent was less precise. Corners were rounded and the ground floor lost its Order, with pilasters undefined from the wall area. A row of first floor balconies, linked by a string course, acted in place of entablature as the division between the floors. Despite these freedoms, the bank was not overburdened with masks and vases, and statuary was confined to a rounded pediment above the central bay. The most elaborate feature of the bank was the cornice, of such a depth as to accommodate an awkward intermediate cornice above the capitals of the pilasters. Among minor points of decorative detail could be noticed shields of arms of bank directors embodied in the capitals of the corner pilasters, an idea borrowed from the Manchester & Salford Bank head office of 1862, which will be discussed below. Other exterior features worthy of mention include the choice of stone — millstone grit for the ground floor and Darley Dale stone for the first — and the splayed, rounded form of the doorway. The latter feature may have developed from the narrow reveals, with similar decoration, of Gibson's windows for the National Provincial Bank's head office.

In the interior, the Bury bank departed from normal practice by not

Plate 42. Blackwell, Son, & Booth's new premises for Bury Banking Company (Lancs.) 1868.

having a domed banking-hall. The reason was to keep the first floor as an integral unit for letting as offices, and indeed part of the ground floor was similarly let to tenants, their entrance being at the side. In other words, the space for banking purposes was restricted: there was no board room, as such, and accommodation was only for a messenger, the space allotted to him being doubtless smaller than would have been granted to a manager. The fire-proofing between floors, on the traditional system of rolled iron joists and concrete, was not revolutionary, but the security arrangements were impressive: the hoist to the bullion safe was hydraulic, the strong room had Chatwood's latest fire-proof and burglar-proof doors, and the windows of the ground floor were double, the inner frames of oak and the outer of iron, protected by steel shutters.

The Italianate tradition of Barry reached the end of its line in banking with the head office of the Worcester City & County Bank, in The Cross, Worcester, built around 1862 to designs by E.W. Elmslie[72] (Plate 43). The inspiration for the main elevation of this building might have been George Alexander's Bath Savings Bank erected 20 years earlier (Plate 27), the main difference being that Elmslie added two more bays and updated the window surrounds of the second floor. The return front was longer than the main elevation and very visible. Lacking a natural focal point, it was given an off-centre, rounded bay of three lights — a radical break with tradition. In other shire towns of the south of England, for instance at nearby Hereford,[73] Italianate designs also lingered, showing an interesting difference of culture from the industrial north. What is difficult to establish is whether bankers themselves recognised this difference, or whether architects suggested it in the proposals they put forward.

The only major bank in the north of England to show vestiges of the Italianate style, in the Barry sense, was the head office of the Manchester & Salford Bank, in Mosley Street, Manchester, designed in 1860 by Edward Walters and opened 2 years later[74] (Plate 44). The bank was therefore of equal date with that at Worcester, just discussed, and the comparison is fruitful if tempered with due regard for differences of urban environment and banking technique: the Worcester bank had more branches but the Manchester bank was richer, with more proprietors. In Manchester the Italianate tradition went no further than the pedimented windows of the *piano nobile*. And yet this was not a design in the formula of Glasgow and Bristol. It was an attempt to give Manchester a unique style of bank, developing and learning from the earlier Italianate designs in the city by Atkinson and

Plate 43. E.W. Elmslie's head office for the Worcester City & County Bank,
Worcester, opened c. 1862, photographed as a branch of Lloyds Bank.

Gregan (Plate 21). Walters, then the leading architect in Manchester, achieved 'a very charming composition, by some considered his chef d'oeuvre . . .'.[75] The cost was around £25 000, exclusive of the site.

Built of Yorkshire stone, Walters's bank was characterised by the strong ground floor with rusticated pilasters — one of several features which seem to have influenced the smaller and later Bury bank, already discussed, and which many later bank architects adopted. With a ground area of 114 feet (34.7 metres) by 78 feet (23.77 metres), and nothing lost for an entrance and vestibule, the bank had impressive space. The banking-hall was 83 feet (25.3 metres) by 49 feet (14.9 metres) with a clear height of 27 feet (8.2 metres), and adequate lighting from the ground-floor windows. The bank did have a small dome, but it lit a large board room on the first floor, rather than the public area. This unusual feature (unusual, at least, for the date) points

Plate 44. Edward Walter's head office for the Manchester & Salford Bank, Manchester opened in 1862. As built, the bank incorporated an extension beyond the entrance which replaced the premises on the left of the picture.

to the planning of William Langton, the bank's manager, who allegedly arranged the interior layout:[76] this was a banker with his directors' interests at heart. The upper floor of the bank comprised private rooms for a submanager, and there is no evidence that such a large building was ever intended to include offices to let. With girders of wrought iron, as opposed to cast iron, and hydraulic hoists for books and bullion, the bank was technologically advanced.

In the innovative tradition of Walters's bank, but losing all trace of the two Roman and Florentine *palazzi* which had had such an enduring influence on bank elevations, was Edward Holmes's head office of the Birmingham and Midland Bank, in New Street, Birmingham, completed in 1869 at a cost of over £25 000[77] (Plate 45). This building showed a superficial resemblance to the Bank of New York, designed by Calvert Vaux and F.C. Withers, which had been illustrated in the *Builder* some 10 years earlier.[78] Both banks were relatively long and narrow, with the public entrance in the middle of a three-bay elevation to the principal street. Stylistically, however, and in interior layout, the two banks were not related. Also the New York building was substantially let, while the Birmingham one was exclusively for banking purposes.

In one of its rare passages about banks which was less than laudatory, the *Builder* called the style of Holmes's bank 'somewhat severe in character, the architect being instructed to avoid all unnecessary ornamentation'.[79] However, it found the result 'at once dignified and bank-like', and certainly the exterior, devoid of masks and vases, was very successful. Both main fronts were of Portland stone while the coupled Ionic columns of the entrance portico were of polished Cornish granite. The ground floor followed the prevailing fashion for pilasters, but with more orthodox grouping and design than had been used at Manchester, and token decoration of the capitals. The floor above carried more embellishment, with Corinthian columns supported by pilasters of the same Order to the windows. The narrow front to New Street was strengthened by doubling the columns between the first-floor windows, while on the return front the increasing depth of the base was relieved by the private entrance in the end bay.

In layout, the bank had the normal division between ground-floor banking-hall, lit mainly from the side in best Gilbartian manner, and first-floor board room, the latter only marginally smaller than that of the Manchester & Salford Bank (which had a more convenient shape of building) and 25 feet (7.6 metres) high. At the south end of the bank, where there was a second floor, as well as a mezzanine, were a variety of offices and rooms for business and residential purposes. One of these was a dining room, while another dining room, for clerks, was apparently in the basement, with the strong rooms. This may have been a novel facility for bank staff.

Another Birmingham bank of this period, the rebuilt National Provincial branch opened in 1869 at the corner of Bennett's Hill and Waterloo Street,[80] was by John Gibson, and leads to consideration once more of probably the most prolific bank architect ever, and the best-known exponent of the classical style. Gibson's commissions were as much the backbone of Victorian bank building as the company for which he worked was the mainstay of Victorian banking. This was the mainstream at its deepest. The Elizabethan style, which he favoured for more domestic commissions, was never used for his banks. Nor was he a particularly Italianate designer, although he had been a pupil of Charles Barry, in London, with whom he stayed on after the completion of pupilage.[81] His move to independent practice was helped by success in the competition for the design of the National Bank of Scotland, mentioned in Chapter Two.

The number of Gibson's branches for the National Provincial Bank has been placed as high as 40.[82] The exact figure is imponderable: some designs, like Birmingham, were to a greater or lesser extent from his studio, while certain branches, such as Hanley, he remodelled rather than built.[83] Furthermore the records of the bank are not sufficiently complete to allow all commissions to be traced at source. Several of his main works, however, are well recorded elsewhere: Tamworth, Southampton, and Bury St Edmunds in the 1860s;[84] Newcastle, Middlesbrough, Durham, Manchester, Stockton, Sunderland, Worcester and Portsea (Portsmouth) in the 1870s.[85] Attributions have been made to Gibson for National Provincial branches as early as about 1860 at Wisbech,[86] and as late as 1883 at Lincoln.[87] But as other architects were working for the National Provincial in 1863,[88] and again by 1883,[89] it is safest to conclude that the main thrust of Gibson's involvement was in a period of some 20 years from 1864.

Gibson was equally successful designing with a single giant Order, as at Bishopsgate and Middlesbrough (Plate 46), with superimposed Orders, as at Durham and Stockton or with Orders on a rusticated base, as at Sunderland and Newcastle (Plate 46). The extent of his versatility is shown also by the absence of Orders at Southampton (Plate 47) and Portsea. There are really no points of architectural style by which Gibson sought to express his individualism or stamp a

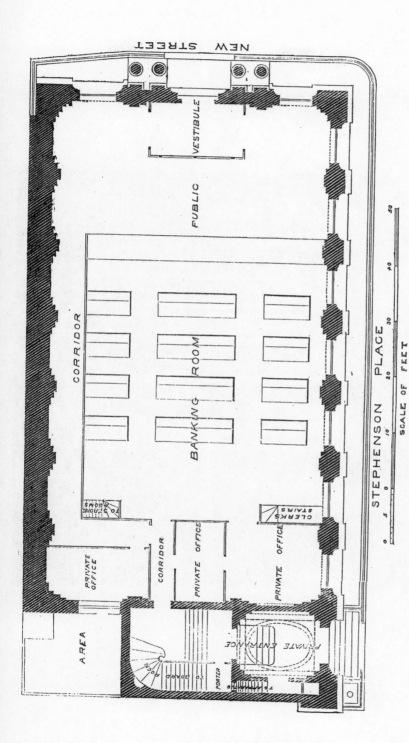

Plate 45. Above: Edward Holmes's head office for the Birmingham & Midland Bank, New Street, Birmingham, opened 1869. Below: ground plan.

Plate 46. Above: John Gibson's Newcastle-upon-Tyne branch of the National Provincial Bank, 1872. Below: the same architect's Middlesbrough branch for the same bank, 1874.

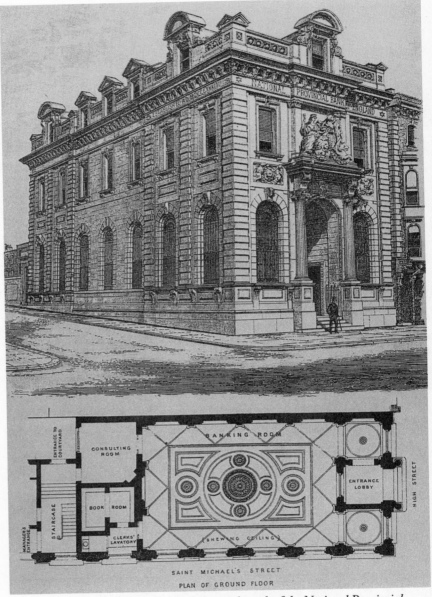

Plate 47. *John Gibson's Southampton branch of the National Provincial Bank, 1867.*

recognisable and cohesive element to his designs; and yet his works have a forceful quality, a dignity, and a lack of otiose decoration which allow attributions to him, or to his studio, to be made with confidence. A.E. Richardson wrote that Gibson's 'buildings are distinguished for their virile character and general appropriateness'.[90] He had the rare ability to build as an extrovert but without extravagance.

One of the earliest of the Gibson banks mentioned above was the National Provincial branch in Southampton, completed in 1867 (Plate 47). This building may be compared with the Birmingham & Midland Bank discussed above. In view of the distance between the two towns, and the fact that Gibson's design (the slightly earlier of the two) was not published until 1875,[91] it is unlikely that one bank could have influenced the other. Although the Southampton building was marginally the smaller, the first thought which occurs is that premises deemed suitable for just a branch in one bank were more than equal in splendour to a head office in another. This comment is made without disparagement to Holmes who, despite working with a more restrictive brief, produced a building with more authority and composure, and therefore more suited to a head office. It is, nevertheless, remarkable that Gibson's branch bank should have shown so much more vigour and style. He retained the established interest in statuary, but brought it down from the cornice or parapet to the porch, complemented by traditional panels of hard-working *putti* at the level of the porch entablature. On the first two bays at each end of the return front were token panels and banded pilaster strips continuing the rhythm of the High Street front. The three middle bays of the return front had no wall decoration, and no bracketed sills to the lower windows. This prevented the bank becoming over-ornate, while the idea of breaking back the entablature added interest to the composition and acted as a foil to the main front, where the centre bay broke forward.

The ground plans of the two banks are also worth comparing. Gibson extended his porch inwards to form an entrance lobby, in this way giving some functional integrity to the powerful columns and entablature applied to the external wall. Holmes, on the other hand, had created more of a portico on the exterior, and therefore had a main door approached directly from the street. He dispensed with a lobby and separated the vestibule from the banking-hall by only a screen. At the other end of the ground floor, the significant difference was the introduction by Gibson of a book room in a space which might otherwise have been occupied by an office or interview room, and a clerks' lavatory, both items more usually found on another floor. These two features were likely to have increased the efficiency of customer service.

An invariable feature of Gibson's designs was the carved name of the bank with the date of its establishment (usually in Roman numerals) on an appropriate entablature. This, with perhaps a town badge or discreet monogram, was as far as Gibson went in the trend towards an archaeological presentation of banking which had been growing since the early 'sixties. This was itself part of a wider movement towards self-advertisement, as apparent in bank stationery as in architecture. With the introduction of perforated cheque forms, for instance, came lists of branches within a decorative cartouche. In the same vein, some banks publicised their branches by badges, and even names, on the front of a building. For instance, the branch of the Gloucestershire Banking Company, erected at Cirencester in 1874, carried the named badges of Cheltenham, Stroud, Redditch and Stow-on-the-Wold.[92] Still more common was the tradition of carving or carrying the words OLD BANK on a façade, denoting a continuity of business bought up from the earliest known private bank in the district. Some examples of this practice can still be noticed.

If lack of imitation by others suggests that Gibson did not give English banking architecture a sense of direction, he nevertheless imparted some stability: his has become the norm against which other styles are measured. It must always be remembered, however, that most of Gibson's commissions were for the National Provincial Bank which operated with a strength and spread of branches which no other bank could match until the last quarter of the nineteenth century. Therefore, in comparing Gibson's buildings with any of the other major banks of the period which might seem stylistically appropriate, there is unlikely to be, in strictly banking terms, a comparison between equals. It is also the case that Gibson's quality of design was far from being general in England in the 1860s, and in some respects there were more promising developments north of the border. Goodhart-Rendel thought Rochead's Bank of Scotland in Glasgow (1865–9) 'exemplifies Scottish superiority in a moment when in England the genius of Cockerell seemed to flame against a dark background indeed'.[93] Although the best years of Scottish bank building were over, the implicit point is well taken that Scotland had achieved a sense of purpose in its building while England was restless and eclectic.

It was partly from this lack of direction, and partly from the acceptability of Gothic witnessed in the work of Waterhouse and Scott, that bank architecture in some areas made a slow move towards the

*Plate 48. Norman Shaw's bank for Knight & Co. at Farnham, Surrey,
opened in 1869.*

picturesque. Nevertheless, it took the combination of an unusual banker and an unorthodox architect to set the movement going. It was bold to design a bank in a style which had no formal antiquarian precedent or associational relevance. And yet, Norman Shaw did more at Farnham, Surrey, than build a bank quite arbitrarily medieval; he placed it in surroundings of a restrained, domestic Georgian nature totally antithetic to his design. And he built it head and shoulders above surrounding property[94] (Plate 48).

Shaw's client at Farnham was the private banker James Knight. Whether Shaw intended this enormous, jettied caprice as a romantic compliment to the name Knight, or a deliberate rebuff to the Italianate style which had produced an orthodox bank at Farnham in 1860, is not clear. At any rate, the building, completed in 1869, was viewed with curiosity, rather than affection or distaste, by local people, who christened it 'Knight's Folly'. When the building was demolished late in the 1920s, Lloyds Bank, as if by atonement, erected a new bank on the site in the safest neo-Georgian. The lack of photographs of the interior of Shaw's building, especially of the banking-hall, is a considerable misfortune.

In the architectural and banking press, this work by Shaw was unnoticed. As far as banking was concerned, the idiosyncracy of a minor bank at Farnham was of no interest to a professional journal steeped in the technicalities of international banking and commercial law. As for the architectural press, attention was directed to technological advances and details of constructional variation. It was the age of the hydraulic hoists, experimentation with passenger lifts, and hot-water heating by Bailey, Haden, Phipson and Boyd. It was a question of granite from Aberdeen, Penryn or Peterhead, stone from Ham Hill, Hollington, Kenton, Mansfield, Portland, Prudhoe or Spinkwell, marble from Devon, Ireland, Sicily or Siena. A reversion to medievalism, particularly for a bank, was not to be taken seriously.

Shaw's particular inspiration may have been the King's Lynn savings bank of 1859, possibly the first bank building of any sort to carry through a medieval or Tudor design to the interior, typified by an enormous fireplace with stone surround.[95] But whatever his model or motive, Shaw seems to have attracted no immediate copyists and he stands at the head of romantic design in the realm of commercial banking without being its leader. It was to be in the 1880s that his style was influential and the picturesque tradition in the 'seventies was kept alive by George Truefitt.

Like Shaw, Truefitt designed in great detail, down to ornamental glass, ironwork, and gas fittings. Unlike Shaw, however, his unorthodox commercial bank designs — all for Cunliffe, Brooks & Co.[96] — could be justified by association or environment. His Manchester bank, completed in 1870 in a mixed Gothic-classical style showing 'much originality'[97] was as far from Cockerell's brand of neo-Greek as he could go because the site had been owned by the Bank of England for some 30 years. If the attribution of Brooks's Blackburn bank to Truefitt, also around 1870, may be suggested, then his originality in this instance was prompted by local cotton riots. Here, the bank was a fortress (Plate 49). As for Altrincham (Plate 49), this was no cosmetic exercise but a dedicated revival of the Cheshire black and white style, in the manner of Little Moreton Hall.[98] The façade was of oak with plaster in-filling (albeit with brick backing), a long way from the 'fire-proof' principles of Dennett, Phillipps, and Fox & Barratt. Both Blackburn and Altrincham, despite contrasting styles, displayed the same technique for handling a corner site, thereby strengthening the attribution of the former to Truefitt. The banks were each composed of two blocks, facing their respective streets with such unity of purpose that the notion of main and return fronts is inappropriate. The two masses were skilfully linked and articulated in each case by the entrance splay, at Blackburn with a round arch matching the windows, at Altrincham with a double arch along each building line, and a smaller central block facing the same way as the banking-hall, as opposed to the residence.

Both Knight and Brooks were private bankers and it was in this type of business, without the complication of responsibility to shareholders, that the picturesque style continued. A notable example, still surviving as a bank, is at Saffron Walden, where W.E. Nesfield's premises for Gibson & Co., complete with Tudor-style Great Hall, is now a branch of Barclays.[99] When such buildings pass out of bank use, it is easy to overlook their importance. A case in point is at Salisbury, where the London architect Henry Hall designed two banks 10 years apart. The earlier, opened in 1869, was the head office of the Wilts & Dorset Bank, a handsome building in the 'Venetian' style.[100] The other bank was for the private firm of Pinckney Brothers, on another corner of the Market Place, which Pevsner, attributing the design to an insurance company, called a 'pretentious . . . sham'.[101] As a former bank, however, it is a building of importance. Characterised by half-timbering, stuccoed plaster, graffito and wood and stone carving by Harry Hems of Exeter, it 'was designed with a view to resuscitating some of the best features of the quaint architecture peculiar to the city.'[102] The *Builder* was only slightly interested, summarising the bank as 'in the domesticated style of half-timbered Tudor work.'[103] And yet the interior had panelling from the Old Weavers' Hall, which the bank had used from 1811, and the ceiling and oak beams came from the Saracen's Head inn.[104] Stained glass symbolised six Salisbury guilds, as well as the goldsmith's profession 'typical of the infancy of banking', and copied famous windows elsewhere in the city.[105] This really was architecture in touch with its environment. The city of inspiration was Salisbury, not Venice.

Plate 49. Above: Blackburn Old Bank (Brooks & Co.), probably by George Truefitt, c. 1870. Below: Truefitt's Altrincham branch for Brooks & Co., also c. 1870.

It was not until 1882, 3 years after Hall's bank at Salisbury, that the architectural press featured in detail a bank in that style, by then known as 'Queen Anne'.[106] This was a bank by William Sugden at Leek, today a rather insignificant branch of the National Westminster Bank, but a building which merited a double-page illustration in the *Builder* when it was completed in 1882.[107] This was perhaps the first bank to have 'Ipswich windows' and pargetted gables, but its real importance is that it was designed by an architect who can be directly linked with a movement which was aesthetic, rather than academic or doctrinaire.[108] The client was a joint-stock bank, the Manchester & Liverpool District Bank, whose neo-Tudor Hanley branch of the 1830s had been the forerunner of all non-classical styles in the realm of commercial banking. It seems unlikely, however, given the extent of Sugden's commissions in the Leek area and his dedication to 'Queen Anne',[109] that the bank itself chose this adventurous design.

The many references in this chapter to branch banks, as opposed to the head offices and one-office private banks which monopolised earlier chapters, calls for some explanation of the way joint-stock banking was developing. The decade of the 1860s was the second great period of branch proliferation. To some extent this was a passive expansion, in the sense that established outlets were acquired by amalgamation with other banks, but at the same time, particularly in London and the northern and midland conurbations, branches were founded both in response to demand from industrialists and petitions from neglected communities. Lloyds Banking Company, for instance, opened at Oldbury at the request of Albright & Wilson;[110] it also received a 'special solicitation' from Longton and a memorial 'numerously and respectably signed' from Halesowen.[111] There was also a degree of speculative expansion, particularly after the failure of a competitor, to prevent or pre-empt the establishment of rival concerns.

At first in this period, banks were hardly interested in domestic business. Profitability lay in advances for industrial growth. There were no banks at Richmond, Surrey, or Southport, until 1852. A bank in the latter town closed again in 1857, 'customers [being] depositors and not borrowers.'[112] But the outlook began to change as High Victorian prosperity boosted the middle classes. The London & County Bank, with no metropolitan branches in 1849, had 17 by 1865, and 2 years later was attracted to the residential suburb of Bromley.[113] By 1881, the board of Lloyds Banking Company in Birmingham, very much in business for the industrialist, could look sympathetically at the following report from a committee: 'Harborne ... contains some fair shops apparently doing good business. It also has a large residential population living in houses of a very good stamp. Your Committee think the inhabitants ought to require and would appreciate Banking accommodation and therefore advise that a Branch should be opened with all convenient speed.'[114] One incentive to this policy for rapid growth by Lloyds was the awakening of local competition from the Birmingham and Midland Bank in the early 1880s.

This was not, however, a time for reckless expansion in the manner of the Northern & Central Bank of the 1830s. The instinct for over-zealous growth was checked by some notable disasters, the most worrying casualties being the banks of Attwood, Spooner and Overend, Gurney.[115] The need now was for a considered response to market pressures. The general manager of Lloyds Banking Company was instructed in 1873 to investigate the position of branches of other banks in principal centres of business, such as Liverpool, Manchester and Glasgow.[116] He chose, in the event, to ignore Scotland 'where the business of banking falls to a lower stratum of the trading population . . .' and found that only Manchester and Liverpool, besides London, had more than two offices of one bank.[117] He was sent to those cities to learn at first hand whether such expansion was considered successful.[118] The strategy of the Birmingham and Midland Bank, a few years later, was to set up a Branch Extension Committee to consider sites for new offices while the bank's board discussed the tactics of growth.[119]

When a new branch was decided upon, temporary premises could be found very quickly and business commenced within 48 hours. Once established, there was time to look around for a better site and discuss the merits of purpose-building. It followed naturally from this that matters such as selection of site, specifications of building, fitting-out, and consistency of appearance, should form a cohesive group of functions suitable for delegation from the work of the main board. Ultimately, there were two consequences of this: the first was the creation of a post of bank architect; the second was the formation of a committee of directors with some responsibility for policy. The latter body, gathering managerial and clerical support, evolved in most banks into a Premises Department, but not within the period of this chapter.

The precedent for bank architect was the position held successively at the Bank of England by Sampson, Taylor, Soane, Cockerell and Hardwick.[120] It is likely that even one-office banks had some more or less formal affiliation with an architect or 'surveyor', in a consulting role, dating from the days of private banking, while Messrs Newnham

& Webb, who designed a branch for the Union Bank of London near Regent Street, were described as 'joint-architects to the bank' as early as 1840.[121]

The best example of a Victorian bank architect, outside the Bank of England, was of course John Gibson, but even in this instance the precise nature of his relationship with the bank is unclear. On 18 November 1862 the National Provincial's Building Committee reported to the main board, or 'Court', that they had appointed Gibson 'Architect to the Bank'.[122] How far this gave Gibson exclusive right to all contracts for new premises, and how far, in return, he was expected to give his whole-time services to the bank, are points which the documentation itself does not clarify. Alfred Waterhouse recollected that the 'company apparently employed nobody but Mr. Gibson as its architect as long as he remained in practice',[123] and yet the bank's important Leicester branch, dated 1869, was designed by Millican & Smith;[124] as for the other point, Gibson's well-publicised designs for an Exeter bank (opened 1877) and for Child's Bank, London (opened 1879), prove that he was not barred from working on banks elsewhere.[125] Probably, the arrangement followed loosely the relationship between Hardwick and the Bank of England:[126] while Hardwick built the Bank's new branches at Hull and Leeds, he was free to accept outside commissions.

More typical than the National Provincial of the position among other banks was the growing Lloyds Banking Company. Having changed in 1865 from a private bank to a joint-stock company, with limited liability, it began a policy of amalgamation which rapidly increased momentum towards the end of the nineteenth century. And yet it opened many more branches itself than it acquired ready made through the mergers.

In Lloyds the post of bank architect was neither premeditated nor immediate. The first involvement of the new company in architectural matters came in 1868, with the question of a larger head office. The bank set up a competition, initially between Edward Holmes, Martin & Chamberlain, and J.A. Chatwin, but Yeoville Thomason was added a little later.[127] Holmes, Chatwin and Thomason had all designed substantial banks then completed, or erecting, in central Birmingham. Chatwin won the competition, although Holmes's ground plan was at first preferred. The bank was eventually opened in 1871 in what was then called Ann Street, the Italian High Renaissance style reflecting Chatwin's earlier work at Temple Row. The success of this design led Chatwin to further work for Lloyds at Rugby branch, and then at

Ironbridge, Coventry, Smethwick and elsewhere.[128] However, his position was not unchallenged: Martin & Chamberlain were employed at Dudley in 1874–5[129] and there is no reason to think Chatwin had all the commissions in the many cases where the architect for alteration or rebuilding is not recorded. Not until 1880 comes the first mention of 'the Bank Architect'.[130] Two years later Chatwin's position was so strong that he was commissioned to design the new London head office as a matter of course, but he was still able to undertake work for other banks, including joint-stock companies.[131]

It was not, therefore, until the 1880s that Lloyds Banking Company gave allegiance to one architect, and this is likely to be nearer the norm for other banks than the 1860s, although with literally hundreds of banks in existence in this period, conclusions can only be speculative. Certainly, the large Wilts & Dorset Bank was earlier,[132] as was the Manchester & Liverpool District Bank:[133] and the *Builder*'s comment of 1871 about the new bank at Bishop Auckland for Backhouse & Co. — that 'We believe this is the third new bank which Mr. Hoskins has built for this same firm'[134] — widens the scope of the question to private banking. The case of George Truefitt, working for Cunliffe, Brooks & Co. in the 1870s, has already been mentioned. The preponderance of examples, however, such as the work of Messrs Hetherington & Oliver for the Carlisle, City & District Bank, Messrs Mills & Murgatroyd for the Manchester & County Bank, Fred Pinches for the Alliance Bank of London, and Messrs J. & J.S. Edmeston for the London & South Western Bank, points to associations forming in the period 1880 to 1884, and then not necessarily with an exclusive commitment on the part of the bank to the services of their chosen architect or partnership.[135]

As regards the administration of premises' affairs, Lloyds can again be taken as representative. There was at first no clear division of practice between directorate and general manager and throughout the 'sixties and 'seventies the minutiae of branch maintenance were quite within the purview of the main board.[136] Alternatively, a subcommittee of directors could be appointed for any *ad hoc* purpose, like receiving the plans in the head office competition, or a single director could exhibit plans for alterations or liaise on site with a builder, functions equally appropriate to the role of the general manager. As for the seeking-out of sites, or of existing buildings for alterations, these were again matters in which the respective roles overlapped. The board was not unaware of the anomalies and as early as 1866 a subcommittee had been formed to consider 'the whole question' of bank premises.

The report of this body, however, was limited to head office problems, and no further progress was made until 1874, when three directors were empowered to undertake the rebuilding of Dudley branch 'and of any branches, where they deem it necessary'. This was not an *ad hoc* group, as temporary, say, as the committee to consider the disposition of available resources, but a standing body, increasingly responsible for the acquisition of sites, as well as their development. Later in 1874 the body was called the 'Premises Committee', and for the next few years this title and that of Building(s) Committee were used interchangeably. By 1878 the committee had its own minutes (but not in a special book until 1890),[137] and members were used as the basis for a brief but important Premises Valuation Committee. In 1879 the practice began of establishing the membership of committees annually, in February, at a meeting of the main board.

As for the committee's functions, it made rapid inroads into the purview of the general manager. The latter, empowered at various times in the 'seventies to oversee a variety of branch affairs at Gt Hampton Street, Tipton, Smethwick, Burton-on-Trent and Aston, lost the whole or part of his authority in all cases to the Premises Committee: at Tipton, for instance, he could finish work only with the committee's sanction; at Burton-on-Trent, his responsibility was totally removed. At no time in this period, however, did Lloyds have anything approaching a Premises Department of full-time officials.

Before all considerations of branch infrastructure are set aside, attention must be given to the first appearance of the in-house style, and to the possibility that bankers were now at last giving published or minuted expression to their preferences in design.

The existence of a house style among metropolitan joint-stock bankers was noticed by the *Builder* as early as 1864: 'One or more of the joint-stock banks in London have adopted a somewhat similar character to that of the City bank we have just now named [i.e. Jones, Loyd & Co., Lothbury], so that each of their branches may be known almost at once, as of the family. The Union Bank of London ... may be quoted as an example of the character, which is also seen in the branches of the London and County Bank.'[138] Outside London, the evidence of homogeneity of design is rather from the 1870s. Styles other than classical were not uncommon. Lloyds marked its individuality with branches in French Gothic vein, like Aston, Deritend, Halesowen and Dudley. Other banks grouped Gothic or neo-Tudor branches around Carlisle and Deeside. Probably the largest and most widespread set of non-classical branches were those of the Manchester

& Liverpool District Bank. Very similar to these were branches of the rival Manchester & County Bank, mostly of the 1880s.

Without entirely removing from their architect's control the initiative for bank design, it seems inconceivable that, in this period, bankers did not exercise a degree of direction in respect of how they wished their premises to look. The introduction of house styles and the degree of interest shown in domestic commissions argue this to a degree which makes the absence of real evidence the more frustrating. Desiccated minuting — simply 'plans discussed' or 'plan seems to be capable of some further improvement', or plans approved 'with certain amendments' — does no more than hint at the richness of discussion which must surely have arisen at board or committee, sometimes with the architect in attendance. It is impossible, for instance, that Lloyds Banking Company, having embarked on a policy of vaguely Gothic branches, should have decided, or agreed, to build certain branches in classical style, all in the 1870s, without reason or discussion. And as the post of bank architect was not yet quite established, this initiative for variation could not lie anywhere outside the directorate.

There is an important hint at increasing board room control buried in an editorial in the *Builder* in 1864. Having earlier referred to architects of City banks 'as comparatively speaking unfettered', the journal was now coming across instances of 'an expression of opinion on the part of directors ...'.[139] It is likely that this position was becoming as applicable away from London as within it.

A parsimonious or negative approach by board or management could affect the style of a new building as profoundly as a constructive interest. It has been noticed above that Edward Holmes's new head office of the Birmingham & Midland Bank was restricted by his client as to ornamentation. The building which resulted might not have been in a style to the architect's liking, successful as it was. Even the limited ornamentation agreed to was perhaps too fancy for some: Henry Edmunds, the bank's managing director 'strongly disapproved of the change of site, and more particularly of the erection of what he regarded as a costly and elaborate set of offices.'[140] The word costly raises another point, especially valid in the context of branch banking: the style of a bank was governed by funds available for its erection, as well as by any aesthetic considerations of board, management or architect. It seems to have been cheaper to build a neo-Tudor branch in brick than a classical one in stone.[141]

In another way, not as yet unduly significant, the plan of a new building was becoming a matter for deliberation with public bodies.

Approval had sometimes been necessary in the past, in various parts of London, and pockets of control continued. The Holborn Circus Improvement Commissioners were responsible for the style of the branch of the Union Bank of London, at the end of Hatton Garden, erected in 1870, the bank's architect conforming with the overall design of Horace Jones, architect to the Commissioners.[142] In provincial towns, the nascent local government bodies, especially the boards of health, had certain elementary duties for town planning, and received drawings for inspection and approval, in a degree of detail which modern bankers would find unacceptable on grounds of security. The powers, and indeed the interest, of such bodies is unlikely to have extended to questions of style and exterior design, but instances of control of frontages (usually setting back) are common and this may indirectly have affected the elevation, as finally agreed between architect and banker. In the Cumbria Record Office is a remarkable series of plans and sections of bank premises, all from the 1870s, and marked: 'Examined and approved by the Health Committee'.[143]

It remains to consider Scotland, so much a feature of the earlier decades of banking architecture, but now of less interest than England. In the late 'sixties and 'seventies, banks, particularly in Glasgow, caused a flurry of building reminiscent of the golden age of some 20 years earlier. Much of this was, of course, branch expansion, and the buildings were as variable in style as those in England: 'Doubtless the majority of the branches are ordinary shops, dignified with a cornice and pair of consoles over the door, but several of them have been built to order, and have very handsome elevations.'[144] Notable among these were the branches of the Clydesdale and City of Glasgow Banks by J.T. Rochead. Two local head offices were also built in Glasgow, one Rochead's Bank of Scotland, so admired by Goodhart-Rendel, the other John Burnet's Clydesdale Bank planned with 'epidemic accidentalism' while Rochead's bank was completing.[145]

In neither of these designs was there any significant departure from the path adopted by Hamilton and Rhind. The Italian, in particular the Venetian, Renaissance was unbeatable: there was no room among Glasgow bankers for neo-Tudor, Gothic or the picturesque. For *Building News* this had all gone on too long. The city had its surfeit of masks and vases, to the extent that an insurance company, about to build there, had 'imposed upon competitors the somewhat singular condition, that in the elevation there was to be neither "storied urn nor animated bust".'[146] The journal looked 'for change even in banks. We are becoming tired of seeing on building after building keystones with

Plate 50. *Mills & Murgatroyd's Blackpool branch of the Manchester & County Bank, 1881.*

heads and pedestals with urns, and getting somewhat ashamed of the poverty of invention . . .'.[147] The fact was that Glasgow, so long the precedent and inspiration for English bank design, was now unable or unwilling to escape from its tradition. In the same way, banks in Edinburgh continued in established style, David Bryce's remodelled Bank of Scotland, completed in 1870 after 6 years' work, being in harmony with the style and character of the old building which it encompassed.[148] It would appear that no bank building erected in Scotland in the period of this chapter could match the kind of handsome, original and functional design achieved by the Manchester

Plate 51. Arnold B. Mitchell's medal-winning design for a bank in a country town, 1885.

& County Bank for a branch as commercially unexciting as Blackpool, opened in 1881[149] (Plate 50). Designed by Mills & Murgatroyd, it embodied the very advanced concept of a single storey building, uncluttered by offices to let or apartments for manager or caretaker. This unity of purpose was summed up by the single round-arched, tripartite window of the main elevation.

The conclusion to this chapter may be devoted to Arnold B.

Mitchell who won the Architectural Association medal in 1885 for his design in the competition 'A Bank for a Country Town'[150] (Plate 51). The building had to comprise a basement and three floors, exclusive of attic, on a level, rectangular site, with two frontages to a market place. The illustration is of great interest. Mitchell's idea was 'to make the design a practical one and yet to give it some distinctive character of its own ....'.[151] In achieving this, he showed a marked Flemish accent and a liking for Norman Shaw. Perhaps predictably, the model design for a bank in a country town met opposition from a practising country architect. Objections were curiously reminiscent of Gilbart, some 35 years earlier. The light was too little and in the wrong place. 'The clerks want it full on their books and on the counter. When a stranger presents a cheque, the cashier looks hard at him ....'.[152]

'Queen Anne' had undoubtedly made its mark but it had yet to prove that it was a satisfactory working proposition.

Chapter Five

Tradition in Disarray

In 1886 the *Quarterly Review* looked back with regret as Lombard Street saw the departure of its last resident banker.[1] There were still a few parlours nearby 'with stiff respectable-looking furniture, fitted up for family life' but this was a far cry from the days when bankers' children were exercised on Blackfriars Bridge and in the Tower Hill enclosure. Some 150 years of banking tradition were passing with consequences affecting the outward appearance of banking as deeply as its practice and philosophy. An old banker's nostalgia humanised the pragmatism of his professional journal: gone were the small house, with low ceiling and uncleaned windows, the elderly chief clerk, and the sense of cosy security.[2] Palatial buildings with 'plate glass, polished counters, and young men smirking behind' made everyone the loser.

Sentimentality aside, it was obvious that something very fundamental was happening to the pattern of banking. London, having asserted its leadership by the bank buildings of the 1860s, was now the centre of wider expansion: the division between metropolitan and provincial banks was breaking down in the wake of national economic and commercial interests. Only the National Provincial and London & County Banks had had any long-standing involvement both in the capital and the provinces. Now, the advantages of a London headquarters were becoming apparent to others, and, with this new base, the wisdom of a title to express the metropolitan anchor. The London & South Western Bank, for instance, was set up in 1862, the London & Provincial Bank in 1870, and the London & Yorkshire Bank in 1872. Later, the London Joint Stock Bank amended its Deed of Settlement to allow country branches to be formed if wanted.

It was equally important for well-established provincial banks to be represented in London and gain a seat in the clearing house. First to do this was the Southampton-based Hampshire & North Wilts Bank which moved its head office to London in 1877, adopting the name Capital & Counties Bank in 1878. By the 1880s, a London office replacing traditional agency arrangements was becoming essential: the important Manchester & Liverpool District Bank took a London office in 1885 and Lloyds Bank, Birmingham based, opened a major building in Lombard Street in 1887 to consolidate a new London connection achieved by amalgamation in 1884. In fact, merger was the easiest route to metropolitan business. The Birmingham & Midland Bank took over the London-based Central Bank in 1891, renaming itself the London & Midland Bank, and then acquired the City Bank in 1898. It was then renamed the London, City & Midland Bank, a title which lasted until 1918. Parr's Bank, a north of England giant, reached the City in 1891 by taking over the private bank of Fuller, Banbury & Co.

The quickening rate of amalgamations was the most obvious symptom of evolution. Both private and small joint-stock banks were swallowed up by growing bodies whose shape and size reflected, as yet, an irregularity of adolescence, not rationalised until full maturity in the 1920s. Accompanying growth was sophistication: an enlargement of the boundaries of banking to include other social strata, an acceptance of new practices, and a recognition that pre-emptive control of new markets was a requirement of progress and even survival. Branch expansion programmes, more determined and comprehensive than those of earlier decades, grew alongside the policy of passive branch extension by the takeover of existing outlets by amalgamation. All these points had their significance in terms of bank design and will be mentioned later. The need here is to warn that the study of bank buildings in an era of rapid professional development must inevitably be complex; and that this complexity was aggravated by evolution and eclecticism in the national architectural context.

That these difficulties were imminent was suggested in the last chapter which ended with the result of a competition in 1885 in which a bank design, far removed from early Victorian prototype, won first prize. That date was rather beyond the confines of the chapter, but the intention there was to suggest that the picturesque styles were a force to be reckoned with; that the conventional view of what was 'bank-like' was coming to an end. Between the early 'eighties and the Great War bank buildings showed all the weaknesses and characteristics of the national situation: a mishmash of historical styles, mannerism, wilful disrespect for established rules, and innovation. The mainstream of bank design had reached a delta where each established style formed its own channel of progress, occasionally breaking banks to mix with

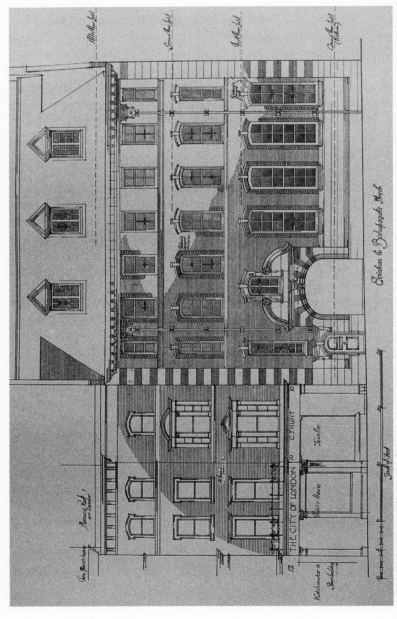

Plate 52. Norman Shaw's new frontage to Baring's Bank, Bishopsgate, London, completed in 1881. This drawing of 1910 was by Gerald Horsley, showing two buildings to the left rebuilt 1913–4, to Horsley's design, as an extension to the bank.

other currents, and deviating into side channels which often dried away to nothing.

It does not necessarily follow from this synopsis of confusion that bank design was irrational or indiscriminate. It would be idle to claim that reasons for styles could be produced as valid and simple as those by which earlier architects had been guided; but a study of national architectural and aesthetic thinking on the one hand, and of the pattern of banking evolution on the other, can account for many vagaries of design.

At the heart of this enquiry is the breakdown of consensus about what was, in ideal terms, the right kind of style for a bank. That such a breakdown had occurred is revealed by the Baring's Bank controversy of 1881. Their building in Bishopsgate Street, London, had just been refronted by Norman Shaw (Plate 52), and the resulting façade was attacked by William Woodward, writing to *Building News*, on grounds of propriety, convenience and even professional competence.[3] 'Raphael's your friend, not Whistler', wrote Woodward, who invited critics to compare Shaw's work with two nearby buildings of acknowledged merit: Gibson's National Provincial Bank, of 1866, and the medieval Crosby Hall. In this context, the substance of the counter-attack by Shaw's supporters and Woodward's detailed defence of his original position do not matter. What is interesting is that, although the bank was the battlefield, recognition of what was inherently suitable for a bank, as distinct from any other kind of building, was not the ground to be conquered. It was hardly even a question of what was suitable for the City. The real quarrel was over something much more general and fundamental. 'What *is* architecture?' asked Woodward. 'Whatever happened to 'reason, symmetry, unity, proportion, and beauty?' Only in his final shot did Woodward champion Gibson's bank as having been designed 'so as to adequately represent the wealth and position in the City of London of an eminent firm'. The breakdown of the tradition of designing banks by historical association, or to impress West End clubmen, had happened and was accepted.

Given that Shaw's frontage of 1881 for Messrs Baring was as generally unsympathetic to traditional banking styles as had been his bank for Messrs Knight at Farnham some 15 years earlier, there was, nevertheless, one point of detail about the Bishopsgate Street bank which is particularly worthy of mention. This was the juxtaposition of large and small entrances. Woodward was understandably confused between 'the poor little doorway at the extremity' and the large opening next to it which he described as 'quite too consummately utter'. In fact,

the large opening was the main entrance and the smaller one was for
ladies — not visitors, but staff.[4] Most banks did not employ women
until the Great War and this was a remarkably early example not only
of female employment in banking but of the sexual segregation which
resulted. It is unlikely, however, that the provision of a separate
entrance for women was anything other than unusual, at least among
clearing banks, and secondary doorways continued for the most part
to give access to bank chambers and, in more rural areas, to accommodation.

The most moderate contributor to the Baring dispute, a correspondent styled 'Evacustes', hoped 'the so-called Modern Gothic, Queen
Anne, and even Renaissance motives may help finally to evolve a true
National Victorian style.'[5] Banks were as involved in this pursuit as any
other homogeneous group of buildings. The search for suitability was
expressed in frequent competitions for branch bank premises promoted by the *Building News* Designing Club (B.N.D.C.), although it is
difficult to judge whether 'these little mutual improvement contests'[6]
followed existing trends or attempted to anticipate new ones. Entries
were under pseudonym and the judges made open comments about
many of the designs, usually publishing one or more of the higher
placings.

The first B.N.D.C. competition for a local bank, held in 1879,[7] is
proof in itself of the breakdown of the classical tradition. 'The
mullioned and transomed windows are appropriate', the judges told the
winner. They praised 'a well-designed elevation . . . in a Late Gothic'
from someone else, and commended 'Late Gothic, with Elizabethan
features, not unsuitable' from a third. Of course, the conceits could
be overdone: the winner was rather too 'quaint', another too 'whim-
sical', and others too 'extravagant'. One competitor was advised to
'moderate his enthusiasm for Queen Anne'. But there was no
doubt that the judges found English Tudor and Renaissance designs
acceptable.

The next two national competitions seem to have been the model
bank design of 1885, mentioned at the end of Chapter Four, and the
'National Silver Medal Design for Bank and Offices', a competition
among Schools of Art in 1887.[8] Although the examiners of the latter
accepted the winning design as Gothic, this time the main inspiration
was from France, while echoes of Norman Shaw's work were apparent
in the gables. From this point, the frequent B.N.D.C. competitions
became an interesting reflection of architectural trends in the country
as a whole. The 1890 competition[9] called for a 'Free Classic' style in

red brick with stone dressings. While the runner-up showed an unremarkable Shavian design (in which Mr Gilbart would not have been happy with the clerks' light), the winner (Plate 53) was more interested in Arts and Crafts style freedom in 'an endeavour to break away from the ordinary commonplace of the regulation type of bank building'. Whatever the merits of the design aesthetically, in banking terms the building was a disaster. While the manager and his family could congratulate themselves on spacious and well-lit accommodation, bank staff farthest from the window were doomed to work in a Stygian twilight; unless the doors were left open — hardly possible in winter — customers would have fared little better. Technologically there was almost a reversion to the eighteenth century. The basement was little more than a cellar, there was no 'fire-proof' construction, of which the Victorians had made such an art, and no central heating. The exterior design, banded into storeys, gave more emphasis to the crow-stepped gable than to the banking floor. The impression created was that the function of the bank was almost incidental to the function of the dwelling-house. Although arguably a pretty contribution to the townscape, the bank had no potential for self-advertisement, indeed no provision for a fascia, or even for window glass, to carry the name of the institution. It may be that the banking interest expressed its dismay with this kind of proposition; at any rate competition designs which followed were far more 'bank-like'.

The next B.N.D.C. competition was for 'A Small Branch Bank' in 1896.[10] The styles, then, moved closer to 'Queen Anne'. In 1899,[11] when the elevation was to be 'English Renaissance', the winner introduced a touch of baroque. In 1902[12] the judges expected 'a picturesque treatment on architectural lines', but the theme was 'Two Shops and a Branch Bank', and so the bank was of subordinate importance. The best and last competition for a bank was in 1907.[13] The judges could 'not remember a more excellent series of designs'. The achievement of the winner was to mount red-brick pilasters on a rusticated stone base to produce a very dignified façade. At last, there was hope. The future seemed to lie, in a sense, in the past — in a neo-Georgian simplicity stiffened with the dignity of classical features. Whatever lip-service bankers may have paid to intellectual and aesthetic interests, only in one form or another of classical style did they feel truly comfortable.

The most noticeable consequence in banking of the Arts and Crafts Movement was not the temporary acceptance of any one style but the tolerance of polychromy. Although contrasts in the manner of

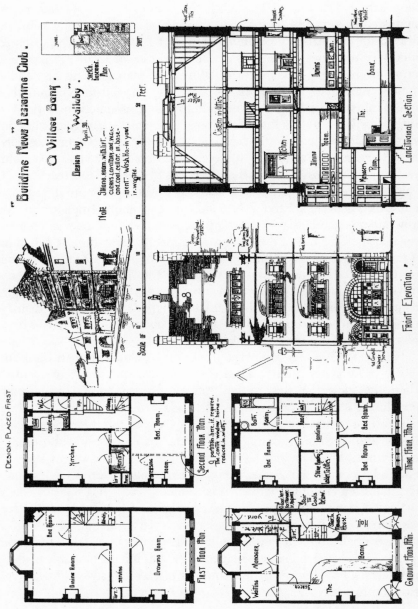

Plate 53. *Winning design for a village bank in the 1890 Building News Designing Club competition.*

Butterfield's work at Keble College, Oxford, were never common in banking, sensitivity to the pleasures of colour and design brought relief from grey façades and unimaginative interior décor. Pink terracotta enlivened St Austell and red bricks around stone dressings smiled in the City. In Leeds, Perkin & Bulmer's National Provincial Bank branch, opened in 1898, mixed black and grey granite with Yorkshire stone and scarlet bricks from Berkshire.[14] Light green Westmorland slates crowned the roof. In fact, green slates became very common, showing to advantage on the steep pitch of Loire-style roof-lines. They even appeared on a bank at Okehampton, on the threshold of Cornish grey-blue, and penetrated deep into London. Most were from Westmorland but Welsh green slates from Llandilo and Preselly were also available.

The main advance in interior design was the admissibility of colourful faience. Tiles appear to have been made most often by Doulton & Co., who provided majolica, for instance, for the massive banking-hall, domed like the Reading Room of the British Museum, in the Birkbeck Bank, in Chancery Lane.[15] Waterhouse, on the other hand, employed Burmantofts of Leeds for banks in the north of England and probably also at Cambridge, where his building of 1891–3, originally for Foster & Co., private bankers, and now a branch of Lloyds, was a matchless example of full interior tiling (Plate 54) which luckily still remains. Another fine survival of work by Burmantofts is the ceiling of what is now the London Chief Office of the Bank of Scotland in Threadneedle Street, a building erected for the British Linen Bank in 1903.[16]

Another boost to polychromy, springing not from the Arts and Crafts Movement but from increasing sophistication of taste, was the interest in light-coloured foreign marbles, advocated by some but considered unnecessary by others, who stressed the availability of multi-hued domestic alternatives. There was discussion, too, about granite, prompted by Lloyds Bank's London office of 1887, the first occasion when granite was used for an entire ground-floor façade.[17] What a pity, some thought, that the colour was a dismal grey-blue; yet, when the Commercial Bank of Scotland attempted to introduce different-coloured granites to the greyness of Union Street, Aberdeen, there was local opposition.[18] For interior work, polished marble was magnificent: delicately veined and subtly coloured, stones from Italy, Spain, France and Numidia, and Norwegian porphyry, led to dramatic and costly banking-halls of chilling beauty.

The best-known polychromatic building was probably Parr's Bank

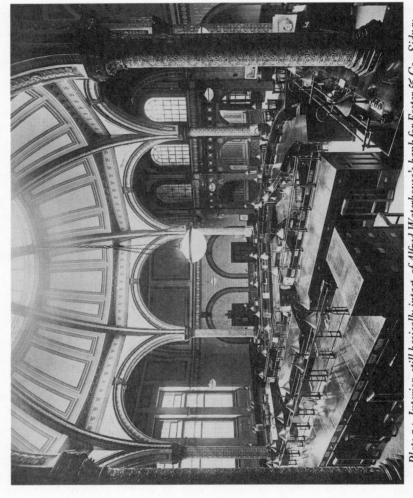

Plate 54. Interior, still basically intact, of Alfred Waterhouse's bank for Foster & Co., Sidney Street, Cambridge, 1891–3. This is now a branch of Lloyds Bank.

(now a branch of the National Westminster Bank), erected 1898–1901 in Castle Street, Liverpool, to designs by Norman Shaw and the local firm of Willink & Thicknesse.[19] Sheeted in Pavonazzo marble, banded with green Cipollino, dressed with red terracotta and roofed with green slates, it reminded C.H. Reilly of a very smart lady standing in the wrong place.[20] This human dimension had already been noted by Halsey Ricardo, a contemporary critic, who welcomed the new building as a 'hopeful augury' of what other bankers might be tempted to commission.[21] He found it dignified and comfortable, looking out benignantly and with tolerance 'upon the small hurrying creatures that scuttle over the pavement before it'. Yet this was exactly why the design was inherently unsuitable. Bankers would certainly wish their buildings to be dignified, even patronising, but benignancy did not meet the spirit of the day.

In short, no deep or lasting contact with 'Queen Anne', the Arts and Crafts Movement, or with any other vanguard of intellectual design, was possible. Harmony of purpose between architect and builder, philosophical motives, the architectural expression of character and emotion, were not matters in the minds of joint-stock bankers. A bank was a business beset by competition: its job was to make money for its shareholders and its reasons for building were worldly. 'Not such was the sentiment that poised the Wingless Victory over the Acropolis . . . or reared . . . the mighty dome of St. Paul.'[22] *Art Nouveau* was similarly unsuitable. The continental base of the movement would have appealed to more ambitious bankers and the new architectural forms lent themselves to exploitation for commercial purposes, a point which soured the new style in the taste of the devotees of Arts and Crafts. But no style which found its chief publicised expression in museums, institutions and centres of learning could have anything but a passing hold on the attention of bankers.

There were, nonetheless, quite a few occasions when bankers built or utilised buildings remarkably unsuitable for their needs. On these occasions they were generally responding to irresistible pressure from conservationist lobbies, now acquiring such organisation and backing that the banks could do nothing but comply. Some banks even acted spontaneously, apparently convinced of the need for environmental protection. A very early example had been set by the directors of the Worcester City & County Bank who, in 1868, bought at Bromsgrove 'one of the finest specimens of the ancient wood-framed structures still left in the county'.[23] This building, the former Hop Pole Inn, dating from 1572, was 're-erected and restored', retaining as many old features as possible.[24] A new manager's house alongside was designed in matching style.[25]

This same bank acquired 'The Old House' at Hereford in 1882. Alterations were entrusted to E.H. Lingen Barker, chosen after a competition 'restricted to half a dozen architects from London and the West of England, selected for their special experience in dealing with works of this kind . . .'.[26] This clearly pleased the *Builder*, dismayed at the demolition, one after the other, of houses on either side.[27] The £1600 which secured the property had been more than the bank intended, but a director 'took upon himself' to bid £1000 more than authorised.[28] 'The Old House' was acquired by Lloyds Bank in 1889 and given by them to the Corporation in 1921. It is still one of the main attractions of central Hereford.

Less troublesome than an old building was a purpose-built bank in a style sympathetic with its site or surroundings. This was, of course, what Hall had already designed at Salisbury and Nesfield at Saffron Walden, but these had been exceptional. Bankers were now prepared to extend a sensitive treatment more widely, and there were notable examples: at Stratford-on-Avon the Birmingham Banking Company built what is now the Midland Bank, in 1883, full of drama, colour and originality, and enriched with Shakespeare's bust and carvings of scenes from his plays.[29] In the same year, the Wilts & Dorset Bank opened a Gothic branch, quite outside their usual style, alongside the *George & Pilgrim* inn in Glastonbury, a famous medieval hostelry.[30] At Canterbury, in 1887, the new High Street bank of Messrs Hammond & Co. was built in a kind of baronial Tudor, a style thought more appropriate, after local intervention, than Early English.[31]

No doubt in most cases the initiative for a meaningful and sensitive design came from the architect rather than the banker. The Liverpool firm of Woolfall & Eccles was particularly good at environmental building, designing a picturesque kind of cottage at Ludlow for the North & South Wales Bank, opposite the famous *Feathers* inn, [32] and a lively Gothic branch for the North & South Wales Bank at Wrexham, to match the church tower. The latter design, however, was rejected by the London, City & Midland Bank who took over the company when building was about to begin.[33]

The main cases of bankers' compliance with local feelings were at Guildford and Chester. The 'Old Guildford Society', a formidable pressure group dedicated to the protection of High Street frontages, persuaded the Capital & Counties Bank in 1899 not to demolish the façade of the old premises of Haydon & Smallpiece, private bankers, which they had taken over in 1883. The event is of some interest. The Capital & Counties Bank was a large, tough company with an unimpressive record of building. It took the combined energy of H.R.H. the Princess Louise, Marchioness of Lorne, and the Lord Lieutenant of Surrey, to defeat the bank's intention. Relief at this success was so enormous that a brass plate was attached to the preserved elevation commemorating the outcome of the struggle.[34] From that date, the Capital & Counties Bank was noticeably more imaginative, taking over an Elizabethan building in Rochester[35] and agreeing to a design at Gravesend as Gothic as anything built in the Revival.[36]

At Chester, the moving force in conservation was the Duke of Westminster. It was he, in 1901, who persuaded the Bank of Liverpool, planning a 'quaint' stone building as its contribution to the redevelopment of St Werburgh Street, to conform to an overall design, involving half-timbered upper floors, conceived by John Douglas.[37] Respect for Chester was something which bankers took seriously, remembering perhaps the incongruity of Parr's bank of 1860. Classical designs were thereafter avoided, with Douglas and T.M. Lockwood bringing bankers into line. It is interesting, too, that Lloyds Bank, having taken over the neo-Greek Chester bank of Williams & Co. in 1897, set about vigorously to redevelop the adjacent shops in a careful black and white revival, carried over the pavement in best local tradition.[38] The bank had built sympathetically before, notably at Shrewsbury in the 1870s, but the development of bank-owned land with the sole aim of the visual improvement of the street was something quite new for Lloyds.

Although Guildford and Chester were exceptional, there were of course other conservationist lobbies and it would have been absurd, for instance in a town like Bath, for a bank to depart from elegant and classical traditions. The south of England generally was becoming well protected. The London & Provincial Bank, building on a famous inn site at Maidstone in 1905, matched the style of the demolished building 'in consideration of public opinion'.[39] At Haslemere, in 1914, the London, County & Westminster Bank, accused of destroying 'quaint old frontages', felt it wise to reuse old materials and follow the earlier style.[40]

At Esher, the London & County Bank, in 1887, had been forced to build picturesquely because their branch was part of a village hall and amenities project originated by the Duke of Albany.[41] This is interesting not as another instance of ducal pressure, but as a sign of the

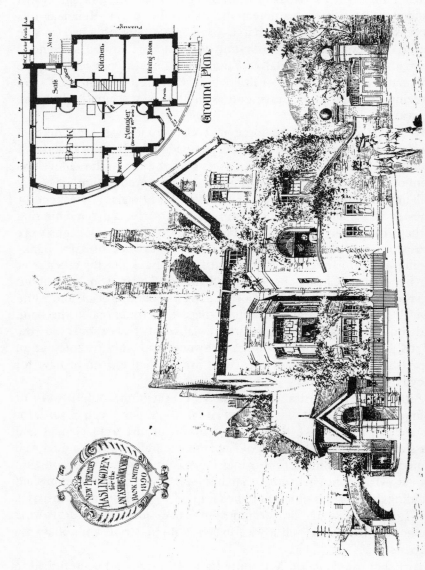

Plate 55. Maxwell & Tuke's 'villa'-style branch at Haslingden for the Lancashire & Yorkshire Bank, 1890.

increasing involvement of banks in wider schemes of rebuilding and development. Again, there was nothing new in a bank being associated with plans for urban enrichment, but the difference now was that redevelopment was usually suburban. Often, associations were formed by agreement, convenience and mutual advantage: this was clearly the case at Esher, and in the outskirts of Manchester and London, where banks were planned in combination with new offices for the nascent district councils.[42] More usually, however, redevelopment was a commercial venture, planned and executed by bankers on land, adjoining a branch, deliberately bought for exploitation. It will be remembered that the subject of the B.N.D.C. competition of 1902 had been two shops and a branch bank. As return on capital investment, banks received substantial rents from shops and offices, the latter usually occupying 'bank chambers' in branches built deliberately too tall for the bank's own purposes. At Reading, in 1898, the Metropolitan Bank planned no less than 10 shops in a terrace adjoining its branch.[43] Even by 1892, the London & Westminster Bank was receiving in rents an income equal to 2¼ per cent per annum on the whole amount at which bank premises stood among its assets.[44]

The architectural point about this involvement is that the design of a bank could be dependent on the style deemed suitable and necessary for the buildings and functions with which it was associated. The London & South Western Bank, for example, built its Wimbledon Common branch as three cells — a central bank and two flanking shops.[45] The bank was obviously the most important unit but the success of the design depended on the integrity of the whole. In the north of England, less interested than the south in Arts and Crafts designs, there were some particularly successful marriages between banking and suburbia. At Haslingden, for instance, the functions of branch bank and managerial residence were skilfully balanced in a design of 1890[46] (Plate 55), and the building could sit comfortably among neighbouring villas. Admittedly, the function of banking was not immediately obvious, but as the site was in a residential district bankers were entitled to highlight the domestic aspect of their premises. In fact, the Haslingden bank gave very generous provision for its banking service and achieved unity of design by interlocking business and domesticity rather than dividing them by layers. Furthermore, the banking-hall had good natural light, the public entrance was sensibly splayed to the corner, and the clerks had a useful private entrance independent of manager and customers. The windowless safe on the ground floor was well positioned for the banking-hall; in practical terms this was a better arrangement for small banks than a safe in the basement, which usually meant problems of dampness as well as the inconvenience of stairs and the expense of a lift or hoist.

Another point is that increasingly, although not yet to any significant extent, questions of the appearance of urban buildings were matters of interest to sectors of local government created by legislation in 1894, and to other supervisory interests. In London, the baroque exterior to Lloyds Bank's St James's Street branch, completed in 1912, was necessary as part of the Crown Estate Commissioners' wider proposals for the block between King Street and Jermyn Street.[47] In Edinburgh, the Dean of Guild Court had approbatory powers, and even urban district councils in England could show a close interest in deposited plans, as W. Watkin & Son of Lincoln discovered when they were designing a new bank at Sleaford.[48] Such interest, however, lay mainly in the enforcement of building regulations and by-laws. Only exceptionally was the style of the elevation a matter for approval, as at Brighton, in 1901, when the Capital & Counties Bank chose not only to build a branch close to the Royal Pavilion but also to redevelop council-owned land nearby.[49]

There were, then, a variety of external factors which influenced bank design, encouraging the breakdown of traditional styles and yet preventing the comprehensive acceptance of new ones. All these factors were significant because branch banking was again in a period of rapid expansion; this internal growth had its own implications for bank design, quite apart from national background movements in architectural taste, and these must now be examined.

The fundamental change in banking, mentioned at the opening of this chapter, was associated with a more liberal interpretation of the scope of the banking service. Some accommodation for the trading classes had been inherent in the philosophy of joint-stock banking, although the North & South Wales Bank was still defending its interest in this class of business as late as 1889.[50] The multiplicity of banks was to the customer's advantage, giving opportunity for competitive pricing. In 1897 the *Bankers' Magazine* was 'told of a large seaport town in which ... merchants ... have gone round from one bank to another, and asked them on what terms they would do their bills'.[51] The move, less specifically, was towards 'the small-propertied body',[52] a term which included middle class suburbia and minor commercial expansion in the wake of improved communications. The Liverpool Union Bank, in 1898, looked forward to branch profits 'from the rapidly growing residential suburbs and country towns served by the

Lancashire & Yorkshire Railway'.[53] In London, the private bankers, unwilling to change their attitudes to overdrafts and the nature of business, left the field unopposed to joint-stock banks which doubled and redoubled their outlets in the boundless conurbation.

In the north of England, too, suburbs and dormitory settlements were increasingly attractive to bankers. Whereas, in the early 1860s, only Manchester and Liverpool had had more than two offices of one bank, Birmingham by 1887 had 32 banking offices, Bradford 12, Leeds 11, Liverpool 47, Manchester 36 and Sheffield 6.[54] By 1893, Birmingham had 44 offices, Bradford 13, Leeds 19, Liverpool 64, Manchester 67, and Sheffield 21.[55] Although suburban competition was the main incentive to growth, banking enclaves were beginning to develop in city centres, as Corn Street had done in Bristol in the 1850s. In Manchester, King Street attracted the best business, while Park Row in Leeds seemed, in 1902, 'almost entirely taken up with bank and insurance buildings'.[56] In such a close and contested environment a considerable influence on bank design was clearly the need for variation. Hence Park Row boasted such diversities as Oliver & Dodgshun's West Riding Union Bank (mingling ground-floor industrial frieze, second-floor French cameos, and upper-floor Corinthian pilasters)[57] and Waterhouse's fortress of a bank for William Williams, Brown & Co., replete with Burmantoft's tiling.[58]

Some surburban expansion was opportunist. The Worcester City & County Bank stepped in without hesitation when mergers left Walsall, a town of 62 000 people, with only two banks in 1888. On the other hand, some banks preferred to expand outlets by takeover and amalgamation. In 1885 the National Provincial Bank, with an unrivalled history of branch development, was publicly cautious about further growth.[59] Clearly, there was room here for tactical advice from leading banking theorists who agreed, with reluctance, on the wisdom of pre-emptive possession: 'if your choice comes to lie betwixt your going there, and allowing another bank to do so ... the choice ceases to be optional. Better the Midgely business, minus fresh expense and trouble, than, so to speak, minus itself.'[60]

In comparison with Scotland, English customers were still 'underbanked'. In 1887, for instance, Edinburgh had 55 offices and Glasgow 100.[61] The figures in relation to population were even more revealing. Manchester, the most 'banked' English city, had an office for every 9484 people: the Scottish equivalent was Perth, with a bank for every 2705.[62] By 1893, however, the gap between England and Scotland had narrowed. Two of the Scottish centres (Dundee and Greenock) had no increase in offices and in other towns the ratio of increase was less than in England.[63]

One of the first banking companies to be interested in suburban expansion in a systematic way, and the first bank to exploit the fabric of its branches as a tool of business, was the London & South Western. If any one bank set a style for building in the late Victorian era it was this one. And yet it was a relative newcomer. Founded in 1862, the London & South Western attempted in its early years to do business in the areas suggested by its name. Its most ambitious building project had been James Weir's Bristol branch, completed in 1880.[64] However the South and West were so unprofitable that the bank had to close eight of its branches, including Bath, Plymouth and Southampton, to stay in business.

With this retrenchment came a wholly new policy of rapid metropolitan expansion, first south of the river, then in the northern suburbs and out to New Barnet. This unhesitant and strategic advance was all the more startling in a bank which had earlier reduced its capital and used up reserves to cover the liabilities of its country branches. Now it swept itself to success, grabbing corner sites and plots near suburban stations, building shops to let, and taking land on lease until there was money to buy the freehold.

In banking terms it was a strategy of colossal risk, succeeding only by a show of solid self-confidence at Annual General Meetings. Competitors thought it took 10 years to bring a new London branch to profitability.[65] While other bankers took annual opportunity to write down the book value of their premises, sometimes by a redemption fund, transferring large sums to capital and reserves to cover increasing exposure, the London & South Western reported with pride to shareholders the yearly increase in the cost of premises. It was splendidly managed. In 1884 the money was said to be 'spread over many branches — some greately enlarged, some newly completed, some in process of erection, and all, in our judgement, good value for the money at which they now stand in our books.'[66] In 1890, as the premises account grew over £200000, the chairman tried a new, more subtle approach, appealing to shareholders themselves to attest to the value of local expenditure. 'There are no persons better able to judge them than the shareholders of this bank, because a great many of them live close to these branches and see the style of buildings there, particularly the new ones.'[67]

This style had been set by the bank's principal architects, James Edmeston (of J. & J.S. Edmeston), succeeded at his death by Edward

Gabriel (of Edmeston & Gabriel). Although Gabriel was called architect to the bank in 1892,[68] and again in 1898,[69] several commissions went to George Truefitt and to his firm, Truefitt & Watson.[70] At least one job, too, went to Eugene Beaumont.[71] The branches themselves were unremarkable, their indifference being all the more apparent from the disproportionate and uncritical attention they received in the architectural press. This attention was, of course, part of the overall strategy for publicity. Bank after bank won description and illustration which the originality of design never merited. For the most part they rehashed Norman Shaw gables, 'Queen Anne' bays and Free Style windows, producing nothing to characterise the bank's new and adventurous approach to the practice of banking.

A significant branch, however, epitomising the bank's interest in corner sites and associated retail development, was Edward Gabriel's Clerkenwell branch [72] (Plate 56), a classic design for metropolitan banking. By the late nineteenth century the commercial advantages of a corner site, attracting trade from two directions, were embodied in an architectural treatment which subordinated the street frontages to the point of their union. The Clerkenwell site was, in banking terms, ideal. The acute angle sharpened perception of the corner, which articulated and controlled two identical façades, the dome serving no other purpose than to focus the eye on the rounded strength of the angle and serve as a landmark. This was a banker's bank: it was truthful to the philosophy of the profession at the date it was designed and the aggressive posture which this philosophy entailed was expressed not by overwrought and excessive decoration but by force of overall design. Unfortunately, Gabriel came a little unstuck with the frieze: the Rosebery Avenue frontage embraced the shop, which meant that the lettering, with two fewer bays available to it, had to bestow on the entrance the rather misleading legend of 'Western Bank'.

What competition there was to the London & South Western's 50 metropolitan branches came from other joint-stock banks: the City private bankers, save two, had no territorial ambitions.[73] The exceptions were Martin's Bank, which began expanding into south-east London and as far into Kent as Sittingbourne, from 1886, and the bank of Messrs Barclay, Bevan & Tritton, which acquired a West End outlet in 1888, by merger with Ransom & Bouverie, and then opened a branch in Cavendish Square in 1894.

By contrast, private bankers elsewhere, more at risk from amalgamations, showed spirit and adaptability. Many chose to publish their accounts and some 200 new branches were opened in the 10 years from

Plate 56. Edward Gabriel's Clerkenwell branch of the London & South Western Bank, 1895.

1886.[74] The most ambitious private banks were the Tyneside rivals, Lambton & Co., and Hodgkin, Barnett, Pease & Spence, owing their strong position to the freak collapse of joint-stock banking in Newcastle in the 1860s. By 1896, Hodgkin, Barnett & Co. had branches at Newcastle, North and South Shields, Morpeth, Alnwick, Rothbury, Shotley Bridge, Jarrow, Amble, Gateshead, High Shields, Westgate Road (Newcastle) and Bellingham.[75] Shortly before this date the bank had begun a policy of purpose-building led by the erection of a grand head office in Collingwood Street, Newcastle, opened in 1891 to designs by R.J. Johnson.[76]

The elevation of Johnson's bank recalled the east front of Houghton Hall in Norfolk. If such a design was meant to suggest the underlying qualities of private banking which distinguished it from the joint-stock practice, then the allusion was destroyed by the interior which typified the administrative regularity which had by now embraced the profession as a whole (Plate 57). Entering by either doorway, the customer was met by a battery of 10 potential service points divided by a low balustrade from the ledger desks. Both in the public area and behind, all the timeless paraphernalia of banking were much in evidence: pewter inkpots, coin balances, pigeon holes, stamps and standard lamps. The ledger desks sloped — the ledgers themselves discreetly removed from the camera — and the clerks sat on stools to gain the extra height necessary to reach the top of a large page. The wall clock was better placed for customers than staff, but the latter were tolerably well off for light and space. It is unlikely at this stage that the architect was involved in the design of furniture and fittings. The market was so strong for office furniture that a wide range of items, even waste-paper baskets, now received the same attention by specialist firms which strong room doors and cashiers' balances had enjoyed for a much longer period.

The policy of Lambton & Co. was to employ J.W. Dyson for plain branches in working class areas, but to give their commissions to other architects in rather better districts, like Wooler or Forest Hall.[77] The practice of extending business to poorer suburbs was not accepted without misgivings by the banking profession as a whole and it is ironical that two private banks, traditionally associated with the landed classes, should have opened the way. 'It is by no means certain', wrote one correspondent to the *Bankers' Magazine*, 'that branches planted in the overcrowded outskirts of a huge city, with its swarms of miners, factory hands, or unemployed, can ever get together so good or lucrative a business as that which offers in a quiet little country

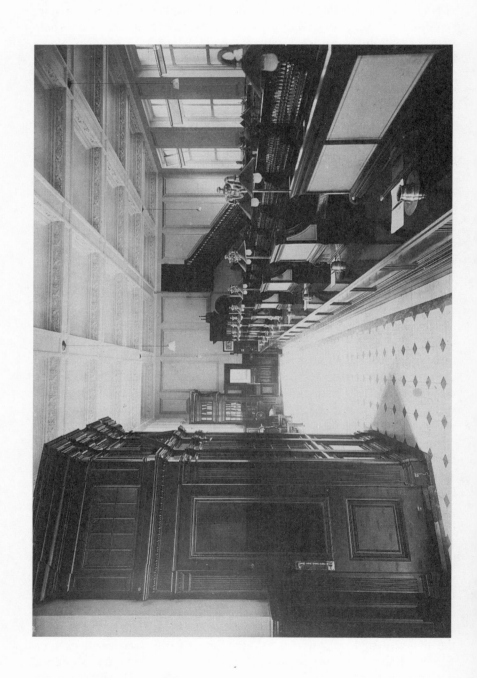

Plate 57. Views either side of the counter in R.J. Johnson's head office for Hodgkin, Barnett, Pease & Spence, Collingwood Street, Newcastle-upon-Tyne, opened in 1891.

town ...'.[78] Most reservations, however, were less contentiously presented as criticism of a 'tendency ... to open branches wherever the slightest prospect of success is held out ...'.[79]

An encouragement to bankers to open in working class districts was the erosion of potential business by the savings banks. It was an annoyance to commercial bankers that a depositor in the Post Office Savings Bank could withdraw his money without paying a penny stamp. It was also apparent to bankers that the independent, local savings banks, although reducing greatly in overall numbers, were holding their own in the northern industrial centres, and even expanding their business with purpose-built branches.[80] Leeds, Liverpool, Hull and Manchester had new savings banks between 1882 and 1884 which could more than match in appearance the branches of their commercial competitors. The Hull savings bank, completed in 1884 to designs by R. Clamp, was a particularly fine example of what could be achieved, albeit with great difficulty, on a budget of £4000.[81]

There was, therefore, a style of building for the working class, as much as for middle class suburbia. Another new phenomenon was building for the retired and for those on holiday. Branches opened at seaside towns like Clacton and Southend, with little in the way of corporate business; the 'rising watering-place' of Newquay was reached by the Devon & Cornwall Bank in 1900,[82] and Frederick Wheeler's London & County Bank branch at Littlehampton was, even in 1901, the 'principal architectural work in the town'.[83] None of these buildings, however, has any significance when compared with the results of the infectious extravagance at Southport.

It was mentioned in the last chapter that Southport lost its bank in 1857 because the customers were 'depositors and not borrowers'. It remained without a bank until 1866, when the Manchester & Salford Bank opened in Lord Street. Nine years later the old post office was sold to Parr's Bank and the competition began in earnest. Late in 1879 the Southport and West Lancashire Bank opened 'very ornate' premises at the corner of Lord Street by the municipal buildings; the architects, Mellor & Sutton, were local, and the cost was around £12699.[84] This was nothing, however, compared with the branch of the Preston Bank, by E.W. Johnson, completed in 1889.[85] This was followed by Parr's Bank's new branch of 1892, a massive Mixed Renaissance building by William Owen, whose 'Queen Anne'-style Wigan premises for the same bank had opened the year before.[86] Then came the opulent Bank of Bolton, 1895, designed by their architects Bradshaw & Gass.[87]

In such a residential district, none of these palaces could have been built with the expectation of profitability. Rather, they were monuments to an uncontrollable competition which showed itself in an unreasoned display of extravagance. It was the philosophy of the 'loss-leader', of marketing to attract potential custom in the knowledge that the gambit of first acquaintance would be unprofitable. This, also, was why newly formed joint-stock banks built quickly and with pretensions: why, for instance, the Mercantile Bank of Lancashire, founded in 1890, chose a rich terracotta design for West Didsbury,[88] recalling features of the façade of the Certosa di Pavia, and why the Palatine Bank of Manchester, established in 1899, and a little too far from King Street for its own good, opted for unusual neo-Norman.[89]

The ultimate result of the introduction of new styles was the impracticability for most banks of continuing the characteristic 'in-house' presentation which many had adopted in the 'seventies and 'eighties. Some harmony was possible for, say, the London & South Western Bank, developing in a relatively small territorial radius; or for the Bucks & Oxon Union Bank, expanding in those and surrounding counties, with a series of rather ugly branches, like Stony Stratford, Watford and Thame. It was possible, too, for the Leicestershire Banking Company, staying faithful to the ideas of 'our friend Mr. Goddard, our architect'.[90] But it was pointless for banks like Lloyds, the London & County, and the London & Provincial, developing nationally, to attempt uniformity even if it were administratively possible to achieve it. The consequence of amalgamations was that banks of different origin, taste and materials became merged in corporate unity. There was therefore a dimension of inherited buildings to complicate the planning of new ones.

The factors which brought about the collapse of in-house styling worked equally to undermine the position of bank architect. The kind of situation which Gibson had enjoyed with the National Provincial Bank and Chatwin with Lloyds never quite returned. In the case of the National Provincial, Gibson appears to have ended his association in the early 'eighties, when he was about 65 years old.[91] He was succeeded for a time by C.R. Gribble, an architect of more contemporary classical taste, who built or altered several major branches, including Cardiff, Hereford and York.[92] His style lacked Gibson's flair and he made little impact. His initials were often miscast by the architectural press, which caused him to write testily to *Building News* in 1893.[93] The interest of this letter lies in the reference to his own position, then and for some years past, as the National Provincial's 'standing architect', a title which did not prevent the bank from passing over him for buildings of real importance, like the branches at King Street, Manchester, and Piccadilly, London. Both these commissions went to Alfred Waterhouse, with Gribble being responsible, at least at Manchester, only for internal arrangements.[94] After 1894, the National Provincial abandoned allegiance to any one architect, employing, for instance, Perkin & Bulmer at Leeds and W.D. Caröe (better known for the Adelphi Bank, Liverpool) at Cambridge.[95]

Lloyds Bank employed J.A. Chatwin as late as 1898 (Stratford-on-Avon) but by then he was approaching 70. His son, Philip, joined him for considerable work in Birmingham, around 1900, but never achieved his father's relationship with the Lloyds Bank directors. By 1891, J.A. Chatwin had developed, in his own words, into 'consulting architect',[96] reporting upon plans and specifications of regional architects — that is to say architects at some distance from Birmingham — and receiving 5 guineas for each appraisal of small works and 10 for the large ones.[97] The architects chosen for these regional branches were often those who had done work for banks which Lloyds took over: for instance, Lloyd Oswell was from the Salop Old Bank and Aston Webb had been commissioned by the Worcester City & County Bank; Thomas Worthington had succeeded George Truefitt as architect to Cunliffe, Brooks & Co. in the north-west, and J.W. Dyson had been with Lambton & Co. of Newcastle, as has been mentioned above.

In the south of England, Lloyds entrusted many branches to A.R. Stenning, who produced the occasional surprise, like an Arts and Crafts design at Caterham,[98] but neo-Georgian branches, such as Enfield, were nearer the norm. Work was also given, before the turn of the century, to Horace Field, beginning an association with Lloyds which was to last for 30 years. It appears that the bank, in these years, had certain 'approved' architects: F.W. Bedford of Leeds wrote to Lloyds in 1903 asking to join their 'list'.[99] He was turned down, but work was given later to his collaborator, Sydney D. Kitson.

The main architect, however, of Lloyds Bank in this period, and the virtual successor to Chatwin, was F.W. Waller, member of a well-known family of Gloucestershire architects. In partnership with his son, Waller designed such prestigious Lloyds branches as Gloucester and Cheltenham, as well as London, St James's Street, one of the chief monuments of Edwardian baroque.[100] At times he reported and explained to the main board, and travelled the south with R.V. Vassar-Smith, who later became chairman, investigating the potential for a good building.[101]

In contrast to the neo-classical palaces of men like Waller, there was an interesting exercise in environmentally sensitive design being conducted in the same period in East Anglia. The bank here was the private firm of Bacon, Cobbold, Tollemache & Co., based at Ipswich, and their branches were mainly in the towns of the Stour and Orwell estuaries. They used the local architect T.W. Cotman who had an affection for the style of the Low Countries and produced some notable designs. For two reasons this was a good choice of precedent. In the first place the commercial and demographic links between East Anglia and the Low Countries had always been strong. If Essex, not strictly part of East Anglia, is included in the reckoning, the connections are even stronger: Colchester, for instance, has its 'Dutch Quarter' once settled by refugee weavers, and Harwich has long been the gateway to Holland. Secondly, the Low Countries developed an early banking system vying with the Italian city states in sophistication and influence. The Bank of Amsterdam had been founded in 1609, while in the same city the Scottish firm of Hope & Co. set up a merchant banking practice whose business was second to none in Europe. Against this background should be seen Cotman's banks like the Felixstowe branch of Cobbold & Co., with crow-step gable and strapwork decoration,[102] and the Ipswich head office of 1880–90 (Plate 58), a potent blend of Gothic and classical features from the Flemish Renaissance.[103] As is clear from the photograph, the bank was not the only building in Ipswich to be treated to such a design. The visiting merchant from Antwerp or Bruges would have liked doing business there.

Among the bigger English banks, the rival to Lloyds in this period was not the National Provincial but the London, City & Midland, another bank of Birmingham origin developing rapidly from a new metropolitan foothold. This company had no purpose-built branches before 1877,[104] but after that date used a variety of local architects, like William Bakewell at Leeds (1892), James Ledingham at Bradford (1893), and F.B. Osborn at Coventry[105] (1897). Their most interesting branch, however, was at Hexham, by George Dale Oliver, opened in 1896.[106] As well as being a pleasing treatment of a difficult site, the external frieze, mingling Renaissance *putti* with dated, contemporary coinage, was refreshingly original. It is therefore the more curious that, also in 1896, plans were being made for Southampton branch which

*Plate 58. T.W. Cotman's head office for Bacon, Cobbold & Tollemache of Ipswich,
opened 1890.*

were to set a style of conservatism unparalleled among other banks in intensity, duration, and extent.

The architect mainly associated with this style was T.B. Whinney of London, although Southampton branch, opened in 1897, had been designed jointly with the local firm of Lemon & Blizard.[107] Whinney's association with the Midland Bank (as it became) was to result in more than 200 branches, work which almost excluded him from outside commissions.[108] In any event, the bank was developing so fast that some work had inevitably to go elsewhere. Most of this was shared by Gotch & Saunders of Kettering, who established the connection by designing the Midland's local branch in 1904,[109] and Woolfall & Eccles of Liverpool, architects to the North & South Wales Bank, taken over in 1908. The drawings of the latter firm are now in the custody of the Midland Bank Group Archivist.[110]

The unusual feature of these three relationships was their comprehensive control of the Midland's architectural presentation until comparatively recent times. This is not to say they were responsible for policy — a point which will be taken up later — but they were able to create a national identity of style out of a background of mergers and inherited traditions as complex as any emerging bank had to face. A branch like Peterborough (Plate 59), dated 1902 on the rainwater heads, had counterparts the length and breadth of Britain, the beginning of a style which even the 1920s and 1930s adapted very little. The main influence on Whinney was clearly the work of Edward Gabriel for the London & South Western Bank, as it had been presented in *Building News*. If Peterborough is compared with Gabriel's Clerkenwell branch (Plate 56), there are obvious similarities. They shared the same ethos of the corner site, the emphasis being placed on the angle; the corners demonstrated their own importance by dome or lantern, to which the identical side elevations were subordinate.

Another of the major modern banks, Barclays, became important in this period as well. Barclay & Company Limited, a joint-stock bank, was formed in 1896 by the merger of 20 private banks, of which the nucleus was the old Lombard Street bank of Messrs Barclay, Bevan & Tritton. The new company had 182 offices at the outset, as varied in style as they were scattered in distribution, and the task of evolving a corporate image for the future was too difficult at first to attempt. Early branches like Hampstead High Street and Leicester showed no obvious direction, and the bank came increasingly to put its trust in Sir Arthur and A.C. Blomfield, architects to the Bank of England.[111] Sir

Plate 59. Peterborough branch of the Midland Bank, 1902.

Arthur Blomfield's first branch for Barclays (although possibly designed before the merger) was the rebuilding of Messrs Gosling's private bank premises in Fleet Street, in 1899.[112] This had very much to conform with the general architectural treatment around Temple Bar, including Blomfield's own branch of the Bank of England, and only in later contracts were the Blomfield family able to develop the style which they felt appropriate, or which the bank requested. The first of A.C. Blomfield's branches was probably Chelmsford[113] (1905; Plate 60), a well-mannered and friendly design adding a welcome contrast in warm red brick to the nearby greyness of the Shire Hall. It was this bank, given wide publicity at the time, which no doubt influenced the B.N.D.C. design of 1907, referred to above, setting the characteristic elevation of the future. Blomfield went on to design similar banks for Barclays at Guildford and Luton, and most of the company's other branches of the Edwardian and later era show the same presentation, even if the architect was local. It was this pleasant, domestic, classical style appropriated by Barclays before the Great War which was to inspire the neo-Georgian revival of the 1920s.

While Barclays were still moving towards self-expression, assisted to a greater or lesser extent by the Blomfields, managers and directors of Lloyds and the London, City & Midland were voicing architectural feelings stronger than those of the architects whom they employed. In the case of the Midland, (Sir) Edward Holden (Joint General Manager, 1891, Managing Director, 1898, Chairman 1908) kept a particularly firm grasp on policy. A man of robust energy, Holden examined Whinney's designs in great detail to ensure the execution of his own vision of the bank's corporate image.[114] This supervision involved site inspections and he had frequent meetings with Whinney to monitor consistency of style.[115] Less easy to bring into line was the Liverpool partnership of Woolfall & Eccles. Their Wrexham branch design, originally prepared for the North & South Wales Bank, was rejected by the London, City & Midland who 'decided to erect a Renaissance façade to correspond with those characteristics which distinguish' their branches.[116] It would seem that Woolfall & Eccles were hurt by this, as their abortive design was eventually exhibited at the Royal Academy.[117] The disagreements did not end there. In 1913 Holden recorded in his diary an interview with 'Mr. Woolfall, Architect of Liverpool' about plans for branches at Warrington, Birkdale, Llandilo and Barmouth. 'I complained', he wrote, 'that he was not working on my lines, but was introducing his own features . . . .'[118]

Plate 60. A. C. Blomfield's Chelmsford branch of Barclays Bank, 1905.

In Lloyds Bank, matters of style were for arrangement by group discussion. In the first instance, approval or rejection lay with the Premises Committee. It was they, for example, who found the elevation of Bute Docks, Cardiff, branch too decorative in 1891 and passed Horace Field's plan for Bournemouth branch in 1899. Thomas Worthington's individualism was particularly difficult to accept: his drawings for Sale were 'of somewhat too ornamental a character for a Bank' and his proposals for nearby Broadheath 'seemed to require considerable alterations and rearrangement . . .'.[119]

Certain decisions, however, were reserved for the main board, although the criteria for submission are not clear. Perhaps guidelines on this were agreed in 1899 when the general manager presented a report to the board on the subject of branch premises. The text of the report has not survived. In any event, it was the board who had agreed in the first place that Field 'may be selected' for the job at Bournemouth[120] and the Premises Committee asked their views on the style of expensive branches like Leicester, Rugby and Swindon. In the case of Rugby, the board considered early proposals capable of improvement.[121] Less clear are the reasons why the board should have been involved in the appearance of minor branches, like Bristol Street, Birmingham, and Byker, near Newcastle. After 1910, the board's involvement in individual branches, even in the major developments at Manchester and London St James's Street, appears to have ceased.

Among the scores of smaller banks it is likely that questions of style were still to a large extent influenced by the architects themselves. As well as freelance specialists, appropriate enough in an age which saw the first purpose-built bank erected as a speculative investment by the freeholder,[122] there were local architects who had such an important regional following that they attracted banking contracts as a matter of course.

With the virtual retirement of Norman Shaw from banking commissions, the only freelance specialist of truly national importance was Alfred Waterhouse, who, in this period, designed premises for the National Provincial Bank at Manchester and London, for William, Williams Brown & Co., at Leeds, and for Foster & Co. at Cambridge. Such a territorial range was beaten only, perhaps, by W.W. Gwyther, a safely classical architect who appears to have made little impact on colleagues in his own profession.[123] Between 1895 and 1899, Gwyther had many prestigious commissions, including the Bishopsgate, London, branch of the Bank of Scotland, the head office of Pease & Co. at Hull, and the Yorkshire Banking Company's office at Leeds.[124] These stolid contracts brought him to the attention of the National Provincial Bank, for whom he designed at least two branches, Aberystwyth[125] and Walsall,[126] and he may have been seen as a successor to C.R. Gribble.

Gwyther died, however, in 1903 when his London position was already being eroded by J. Macvicar Anderson, an architect whose Renaissance style, even more conventionally Italian, was popular with banks, discount houses and insurance companies. Among his main bank commissions were the Commercial Bank of Scotland, at the corner of Birchin Lane and Lombard Street, and premises, since demolished, for Coutts & Co. in the Strand.[127]

Another London architect of importance was W. Campbell Jones. Although his more important commissions were in the 1920s, his long career had begun with the London & County Bank in the early 'nineties. For this company he did certain London-area branches, working as far into the provinces as Henley-on-Thames and Colchester. He designed the bank's new Lombard Street head office in 1907.[128] By this date he had already attracted the notice of other banks, having designed the Grimsby branch of Smith, Ellison & Co. of Lincoln, opened in 1899.[129] His largest commission in London, in the period of this chapter, was the head office of the Hong Kong & Shanghai Bank, completed in 1914.[130] When the London & County Bank joined with the Westminster Bank in 1909, he continued to do some work for the new company (the London, County & Westminster Bank),[131] his style moving from Renaissance towards neo-Georgian, perhaps under the influence of Blomfield's work for Barclays.

In Sussex, the London & County Bank, and later the London, County & Westminster, showed continuing allegiance to the talented Frederick Wheeler, of London and Horsham.[132] On the evidence of Chichester, Littlehampton, Petworth and other places, Wheeler designed no two banks alike. He is a good example of the type of architect mentioned above whose regional importance was so strong that his employment for local banks was inevitable. Another instance is G.J. Skipper of Norwich, whose Norfolk & Norwich Savings Bank of 1903[133] and Norwich branch of the London & Provincial Bank, 1911,[134] were each more expensive, no doubt, than the bankers would have wished. In Wales, the London & Provincial used J. Glendinning Moxham of Swansea until around 1915; he had come to notice in 1890 on the publication of an interesting Free Style design, prepared jointly with J. Buckley Wilson, for the Llanelly branch of the South Wales Union Bank.[135]

In North Wales, the Wirral and Merseyside, most work was done by

John Douglas of Chester (the firm of Douglas & Fordham, later Douglas & Minshull), and the Liverpool practices of Grayson & Ould, Willink & Thicknesse, Woolfall & Eccles, J. Francis Doyle and Edmund Kirby. Kirby had a private association with the North & South Wales Bank, for whom he did an early Gothic branch at Llanrwst[136] (1880), and a very late one at Laird Street, Birkenhead[137] (1908), but the bank gave most work to Woolfall & Eccles. The best-known bank by Kirby is actually at York, the present-day Barclays Bank, in Mixed Renaissance style, at the corner of Parliament Street and High Ousegate. As this is believed to date from 1901,[138] it must have been commissioned by the York Union Bank and completed just before its merger with Barclays in 1902.

Other Lancashire architects associated with banks were Briggs & Wolstenholme of Blackburn and Liverpool, Bradshaw & Gass of Bolton, and Maxwell & Tuke of Manchester. Among clients of the last-named were the Lancashire & Yorkshire Bank, the Manchester & Liverpool District Bank, and the Preston Banking Company. The main firm in Manchester, however, were Charles Heathcote & Son (earlier, Heathcote & Rawle), who designed the head office of the Lancashire & Yorkshire Bank[139] (1889), the Spring Gardens branch of Parr's Bank (1903)[140] and the enormous Lloyds Bank branch at the corner of King and Cross Streets (1914).[141] Elsewhere, they prepared drawings for a major branch of the National Provincial Bank at Worcester, opened in 1906.[142]

Two other practices in the north of England deserve particular mention, the first being Perkin & Bulmer of Leeds, whose work for the Yorkshire Penny Bank will be mentioned later, although they worked for other bankers too, at least in Leeds. The other practice was the York firm of Demaine & Brierley whose association with the York City & County Bank began when the partnership was still Atkinson & Demaine, and lasted nearly 40 years. Later banks were built in the name of the London Joint Stock Bank with which the York City & County merged in 1900. The leading partner was Walter H. Brierley who was responsible for important banks at Doncaster (1896) and Sunderland (1902) and from whom the firm, as Brierley & Rutherford, was to develop a wider banking clientele in the 1920s.[143]

With such strong local firms handling a fair proportion of branch bank development it can be appreciated that designs were more likely to reflect the wishes and experience of the local architects than preconditions of the bankers. The latter, however, would have been more sensitive to accusations of extravagance than the evidence of a score of publicised major branches might suggest. The cost of the average branch bank, in the 1890s, appears to have been between £5000 and £6000.[144] With the larger banks reporting global assets of around £35 million, several average branches could be built in a year, with still enough money for the occasional big one in a position of importance. The trouble was that the larger branches attracted disproportionate attention and this level of spending was taken as representative of the joint-stock philosophy. Banks therefore suffered in the wider intellectual attack on materialism. 'Our modern buildings ... are ... only artifice ... to mislead the undiscerning', thought the *Quarterly Review*.[145] 'Throughout England the professional expenditure on country seats, and highly ornamental banks, and warehouse buildings, is a melancholy show of ignorance and waste.'[146]

It must not be forgotten that bankers were accountable to shareholders, having to justify ever-increasing expenditure on material matters with money which might otherwise have contributed to profits and boosted dividends. Although no other bank appears to have attempted the bravado of the London & South Western, referred to at length above, others were anxious to convince shareholders that they 'always acted on economic principles' before building.[147] The constant transfer of profits to capital and reserve funds, in proportion to the rising risks of branch proliferation, and the marking down of property values to levels well below the probable market value of sale, seemed to add an element of professional mystique which bankers took pains to explain.

A major discomfort for bankers, however, was that they had lost some of the moral support of their own lobby. Whereas Gilbart, in his early textbook, had argued without reservation the case for good premises, George Rae, in some respects his successor, was more cautious. First published in 1885, Rae's book, *The Country Banker*, was in the form of a compendium of letters on what he called 'the machinery of banking in motion'. Being therefore less philosophical than Gilbart's, his ideas on practical matters, like choice of premises, were the more important. Rae was able to accept that to some people a large, expensive building was reassuring, and others experienced 'a sense of reflected dignity, as they pass under the Grecian portico of your rivals with the eyes of the Market Square upon them.'[148] But why, he questioned, do people enter a bank in the first place? — either to borrow money or deposit it. In the former case, they did not want to appear to be short, in the latter, they did not want to be touched 'by needy neighbours'.[149] In short, an insignificant bank was likely to be as popular as a big one.

To re-establish their confidence, bankers had at first to retreat behind the kind of unexceptionable clichés which had been used 40 and 50 years earlier. New premises were reported as 'good, useful and substantial' or just 'a good piece of work'.[150] In the 'nineties, however, came sentiments of pride and a sense of contribution to urban improvement, again echoes of earlier defences. The City Bank, in 1890, invited shareholders to an inspection of their remodelled chief office;[151] in 1891, the London Joint Stock Bank, at its jubilee dinner, presented staff with a lithographed card comparing the original bank of 1840 with the 'present handsome structure'.[152] In the same year, the London and Yorkshire Bank reported their new Scarborough branch as a 'great ornament to the town'.[153] Then the Leicestershire Banking Company began routinely to describe new branches as 'handsome',[154] and in the end the North & South Wales Bank, Rae's own company, could not resist self-advertisement: Rae himself, as chairman, reported a new Birkenhead branch, in 1894, as a 'model' bank, combining 'beauty, efficiency and economy'.[155]

But these were hardly admissions of extravagance. The only bank openly to argue the case for a grander style of building was Lloyds, whose chairman, Thomas Salt, told shareholders in 1896 'that it is an absolute necessity for our business to have good and commodious premises.'[156] In the following year, his address expanded this theme, arguing with force and conviction that it was essential 'if you are to do successful banking, to have expensive and convenient premises. You cannot help it. I could point out places where, with a small bank, we were doing only a moderate business: and when we improved our premises, and made them more convenient and handsome ... we increased our business very profitably and very rapidly.'[157]

Shortly afterwards, the *Bankers' Magazine* sided with Lloyds, without expressly making the association, by criticising 'a tendency to underrate the importance of first class premises. We are no advocates of mere palatial buildings and shining mahogany counters minus ... brains and integrity ..., but there is undoubtedly very much to be said in favour of the banking management which endeavours, so far as possible, to secure for the basis of operations in a particular town the best site and the best building consistent with the funds of the institution.'[158] Such a building would, in the provinces, overawe 'that portion of the population least conversant with banking principles and methods ...'[159] — a view of the naivety of country people contrasting with Rae's appraisal of their shrewdness. The underlying point was that, as canvassing by banks was still professionally unacceptable, an imposing building was as good a substitute as any for a three-column advertisement in the newspaper.

Salt's ultimate justification had been the welfare of his staff: 'we must have commodious premises, not only for the purpose of carrying on our business conveniently, but also for the health and comfort of our clerks, who deserve so much at our hands.'[160] No shareholder aware of his own conscience could take exception to this, however unconvinced he might be by the broader logic. Improvement in the working conditions of staff was an issue as old as Gilbart. That conditions in many urban banks, with their crowded, dusty, gas-lit rooms, were unsatisfactory, was hardly a contentious proposal. And yet the only person, other than Salt, who seems to have argued the point directly, was Rae. In 1888, at the annual meeting of the North & South Wales Bank, Rae claimed that his bank's new Castle Street, Liverpool branch would 'save much in the improved health of our staff.'[161] Shareholders were given earlier statistics of sick leave, amounting to 10 per cent of the staff at any given time. 'At present there is only one on the sick list. We must congratulate ourselves on this satisfactory state of affairs, and we believe the recent introduction of the electric light will be a further improvement in this respect.'[162] A similar defence was made for their Seacombe branch in 1896, described as handsome premises enlarged and improved 'for the convenience of our customers and the welfare of our staff.'[163]

The mention above of electricity is a pointer towards one of the technological developments of the late nineteenth century which complicated the costing and planning of larger buildings. A patented system of electric bells and alarms had been available in 1879, installed by Julius Sax in the Paddington branch of the London Joint Stock Bank.[164] But the use of electricity for lighting seems not to have been used in a bank before the new Lombard Street office of Lloyds, completed in 1887. Here, 246 Edison-Swan lamps were powered by a dynamo coupled to a 16 h.p. Otto gas engine, 'with secondary batteries in case of need.'[165] The installation was by Clark, Muirhead & Co. under the superintendence of Henry Lea & Thornbery of Birmingham.[166] In the following year, the new London & South Western Bank's head office was built with fittings designed for both electricity and gas,[167] and from 1890 it became quite normal to build large new banks with dynamos, or wire them for electricity, in cities like Cardiff, Coventry and Lincoln, and wait until the Coporation could supply the current. The cost of installation in a building already erected, estimated at £500 for a relatively small London bank in

1893,[168] was too much to make conversion attractive. Even after 1900 electricity was only sanctioned for large new urban branches, acceptable at Leicester, for example, in 1904, but not for Burford or Sandgate in the same year.[169] The supply was often unreliable in any case, too defective at Cheltenham in 1902 to power a lift.[170] Nevertheless, it is surprising, in view of the overall improvements in safety, cleanliness and working conditions which electricity made possible, that its adoption in many branches was delayed until as late as the end of the 1920s.

There was a similar reluctance to install central heating. Lloyds Bank approved a tender of £86 for warming Ludlow branch in 1890, only if two of the six radiators were omitted.[171] At Cardiff, in the following year, the same bank would agree to warm only the public area of a new dockland branch.[172] The cost of installing full central heating in a large new branch, like Cheltenham, in 1902, was £435.[173] Cheltenham was also one of the first country branches of Lloyds to have a telephone: the estimate for installation was £37 and the receiver was placed in the submanager's room.[174] It was therefore regarded as an instrument of utilitarian and emergency use, rather than a medium of routine business by senior branch management. This was confirmed by a letter of the Premises Committee to the manager of Heswall branch, who asked for advice in the case of fire: 'he should communicate by telephone with the Birkenhead Fire Brigade and ask for their services.'[175]

Technology reached also the strong room. Dalton & Co. produced a time lock in 1885, and in 1890 Hobbs Hart & Co. manufactured a safe door 7 feet (2.1 metres) high, 3½ feet (1 metre) wide, 3 feet (0.9 metres) deep, and weighing nearly 4 tons.[176] Circular doors were being marketed in 1900. As had been the case 100 years earlier, safe doors were the most expensive and specialised equipment which banks possessed; a redundant door was worth hauling from London to Manchester for reuse, or stock-piling indefinitely against future need. At the same time, banks were becoming less complacent about the ability of technology to resist criminal intentions. Whereas 40 years earlier the finer details of strong rooms were offered for publication with pride and confidence, caution had set in to such a degree that basement plans were now seldom available. On the other hand, bankers appear to have accepted without protest, or at least without publicity of protest, the right of local government bodies to scrutinise and file building plans which included the thickness of strong room concrete.

Electricity, central heating, telephones and safe doors were all aspects of the increasing range of premises matters which might have been thought suitable for a defined head office function. And yet such a service department, not directly concerned with profitability, was slow to reach definition. Lloyds Bank had a premises committee, but this was, of course, composed of directors. In the London, City & Midland Bank, outside architects exercised the administrative function until 1920.[177] Similarly, Barclays Bank had no formal premises department until that year.[178]

At Lloyds Bank a building inspector, at first under the chief inspector but later under the secretary, had been appointed in 1902. He liaised with local authorities and such bodies as the London Sanitary Protection Association who made recommendations for the installation and maintenance of lavatories. He was not concerned with bank design but travelled widely among branches to improve and standardise working conditions. He also responded to regional alarms: in 1905, when diphtheria broke out at Aberdare, he visited the branch and reported back on the drainage to the premises committee.[179] As his duties widened, the building inspector gained support staff. When his assistants were increased to three, in 1912, the small team was officially recognised as the premises department, although independence from the secretary took a little longer.

There was, then, among late Victorian and Edwardian banks, no unity of architectural presentation and no common approach to central control. Perhaps the darkest years had been in the middle 'nineties when a bank competition at Halifax, responsible for the publication throughout the architectural press of extravagant and ambitious designs, seemed to promise a future of building as profligate as funds would allow.[180] It should have been a shock to mainland bankers that the directors of the Isle of Man Banking Company, searching Britain in 1899 for an exemplar on which to base their new premises at Douglas, decided to follow the French neo-classical lines of an assurance company's office in Aberdeen, commissioning the same architect.[181]

Scotland, in fact, was now developing more sensibly than England in terms of its banks, although for many years the trammels of High Renaissance splendour seemed inescapable. This exuberance was not only so with commercial banks, like the Clydesdale's Dundee branch of 1881,[182] but even with the new Glasgow Savings Bank of 1896.[183] The £25 000 spent on this little building could only have been an embarrassment to the National Debt Office, keeping expenditure on English savings banks down to one-fifth of that figure, but by Glasgow standards this was a building of a plain and simple character.[184] But the style of Scottish banks was already moving quickly in other directions, while its legacy of masks and vases was still influencing London, decorating buildings like Kidner & Berry's head office of the Capital & Counties Bank, completed in 1893.[185] The most exciting designs were coming from the National Bank of Scotland for whom T.P. Marwick introduced a free and original interpretation of Italian Renaissance motifs for a branch at Kilmarnock,[186] so solid and monumental that it recalled the work of Cockerell for the Bank of England. Even more interesting was the major Glasgow branch of the same bank built in 1910 to designs by A.N. Paterson[187] (Plate 61). Here the only concessions to Glaswegian tradition were the sculptured figures of Prudence, Adventure, Commerce and Security, symbolic of banking. Influenced by Mackintosh's modern style, the branch was a foretaste of the steel-framed regularity, imitative of North America, which was to become popular in Glasgow and Liverpool nearly 20 years later. Although not characterised overall by an absence of decoration, the bank had six windows in the three central bays which had plain architraves and were set in a plain wall space. It is difficult to believe that any bank before this date had its main windows deliberately unadorned as a focal point rather than deliberately decorated.

In England, too, the Edwardian era was showing some hopeful signs, but recovery was fitful. Respect was growing for heritage and environment, but it did not stop the replacement of Crosby Hall in Bishopsgate by premises for the Chartered Bank of India, Australia and China. Martin's Bank commissioned Ernest Newton and Professor Beresford Pite to produce choice little branches unfettered by tradition and precedent.[188] Originality was shown by the young Edward Maufe, apparently prompted by Edwin Cooper's premiated design for Marylebone Town Hall[189] to attempt an icy classicism for the Capital & Counties Bank branch in St Albans, opened in 1914.[190] But men like Webb, Voysey and Lethaby, the intellectual vanguard of architectural thinking, were never commissioned. Banking, once a legitimate and favoured area of work for leading architects of the day, was now at some distance from the profession's cultural centre.

If the reasons for optimism were therefore qualified, there was at least one happy story, one pointer to better times, which it is fitting to end on. Although not in itself a story of architectural advance, it was a measure of the maturity of banking, of an outlook which promised to lay for good the last ghost of immoderate spending.

The story concerns the Yorkshire Penny Bank. Founded in 1856 as

Plate 61. A.N. Paterson's Glasgow branch of the National Bank of Scotland, 1910.

a provident association, it functioned at first as both a provident society and a savings bank, although the latter role soon became dominant. The constraints of the 1863 Savings Bank Act made it advisable for the bank to be reconstituted as a company limited by guarantee, with the name of The Yorkshire Penny Bank. By the end of 1893 it had 947 branches and owed £7.3 million to depositors.[191] In other words it had become a huge organisation locked in competition with commercial banks among the suburbs and townships of the industrial West Riding. With the confidence of paper wealth, the bank built some fine branches, including large, Gothic buildings at Sheffield, Halifax and Leeds all by Perkin & Bulmer.[192] Leeds, the last of these, was opened by the Duke of Devonshire in 1894. Building work had taken many years, the cost was said to be around £50000 to £60000,[193] and the fairy-tale design was published in Germany as an example of contemporary British architectural thinking.[194]

With such obvious marks of prosperity, money again poured in from working class depositors, to such an extent that the bank's constitutional structure seemed precariously inadequate for liabilities which, in 1911, exceeded £18 million. It was too risky to go on. Co-ordinated by the Bank of England, two groups of commercial banks stepped in, the one subscribing capital for a new company, the Yorkshire Penny Bank Limited, to take over the liabilities and assets, the other giving individual guarantees to underwrite depreciation of securities.

The press were very heartened. Bankers could now show unity, compassion and collective responsibility. By the same token they were, unwittingly, concluding an era of banking architecture as effectively as its interruption a little later by the Great War.

Chapter Six

The Twentieth Century: Prestige Gained, Lost and Coveted

In a history spanning two centuries, the architecture of British banking reached the summit of its achievement in a brief space of 10 or 12 years after the Great War. In this decade a number of factors came together: wartime building restrictions were lifted; banks merged and entered another period of branch expansion on a scale which has shaped the distribution of today; and there was informed and persistent analysis of policy and construction. It was not possible before the 1920s to explore the architecture of banking in such depth, and it has not been possible since.

The fact that this golden age should have happened at all was a matter of surprise to banker and architect alike. The banking profession, finding it was behaving in a way satisfactory to the architectural press, tried even harder to win support and approbation. Never had goodwill between the two professional bodies been so strong and never had the inclination to spend on material matters been matched by such availability of funds, and the internal administration to employ them.

The factor which contributed most to this happy state of affairs was a new round of mergers which rid the profession of some of the worst consequences of frenetic competition. Against the colossal significance of the end of the war, the constitutional importance of 1918, in terms of banking, has been understandably overlooked. Yet in that year the National Provincial amalgamated with the Union of London and Smiths Bank; the London, City & Midland joined with the London Joint Stock Bank; Lloyds merged with Capital & Counties; Barclays with the London, Provincial & South Western; and the London, County & Westminster with Parr's. The banking empires of today were beginning to take shape. In the case of some of these amalgamations, rationalisation of title took a little longer, but the mainstream of development had reached an enormous, serene estuary, virtually untroubled by other merging waters for another 50 years.

Serenity could almost be called the keynote of the 'twenties architectural scene: it was not a complacent uninterest, but a state of mind confident that past mistakes had been understood and corrected. Fewer banks meant that the need for aggressive, competitive building had largely passed, while the policy of each company was open to greater critical exposure. Mindful of this, the banks put into practice the lessons taught by conservationist lobbies at Chester, Guildford and elsewhere. In some towns this kind of unofficial local pressure had never died away. The National Provincial, for example, had little choice of styles at Stratford-on-Avon and Ludlow in the early 'twenties, where 'the inhabitants ... through the medium of the authorities and societies interested in the preservation of local amenities, approached the directors of the bank with a request that half-timber buildings should be erected.'[1]

The difference now was that such pressure was largely unnecessary. Banks were only too pleased to build a half-timbered design whenever an aura of medievalism brought it to mind. In other places an historical style complimentary to a particular local monument might be chosen, often planned with sensitivity and executed without stint. There is a good example at Ely[2] and an even better one in London, where the Midland commissioned Sir Edwin Lutyens to design their branch at 196a Piccadilly in a red-brick seventeenth century style echoing St James's Church nearby, rather than the twentieth century commercialism which overshadowed it.[3] Less conscientious were the sham-Tudor frontages widely adopted by banks in suburban parades. But this trend was no more than conformity with reigning taste and banks were not specifically responsible for its adoption.

The facet of conservation which won bankers most respect was the rescue and conversion of old buildings, some inherently unsuitable for banks, and their use as branches in a way which subordinated the image of the bank to the original character or purpose of the building. This was a tradition dating back to the Worcester City & County Bank, whose renovations at Bromsgrove and Hereford were recorded in Chapter Five. Most of the major banks can produce first-class examples from between the wars in a wide range of buildings: Barclays, for instance, rescued the Victorian Corn Exchange at Romsey,[4] the Westminster preserved the Elizabethan 'Golden Lion' ceiling at Barnstaple,[5] and Martin's restored a medieval house at York.[6] Environmental concern extended to far less spectacular matters, like reusing tiles from an old house at Andover,[7] and building with local flints, Chilmark stone and sand-faced tiles at Amesbury.[8] One bank even went to the trouble of remodelling a sound and serviceable branch which was considered ugly and out of character, replacing it with a more suitable external design.[9] In the rare case when an existing building of note was demolished for a new branch, banks took pains to explain the reason. Lloyds only pulled down the *George* inn in Northampton because it was 'very badly built; great expense would have been necessary to make it habitable or even safe.'[10] For other banks, however, cost was not the first consideration, even in speculative reconstruction. In 1925 Barclays created a branch in Faversham in a building expensively 'restored ... to what was conceived to be its condition before it was converted into a shop.'[11]

This kind of sensitivity contributed in large part to the banks' good relations with the architectural press: '... in almost all the cases of modern bank rebuildings it is only fair ... to mark the very high standard of architecture which is maintained in this class of building. It would indeed be hard to find another class of modern building in which there are so few enormities, such a small proportion of mediocrity, and so many really great expressions of architecture.'[12] This observation in the *Builder*, typical of many in other journals, was not of course based solely on acts of conservation. It reflected a broad architectural policy for improvement characterised, especially in provincial branches, by the use of neo-Georgian designs.

The Georgian Revival was particularly suited to the bankers' new image. The reason for this suitability was open to conjecture. To some people neo-Georgian was representative of the age in which British banking developed; to others it was appropriate as the last true period of native design before architecture lost its way; to others again it was the style most compatible with the nature of country towns. No doubt there was some truth in all these views but they miss the central point that neo-Georgian had also evolved by a process of natural selection. Rooted in the 'Queen Anne' resurgence of some 40 years earlier, the style, as appropriate for banking, had been forming in Edwardian times under the influence of Barclays. With the phasing out of less suitable designs, like baroque and *Art Nouveau*, neo-Georgian was inevitable for the 1920s. It offered taste, well-being, and a happy camouflage for the less beneficent activities within.

The bank which had to move most to accommodate neo-Georgian was the Midland Bank (so-called from 1923), which left the war years with a policy of consistent design based on the Italian Renaissance. Branches were to be 'at once recognisable'.[13] In 1926 the bank had a scheme to introduce an even more rigorous exterior conformity, based on designs by Sir Edwin Lutyens, but this was abortive.[14] Three years later, J. Alfred Gotch, one of the more important architects regularly commissioned by the Midland, explained their corporate philosophy. Except in large towns, they were not in favour of associated shops or offices built to let. 'We are bankers,' said Gotch, 'not property owners', and their branches were often of one storey, forming a single entity.[15] Gotch also 'confessed that he was not a great believer in the doctrine that a bank ought to conform closely to the style of the town in which it was built. If it was quietly and sensibly designed it would not jar with anything . . .'[16]

If the Gotch doctrine accounts for the majority of Midland's branches in this era — and for no other bank can buildings be recognised almost anywhere without recourse to the name — the veteran T.B. Whinney nevertheless produced some notable and distinctive neo-Georgian. His Henley-on-Thames branch[17] (Plate 62), opened in 1924, had many imitators, among them the Midland's architects commissioned to build at Eccles some years later.[18] The success at Henley derived from the balance of the architectural features and the neighbourly restraint from commercialism. On the ground floor, tall sash windows and pedimented entrance gave a vertical thrust, continued in the centre bay by window and coat of arms linking directly from porch to cornice, and terminated across all three bays by the sunken panels of the parapet. At the same time, the parapet, cornice and string-course added a horizontal emphasis, the small first-floor windows articulating both lines of direction by participation in each. As for self-advertisement, the string-course was adapted to take the name of the bank, more usually presented with less modesty on a frieze between ground- and first-floor windows. This extra height softened the brashness of advertisement in an essentially domestic façade, while giving a subtle superiority over the level of surrounding shop names.

Despite Georgian predominance, purely classical designs never died away absolutely. Sometimes the environment gave little scope for anything else. The Midland, while loosening allegiance to Italian Renaissance in the provinces, found it inevitable for Pall Mall, where T.B. Whinney's branch, opened in 1926, captured all the grandeur of St James's.[19] Likewise, the extraordinary tradition of Southport led to a National Provincial Bank of 1933 'out to beat the band'[20] and worthy of Milsom Street, Bath. At other times, however, it was simply a matter of local preference, as with the National Provincial at Wolverhampton in

Plate 62. T.B. Whinney's Henley-on-Thames branch of the Midland Bank, 1924.

1920,[21] and the Westminster at Maidstone in the 1930s, criticised as 'very vulgar'.[22]

Another distinct style was brought about by contemporary American trends. One of the earliest examples was the National Bank at Liverpool, a building still standing at the junction of James Street and Derby Square.[23] The actual bank was confined to the ground floor and basement of the nine-storey building, the remaining floors being let at lucrative city rents. The importance of this structure is that it was planned in 1920, before Philip Sawyer's seminal paper in the New York journal *Architecture*[24] had time to influence British designs. Liverpool's transatlantic connections made it particularly receptive to American influence, and the Bank of British West Africa in the same city was another early example of what later became nicknamed the 'Classic-cum-steel frame manner'.[25]

The article to which Sawyer made the first and most thoughtful contribution was a wide-ranging analysis of American bank architecture presented by practising architects in March 1921.[26] That British architects of banking were ripe for the influence of their transatlantic colleagues was proved by the appearance, in exactly the same month and year, of an article in the *Architects' Journal* which admitted the better quality of American design.[27] Not unnaturally, it was McKim who was held up as the ultimate model, praised for his grasp of classical precedent and the virtues of reticence and restraint which governed his translation of their features to suit North American practice: 'he was big enough to pick up the European tradition, strong enough to make it American, wise enough to sink his personal likes and dislikes for the fulfilment of a vast idea.'[28] But it was Sawyer who pointed beyond the external presentation of design to the big changes in the philosophy and practice of banking which were causing a revolution in bank architecture beginning from within.

There has to be some caution in evaluating Sawyer's comments because the layout of American banks differed from those in Britain. In the former there were traditionally places for 'officers' and 'tellers' on the ground floor, both being accessible to the public, with a 'loan cage' near the officers. There were different tellers for receiving and paying, whereas in Britain the tellers (cashiers) performed both functions and presented the only interface with the public. The manager(s) and other clerks were usually unapproachable and often out of sight. What Sawyer was finding was that banks were now so big and busy that officers and tellers were being separated; instead of jockeying for space on one floor they were rising up the building in hierarchical order, the highest, and therefore the quietest, rooms being reserved for the most senior officers. The key to this new disposition was, very simply, the elevator.[29] When Sawyer was designing his banks the first point he established was the position of the elevators, the second was the internal arrangement of the various departments of banking; and then he decided what style of building to put them in. Symptomatic of this change was the new attitude of bankers themselves. 'A few years ago', wrote Sawyer, 'a banker said to his architect: "There's no use telling me of your experience in bank planning — no architect knows any thing about it; you build the building and we'll move in and put the desks in place . . .". That attitude is rarer now . . .'[30]

In Britain, such an attitude had been rare for much longer but what evidence there is of discussion between banker and architect has tended to show more involvement by the former in the layout than the appearance, at least in matters of detail. Ironically, therefore, it was the appearance of American banks, in particular their monumentality, which seems to have most influenced British ideas, although the thrust of Sawyer's comments was directed at the totality of planning. The copious plates to the *Architecture* article added a minor new reservoir of sources for British inspiration, the District Bank at Southport,[31] for instance, using a temple-form entrance style (two giant columns *in antis*) reminiscent of the First National Bank at Appleton, Wisconsin, as Sawyer had illustrated it.[32] The Americans had even produced their own version of a one-storey neo-Georgian bank by 1921, for suburban branches, and if the reasons for the acceptability of this style among British bankers and architects have been found to be properly domestic, there is nevertheless the possibility of some influence on the Midland Bank in the manner of execution.[33]

Despite such cross-fertilisation, the impact of American design on British, or at least on English, banks, was not widely advertised. For one thing it was clear that there were differences between Britain and America in banking which went much deeper than the nomenclature of staff or the disposition of the banking-hall, a fact which struck an American architect contributing to Sawyer's review: 'One very conspicuous condition impressed me everywhere in England', he wrote, 'and that was the abnormal amount of time the bankers wasted in their efforts to be polite.'[34] Appropriate to this attitude were 'antiquated and mid-Victorian buildings, structures that do not convey the impression that they were intended to be banking-houses in any way whatever.'[35] The American fondness for a massive, lofty banking-hall, with open plan seating, was suited to their 'rapid-fire methods' of business. If English bankers as a whole were unimpressed by the Americans' *savoir faire*, they were all the less likely to admit the adoption of their building style.

Where the American influence did take hold it was not through any change of banking ethics but because high inner-city rates made it attractive to maximise income. The taller the building, the more lucrative the return from rented offices, and the greater the temptation to follow American styling. In fact, at Glasgow, which was the first British city after Liverpool to adopt the American philosophy, it was overtly copied. Here, two such banks were built in the late 1920s, one the Renfield Street branch of the Bank of Scotland by Andrew Balfour & Stewart,[36] the other the St Vincent Street head office of the Union Bank of Scotland by James Miller.[37] The more interesting of the two was the latter (Plate 63).

The St Vincent Street bank had not only to demonstrate the permanence and solidity of a head office, but also to characterise the westward shift of Glasgow's business and shopping centre; in particular, it was necessary to upstage the bank's existing head office in Ingram Street, part of the old commercial quarter of the city. Uncertainty as to the style which would best reflect these elements deferred the decision to rebuild until 1923, the site having been acquired in 1918. The building which resulted owed much to Norman Hird, the bank's general manager, who was sent to the United States by his directors.[38] Thus the city which itself had been the Mecca for Ulster bankers sought its own architectural fulfilment in the sky-scrapers of North America. As the new bank was called 'a very happy combination of American lay-out adapted to British conditions',[39] it is reasonable to suppose that Hird was primarily concerned with the internal arrangement, leaving Miller the formidable task of executing his ideas within a suitably American elevation. Miller's own indebted-ness to Sawyer seems proven by the similarity of his lower storey to that of the Broadway Trust Company's building at Camden, New Jersey, designed by Phillip Merz and featured in the article in *Architecture*.[40] Another inspiration was probably the New York office of the National City Bank by McKim, Mead and White.

Miller's bank had two basement levels and seven storeys above ground. Only the ground and first floor were occupied by the bank, and indeed part of the former was let to shops. However, occupancy by the bank could never be doubted by anyone, the giant Ionic columns rising 40 feet (12.2 metres) from their plinths of polished granite, embracing both the banking-hall and the first floor of offices, managerial rooms, and board room. Belying appearances, the banking-hall was lit not only from the two main frontages but by a lantern, the building being cleft by a light well, open on the north side. The Order within the banking hall was Doric, the frieze being restricted to triglyphs above the columns, while the walls were lined with Forêt de Brousse marble. Although hardly welcoming, the interior was bright, spacious and redolent of the better qualities of banking. In wider terms, the building

Plate 63. Above: James Miller's Glasgow head office of the Union Bank of Scotland, 1927. Opposite: interior.

was even more successful — a powerful and stylish contribution to downtown Glasgow upon which many businesses, even department stores, must have cast an envious eye.

While Glasgow, Liverpool, and to a lesser extent Manchester, were under American influence, the City of London resisted the squareness and austerity of detail which such designs entailed. Late in 1921 Professor A.E. Richardson's published skyscraper 'Fantasy' for the Bank of England,[41] erupting like a space-rocket behind Soane's perimeter wall, must have awakened fears of Manhattan or Chicago taking hold of the Square Mile. But the major banks had no intention of building their new head offices in styles other than those which were proven and safe, even if the local authority had allowed it. Being at peace with the world on account of the suitability of their branches, bankers were in no mood for spoiling this harmony in London: they were out to prove, once and for all, that their Philistine image was behind them. It was no coincidence that all the big banks, except Barclays,[42] felt the need to rebuild their head offices at the same time: a substantial increase in business had arisen from the 1918 amalgamations, and a large expansion of branch networks had brought a need for tighter co-ordination at the centre, outstripping the space and resources of existing departments.

The first of the major new buildings was the Westminster Bank in Lothbury, designed by Mewès & Davis[43] (Plate 64) and replacing the

Plate 64. Above: head office for the Westminster Bank, Lothbury, London, by Mewès & Davis, opened 1930. Opposite: head office for Lloyds Bank, Lombard Street, London, by Sir John Burnet & Partners in association with Campbell Jones, Sons & Smithers, opened 1930. The view shown is the Cornhill frontage.

earlier building by Cockerell & Tite. The drawings were exhibited at the Royal Academy in 1921, some years before the commencement of building, which lasted until 1930. Also completed in 1930 was the head office of Lloyds Bank between Lombard Street and Cornhill, designed by Sir John Burnet & Partners in association with Campbell Jones, Sons & Smithers[44] (Plate 64). The drawings had been exhibited in 1927, the year after building was started. Much longer in construction was the head office of the Midland Bank between Poultry and Princes

Street (Plate 65), designed by Sir Edwin Lutyens with the interior planning by Gotch & Saunders.[45] The drawings were exhibited in 1925 and 1928. The Poultry section was completed in 1930 but the extension into Princes Street was not opened until 1939. Such long periods of construction gave the opportunity for exhaustive reporting by the architectural press, but with little comparative analysis. Scarcely less awesome were some of the major City branches, like Mewès & Davis's Threadneedle Street branch of the Westminster,[46] and Sir Edwin Cooper's office for the National Provincial Bank[47] (Plate 65) abutting Lutyens's new bank for the Midland. This was virtually a head office to supersede Gibson's bank in Bishopsgate Street which, as well as becoming too small, was too far from the new centre of activity: scarcely 200 yards now separated the dynasties of banking.

Discussion of these banks must be prefaced by an understanding of

Plate 65. *Above: head office for the Midland Bank, Poultry, London, by Sir Edwin Lutyens in association with Gotch & Saunders, opened 1930. Below: Sir Edwin Cooper's new office for the National Provincial Bank, junction of Poultry and Princes Street, opened 1931.*

their sites. The Midland and the National Provincial were in the best locations inasmuch as the former was readily visible from both its frontages and the latter occupied perhaps the most prestigious corner site in the City. A drawback for the Midland, however, was that someone admiring the elevation in one street had no inkling of the other frontage in the street beyond and therefore no immediate grasp of the vastness of the building. Lloyds was in the same predicament, but at least the Midland faced two streets with an open vista; the problem for Lloyds was that the frontage which carried the address was in prestigious but very narrow Lombard Street, while the one in less fashionable Cornhill was by far the more visible. As for the Westminster, the only perspective of its Lothbury office was down Bartholomew Lane, while the new Threadneedle Street branch required a difficult curved frontage. The Westminster was therefore in the trickiest position, and Mewès & Davis resorted to established solutions. For the Lothbury head office they chose an Italian Renaissance design, not based on any specific precedent, which allowed for a three-bay central block, breaking slightly forward and closing the view from Threadneedle Street. The main feature of this centre was a massive doorway, making Bartholomew Lane seem almost to disappear into the bowels of the bank. For the office in Threadneedle Street itself, Mewès & Davis borrowed heavily from the Palazzo Massimi, the archetypal treatment of a curved building line. The branch, completed in 1925, was extended in the 'thirties continuing the style, of course, but making the building almost as difficult to photograph as its Roman precedent.

In contrast to the Westminster, Lloyds opted for a more broadly classical design, massive and monumental, by far the most bank-like of the head offices, in so far as it exuded the virtues of strength and permanence. No attempt was made to design identical elevations for the two frontages and for the reason of greater visibility, noted above, the Cornhill side was given the stronger treatment. Thirteen giant Corinthian columns, linking a robust base and powerful superstructure, stood up well against the Royal Exchange, across the street, and controlled the Cornhill perspective from the Bank intersection. The Lombard Street frontage, on the other hand, was given pilasters, with the main door at the western end where the street was most open and the hanging sign seen to best effect. In a quite different style again was the Midland's head office, which had almost identical frontages to Poultry and Princes Street. This was unquestionably the most important of the buildings now being discussed. This was not Lutyens's only involvement with the Midland: his branch in Piccadilly has already been referred to, but the three later commissions[48] — i.e. head office, Leadenhall Street branch (opened 1931) and King Street, Manchester branch (opened 1935) — were different in style from Piccadilly and interrelated, in so far as they carried the architect's hallmark of roof-line pavilions, like little classical temples, and an artistic conception of the treatment of mass.

Lutyens had come to work for the Midland through the influence of their chairman, Reginald McKenna, for whom he had already designed a house.[49] Thus the Midland's tradition of strong one-man leadership in the area of architectural taste was continued, while the appointment of the bank's normal architects to work alongside Lutyens ensured favoured configurations of layout. Most striking about the Midland's head office was the exquisite sense of balance and proportion, to which a degree of imaginative classical detail added rhythm without impairing the originality of the design. This was a façade very sensitive to the banking traditions of the City: the banded rustication recalled Soane's perimeter wall of the nearby Bank of England, which had itself reminded Ruskin of pages in a ledger;[50] the old London & Westminster Bank head office by Cockerell & Tite (being demolished while Lutyens was working for the Midland) also used this treatment, and featured distinctive sculptured figures at each side of the elevation. Lutyens followed the same idea with his flanking sculptures of a boy and a goose, carved by Sir William Reid Dick, at each end of the Poultry frontage; it is interesting to see their inclusion as a token of his respect for the passing of one of the City's worthiest buildings, while the representation was appropriate for 'the street of the poulterers'.

Juxtaposed to Lutyens's genius, Cooper's National Provincial Bank looked very pedestrian. Although well-enough received at the time, and politely complimentary to its neighbour in the uniform height of the lower cornice and frieze, the building seemed to be a regression to out-moded concepts of what a bank ought to look like. Critics were soon bringing the allegorical statuary into disrepute. Too many figures in bewildering nightgowns with irrelevant cornucopiae were dismissed by Goodhart-Rendel as 'tiresome pomposities' and a large waste of money.[51] 'If the purpose of external walls in a city building', he wrote, 'were to display figure-sculpture and to keep out the light, those of the National Provincial Bank would be hard to better.'[52] But if the bank was a reversion to High Victorian decorative detail, it was an interesting modernisation of the traditional treatment of the corner site: there was no extravagant emphasis of the angle, crowned by dome or lantern, and the three faces received equal architectural weight in a skilful manipulation of the site.

Before this discussion of head offices is closed, something must be said of the quality of interior work: if the banks were employing in-house or regular architects for internal planning this did not prevent the main architect from stamping his personality not only in the style of the banking-hall but in the minutiae of ornamentation. The Midland was the classic example with the axes of entry and communication articulated by a circular light well (for the basement), as spokes join a hub, the banking-hall and certain other areas being finished in green and white marble. Clocks and door handles were among other features of Lutyens's own design.[53] Lloyds opted for cream marble, with a delicate interplay in counter screens and floor pattern between the bank's two corporate symbols — the beehive reminiscent of Birmingham private banking and the black horse inherited from a Lombard Street goldsmith and expressive of the bank's new London interests. The National Provincial had a domed banking-hall, partly coffered in the style of the Pantheon.

A different kind of building was preferred by the London merchant bankers marking their commercial independence by an architectural uniform based on the use of red brick. The precedent for this had been Norman Shaw's Bishopsgate office for Baring Brothers (extended sympathetically by Gerald Horsley in 1912–3), but the connection was overlooked by commentators in the excitement of so much rebuilding. Indeed, Messrs Schroder's premises of 1924, the first in the new style and designed by Messrs Joseph, were thought to have introduced red brick to the City.[54] The banks of Messrs Hambros and Messrs Lazard followed in 1926 and 1927, the former using pilaster strips to add a certain dignity,[55] the latter deliberately informal, as the 'directors suggested that it should give the impression of a country bank moved to London, and expressed a preference for red bricks, simple lines, and the elimination of unnecessary ornament.'[56] The bank of Messrs Morgan & Grenfell, designed on a difficult site in Great Winchester Street by Mewès & Davis,[57] moved more towards classical lines, but the red-brick tradition was kept alive in Lombard Street, in 1931–3, by two clearing banks — Martin's, and its neighbour Williams & Glyn's — both rebuilding to designs by Sir Herbert Baker and A.T. Scott.[58]

Mention of Baker draws attention to the greatest of all rebuildings in this period, that of the Bank of England. The demolition of most of Soane's work and the systematic reconstruction within his perimeter wall produced the only storm cloud in this summertime of bank design.

Dismissed by Goodhart-Rendel as 'incongruous and ignorant',[59] castigated by Summerson as a 'tragi-comedy of incompatibles',[60] Baker's work was spoilt from the outset by a certain reluctance to publicise the intended design. This 'portentous silence' led to an article on the 'Destruction of the Bank of England' as early as 1921.[61] Yet when Baker's plans were revealed they seemed, in the short term, to show that fears were unfounded. There was respect and even approval,[62] although the resilient ghost of Soane ensured a level of support well below that accorded for the contemporary clearing bank reconstructions. Furthermore, the Bank of England's unique constitutional status led to its criticism more as a department of state than a bank, and public buildings were, in the nature of things, more susceptible to critical review than those in the private sector.

The interest shown generally by the architectural press in the progress of bank design was one of the phenomena of the age. At first reflecting and reporting the bank architectural scene, the journals later took an active and less dispassionate stance in the direction it was going. The subject as a whole broke in 1921 with a small article in the *Architectural Review* by F.H. Shann, a Lloyds Bank building inspector.[63] Shann thought the first bank, ever, had probably been a hole in the ground, in contrast to which were 'the magnificently decorated and lavishly equipped banks in the chief cities of America ...'.[64] As if on cue, came the article in the New York journal *Architecture*, already mentioned above, while at the same time in Britain an even more comprehensive article appeared in *Architects' Journal*.[65] Spanning 43 pages, the treatment was very broad, beginning with comments by 'Aero' on the design of banking premises, describing specific new banks in London, Liverpool and elsewhere, and discussing layout, equipment, strong rooms, and questions of ventilation, heating and lighting. The same periodical published 'Corner Sites and Banks' in 1924, lamenting that the post office had not beaten the banks to it.[66] The *Builder* featured 'Bank Façades and Their Influence' in 1923, a thoughtful article on whether any design can say unequivocally 'I am a banking establishment' to the man in the street, and whether branches should be committed to a uniform style.[67] This was followed closely by 'The Design and Planning of Banks' by J. Hembrow, also in the *Builder*.[68] A partner in Mills & Murgatroyd, Hembrow became the national authority on strong room design, as well as an advocate of the windowless bank, an idea which he floated with little success in 1927.[69]

The question of the security of strong rooms was obviously one of the reasons why major banks employed favoured architects for internal work while commissioning a famous name for the overall design. The old attitude that a secure area could be burglar-proof was now little supported and the Great War had taught that aerial bombing was another danger to be reckoned with. There developed quite a science in the planning and execution of strong rooms of reinforced concrete designed to be resistant to attack not indefinitely, but for such time as the bank was unattended. Hembrow reckoned that strong rooms should be planned according to the number of hours in which a burglar might have the bank to himself.[70] Of course, if the bank was patrolled day and night the risk was minimal, but smaller branches he found particularly vulnerable. Strong rooms of blue Staffordshire brick could be systematically dismantled, even if laced with steel rods, while fine concrete was better than coarse, because round, smooth pebbles in the latter could allegedly be picked out with a cold chisel.[71] Such considerations bore out all Sawyer's comments about banks now being designed from the inside out. For instance, it was the Midland's confidence in the virtual impregnability of their branch strong rooms which encouraged them, according to Gotch, to build one-storey banks with no manager or caretaker above, or no associated shop or chambers.[72] In this belief, Gotch was openly criticised by Arthur J. Davis at a meeting of the R.I.B.A.;[73] Gotch immediately retracted his absolute comment, but insisted that strong rooms could be made 'safe for the period of time during which banks were likely to be unoccupied'.[74] Davis, in an uncannily prophetic question at the same meeting about making strong rooms bomb-proof, 'inquired whether it was to resist the 1914 bomb or the 1940.'[75] The meeting was in 1929.

An attempt to classify bank design was made by the *Architect & Building News* in 1928.[76] First came the banks proper, undistorted by chambers or living accommodation above; then the composite banks, which divided themselves architecturally according to the inclusion or omission of a horizontal break, to indicate the change of function. The most satisfactory kind was obviously the self-contained bank, as it was an architectural unit fulfilling a single function. When a building failed to indicate the break of function between bank and chambers (or whatever else was above) the 1920s mind saw something of a moral dilemma which had not troubled the Victorians: there was talk of 'architectural pretence', despite the aesthetic success of many of the designs.[77] A more practical issue for banks, however, was to find the calibre of architect who could cope with a composite building. It was not easy to blend a ground-floor bank with upstairs rented flats and ensure the unity of expression which commercial self-advertisement made desirable.

From this point, the architectural journals tended only to exhibit the extraordinary fecundity of branch building, or reiterate established canons of bank design. The scope for illustration was so wide and interest so contagious, that the *Bankers' Magazine* began its own series on premises in 1925. The initial article[78] is of value because the topics were geared very much to the kind of issues then exercising premises' managers, that is to say, the benefits of a corner site, the disadvantages of a plot in a suburban terrace, and the question of housing for the manager.[79] As Gilbart and Rae had shown in the nineteenth century, there were certain questions affecting banking premises which bankers themselves were in the best position to raise. But then philosophy grew stale: the few articles which followed, in later issues, discussed particular buildings in much the same way as did the architectural journals.

A chief cause for the magazine's retreat from architectural matters was the appearance of the rival journal, the *Banker*, in 1926. Less ponderous than other banking periodicals, the *Banker* set out from the beginning to win a wider market than finance and banking law could ever attract. The medium of bank buildings was already a source for popular interest: when augmented with advertisements by builders and strong room contractors, and stiffened by a regular series of articles by C.H. Reilly, Professor of Architecture in the University of Liverpool, the formula for success seemed all too easy.

It is difficult to exaggerate the richness of Reilly's early contribution to the evolution of bank design. A man of proven academic stature, with considerable knowledge of banking, Reilly wrote nearly a hundred articles in the *Banker* over a period of some 18 years, a tireless marathon which the outbreak of war could scarcely interrupt.[80] His technique was to examine new branches of all the major banks individually, although not necessarily in sequence. When his appetite outstripped supply, he turned to Europe, Australia, America and Canada. When new building ceased entirely in the Second World War, he rehashed his earlier material. Working wholly from photographs (which occasionally misled him),[81] never meeting the architects whose work he discussed, Reilly sat in self-imposed, isolated judgement on the policy of the banking dynasties. Anecdotal, amusing, always frank, sometimes caustic, his opinions were unchallenged and bankers took them seriously. Never had the profession been so susceptible to outside views, and never had there been a man of such authority to give them. It was due to Reilly that the mood of change ultimately came about, that acquiescence in the 'serene' stance turned to impatience for something new. And yet it had not been Reilly's original intention to upset or embarrass his readership. The motive which inspired him was an honest belief that bankers could break with their traditional caution and afford, literally, the role of the *dilettante*. 'Surely it is time', he wrote, 'that the leaders of the banking world should, as the greatest builders in the country, make a study of modern English architecture, and discover who are the good architects and who are the bad . . .'[82]

The difference between Reilly and the many other critics and commentators was, therefore, idealism. He craved for the personal element to reveal itself in a world of corporate insensitivity. He was little interested in fitting-up and problems of internal security: for these he gave space to Hembrow. Nor was he concerned particularly with the concept of what was 'bank-like', a point which had interested the architectural press. Indeed, in the first sentence of his first paper he dismissed the notion of 'bank architecture', arguing that architectural styles and treatment should be all-embracing.[83] Reilly looked for architecture good in its own right by companies who had the resources to achieve it. 'It seems to me', he continued, 'that bank directors have the most delightful task in the world. They alone can be patrons of architecture in the Renaissance manner . . . let them enjoy the pleasure of discriminating connoisseurship. Let each director have his pet architect, searched for like a Derby winner, and run him against his colleagues' candidates.'[84]

To appreciate Reilly's early achievement it is necessary to understand the overall position before 1926. Most banks distinguished between architects for branches and architects for head offices, or offices of exceptional importance. The mention already made of London shows the calibre of architects chosen for the more prestigious commissions, although in-house or trusted external architects advised on interior layout. For more normal branches, the practice varied considerably, as the following résumé indicates.

The Midland gave nearly all work to T.B. Whinney (of Whinney, Son & Austen Hall), Woolfall & Eccles of Liverpool, and Gotch & Saunders of Kettering. However, two new firms were added: Brierley & Rutherford of York, introduced by the London Joint Stock Bank in 1918, and Elcock & Sutcliffe, who did branches as far apart as Harrow and Ripon. Lloyds had a less rigid policy, using a variety of contract and staff architects for small branches, reserving more important commissions for Edward Maufe,[85] introduced via the Capital &

Counties Bank in 1918, and Horace Field, Lloyds' own discovery in the late nineteenth century. The Westminster Bank had much the same policy as Lloyds using W. Campbell Jones and E. Guy Dawber for normal branches, and Mewès & Davis for important work in London. Barclays were quite eclectic, giving local branches to architects who were also customers.[86] In the north, the District Bank used Francis Jones, the very talented partner in Jones & Dalrymple, continuing a policy of imaginative building which stretched back more than 50 years.

A different policy was pursued by the National Provincial Bank. After experimenting with various architects between 1920 and 1922, the bank gave virtually all subsequent work to two salaried officers who rapidly gained great experience. These men were F.C.R. Palmer and W.F.C. Holden. At first known as surveyor and assistant surveyor, they were retitled architect and assistant architect from about 1923.[87] This was an astonishing partnership. No more fitting sequel to the rich period of Gibson could possibly have been found and Reilly never mastered his own amazement.

By definition alone, the position of salaried architect was disliked by Reilly. Running against his principles of patronage, it suggested an element of cautious subservience, hardly conducive to free-ranging architectural expression.[88] And yet Palmer and Holden were so good that time after time he could only admit their success, groping for points of criticism, marvelling at the consistent standard of such a formidable output, scratching his head at their versatility. 'I do not know the history of Messrs. Palmer and Holden,' he wrote in 1932, 'but . . . they must have been caught young.'[89] In fact, it is impossible to generalise on the characteristics of their work. They seemed equally at ease with a three-gabled, jettied, and half-timbered bank at Ludlow;[90] a classic neo-Georgian branch at Edgware — more a town house than a bank;[91] and a scholarly, delicate interpretation of Palladio's Loggia del Capitanio at Vicenza for a routine branch in Chelmsford[92] (Plate 66).

When Palmer died in 1935, Reilly wrote a touching tribute to the man he had never met and wondered if the standard could continue.[93] But Holden rose to the occasion, producing in Osterley[94] (Plate 67), the following year, the kind of branch which Reilly had always wondered if the partnership could produce — a bank in a really modern style. Osterley was a triumph, a thoroughly purposeful bank, neither too big nor too small, original in design, functional without austerity. The banking area was bright and spacious, the light falling

Plate 66. *Palmer & Holden's Chelmsford branch of the National Provincial Bank,
1925. This building is now a branch of the Midland Bank.*

full in the customer's face (without dazzling him), the great desider-
atum of Gilbart and, more recently, of Hembrow.[95] The doors were of
teak, the counter fronts of laurel-wood veneer, and the public space
laid in slabs of travertine, which was beginning to replace the more
expensive marble in most branches. (The alternative to travertine was
rubber but it was meeting customer resistance.[96]) Above all, the bank
was sympathetic to its environment, harmonising with the new factory
for Gillette nearby; apparently the architects collaborated on the siting
of the bank and the choice of materials.[97] Reilly was beaten, without
regret, recrimination, or even, it seemed, awareness of his own past
prejudice. 'By virtue of his salaried position', he wrote in 1939,

'Holden is freer in his attack than usual bank architects ... he can suggest all kinds of new things.'[98] Never had a *volte-face* been so painless.

In the case of the other banks, Reilly was very much the winner, gradually raising the tempo of his criticism. He disliked the architect who had 120 branches in hand at once (in Reilly's eyes 100 too many), but it was some years before the culprit could be identified with the Midland.[99] By then, in any case, the work of Lutyens had softened most of Reilly's dislike for the bank's past habits: he reckoned Lutyens's commissions 'may alter the whole outlook in England towards bank buildings.'[100] Lloyds he favoured more from the start, but had no time for their use of so-called building inspectors. His attack culminated in 1937, when he described them as 'largely ex-office boys and bank clerks who had drifted into the department and waited there to be promoted by seniority ...'[101] This was unkind, and partly inaccurate,[102] resting on the information of one of Reilly's ex-students who had had a temporary job in their department. Reilly did not name Lloyds in his attack, but took pains to eliminate the alternatives. Barclays, in the early years, fared worse than anyone. Reilly was deeply troubled by a situation where scarcely two banks together were by the same architect. Only pleasant standard lettering saved Barclays' 2000 local branches from total disharmony.[103]

His influence was quick and positive. The Westminster discovered Septimus Warwick, whose designs found favour at the Royal Academy,[104] and Barclays gave more and more work to Peacock & Bewlay, particularly in the Midlands where they showed versatility and taste. As for Martin's Bank, Robert Holland Martin, president of the Architecture Club, delighted Reilly with a policy statement in 1927 that his company would in future take the greatest care in the selection of architects.[105] Their best work was done by Darcy Braddell, of Braddell & Deane, whose Maidstone branch was a particular favourite of the contemporary press.[106]

But Reilly's greatest success was with Lloyds. In his opening article, entitled 'Bank Directors and Architecture', Reilly had thrown down a challenge: 'Which of the five great banks', he asked, 'has yet had the good sense as well as the distinction, and even the appreciation of advertisement value, to employ one of the returned Rome scholars in architecture?'[107] The idea appealed immediately to Sir Austin Harris, Lloyds' deputy chairman, and the case was argued through the Premises Committee in October 1926.[108] In future, Lloyds would give one branch bank design to every returning Rome scholar, and in

Plate 67. Above: W.F.C. Holden's Osterley branch of the National Provincial Bank, 1936. Opposite: interior.

practice this arrangement included at least one man who had returned some years previously.[109] The early commissions were wholly successful, as Reilly had predicted. The *Banker*, in an editorial, paid tribute to the acceptance of 'a duty which, in any other country, would fall to the Government.'[110] Reilly himself, even many years later, never lost sight of his gratitude.

This was a spectacular boost for Reilly's new series, a triumph for architect and banker alike. The first Rome scholar employed was H.C. Chalton Bradshaw, for Caversham branch.[111] His orthodox style pleased Lloyds, who gave him other work later at Crowborough and

Caterham-on-the-Hill. Even better was the work of P.D. Hepworth, whose memorable Southwark branch was completed in 1928[112] (Plate 68). Hepworth used his experience in house designs to good effect, producing a three-floor, three-bay building with all the reticence of the best neo-Georgians and yet enough classical features and a skilful use of stone facing to remove any domestic ambiguity. This was demonstrably a bank, even without the name on the fascia carried through the arches — a novel idea in itself. In this year, Lloyds, with their more-established architects like Horace Field and Edward Maufe doing fine work at Richmond and Muswell Hill, must have felt they could do little wrong.

And yet even here was the seed of disillusion. Ten years of variation on a Georgian theme were too much for some sectors of architectural opinion. On the one hand, students' designs, 30 years earlier the barometer of taste, were still neo-Georgian in 1931 and 1932;[113] on the other hand, reporting of new branch banks had almost ceased in the architectural journals. As far as Lloyds was concerned, the Rome scholars brought the problem home. Staines branch of 1930[114] by S. Rowland Pierce, gave ominous notice of something more modern. Then came Orpington in 1931,[115] by Edwin Williams, and the bank was facing a problem.

Plate 68. P.D. Hepworth's Southwark branch of Lloyds Bank, 1928.

Lloyds, who would have been looking to the Rome scholars for other branches like Southwark, could not really have wanted at Orpington a building which local people called 'Hindenburg's pill-box'.[116] The architectural press tried weakly to make the best of things, suggesting the nickname was a compliment to security and strength: 'Has not the quick wit of the general public seized unconsciously on a merit of the design, and emphasized it by a somewhat crude label?'[117] Reilly liked it, not least because Williams had been his pupil.[118] But the untrained eye saw just a plain little box, with a door to the left, two three-light steel windows, a flat roof, and a paved forecourt. This was acceptable functionalism, but was it Orpington?

The discomfort of Lloyds was not helped by Teddington branch, designed by A. Randall Wells, today a 'listed' building, but at the time (1929) a challenge to the limits of bankers' tolerance (Plate 69). Seen 'with surprise and pleasure' by one journal,[119] Teddington was quite out of character with Lloyds' traditional building styles. The recessed curve of the external wall was enhanced and complimented by every surrounding feature. The windows and doorway were round-arched, the latter supporting a sphere like a globe in a cage, the whole suggesting a sculptor's feel for the expression of form and mass. This was a new geometrical form for a bank, but one which was appropriate. The circle expressed continuity, self-containment and endlessness, aspects which had endeared it to the architecture of religion for centuries, while the globe gave more worldly insight into the ubiquity of banking. With proper conformity, the interior was characterised by rounded arches and ceiling vault. Again, Reilly was delighted. Other banks, he thought, found it easier to be dull than to be brave;[120] to Lloyds he gave the title of the most adventurous of the Big Five,[121] a title they may not have wanted. On the rare occasions when Lloyds wished to be really different, as with Church Street, Liverpool branch, they first asked Reilly for his opinion.[122]

The last Rome scholar branch to be completed seems to have been Welwyn Garden City, designed by Marshall Sissons in 1929 and opened in 1931.[123] The style was safely neo-Georgian but it was too late to rediscover the mood of 6 years earlier. Reilly soon began to worry that the Rome scholars scheme had been abandoned by Lloyds,[124] and there is certainly no evidence of later commissions. Meanwhile, neo-Georgian became deeper in disgrace and one journal was openly referring to 'the stupidities of the Georgian revival'.[125] Comparisons were now being made once again with America where the premises of the Philadelphia Savings Fund Society, designed by Howe and Lascaze, were described by Reilly as the 'First Great Modern Bank Building'.[126]

Ironically, the banks were saved from further problems by the Great Depression. By 1934 the rate of new building, which had stood in the late 'twenties at around 300 branches a year, had fallen so low that Reilly had to cast around for his material. He, too, was now rejecting revivalism and making open and urgent requests for a totally modern style. Each little pointer to a contemporary trend, like the use of steel windows in Mitchell & Bridgwater's otherwise conventional branch of Barclays at Horley,[127] was analysed and welcomed. When rebuilding picked up in the late 1930s the good relations of 10 years earlier

Plate 69. Above: A. Randall Wells's Teddington branch of Lloyds Bank, 1929.
Opposite: interior.

between the professions of banker and architect, as expressed in the journals, had broken down. A new surge of Georgian-style branches was largely ignored; the extravagant coverage of 1928 was replaced by neglect, punctuated only by comment on a few banks of unusual size or significance.

Perhaps the most important of these was the new Liverpool headquarters of the Bank of Liverpool & Martins, opened in 1932. The six competitive designs, of which Reilly had been an assessor, were on view at the Royal Institute of British Architects in 1926.[128] Some, particularly the drawing by the local firm of Willink & Dod, showed more than a hint of American influence. The winning design was by Herbert J. Rowse, who was thereby assured of continued local commissions, the most important being India Buildings in Water Street.[129] However, this was in every sense a 'twenties design and Reilly kept looking in vain for something wholly expressive of the 1930s. Certainly there were good banks being built, such as the Municipal Bank in Birmingham by Cecil T. Howitt, opened in 1933,[130] and Lutyens's Midland Bank branch in King Street, Manchester, opened in 1935.[131] The Birmingham building represented, in banking terms, a new kind of institution. The result of this was an appearance which distinguished it from the contemporary styles of the competitors. The treatment was a clean neo-Greek, influenced by the nearby Masonic Temple and smacking of the savings banks of 100 years earlier, as well as of American provincial designs which were much more recent. The press saw a pleasing contrast with the nearby 'grotesque' and misapplied Victorian Gothic.[132] Likewise, the Midland's Manchester branch, in bluff, white contrast to its surroundings, was 'a further step in the reclamation of the city centre from its 19th century architectural gloom.'[133] The design, however, dated from 1928, and Reilly remained restless.

In 1936, however, the year in which he was gratified by Holden's National Provincial Bank branch at Osterley, Reilly was also much heartened by an Edinburgh bank. This building, in George Street, was to provide temporary accommodation for the National Bank of Scotland while its headquarters were rebuilt in St Andrew Square.[134] The architects of the George Street bank were Thomas P. Marwick and Son, who produced a striking elevation (Plate 70), the bank's board having decided on a modern design. 'For a great British Bank', said Reilly, 'to think of clothing itself in anything but the fancy dress of some ten generations back and to show faith instead in the materials and manners of its own time, is . . . a very novel experiment.'[135] It was, of course, safer to do this for a temporary head office than the real thing, but Reilly's comment was fair. If the architects had not been constrained to some extent by the need to retain parts of the building already existing — which affected the interior planning and the site of the George Street entrance — perhaps something even more radical would have ensued. As it was, there were innovations enough for banking eyes: a stone-faced façade of restraint and clarity, reducing traditional figure sculpture to five panels by Thomas Whalen above the second floor windows, and limiting self-advertisement to the name of the company reproduced in the railings. The wall spaces above dazzled in their inviolacy. Within, arrangements were planned with the same level of imaginative treatment. The banking hall was not to the left of the entrance, where it might have been expected, given the length of the window-range, but towards the rear where confidence in modern lighting techniques outweighed conventional reliance on the benefits of natural light. The rounded, sculpturesque forms and colour variations matched the boldness of the planning. The walls were finished with Indian red gum veneer, the ceilings with textured paint applied to canvas over wallboard, or direct to wallboard in the panels of the banking-hall ceiling. The floor was laid with linoleum of various colours, giving a sense of circulation and direction. Furniture was generally of mahogany blockboard, finished in walnut, while chairs were upholstered in dark green corduroy or natural hide, and desk tops inset with green rubber.

It is impossible to disagree with Reilly's assessment of the general sterility of bank design towards the end of the 1930s — a sterility which

Osterley and Edinburgh, and a few other exceptions, served only to accentuate by their relative success. Fortunately, the Second World War brought a cessation of building and therefore, viewed with hindsight, a reprieve from the disaster which would have overtaken many of the clearing banks if their architectural practices had continued. The Georgian grip was inescapable. In a society still structured by class, where a bank account for non-business reasons was a mark of the bourgeoisie, it was impossible in bankers' eyes to find any formula of derivative design which expressed sentiments more proper and at the same time more domestic. Yet with the architectural press on another course, with Reilly looking more each year like a malevolent headmaster, a total alienation between banker and critic was very much a possibility.

It can be argued that Reilly's influence in the war years was less than constructive. By clinging to his series until 1944, repeating comments and photographs of 10 years earlier, he gave the banks little guidance for their policy of the future. Reilly's last article attempted a prophetic look at post-war urban conditions.[136] Set in some planned new-town environment, banks would build and finance massive buildings, occupying only the ground floor but seeming to inhabit the whole. While in some ways anticipating the work of the later bank property companies, the vision was closer to the style of building which Liverpool had experienced more than 20 years earlier, with such buildings as the National Bank in James Street. So in the end it was Reilly himself who seemed incapable of escaping the trammels of the past, while his lack of interest in the layout and decoration of interiors doomed the formidable collection of his writings to have no relevance in the issues which were to dominate the post-war years.

In the analysis of those years, the temptation must be resisted to over simplify. And yet the growing interest and involvement of traditionally unadventurous clearing banks in overseas business and branches, the equally strong interest of foreign banks in the British market, and the steady erosion of definition between banks and other financial institutions, has created a complexity of background not necessarily irrelevant to building design but impracticable to analyse in a study of this kind. Instead there are three factors of quite a different nature which must steer the study of bank buildings in the second half of the twentieth century into new considerations.

The first factor is the rise of planning control. Certain elementary planning powers have been mentioned in earlier chapters and wider powers became available pre-war if authorities chose to adopt the

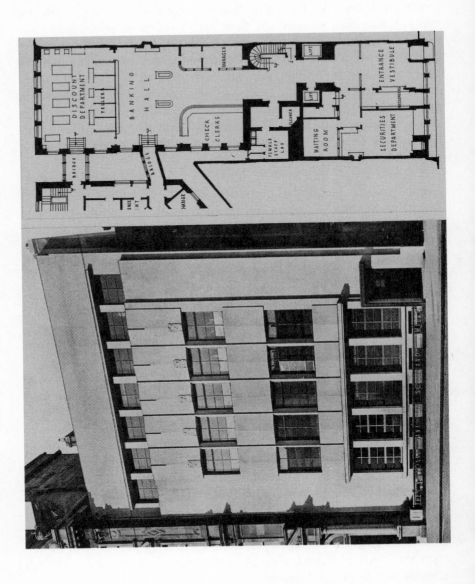

Plate 70. Elevation, ground plan, decorative panel, and interior of Thomas P. Marwick & Sons's temporary Edinburgh head office of the National Bank of Scotland, 1936.

provisions of the 1932 Act. But the post-war legislation introduced new dimensions of control, including the preservation of buildings of architectural or historic interest.[137] Although not at first intended for the preservation of Victorian buildings such as banks, the Acts led to a growing awareness of the importance of commercial monuments and the preservation of many fine urban façades which might otherwise have been demolished by the companies who built them, or their successors.

What this represented essentially was the transfer to officialdom of the aims of the pressure groups and conservationist lobbies of earlier times. Unfortunately, the loss of amateur status was not marked by a consistency of attitude and action on the part of the professionals. A national bank, negotiating changes and alterations through several scores of local councils, found variations of policy which could scarcely have been predicted.

The Chichester controversy of 1958 was a case in point.[138] Barclays wished, as others had done before them, to rebuild their East Street branch in a neo-Georgian style harmonious with the character of the city. But the City Council, acting on behalf of West Sussex County Council, refused planning permission. They wanted a twentieth century design. There was a danger, they thought, of Chichester becoming 'merely a pseudo-Georgian city lacking the refinements of 18th-century architecture.'[139] The authorities were supported by the Georgian Group and the Royal Fine Art Commission. The logic of this aesthetic stance was no help to bankers in establishing their architectural policy when, with their next project, they might face a determinedly conservationist council at Totnes or Tewkesbury.

It is against this background that branches such as the National Provincial Bank at Canterbury (Plate 71) must be seen. Completed in 1956, it was designed to stand alongside a future open market place.[140] The cladding was Portland stone, slate, and Roman stone, the window frames were generally of aluminium, with bronze for the curved bay lighting the banking-hall. The clock was in blue faience. Within, the emphasis was on teak veneer and joinery with travertine-lined walls and a marble floor. The building was composite, in that other floors were let to shops and offices. Today, of course, this is exactly the sort of development which tops the league of unpopularity. Such colours and materials are found garish, even tawdry, the building as a whole more evocative of suburban Staines than medieval Canterbury. Unfortunately, this style of presentation had a long vogue and, allowing for some technological improvements, would have been broadly acceptable even 10 or 15 years later. In judging this, with hindsight, to have been a regrettable building, we should nevertheless give the bank credit for conscientious and responsible behaviour. The location had not been forgotten. Cast bronze medallions in the main door were replicas of old coins, one of which had been found in Canterbury itself, and a large, interesting mural in the banking hall had been commissioned from the Canterbury College of Art. There was opportunity for comment and consultation at every stage of the planning and approval. What has changed is not the environmental concern of the banks but our perception of concern for the environment.

As far as 'listed' buildings were concerned, the problem was at first no easier. It has been suggested in one article that 'bankers like other urban property interests find ... restrictions ... unpalatable, and have been heard to instruct their architects to design nothing that could conceivably ever be listed at any point in the future.'[141] If this was so, then it was as much a reaction to inconsistencies of attitude to the merits of commercial buildings as a statement of insensitive policy on the part of the bankers themselves. Gibson's National Provincial Bank head office and Mewès & Davis's Threadneedle Street branch were saved, but not before the demolition of the Birkbeck Bank in Chancery Lane, and of the Westminster and Lloyds Bank branches in Colmore Row, Birmingham, part of what was considered in the late 'sixties to be 'a frontage badly scarred by third rate architecture.'[142] If Colmore Row were intact today it would be regarded as a magnificent example of Victorian urban exuberance. But if better national guidelines now exist for the identification of valuable façades, there has been little outcry beyond the ranks of specialist societies against the destruction of mahogany counters and pillared domes, leaving interiors aesthetically divorced from the street elevation so that the architectural integrity of the latter is that of a propped façade in a film set. It will be shown below how the interior of a bank has become, as it had never been before, a more potent marketing tool than the exterior.

The second major factor to influence post-war bank design was part of the wider interest in the management and exploitation of urban buildings. From the late 1950s, speculating financiers were buying up retail businesses, selling freeholds to other companies who would lease them back the buildings. In this way, extensive capital was gained for improving retail trade or buying up other concerns.[143] Banks could stay aloof from this movement until town or city centre redevelopments embraced their own premises. Involvement in property speculation was an area of which banks had traditionally fought shy, but the temptation

Plate 71. Above: B.C. Sherren's Canterbury branch of the National Provincial Bank, 1957. Below: interior.

to redevelop their own freehold land for wider commercial advantage was, in the end, irresistible, and coincided with other impulses to expand and update the branch network. The result was that banks set up their own property companies in the early 1960s, demolishing established buildings and replacing them by a functional unit of shops, bank and offices, usually to the detriment of the townscape. The scale and speed of these creations militated against architectural representations being anything better than perfunctory.

Similar considerations of property management were responsible for a number of first-floor banks, reached from the ground by escalators, a principle which Barclays had pioneered at Cardiff in 1956.[144] The rationale for first-floor banking was that high city centre rents made it more profitable to lease the ground floor for retail shops than to bank on the ground floor and lease the upper floors as offices. By the same logic, Martin's Bank, choosing a site in Watford in 1962, leased the ground-floor front to a shop and placed themselves behind it.[145] This was, of course, a negation of one of the traditional philosophies of banking, that premises were a legitimate and necessary form of self-advertisement. Other values were undermined by the mood of the architectural press. One bank in London, for instance, was said to have departed 'from the worn-out banking tradition of the corner entrance ... which no longer makes commercial or functional sense.'[146] Victorian architects 'whose banking architecture did so much to de-value classicism in England'[147] were treated as roughly as their buildings.

The third, and most elusive factor has been changes in technology. If the basic element common to all banking-halls was the counter, so the importance of this division diminished as cash gave way to alternative systems of credit transfer, and to machine-dispensed money. At the heart of this change has been the computer, breaking down traditional office designs as surely as it has removed from sight the mechanics of calculation, payment and control. This technology coincided with competition from the building societies and the arrival in London of American banks, with their open and informal relationships between staff and customer precincts. British banks tried various experiments in return, juggling with the arrangement of desks and service points, brightening the public space with murals, and even, at Lowestoft, attempting something like a maritime museum.[148]

The most determined attempt to modernise was by the Midland, even before the computer was in any way common. Following half a century of devolution of work to outside architects, its premises department was the smallest among the major banks. It lacked, for instance, the wide-ranging brief of Lloyds', where managerial function had divided into estates' and architects' departments in 1945, the former dealing with the interpretation of the policy of the directors and general management, the latter with expenditure upon buildings and their contents. To keep pace with the renovation and expansion of its branches, the Midland was using over 60 firms of local architects by 1961,[149] compared with their traditional use of just a handful. But there was more to modernisation than changing the appearance of a building, and every aspect of the bank's presentation needed scrutiny. The Midland were warned in 1964 that their publicity booklet was still advocating a bank account that 'lifts you several degrees up the social scale in the eyes of a lot of people.'[150] In the same year, the bank set up a design panel, responsible to the Management Committee, 'to initiate and maintain a consistent corporate image throughout all printed communication, equipment and premises.'[151] One result of this was a new concept in bank design based on the use of a flexible system of components. The scheme was tried first at Loughton, then at Cambridge, and later extended to about a hundred branches.[152] With wall-to-wall carpeting uniting public and staff areas, with freedom from the linear prison of a running counter, the Midland publicised a breakthrough.[153] But then security became the overriding factor, and, with the universal introduction of the bandit screen, informality of contact seemed as far away as ever.

The way forward from this stalemate in all banks has been indicated by information technology. As the counter-run has become redundant, so has the need for staff to maintain many of the services with which the counter has so long been associated. Machines can receive and dispense money faster than people and with more accuracy. They cannot (yet) say 'Good morning, Mr Jones, How nice to see you!' while they do it, but Mr Jones is believed to be no longer in the mood for these traditional courtesies when making minor transactions. For instance, there exist lobbies, operated by plastic card, which dispense money when the Mr Jones of past generations was probably in bed. But is such a lobby a 'bank' in itself? And as we look forward to the introduction, before the turn of the present century, of outlets of retail banking — not simply cash lobbies — automated to the exclusion of most, or even all, staff, will not this dilemma of identity get worse?

Against this trend, however, run other more humanising factors and it is here that the blurring of functions between the practitioners of money is working to continue the last vestiges of local banking relationships. As competition increases, so banks have had to lose their image of domination of the customer (which the marble-halled head offices of the 1920s had done nothing to diminish) and replace it by customer enticement. The emphasis is not on banking, but on banking services, expressive of the multiplicity of activities, which have replaced the passive introversion of earlier years. In the fight for business, an open-planned office, comfortable chairs, a smiling face and a corporate uniform are much more effective than echoes from a cold floor and voices strained through a bandit screen. Win over the *person* and the business will follow automatically. Although the attitude, practice and premises of the private banker may be gone for good, the local bank is now a money shop in a way even more literal than the connotation he had intended and understood.

As the trends in the last paragraph become fully realised then the future for bank design in Britain during the next century will lie not in branches but in the building of regional centres for handling marketing functions or responsibilities devolved from head office. The new Bristol headquarters of the United Kingdom Retail Banking Division of Lloyds Bank are a case in point. As for head offices themselves, it may be that the recent (1986) building for the Standard Chartered Bank in Bishopsgate, designed by The Fitzroy Robinson Partnership, marks the end of the line, in so far as integrated central control is concerned. If so, then the success of the design, championing the cause of urban foliage within outer walls in a manner pioneered amongst bankers by Coutts in the Strand, is a fitting valediction.[154] In scale, however, the Standard Chartered Bank premises are likely to be nearer the concept for future bank offices than the famous National Westminster Tower, opened in 1981 (Plate 72). Designed by R. Seifert & Partners, the tower epitomises the confidence of the City in the heady years before Big Bang, the stock market collapse, and the millstones of Third World debt and recession. Ironically, the tower was opened not as a head office for the National Westminster Bank (that remained at Lothbury) but as a centre for the bank's international arm. It is unlikely that another such conspicuous dedication to overseas business will be seen in the City for a very long time to come, or indeed that any clearing bank will ever build on that scale again.

So if underlying assumptions of confidence and success will not be the hallmark of bankers' buildings to come, what qualities will they portray? The answer lies in the other less dramatic virtues of permanence, stability and respectability by which bank designs have

Plate 72. R. Seifert & Co.'s National Westminster Tower, opened 1981.

traditionally been governed. From these will be distilled only a bland essence of 'safeness', mixing comfortably with a new ingredient of user-friendliness from which customers, staff and the environment should have everything to gain.

References

The following abbreviations have been used:

A.	*Architect*
A. & B.N.	*Architect & Building News*
A. & B.J.	*Architects' & Builders' Journal*
A.J.	*Architects' Journal*
A.M. & J.	*Architectural Magazine & Journal*
Ann. Reg.	*Annual Register*
A.P.S.D.	*Architectural Publication Society Dictionary*
A.R.	*Architectural Review*
B.	*Builder*
Ba.	*Banker*
B.M.	*Bankers' Magazine*
B.N.	*Building News*
B. of E.	Bank of England
B.P.P.	*British Parliamentary Papers*
C.E. & A.J.	*Civil Engineer & Architect's Journal*
C.L.	*Country Life*
Colvin	the appropriate entry in H.M. Colvin, *A Biographical Dictionary of British Architects 1600–1840* (London, 1978)
D.N.B.	*Dictionary of National Biography*
G.M.	*Gentleman's Magazine*
I.L.N.	*Illustrated London News*
J.H.C.	*Journal of the House of Commons*
J.I.B.	*Journal of the Institute of Bankers*
J.R.I.B.A.	*Journal of the Royal Institute of British Architects*
Pevsner	the appropriate volume of N. Pevsner *et al.* (eds), *The Buildings of England* series or *The Buildings of Scotland* series
P.R.O.	Public Record Office
Q.R.	*Quarterly Review*
W.R.	*Westminster Review*

Chapter One

1 The commentary in W.S. Lewis & A. Dayle Wallace (eds), *Horace Walpole Correspondence* ... Vol. 32 (London & New Haven, 1965) does not refer to the

definition of shop, but the point was made in the extract from the letter in P. Clarke, *The First House in the City* (London, 1973).

2 *I.L.N.*, Vol. 1 (1842), p.344.

3 Named after the merchants and financiers of Lombardy who settled there in the twelfth century.

4 Mynors Bright (ed), *The Diary of Samuel Pepys*, Vol. 3 (London, Everyman Library, 1953), p.189.

5 J. Strype, *A Survey of the Cities of London and Westminster . . . written at first . . . by John Stow . . .*, Vol. 1 (London, 1720), pp.162, 163.

6 This was the effect of the provision in 6 Anne, c.22, s.9 which prevented more than six persons uniting in partnership to issue banknotes. See Chapter Two for more detailed commentary.

7 Under 7 Anne, c.30, s.58.

8 Sir J. Summerson, *Georgian London* (London, 1962), p.64. See also Colvin, *sub* Sampson.

9 W. Marston Acres, *The Bank of England from Within*, Vol. 1 (London, 1931), pp.167, 168. This book is very useful for all questions affecting Bank of England properties.

10 B. of E., Court Book, 16/11/1727–27/7/1732, p.241.

11 Ibid., p.242. Marston Acres, op. cit., p.168, writes: '. . . they reported to the Court that they "could not agree upon which to choose but they had several objections to both".' The wording is not quite accurate and is formed by an elision of two clauses, but the sentence as a whole is a good precis of the committee's report.

12 B. of E., Court Book, loc. cit.

13 Ibid.; cf. Marston Acres op. cit., p.168.

14 B. of E., Ancillary Papers to Court Book, 16/11/1727–27/7/1732. For Joynes, see Colvin, *sub* Joynes.

15 Reproduced in *An Historical Catalogue of Engravings, Drawings and Paintings in the Bank of England* (1928), p.3, No. 10. See also, M. Binney, 'Sir Robert Taylor's Bank of England' in *C.L.* 13/11/1969, p.1247, and Colvin, *sub* Jacobsen.

16 Marston Acres, op. cit., p.170. Sampson was paid £200 as surveyor and a gratuity of £105.

17 Ibid., pp.168, 169; cf. *G.M.*, Vol. 2 (1732), p.925.

18 Marston Acres, op. cit., p.198.

19 T. Malton, *A Picturesque Tour through the Cities of London and Westminster . . .* (London, 1742; plates 1792–1801), p.76: 'The Bank next claims our attention . . . The central part was erected . . . by Mr. George Sampson; it is designed in a tolerable good style, and the parts are simple and bold. The wings, which have been added . . . by the late Sir Robert Taylor, are uncommonly elegant; but they certainly do not harmonize with the central building, nor are they properly subordinate' (plate LXIII).

20 Talor's obit. in *G.M.*, Vol. 58 (1788, ii), p.930.

21 By 3 & 4 Anne, c.9.

22 In 1714.

23 Extracts from 'Banking in London', prefatory chapter in M. Phillips, *A History of Banks, Bankers & Banking in Northumberland, Durham and North Yorkshire* (London, 1894).

24 D. Hardcastle, jr, *Banks and Bankers* (London, 1842), pp.22, 23.

25 Colvin, *sub* Taylor, states the few places where a copy of Malton's aquatint can be found.

26 F.G. Hilton Price, *A Handbook of London Bankers* (London, 1890–1), pp.88, 123.

27 J.F. Wadmore, *Some Account of the Worshipful Company of Skinners* ... (London, 1902), p.189.

28 Wadmore, op. cit., p.149; Hilton Price, p.123.

29 C. Hussey, 'Asgill House, Richmond, Surrey', in *C.L.*, 9/6/1944; M. Binney, 'The Villas of Sir Robert Taylor' in ibid., 6–13/7/1967.

30 *G.M.*, Vol. 58 (1788, ii), p.930.

31 F.G. Hilton Price, 'Some Account of Lombard Street ...', in *J.I.B.*, Vol. 7 (1886), p.342.

32 Hilton Price, *Handbook* ..., p.66; R. Fulford, *Glyn's 1753–1953* (London, 1953), pp.2, 7.

33 Fulford, op. cit., p.9.

34 H. Bolitho & D. Peel, *The Drummonds of Charing Cross* (London, 1967) pp.45, 191.

35 Ibid.

36 Ibid., p.45; L.C.C., *Survey of London*, Vol. 16 (London, 1935), pp.103, 109, 110, quoting P.R.O., Works 6/35, pp.144, 152, 153.

37 Bolitho & Peel, op. cit., p.44, who refer to an abortive drawing now at the Soane Museum 'of an elegant façade with an elaborate horizontal plaque'.

38 Bolitho & Peel, loc. cit.

39 Hilton Price, op. cit., p.47; Cunningham, *Hand-Book of London Past and Present* (London, 1850), p.476; A.T. Bolton, *The Architecture of Robert & James Adam*, Vol. 2 (London, 1922), p.39.

40 Colvin, *sub* Paine, quoting also unpub. Oxford D.Phil. thesis on Paine by Peter Leach (1975). See also E.H. Coleridge, *The Life of Thomas Coutts Banker*, Vol. 1 (London, 1920), p.72n. However, Coleridge, Vol. 1 (pp. 43, 44), perpetuated the belief that the Adam brothers had been employed 'to rebuild or reconstruct' No. 59, The Strand.

41 Summerson, op. cit., p.64.

42 14 Geo. III, c.78 (1774).

43 By Herries, Farquhar & Co., bankers at 16 St James's Street.

44 Sir J. Clapham, *The Bank of England*, Vol. 1 (Cambridge, 1944), p.215.

45 Coleridge, op. cit., pp.43–6.

46 Colvin, *sub* Paine.

47 Coleridge, loc. cit.

48 Ibid.

49 Fulford, op. cit., pp.59, 60, 165.

50 Ibid.

51 Ibid., pp.61, 164.

52 Clarke, op. cit., pp.15, 16.

53 P.W. Matthews & A.W. Tuke, *History of Barclays Bank Limited* (London, 1926), p.83.

54 *Survey of London*, loc. cit.

55 Bolitho & Peel, op. cit., p.111.

56 Ibid., p.75.

57 Ibid., p.95; D. Stroud, *Henry Holland* (London, 1966), pp.23, 39, 40, 53;

D. Linstrum, *Sir Jeffry Wyatville* (Oxford, 1972), pp.137–40, 232–3, etc., pl. 108, fig. 19.

58 K. Woodbridge, *Landscape & Antiquity* (Oxford, 1970), pp.1, 19–21, etc.; *C.L.*, 6/3/1958, pp.450–3.

59 *C.L.*, loc. cit.; but see Colvin, *sub* Flitcroft, for problem of New Hall. For Luscombe, see C. Hussey, *English Country Houses: Late Georgian 1800–1840* (London, 1958), pp.18, 55–65.

60 Colvin, *sub* Paine.

61 Colvin, *sub* Basevi; D. Stroud, *The Architecture of Sir John Soane* (London, 1961), p.80.

62 Colvin, *sub* Soane.

63 *B.N.*, Vol. 26 (1874, Part 1), p.228.

64 *A.R.*, Vol. 15 (1772), p.110.

65 Letters in Northumbs. R.O. (ref. 2DE. 36/2/1–88) from Oliver Farrer of Chancery Lane to Sir John Hussey Delaval, Bart., inform him of the imminent bankruptcy of Messrs Glyn & Hallifax. cf. Fulford, op. cit., pp.14–37.

66 From 1797 to 1821 the Bank of England did not honour its promise to convert its banknotes into cash on demand.

67 G. Chandler, *Four Centuries of Banking*, Vol. 1 (London, 1964), p.218.

68 A.D. Gayer, W.W. Rostow & A.J. Schwartz, *The Growth & Fluctuation of the British Economy 1790–1850*, Vol. 2 (Oxford, 1953), p.535.

69 Stroud, op. cit., pp.65–79; Summerson, op. cit., pp.155–8; Marston Acres, op. cit., Vol. 2 (1931), pp.392–411. See also H.R. Steele & F.R. Yerbury, *The Old Bank of England* (London, 1930) and descriptions in A.C. Pugin & J. Britton, *Public Buildings of London* (London, 2nd ed., 1838).

70 Many of these criticisms are detailed in Marston Acres, op. cit., pp.409, 410.

71 Colvin, *sub* Soane.

72 Cunningham, op. cit., p.29.

73 D. Stroud, *George Dance Architect 1741–1825* (London, 1971), p.159.

74 The illustration in Miss Stroud's book differs from the plate in J.B. Martin, 'The Grasshopper' in Lombard Street* (London, 1892), while a third variation exists in a drawing in the Guildhall Library.

75 Colvin, *sub* Leverton.

76 Hilton Price, op. cit., p.143.

77 A. Graves, *The Royal Academy of Arts. A Complete Dictionary of Contributors ... 1769–1904*, Vol. 5 (1906), p.48.

78 However, designs for the National Bank of Ireland were exhibited in 1800 and for the Bank of Scotland in 1807, and many of Soane's plans for the Bank of England were shown from as early as 1792 (Graves).

79 Colvin, *sub* Leverton.

80 Malton, op. cit., p.32.

81 *B.N.*, Vol. 7 (1861), p.359.

82 Stroud, *Soane . . .*, p.82, and plates. Miss Stroud states No. 90, Fleet Street, and according to Hilton Price, op. cit., p.132, it became No. 71 in 1810. But directories have No. 189 from 1812, the year in which Soane made certain alterations to the rear of the bank (Stroud, loc. cit.).

83 Stroud, loc. cit.

84 *Times*, 5/1/1802: 'That elegant new Building just erected in Fleet Street . . .'.

85 Letter from Thos. Salt to Howard Lloyd, 17/3/1893: 'We do not require C. Praeds house ... I have no fear of a good purchase ... but I am terrified of the Architect.' (Lloyds Bank Archives, ref. file 5460).

86 The virtue of seating clerks sideways to natural light was first expounded by J.W. Gilbart in 1849. See Chapter Two.

87 Hilton Price, op. cit., p.99.

88 Malton, op. cit., plate LIX. His illustration reveals the first half-dozen houses in Lombard Street, all similar with 'shop' ground floors and three or four storeys above, but he does not comment.

89 J. Tallis, *London Street Views* ... (London, 1838–40). When Lombard Street is shown, it is a passing glimpse from an adjacent thoroughfare.

90 *B.N.*, Vol. 7 (1861), p.359.

91 Colvin, *sub* Smirke.

92 P.R.O., CRES 6/93 (formerly L.R.R.O. 63/93), pp.275–82; L.C.C., *Survey of London*, Vol. 29 (London, 1960), p.381; *Monthly Magazine*, Vol. 43 (1817, i), p.399. The house was originally numbered 76, Pall Mall, but became No. 69 in about 1822 (directories).

93 *Monthly Magazine*, loc. cit.

94 Ibid.

95 Sir J. Summerson, *John Nash, Architect to King George IV* (2nd ed., London, 1949), p.206; *Appendix to Report from the Select Committee on the Woods, Forests and Land Revenues of the Crown* (London, 1848), p.136, refers to 99-year lease from 5/1/1819. For G.S. Repton, see Colvin, but bank is not listed among his works.

96 *A.P.S.D.*; Colvin, *sub* Atkinson.

97 Lloyds Bank Archives, ref. file 5180.

98 Hardcastle, op. cit., p.23.

99 Illus. in Summerson, *Georgian London*, plate 33.

100 J. Weale, *The Pictorial Handbook of London* ... (London, 1854), p.106.

101 *B*, Vol. 35 (1877), p.5.

102 Cf. E.B. Chancellor, *The London of Charles Dickens* (London, 1924).

103 See further, Chapters Two and Four. Another 'unpretending' nearby frontage was the ancient bank of Strahan, Paul & Co., at Temple Bar. This was rebuilt by the London & Westminster Bank in 1874 (*B*, Vol. 32 (1874), p.171).

104 L.S. Pressnell, *Country Banking in the Industrial Revolution* (Oxford, 1956), pp.4, 5.

105 C.H. Cave, *A History of Banking in Bristol* (Bristol, 1899), p.3.

106 The fullest discussion of these matters is in Pressnell, op. cit., pp.12–74.

107 Ibid. The modern clearing bank most closely connected with brewing is Barclays.

108 H. Ling Roth, *The Genesis of Banking in Halifax* ... (Halifax, 1914), pp.18, 19.

109 Ibid.

110 Ibid.

111 Ibid.

112 J. Hughes, *Liverpool Banks and Bankers 1760–1837* (Liverpool & London, 1906), p.56.

113 Ibid.

114 B. Trinder, *The Industrial Revolution in Shropshire* (Chichester 1973), p.234.

115 L.H. Grindon, *Manchester Banks and Bankers* ... (Manchester & London, 1877), p.38.

116 Cave, op. cit., p.43.
117 The articles of partnership of Hardy & Co. are reproduced as a plate in W.F. Crick & J.E. Wadsworth, *A Hundred Years of Joint Stock Banking* (London, 1936), opp. p.246.
118 Report in Harrop's *Manchester Mercury*, 12/11/1771, cit. Grindon, op. cit., p.4.
119 C. Brown, *The Annals of Newark-upon-Trent* (1879), p.2: 'Potter's ditch ... became Potter dike, but a banking-house being established there it changed its name to Lombard Street ...' The Portsmouth Lombard Street may have been named after Grant & Burbey, est. nearby in 1787.
120 *B.P.P.* (1831–2), vi, Q. 1155.
121 H. Clarkson, *Memories of Merry Wakefield* (Wakefield, 1887), p.163.
122 Ibid.
123 R.E. Leader, *Sheffield in the Eighteenth Century* (Sheffield, 1901), p.108.
124 J.A.S.L. Leighton-Boyce, *Smiths the Bankers 1658–1958* (London, 1958), pp.52, 140, 189.
125 Lloyds Bank Archives, A53/58b/1.
126 Cave, op. cit., p.100.
127 Now Lloyds Bank, Cirencester branch. Deeds (at branch) show occupation as bank at least by 1797.
128 Grindon, op. cit., p.79.
129 H. Heginbotham, *Stockport Ancient and Modern*, Vol. 2 (London, 1892), p.425.
130 At Tewkesbury, the building near the Cross still marked BANK was probably the premises of the Tewkesbury Old Bank, founded 1790; for Tavistock, article in *Western Morning News*, 27/4/1982, refers to 'purpose-built bank building from 1791'.
131 Booklet, 'Links with the Past. National Provincial Bank Limited, Sherborne', in paperback 'Banking in the South West of England' (Institute of Bankers' Library).
132 C.J. Billson, *Leicester Memories* (Leicester, 1924), p.27.
133 C. Mackie, *Norfolk Annals, vol. 1. 1801–1850* (Norwich, 1901), p.255.
134 Pevsner, *Yorkshire. The West Riding*, p.232, refers to 'John Royds, the banker'. For a study of the building, see D. Linstrum, *West Yorkshire Architects and Architecture* (London, 1978), pp.98, 99. See also Colvin, *sub* Carr.
135 At least by 1836: see Halifax town plan in J. Crabtree, *A Concise History of ... Halifax* (Halifax, 1836), marking 'Rawson's Bank'. cf. Ling Roth, op. cit., pp.28, 30–4.
136 Pressnell, op. cit., pp.50, 51; J. Ryton, *Banks and Banknotes of Exeter 1769–1906* (Exeter, 1984), p.23.
137 R.E. Leader, 'The Early Sheffield Banks' in *J.I.B.*, Vol. 38 (1917), p.231.
138 Cave op. cit., p.12.
139 Ibid., pp.17, 51.
140 I am grateful for information from Dr D. Linstrum and from Miss M.E. Williams.
141 Ex inf. Mr K. Lampard, University of Kent.
142 Hughes, op. cit., p.173.
143 A.G.E. Jones 'Early Banking in Ipswich' in *Notes and Queries*, Vol. 196, No. 19 (1951), p.403.
144 Hughes, op. cit., p.95; Chandler, op. cit., Vol. 1. p.185.
145 Plates in Hughes, op. cit., opp. pp.58 (background) and 96. See also, Chandler, op. cit., p.183.

146 Cf. Liverpool Heritage Bureau, *Buildings of Liverpool* (Liverpool, 1978), p.30.

147 Hughes, op. cit., pp.192, 195. He dates the newspaper to 16/9/1811 but does not name it.

148 Ibid.

149 See Chapter Two.

150 J. Broster, *A Walk Round the Walls and City of Chester* (1821).

151 Lloyds Bank Archives, A30d/133.

152 In Colvin. Lloyds Bank Archives has refs to Benjamin Wyatt in the context of the bank itself, and to Lord Penrhyn.

153 Grindon, op. cit., p.111.

154 Ibid., p.128.

155 Ibid., but the improvements in Market Street began in June 1822 (W.E.A. Axon, *The Annals of Manchester* (Manchester & London, 1886), p.165) and Grindon may be rather late in his dating.

156 Grindon, op. cit., pp.128, 242.

157 Ibid.

158 W. Westall & T. Moule, *Great Britain Illustrated* (1830), p.14; Colvin, *sub* Royle. The illustration here (not the one in Westall & Moule) was reproduced in the *Guardian* 8/12/1969, dating the building to 1819, but that date is impossibly early.

159 C.B. Knight, *A History of the City of York* (2nd ed., York, 1944), p.590.

160 Colvin, *sub* Taylor; Linstrum, op. cit., p.385.

161 J.J. Sheahan, *History of . . . Kingston-upon-Hull* (London, 1864), pp.517, 518.

162 Billson, op. cit., p.13; Marston Acres, op. cit., Vol. 2, p.437n.

163 *Extracts from the Minutes and Advices of the Yearly Meeting of Friends held in London . . .* (1783), pp.247–50; *Rules of Discipline of the Religious Society of Friends* (1834).

164 Illus. in J. Booker, *The Face of Banking* (London, 1979).

165 At least, that was the quotation (Marston Acres, op. cit., Vol. 1, p.168).

166 Stroud, *Dance*, p.159.

167 Lloyds Bank Archives, A56b/112.

168 Fulford, op. cit., p.61.

169 J.W. Gilbart, *A Practical Treatise on Banking*, Vol. 1 (London, 1849), p.196.

170 The expression waste book is still familiar to bankers (signifying a draft record of business before the copying up or 'posting' of ledgers) but the origin of the term is obscure. The most likely derivation is from the Latin *vastus*.

171 Cf. Gilbart, op. cit., p.215: 'We think it is better for [a clerk] to stand than to sit at his work . . .; [The] cashier . . . is generally standing . . .'

172 Bolitho & Peel, op. cit., p.44.

173 Bramah's first patent was 1784, with another in 1798; Jeremiah and Charles Chubb took out patents in 1818 and 1824 (B. Woodcroft, *Alphabetical Index of Patentees of Inventions* (London, 1854).

174 Lloyds Bank Archives, A47a/1.

175 Ibid., A53/60b/4.

176 Ibid., A26b/1.

177 Ibid., A50b/1.

178 Ibid.

179 Pressnell, op. cit., p.228.

180 The Manchester Bank failed and the Heywoods immediately purchased their premises, even adopting their title of The Manchester Bank (W.A. Shaw,

Manchester Old and New, Vol. 2 (London 1896) p.68). At Sheffield, Messrs Walkers, Eyre & Stanley took the premises of Roebuck's Bank which had stopped trading in 1778 (A. Galty, *Sheffield Past and Present* (Sheffield & London, 1873), pp.135, 136).

Chapter Two

1 The principle of limited liability was not extended to banking until 1858.

2 Cf. comments in Colvin, *sub* Barry: 'His success in adopting the features of the Italian *palazzo* to English architecture ... provided an acceptable alternative to the extremes of Greek and Gothic ... The Italianate style also permitted a greater richness of detail ...' See also *Q.R.* Vol. 95 (1854), p.362, for suitability of the Italian Style for street architecture.

3 Wrongly attributed to Sir Robert Smirke in *B*, Vol. 108 (1915, Part 1), p.135.

4 See C. Hussey, 'Hoare's Bank, Fleet Street, E.C.4' in *C.L.*, 6/3/1958, pp.450–3; Colvin, *sub* Parker; C. Hoare & Co., *Hoare's Bank. A Record 1673–1932* (London, 1932).

5 *G.M.*, Vol. 99 (1829, Part 2), p.637, which adds: 'a fund has been long accumulating'.

6 Hussey, op. cit., p.451.

7 *G.M.*, loc. cit.

8 I.e. banks set up by a specific royal charter.

9 *Q.R.*, Vol. 12 (1814–5), p.416.

10 For the general background, see S.G. Checkland, *Scottish Banking. A History 1695–1973* (Glasgow & London, 1975).

11 Colvin, *sub* Adam and Neilson.

12 Ibid., *sub* Crichton and Reid; *B.M.*, Vol. 52 (1891, Part 2), pp.396, 397; C.A. Malcolm, *The Bank of Scotland 1695–1945* (Edinburgh, 1948).

13 Malcolm, op. cit.

14 Malcolm, *The History of the British Linen Bank* (Edinburgh, 1950), pp.161, 162, 165.

15 Ibid., p.168.

16 Ibid., Colvin, *sub* Reid.

17 Malcolm, p.170.

18 Colvin, *sub* Graham.

19 C.W. Munn, *The Scottish Provincial Banking Companies 1747–1864* (Edinburgh, 1981), pp.148, 149.

20 Ibid.

21 Colvin, *sub* Paterson.

22 Ibid., *sub* Burn.

23 D. Walker, 'Era of Banks and Churches' in *C.L.*, 28/8/1969, p.503.

24 Colvin, *sub* Simpson.

25 Ibid., *sub* Elliot; *B.M.*, Vol. 117 (1924, Part 1), p.227; J.M. Crook, *The Greek Revival* (London, 1972), plate 246. Measured drawings were published in *B.N.*, Vol. 77 (1899, Part 2), pp.163, 164, 181, 186.

26 7 Geo. IV, c.46.

27 3 & 4 Will. IV, c.98.

28 6 Anne, c.22, s.9.

29 See 'Memorial to the Treasury from country bankers respecting establishment of Branch Banks [of England],' *B.P.P.*, 1828 (xvi), p.481, and 'Memorials of Country Bankers to Government, 1828–33', *B.P.P.*, 1833 (xxiii), p.319.

30 L.H. Grindon, *Manchester Banks and Bankers* (Manchester, 1877) p.235.

31 See T.E. Gregory, *The Westminster Bank Through a Century*, Vol. 1, (London, 1936).

32 Ibid., pp.122–50.

33 Without this provision, banks were obliged to quote the name of every shareholder in any legal action.

34 7 & 8 Vic., c.113, s.47.

35 Gregory, op. cit., pp.150–67.

36 Ibid., pp.167–74; *B.M.*, Vol. 14 (1854), pp.192, 254, 326, 384.

37 P.R.O., CRES 6/153, pp.58–110 *passim*; H.T. Easton, *The History of a Banking House* (London, 1903), p.88.

38 Colvin, *sub* Kempthorne; *C.E. & A.J.*, Vol. 2 (1839), p.28, and Colvin, *sub* Hopper.

39 S.H. Twining, *Two Hundred and Twenty-Five Years in the Strand* ... (London, 1931), p.32.

40 *B.M.*, Vol. 16 (1856), p.258.

41 J.W. Gilbart, *A Practical Treatise on Banking* (new ed., Philadelphia, 1860), Section 111, pp.271, 272.

42 Ibid., p.277.

43 Ibid., pp.274, 280.

44 In April 1836 the North Wilts Bank had a letter from the Bank of England's solicitors asking 'the grounds on which the directors think themselves justified in transacting business at Hungerford' 67 miles from London (Lloyds Bank Archives, A53/9b/1).

45 Illus. in H. Withers, *National Provincial Bank 1833–1933* (London, 1933), opp. p.67.

46 T.E. Gregory, op. cit., pp.288, 289; *I.L.N.*, Vol. 2 (1843), p.159; *W.R.*, Vol. 46 (1846–7), pp.95, 96; D. Watkin, *The Life and Works of C.R. Cockerell* (London, 1974), pp.221–5; J.W. Gilbart, op. cit., p.261.

47 Watkin, loc. cit.; Colvin, *sub* Cockerell.

48 Watkin, op. cit., p.221.

49 Ibid.

50 Cf. ibid., p.225; the bank 'had little or no influence' in the development of styles.

51 For the importance of the domed banking hall, cf. N. Pevsner, *A History of Building Types* (London, 1976), p.200.

52 R. Chambers Jones, *Arian* (Swansea, 1978), p.78.

53 J.J. Sheahan, *History of ... Kingston-upon-Hull* (London, 1864), pp.517, 518; I. & S. Hall *Georgian Hull* (York, 1978–9), fig. 150; J.A.S.L. Leighton-Boyce, *Smiths the Bankers 1658–1958* (London, 1958), plate opp. p.210; etc.

54 Illustrations of both buildings are in the National Monuments Record.

55 Bentley's, *Worcestershire Directory*, Vol. 2 (1840), p.66.

56 *B.P.P.*, 1831–2 (vi), p.323; *B.P.P.*, 1836 (ix), pp.181–245.

57 Question 12 in a circular to all joint-stock banks, 1836, from a parliamentary committee asked if their Deeds of Settlement had been printed and published (*B.P.P.*, 1836 (ix), pp.181–245).

58 Lloyds Bank Archives, A24/1b/1.

59 Ibid., A8b/2.

60 Ibid.

61 A29b/1.

62 By 1854 only £1 million of the £5 million subscribed capital of the London & Westminster Bank had been paid up (*I.L.N.*, Vol. 25 (1854), p.514); for the earlier position with regard to all joint-stock banks see *B.P.P.*, 1836 (ix), pp.181–245.

63 These more specific reasons (with 'fluctuations' written in place of the more honest 'reductions') were found only in one Deed of Settlement, that of the Hampshire Banking Company, out of 15 examined.

64 Grindon, op. cit., p.244.

65 Lloyds Bank Archives, A54/17b/1, from which all refs in this paragraph are taken.

66 For these, see *B.P.P.*, 1836 (ix), pp.181–245; cf. L.H. Grindon, op. cit., p.302, and H. Ling Roth, op. cit., p.40.

67 *B.P.P.*, 1831–2 (vi), p.323.

68 Lloyds Bank Archives, A53/9b/1.

69 Ibid., A46b/1.

70 *B.M.*, Vol. 14 (1854), pp.264, 265.

71 *B.P.P.*, 1836 (ix), p.131.

72 P.H. Fisher, *Notes & Recollections of Stroud, Gloucestershire* (1891), p.142.

73 *A.M. & J.*, Vol. 4 (1837), p.80.

74 J. Ward, *The Borough of Stoke-upon-Trent* (London, 1843), p.267.

75 *B.P.P.*, 1836 (ix), p.226.

76 Ibid., p.236 (the figure includes 23 'sub-agencies'); *B.P.P.* 1843 (L11), p.14.

77 Colvin, *sub* Edge.

78 Nat. West. Bank Archives, Nat. Prov. Bank Branch Committee Minutes, 2 vols, 1845–89 (incomplete).

79 Ibid., Nat. Prov. Bank Court Minutes (1839–42) pp.296, 303.

80 Grindon, op. cit., p.270.

81 See *B.P.P.*, 1836, (ix), pp.1–180 *passim*. Viscount Stuckey would have no branch more than 50 miles from head office (ibid., p.81).

82 'S', *British Losses by Bank Failures 1820–57* (London, 1858), p.27.

83 *B.M.*, Vol. 17 (1857), p.773.

84 Grindon, op. cit., pp.251, 252, 255.

85 Colvin, *sub* Atkinson.

86 *B.*, Vol. 19 (1861), p.590.

87 Ibid., Vol. 5 (1847), p.526; the bank 'was the most complete change yet attempted'. See also ibid., Vol. 30 (1872), pp.199–201.

88 Colvin, *sub* Rickman; B. Little, *Birmingham Buildings* . . . (Newton Abbot, 1971), p.21; D. Hickman, *Birmingham* (Studio Vista Series, London, 1970), plate 31 and text; Pevsner, *Warwickshire*, p.127.

89 Lloyds Bank Archives, A5c/3; Hickman, loc. cit.

90 Colvin, *sub* Edge. His drawings are in Birmingham Library.

91 Lloyds Bank Archives, A53/17b/1; A29b/1.

92 H.S. Goodhart-Rendel, *English Architecture Since the Regency* (London, 1953), p.155.

93 Cf. M. Girouard, 'All That Money Could Buy' in A. Clifton-Taylor *et al.*, *Spirit of the Age* (1975), pp.164, 165.

94 W. Bagehot, *Lombard Street* . . . (London, new ed., 1917), p.90.

95 Cf. Pevsner, *Building Types*, p.193.

96 S. Bagshaw, *Derbyshire Directory* (1846), p.84; Colvin, *sub* Wallace, notes that the bank was altered in 1850.

97 *C.E. & A.J.*, Vol. 1 (1837–8), p.235; Grindon, op. cit., p.282; Colvin, *sub* Tattersall.

98 R.E. Leader, 'The Early Sheffield Banks' in *J.I.B.*, Vol. 38 (1917), p.240.

99 Pevsner, *Cumberland and Westmorland*, p.205.

100 C. Nicholson, *The Annals of Kendal* (2nd ed., London and Kendal, 1861), p.152; J.F. Curwen, *Kirkbie-Kendall* (Kendal, 1900), pp.129, 130; H.M. Colvin, *sub* Webster.

101 This statement ignores a bank possibly built in Plymouth in 1835. See below.

102 Marston Acres, Vol. 2, pp.428–33.

103 Ibid.

104 Ibid., pp.433, 434.

105 Ibid., pp.435, 436.

106 Ibid., p.434.

107 M. Phillips, *A History of Banks, Bankers & Banking in Northumberland, Durham and North Yorkshire* (London, 1894), p.202.

108 Marston Acres, op. cit., p.435.

109 Grindon, op. cit., pp.222, 223.

110 Marston Acres, op. cit., p.436.

111 Ibid., p.471. Cockerell succeeded Sir Joan Soane in October 1833 and held the post until 1855.

112 Ibid., p.571.

113 For designs, see Watkin, op. cit., p.216 and Colvin, *sub* Cockerell; but Marston Acres, op. cit., p.571, is definite that Newcastle was the first Bank of England branch for which premises were especially erected.

114 Watkin, op. cit., p.217; Colvin, loc. cit.

115 Marston Acres, loc. cit.: '. . . the Directors seem to have decided . . .' to purpose-build.

116 Ibid., p.570. Before being renamed Grey Street, the new location was called Upper Dean Street.

117 *B.*, Vol. 75 (1898, Part 1), pp.306–9; Ministry List; Colvin *sub* Grainger. For the general development of inner Newcastle see L. Wilkes & G. Dodds, *Tyneside Classical* (London, 1964). The authors have a plate of the Bank of England (p.85) but the attribution of the design is not particularly discussed.

118 *C.E. & A.J.*, Vol. 4 (1841), p.18.

119 Ibid., p.17.

120 H.-R. Hitchcock, *Early Victorian Architecture in Britain* (London & New Haven, 1954), pp.353, 354; J. Quentin Hughes, *Liverpool* (City Building Series, London, 1969), p.34; *B.N.*, Vol. 3 (1857), pp.582, 583; Liverpool Heritage Bureau, *Buildings of Liverpool* (Liverpool, 1978), p.35; Colvin, *sub* Rowland.

121 C.H. Reilly, *Some Liverpool Streets and Buildings in 1921* (Liverpool, 1921), pp.42, 43.

122 *C.E. & A.J.*, op. cit., pp.17, 18, 76. The bank survives, but with an altered

frontage, as Castle Moat House, Derby Square (Liverpool Heritage Bureau, op. cit., p.28).

123 Ibid., p.18; Lloyds Bank Archives, A35b/1; Colvin, *sub* Cunningham.

124 Lloyds Bank Archives, loc. cit.

125 Leader, op. cit., p.238.

126 At Liverpool, Cunningham was told to resubmit his plans because they included no scale or dimensions (Lloyds Bank Archives, A35b/1). For 'respectability', see minutes of Gloucestershire Banking Company 1837 (ibid., A53/17b/1), and letter 1853, from director of Bucks & Oxon Union Bank (ibid., A40b/40).

127 Lloyds Bank Archives, A35b/1.

128 Ibid., A53/17b/1. Tenders between £5700 and £4922.

129 *B.P.P.*, 1836 (ix), p.210.

130 'S', op. cit., p.38.

131 *Times*, 2/1/1843, p.3.

132 *B.M.*, Vol. 2 (1845), p.196; cf. 'S', loc. cit.: 'Palatial and most extravagant premises'.

133 *C.E. &A.J.*, Vol. 13 (1850), pp.284, 285, 312, 313.

134 I.e. £1600 at Whitby, including fittings, and nearly £4000 at York, exclusive of counters and fittings.

135 *A.M. &J.*, Vol. 4 (1837), p.80.

136 Ibid.; *B.M.*, Vol. 87 (1909, Part I), opp. p.423; W. & J. Hargrove, *The New Guide . . . [to] The City of York* (York, 1838), p.159; C.B. Knight, *A History of the City of York* (2nd ed., York, 1944), p.624. Parliament Street was earlier called New Market.

137 By J.B. & W. Atkinson (*B.*, Vol. 33 (1875), p.38).

138 *A.M. &J.*, loc. cit.; on the site is now Barclays Bank.

139 7 & 8 Vic. c.32. In the event, the main effect of this Act was in the realm of note circulation.

140 Marston Acres, op. cit., p.571. For dates of the contract drawings, see Watkin, op. cit., p.217.

141 Watkin, op. cit., p.214.

142 Hitchcock, op. cit., p.357.

143 E.g. for Bristol: C.H. Cave, *History of Banking in Bristol from 1750 to 1899* (Bristol, 1899), p.171 (but refers to 'heavy looking edifice'); T.H.B. Burrough, *Bristol* (Studio Vista Series, London, 1970), plate 86 and text; Pevsner, *North Somerset & Bristol*, p.426; A. Gomme, M. Jenner & B. Little, *Bristol, an Architectural History* (London, 1979), pp.8, 249–52; for Manchester: C.H. Reilly, *Some Manchester Streets and Their Buildings* (Liverpool & London, 1924), pp.30, 31; for Liverpool: *B.*, Vol. 6 (1848), p.613; ibid., Vol. 7, (1849), pp.42, 43; Watkin, op. cit., p.218; Reilly, op. cit. (Liverpool Streets and Buildings), p.36; Quentin Hughes, op. cit., p.45. It should be noted that Cockerell had very great funds available: Bristol cost less than £6000, but Manchester nearer £20000 and Liverpool over £24000 (Watkin, op. cit., pp.217, 218).

144 Sheahan, op. cit., pp.517, 518.

145 Watkin, op. cit., p.224.

146 *C.E. &A.J.*, Vol. 4 (1841), p.18.

147 Whellan's *History, Gazetteer & Directory of Northamptonshire* (London, 1849), p.157, makes the attribution to Law and mentions phoenix as the bank's crest.

148 Colvin, *sub* Burn, Robertson, Simpson and Graham. A. Keith, *The North of Scotland Bank Limited 1836–1936* (Aberdeen, 1936), p.45, mentions that Simpson's costing of £7200 for a bank at Aberdeen in 1842 was the highest submitted.

149 Colvin, *sub* Elliot.

150 'Glasguensis', *Banking in Glasgow During the Olden Times* (Glasgow, 1884), p.22.

151 Colvin, *sub* Hamilton.

152 Ibid.; R.S. Rait, *The History of the Union Bank of Scotland* (Glasgow, 1930), p.211; 'Glasguensis', op. cit., pp.23, 24.

153 *B.*, Vol. 37 (1879), p.267; Rait, op. cit., p.308; Checkland, op. cit., p.331.

154 Rait, op. cit., p.211.

155 'Glasguensis', op. cit., p.28n; cf. R. Gunnis, *Dictionary of British Sculptors 1660–1851* (London, 1951).

156 *B.*, Vol. 5 (1847), p.211; Hitchcock, op. cit., p.360.

157 *B.*, Vol. 8 (1850), p.415; Malcolm, op. cit., p.170. The bank cost around £30000.

158 *B.*, Vol. 5 (1847), p.480; ibid., Vol. 6 (1848), p.613.

159 *B.M.*, Vol. 7 (1847), p.45.

160 *B.*, Vol. 7 (1849), p.18; ibid., Vol. 30 (1872), pp.199–201; Grindon, op. cit., p.186; Pevsner, *Lancashire. The Industrial and Commercial South*, p.297; D. Sharp, *Manchester* (Studio Vista Series, London, 1969), p.19.

161 Reilly, op. cit. (Manchester Streets and Buildings), p.38.

162 Ibid., p.39.

163 This building was the head office of the Gloucestershire Banking Company, later the Gloucester branch of the Capital & Counties Bank.

164 *I.L.N.*, Vol. 15 (1849), pp.11, 12; A. Graves, *The Royal Academy of Arts. A Complete Dictionary of Contributors . . . 1769–1904*, Vol. 3 (1905), p.230; Hitchcock, op. cit., pp.361, 362.

165 *I.L.N.*, loc. cit.

166 Ibid.

167 The Hall of Commerce was illustrated in *I.L.N.*, Vol. 27 (1855), p.776, after it had been taken over by the Bank of London.

168 *I.L.N.*, Vol. 15 (1849), pp.11, 12.

169 Ibid.

170 Cf. J. Kirshner (ed.), *Business, Banking, and Economic Thought . . . Selected Studies of Raymond de Roover* (Chicago and London, 1974), pp.225, 226.

171 *C.E. & A.J.*, Vol. 4 (1841), p.76; for this countered, and Corbett's indignant reply, see ibid., pp.119, 120, 161.

172 *W.R.*, Vol. 46 (1846–7), p.61.

173 *Q.R.*, Vol. 95 (1854), p.340.

174 Such as Cunningham's Liverpool Commercial Bank (Vols 5 (1847), p.480, and 6 (1848), p.613), and Burn & Bryce's British Linen Bank, Edinburgh, of which 'more should have been made' (Vol. 8 (1850), p.415).

175 This was R.H. Potter who exhibited at R.A. in that year (Graves, op. cit., Vol. 6 (1906), p.189).

176 *B.*, Vol. 7 (1849), pp.608, 609.

177 For full career, see *D.N.B.*

178 *B.*, loc. cit.

179 Ibid.

180 For Rae's important career, see E. Green's introduction to Rae's *The Country*

Banker, first published in 1885 and republished in 1976 for the British Bank of the Middle East.

181 *B.M.*, Vol. 9 (1849), pp.421–3. However, as the correspondence developed there was some mellowing of opinion: '... when a branch is fairly established in a town ... the Directors act wisely in procuring, by building or otherwise ... suitable premises ... The Scotch people have found this out, the branch banks of the sister Kingdom being the handsomest edifices in the country towns' (ibid., Vol. 12 (1852), p.208).

182 *A.M. & J.*, Vol. 4 (1837), p.324.

183 Ibid.

184 See D. Watkin, op. cit., p.222, who quotes from Cockerell's diary: 'Light is the soul of offices and houses in the city. If I ever have anything to do there I will create an architecture expressly for this end.'

185 *B.*, loc. cit.

186 The foundation and early years of the Institute are recounted in E. Green, *Debtors to their Profession* (London, 1979).

187 Green, op. cit., p.12.

188 G. Sharp, *The Gilbart Prize Essay on the Adaptation of Recent Discoveries and Inventions in Science and Art to the Purposes of Practical Banking* (London, 1854); the abbreviated text appeared as an appendix to *B.M.*, Vol. 12 (1852).

189 In the letter published in *B.M.* in Dec. 1850 the questions, *inter alia*, were asked: 'May not the Exhibition contain some architectural models that may lead to improvements in the construction of our bank-buildings? or, some instrument or machine by which light, heat, and ventilation may be secured, so as to promote the health of our clerks? or, may there not be exhibited some improvements in the fine arts, by the use of which, we may so decorate our public offices, our board-rooms, and even our waiting-rooms, as to give them all a more attractive appearance? ...'

190 In the *B.M.* version of the essay the words *not fail to combine* are replaced by *take care shall be combined*.

191 These comments are omitted entirely from the *B.M.* version.

192 In this area the two versions of the text have no significant variations.

193 *B.M.*, Vol. 3 (1845), pp.26, 27.

194 Ibid.; Sharp, op. cit.

195 Green, op. cit., pp.16–20; *B.M.*, Vol. 11 (1851), pp.134–40, 296–300, 632–6.

196 For all patents to end of 1852, see B. Woodcroft, *Alphabetical Index of Patentees of Inventions* (London, 1854).

197 *B.M.*, Vol. 3 (1845), p.28.

198 Ibid., cf. Woodcroft, op. cit.

199 Progressive No. 10047, 10 Feb. 1844.

200 Ibid.

201 *B.M.*, Vol. 12 (1852), p.547. The use of iron in the roof of Hoare's Bank, Fleet Street, had been noted in *G.M.*, Vol. 99 (1829, Part 2), p.637.

202 *B.M.*, loc. cit.

203 Woodcroft, op. cit. Progressive No. 7123, 18 June 1846. See also letter in *C.E. & A.J.*, Vol. 1 (1837–8), p.108, and report in ibid., Vol. 8 (1845), p.261, on alleged infringement of patent.

204 Cf. Sharp, op. cit., who unjustly describes Bunnett's shutters as 'only a modification of' Quincey's.

205 Addresses given in London *Directories*.

206 Descriptions and illustrations are in Sharp, op. cit.

207 *B.M.*, Vol. 3 (1845), p.28.

208 Munn, op. cit., p.149, found that in the 1850s the Dundee Banking Company deducted £100 from its property account, but traced no other similar examples before 1864.

209 Lloyds Bank Archives, A53/17b/1.

210 Cf. *B.M.*, Vol. 14 (1854), pp.264, 265, for case of West of England and South Wales District Bank.

211 Ibid., Vol. 70 (1900, Part 2), p.13.

212 *C.E. & A.J.*, Vol. 3 (1840), p.183.

213 Ibid.

214 *I.L.N.*, Vol. 27 (1855), p.774.

215 I.e. the acquisition of the Hall of Commerce in Threadneedle Street by the Bank of London.

216 *B.*, Vol. 11 (1853), pp.260, 392, 393; *I.L.N.*, Vol. 25 (1854), p.513.

217 *B.*, loc. cit., lists competitors.

218 Graves, op. cit., Vol. 7 (1906), p.165.

219 *B.N.*, Vol. 7 (1861), p.360; *B.*, Vol. 18 (1860), p.268.

220 *I.L.N.*, loc. cit.

221 Ibid.

222 *B.*, Vol. 13 (1855), pp.78, 79.

223 Colvin, *sub* Moseley. Now a branch of the Midland Bank.

224 Graves, op. cit., Vol. 3 (1905), p.384, and Vol. 5 (1906), p.311.

225 Established in Dec. 1834, it had set up 17 branches or agencies within 18 months, up to 110 miles from Bristol (*B.P.P.*, 1836 (ix), pp.193, 194).

226 *B.*, Vol. 12 (1854), p.277.

227 Ibid.; ibid., Vol. 16 (1858), pp.334, 335, 337.

228 £50 to Barry; £30 to Gibson.

229 *I.L.N.*, Vol. 29 (1856), p.135; J. Latimer, *The Annals of Bristol in the Nineteenth Century* (Bristol, 1887), p.201; Gomme, Jenner & Little, op. cit., pp.351 ff., 372, 428, plates 183, 276; Ministry List. The comparison with Smirke, for whose clubhouse see *B.*, Vol. 5 (1847), pp.218, 219, is made in *I.L.N.*, loc. cit., and *B.*, Vol. 16 (1858), p.337.

230 *I.L.N.*, loc. cit.

231 Latimer, loc. cit.

232 Pevsner, *North Somerset and Bristol*, pp.368, 424.

233 J. Latimer, op. cit., p.324; N. Pevsner, op. cit. p.425; Gomme, Jenner & Little, op. cit., p.351; Ministry List.

234 It failed in 1878, but was reconstituted in the following year as the Bristol and West of England Bank Limited.

235 *B.M.*, Vol. 17 (1857), p.937.

236 *Q.R.*, Vol. 95 (1854), pp.338 ff.

237 *C.E. & A.J.*, Vol. 19 (1856), p.1; A.E. Richardson, *Monumental Classic Architecture* ... (London, 1914), p.84, who thinks the design was influenced by the Royal College of Surgeons building of 1830.

238 A. & C. Black & Co., *Guide to Glasgow* ... (Edinburgh, 1885) p.391.

239 *C.E. & A.J.*, loc. cit.

240 Ibid., Gunnis, op. cit., pp.388–90.
241 *B.*, Vol. 16 (1858), p.334; *I.L.N.*, loc. cit.: Gunnis, loc. cit.

Chapter Three

1 E.g. Leeds Savings Bank of 1834 in Pevsner, *Yorkshire. The West Riding*, p.58.
2 E.L.S. Horsburgh, *Bromley, Kent*... (London, 1929), p.303.
3 The last major work on savings banks was in 1947 (see Bibliography).
4 Bentley's *Worcestershire Directory*, Vol. 1 (1840), p.31.
5 Ibid., Vol. 2 (1840), p.112.
6 *B.M.*, Vol. 2 (1844/45), p.277.
7 5 & 6 Will. IV extended to Scotland the provisions of 9 Geo. IV, c.92.
8 *B.P.P.*, 1857–8 (xvi), p.4.
9 57 Geo. III, c.130.
10 This figure was reduced to £3 16s. by 9 Geo. IV, c.92 (1828).
11 Most paid £3 6s. 8d. per cent per annum (*Hansard* (New Series, 18), col. 1283).
12 Especially in 1828 and 1838. See *Hansard* (New Series, 18) cols 258, 259, 1123–6, and (New Series, 43) cols 1283–91.
13 5 Geo. IV, c.62. But only after the bank had been established 10 years (s.11).
14 P.R.O., NDO 9/7, 9/8.
15 P.R.O., NDO 9/7, p.191.
16 P.R.O., NDO 9/8, pp.87, 88.
17 *B.P.P.*, 1857–8 (xvi), pp.1–438.
18 Ibid., p.70.
19 Joseph Hume (1777–1855), a champion of savings banks in 1817, led the movements for their reform in 1828 and 1838: See *D.N.B.* for his career.
20 *Hansard* (New Series, 18), col. 1125, 12 March 1828.
21 9 Geo. IV, c.92. There had been Acts in 1818 (58 Geo. III, c.48) and 1820 (1 Geo. IV, c.83) as well as the 1824 Act already mentioned.
22 The duties of this post were analysed in *B.P.P.*, loc. cit., pp.45, 57, etc.
23 W. Lewins, *A History of Banks for Savings* ... (London, 1866), p.67. For Pratt's career as a whole, see *D.N.B.*
24 Approved by the Commissioners, 27 Feb. 1830 (P.R.O., NDO 9/9, p.140).
25 In the worst cases of misappropriation, Pratt was sent personally to investigate, as at Cuffe Street (Dublin) and Rochdale.
26 P.R.O., NDO 9/10, pp.229, 230; 9/11, pp.361, 362.
27 7 & 8 Vic., c.83.
28 *J.H.C.*, Vol. 86 (1831), *passim*.
29 *Hansard* (New Series, 43), cols 1283–91; *J.H.C.*, Vol. 93 (1838), pp.679, 680.
30 The editorial remarks and correspondence in the *Times* were published by E. Wilson in 1843.
31 Savings banks were enabled to act as a medium for the purchase of Government annuities by 3 Will. IV, c.14 (1833).
32 Letter signed 'A.B.C.', dated 10 Sept. 1842, and published in the *Times*, 14 Sept. 1842.
33 *B.P.P.*, 1844 (xxxii), pp.801–4.
34 *B.M.*, Vol. 2 (1844/45), p.277.
35 Savings banks were established also in Scotland, Wales and Ireland but their

development was rather different. For Ireland there was *ad hoc* legislation; Scotland, aloof from English savings bank law until 1835, had virtually no surplus fund accumulations (*B.P.P.*, 1857–8 (xvi), pp.244, 247); in Wales, savings banks were sparse and late established (H.O. Horne, *A History of Savings Banks* (Oxford, 1947), p.69).

36 P.R.O., NDO 9/13, pp.188, 189.

37 *J.H.C.*, Vol. 107 (1852), p.170. The return was published as *B.P.P.*, 1852 (xxviii), pp.757–817.

38 *J.H.C.*, loc. cit., p.55.

39 Ibid., Vol. 108 (1853), pp.550, 555, 559, 565, 575, etc.

40 17 & 18 Vic., c.50.

41 Section 64 of the first Bill (s.63 of the amended Bill) made certain provisions about freehold tenure which will be discussed later in this chapter.

42 All references in this paragraph are to *B.P.P.*, 1852 (xxviii), pp.757–817.

43 *B.P.P.*, 1837–8 (xxxvi), pp.493–5; 1844 (xxxii), pp.801–4; 1849 (xxx), pp.403–25.

44 One even in 1844, published in *B.P.P.*, 1844 (xxxii), p.867.

45 Manchester savings bank, very large and prosperous, was the subject of a specific report published in *B.P.P.*, 1847–8 (xxxix), pp.513–5.

46 P.R.O., NDO 9/12, p.94.

47 A clergyman had embezzled £24 000 at Hertford (see Horne, op. cit., p.122).

48 Although Worcester was apparently built by 1825 (see Appendix One).

49 A. Harrison, *West Midland Trustee Savings Bank 1816–1966*, p.91. Subscriptions amounted to some £152.

50 That is to say that no withdrawals are noted in *B.P.P.*, 1844 (xxxii), pp.801–4. Trustees at Worcester had not withdrawn money either but as their bank was built before 1828 it might well have been financed by surplus fund money manipulated without the knowledge of the National Debt Office. In 1827, for instance, they had £2639 in a local commercial bank (*Worcester Herald*, 22/12/1827). This was perhaps the case at Stone and Ellesmere, although the 1828 legislation would in theory have prevented it.

51 M. Phillips, *A History of Banks, Bankers & Banking in Northumberland, Durham and North Yorkshire* (London, 1894), pp.368–70.

52 *B.P.P.*, 1857–8 (xvi), pp.104, 105.

53 Ibid. The fund continued after 1828, despite the prevailing legislation. By 1849 it amounted to £5630, invested in stock, from which dividends accrued to the officers' superannuation fund (*B.P.P.*, 1849 (xxx), pp.403–25, footnote).

54 *B.P.P.*, 1857–8 (xvi), pp.104, 105.

55 *B.P.P.*, 1852 (xxviii), p.749–52, lists 20 savings banks discontinued since 1844.

56 *B.P.P.*, 1857–8 (xvi), pp.253–61, contains evidence of the Rochdale bank manager submitted to a parliamentary select committee and deals with most aspects of the bank's business.

57 Harrison, op. cit., p.91.

58 G. Tate, *The History of . . . Alnwick*, Vol. 2 (Alnwick, 1868/9), p.219.

59 See Appendix One.

60 At Birmingham and Sheffield in the public libraries. For Ulverston, see article by A. Taylor in *Transactions of the Cumberland and Westmorland Antiquarian & Archaeological Society*, Vol. lxxiv, New Series (1974), pp.147–58.

61 These are listed in Horne, op. cit., pp.394–6.

62 *Hull Advertiser*, 6/6/1828.

63 *West Briton*, 12/9/1845.

64 *Doncaster, Nottingham & Lincolnshire Gazette*, March 1843; *Sheffield & Rotherham Independent*, 15/11/1851.

65 Publication began generally after the 1828 Act (9 Geo. IV c.92) which made it necessary (ss.46, 47) for an annual set of accounts to be sent to the National Debt Office and for a duplicate to be displayed in the savings bank office. However, Worcester had published its balance sheet from as early as 1825 (*Worcester Herald*. 17/12/1825).

66 *Windsor & Eton Express*, 30/1/1830, 28/12/1833, 30/1/1836, 4/2/1837, 17/2/1838.

67 *A.M. & J.*, Vol. 1 (1834), p.142.

68 *C.E. & A.J.*, Vol. 3 (1840), p.217 (Finsbury), and Vol. 14 (1851), pp.330, 331 (Chester).

69 *B.*, Vol. 6 (1848), p.477 (Newbury), and Vol. 8 (1850), pp.138, 139 (Gloucester).

70 *I.L.N.*, Vol. 16 (1850), p.32.

71 Graves, op. cit., Vol. 1, p.20; Vol. 2, p.178; Vol. 8, p.23.

72 See Appendix One.

73 Ditto.

74 H.-R. Hitchcock, *Early Victorian Architecture in Britain* (London and New Haven, 1954), pp.356, 369.

75 Taylor, loc. cit.

76 Some directories called it Castle Street, which ran into Back Lane, and it was probably unclear where the boundary lay.

77 Or Paul's Ward, which was a local government district.

78 A footnote to *B.P.P.*, 1849 (xxx), pp.403–25, *sub* Ashford, refers to expenses 'at the time of the alterations'; the inference from this is that the building was adapted for bank use and not purpose-built.

79 The bank acquired this property in 1844/45. I am grateful to Mr C.J. Pickford, Assistant (now County) Archivist of Bedfordshire for much help with the Bedford bank.

80 T.A. Blyth, *History of Bedford* (London & Bedford [1873]), p.167. Blyth deals with the savings bank under the heading of the Assembly Rooms. Bedford Central Library: Minutes of Bedford Rooms Committee, 15 April 1835.

81 Slater's *Directory* (1850).

82 Ministry List.

83 See Appendix One.

84 Ditto.

85 Ditto.

86 B.P.P., 1852 (xxviii), pp.757–817.

87 See Appendix One.

88 Ditto.

89 All refs in this paragraph are from *B.P.P.*, 1852 (xxviii), pp.757–817.

90 Evidence for costs is given in Appendix One.

91 Multiplicity of banks in one area was effectively prevented from as early as 1824 (5 Geo. IV, c.62) by the ruling that subscribers to one savings bank were not to subscribe to another. Apart from London, only Ipswich seems to have had two savings banks and there it appears to have been a parochial division.

92 Neither did they communicate less formally. A periodical called the *Savings Bank Circular* lasted only from Oct. 1844 to Sept. 1847, and there was only one issue (March 1857) of the *Savings Banks' Magazine* (Horne, op. cit., pp.106, 152, 398).

93 See surplus fund figures in Appendix One.

94 Liverpool in 1864 in Bold Street (City Heritage Bureau, *Buildings of Liverpool* (Liverpool, 1978), p.61; Southampton, in West Marlands between 1859 and 1863 (directories).

95 *B.M.*, Vol. 3 (1845), pp.30–2.

96 *A Century of Thrift* . . . (Stockport, 1925), p.28.

97 Lloyds Bank Archives, Stafford trustees' minute book. Their plans to build in the 1840s were abortive and premises were not erected until 1862.

98 Cf. Ministry List: 'Dignified building in an important position at the end of the High Street and beside the entrance gates to Vivary Park.'

99 Gloucestershire Record Office, D2405/1.

100 Taylor, op. cit., p.147.

101 The bank with most staff was probably Manchester, where the annual salary bill came to £1053 in 1842 (*Manchester Guardian*, 11/1/1843).

102 All refs in this paragraph are from *B.P.P.*, 1852 (xxviii), pp.757–817.

103 P.R.O., NDO 9/13, pp.188, 189.

104 *B.P.P.*, loc. cit.

105 Ibid.

106 *B.M.*, loc. cit.

107 Particularly as he had strong feelings about the kind of customer the savings banks were established to serve and protect.

108 Like the 2 guineas subscribed annually by Louth Corporation until the local savings bank 'could support itself' (W.R. Goulding, *Louth Old Corporation Records* (Louth, 1891), p.64). Horne (op. cit., p.66) thought the highest total of voluntary subscriptions was at Exeter (£468).

109 See Appendix One. At Cambridge, in 1848, trustees had subscribed £700 (footnote to *B.P.P.*, 1849 (xxx), pp.403–25) but that was only 22 per cent of the building costs.

110 See Appendix One.

111 At Stafford, in 1862, premises were erected and paid for by a local philanthropist (Lloyds Bank Archives, trustees' minute book), but that was a quite exceptional event. In the period to 1852 the only bank which might have received a large cash sum towards building expenses was Rotherham which, founded in 1846, erected premises in 1851, with a building lease from the Earl of Effingham (see Appendix One).

112 *B.M.*, loc. cit., from which all refs in this paragraph are taken.

113 See Appendix One.

114 Lloyds Bank Archives, Swindon trustees' minute book; Gloucestershire Record Office, D2405/1.

115 *Preston Savings Bank 1816–1907* (1907), pp.19, 20.

116 Whitchurch bought a subsisting 999-year lease of the site (Harrison, op. cit., p.91). C. Donald Hebden, *The Trustee Savings Banks of Yorkshire & Lincoln* (1981), p.374, states that Wakefield trustees, told they could not legally own property, took a 1000-year lease in 1830.

117 For instance, a leasehold in two 'good lives' was offered to Taunton bank in 1829

(E. Barnard, *The Somerset & Wilts Trustee Savings Bank 1817–1967* (Taunton, 1967), p.13).

118 *B.P.P.*, 1852–3 (vi), pp.95–131 (s.64) for clause in first Bill; ibid., pp.135–70 (s.63) for clause in Bill as amended in Committee.

119 *B.M.*, loc. cit.

120 Lloyds Bank Archives, loc. cit.

121 Minet Library, IV/44/2,4.

122 R.E. Leader, *Sheffield Savings Bank — A Century of Thrift, 1819–1919* (Sheffield, 1920), p.15.

123 For instance at Bridport, Chelsea, Ellesmere, Montague Street and Rotherham (see Appendix One).

124 *B.M.*, loc. cit.

125 Gloucestershire Record Office, loc. cit.

126 *Doncaster, Nottingham & Lincolnshire Gazette*, March 1843.

127 Lloyds Bank Archives, loc. cit.

128 Some errors in directories may be typographical. The cost of Worksop bank, for instance, was given in White's *Directory* (1864), p.630, as 'about £300', whereas the surplus fund withdrawal figure was £1300.

129 White's *Directory* (1855), p.190; Lloyds Bank Archives, Clb/51.

130 *B.P.P.*, 1844 (xxxii); *Essex Standard*, 10 June 1842.

131 *B.P.P.*, loc. cit.; Bagshaw's *Directory* (1850), p.214.

132 *B.P.P.*, loc. cit.; J. Latimer, *The Annals of Bristol in the Nineteenth Century* (Bristol, 1887), p.54.

133 *B.P.P.*, loc. cit.; Leader, op. cit., p.16.

134 Gloucestershire Record Office, loc. cit.

135 White's *Directory* (1845), p.143.

136 Phillips, op. cit., p.369.

137 *B.P.P.*, loc. cit., and 1847–8 (xxxix), pp.513–5; P.R.O., NDO 9/11, pp.361, 362.

138 *Manchester Guardian*, 11/1/1843, publishing annual report.

139 Taylor, loc. cit., p.149.

140 Gloucestershire Record Office, loc. cit.

141 Ibid.

142 Lloyds Bank Archives: C1b/51. The clerk to the bank, 17 Aug. 1846, was 'to express to Mr. Cottingham the astonishment of the Committee that any alterations attended with increased expense should have been made ... without first having received the approval of the Committee.' He was 'distinctly to understand' that they had no power to increase expenditure. On 1 Sept. 1846 Cottingham attended at Bury 'and gave so satisfactory an explanation' that the Committee could only pass a resolution of thanks.

143 *C.E. & A.J.*, Vol. 3 (1840), p.217.

144 This was certainly the case at Tewkesbury (Gloucestershire Record Office, loc. cit.).

145 The owner, Gregory Gregory, was also a trustee of the savings bank (*B.P.P.*, 1852 (xxviii), p.849).

146 Salvin's obituary in *B.*, Vol. 41 (1881), pp.809, 810. Since this was written, there has appeared Dr Jill Allibone's definitive work *Anthony Salvin. Pioneer of Gothic Revival Architecture* (Cambridge, 1988), of which p.165 is particularly relevant.

147 Pevsner, *Suffolk*, p.150.

148 Lloyds Bank Archives, C1b/51.

149 I am grateful to Dr Arthur Channing Downs of Pennsylvania for helpful advice on the respective works of the Cottinghams.

150 Graves, op. cit., Vol. 2 (1905), p.178.

151 *B.*, Vol. 1 (1842/43), p.553; *G.M.*, Vol. 38 (1852, Part 2), pp.608, 609.

152 On the basis that the winning design was approved in 1848 (*B.*, Vol. 6 (1848), p.477).

153 For Wakefield, see sources in Appendix One; for Newcastle, *B.*, Vol. 18 (1860), p.268.

154 Three-quarters of his work was from this source: obit. in *J.R.I.B.A.*, Third Series, Vol. 1 (1902), p.461.

155 *B.*, Vol. 5 (1847), p.242.

156 See Chapter Five.

157 Pevsner & Harris, *Lincolnshire*, p.548. Even this style was called 'Elizabethan' in White's *Directory* (1842).

158 M. Girouard, *The Victorian Country House* (2nd ed., New Haven & London, 1979), pp.130–6. See also plate in *B.N.*, Vol. 4 (1858), p.11.

159 Taylor loc. cit., p.149.

160 Published annual report in the *Royal Devonport Telegraph & Plymouth Chronicle*, 27/2/1830, referring to interim premises acquired on a 21-year lease and fitted out 'with every convenience necessary'.

161 [T. Clarke], *History of . . . Howden* (Howden, 1850), p.59.

162 *Doncaster, Nottingham & Lancashire Gazette*, March 1843.

163 *B.*, Vol. 30 (1872), pp.199–201 (obit. of Edward Walters).

164 *Manchester Guardian*, 11/1/1843.

165 Phillips, op. cit., p.369.

166 Leader, op. cit., p.17.

167 *West Briton*, 12/9/1845.

168 Pevsner, *Yorkshire. West Riding*, p.320.

169 H.-R. Hitchcock, op. cit., p.356.

170 Ibid.

171 T. Hughes, *The Stranger's Handbook to Chester . . .* (Chester, 1856), p.69.

172 Devon County Library, press-cutting in Westcountry Studies Library.

173 *B.*, Vol. 8 (1850), pp.138, 139.

174 Post Office *Directory* (1855), p.44.

175 W. & J. Hargrove, *The New Guide . . . [to] The City of York* (York, 1838), p.70.

176 *C.E. & A.J.*, Vol. 3 (1840), p.217.

177 Ibid.

178 *An Outline of the 150 Years History of the London T.S.B., 1816–1966* (London, 1966), p.6.

179 P. Nuttgens, *York* (Studio Vista Series, London, 1971), p.55, perhaps following Victoria County History, *Yorkshire. City of York* (London, 1961), p.260.

180 H.W. Brace, 'Gainsborough. Some Notes on its History' (typescript, 1966), p.98, quoting from *Gainsborough Evening News*, 8/1/1957. This was again the date of the bank's establishment.

181 References below are taken from Ministry Lists, researched 1981–4. It is possible that since then some lists have been amended.

182 See Appendix One.

183 I.e. Bath, Bolton, Cockermouth, Colchester, Devizes, Gloucester, Lancaster, Newark, Nottingham, Ormskirk, Portsmouth, Swindon, Tewkesbury, Truro, Wakefield and Wirksworth.

184 See Appendix One.

185 *Manchester Guardian*, 4/1/1840. The trustees reported also a 'mischievous attempt . . . to shake . . . confidence'.

186 P.R.O., NDO 9/13, pp.188, 189. Marlborough backed down immediately, and it is clear that Portsmouth continued to work from its premises at No. 88, St Thomas's Street, built only in 1837.

187 Harrison, op. cit., p.57.

188 In G.F. Townsend, *The Town and Borough of Leominster* (Leominster [1863], p.202.

189 Lloyds Bank Archives, Trustees' Minute Book; *Worcestershire Chronicle*, 29/6/1853; title deeds; Pevsner & Hubbard, *Cheshire*, p.331; White's *Lincolnshire Directory* (1856) and P.O. *Directory* (1861); Townsend, loc. cit.; P.O. *Directory*, loc. cit.; H.J. Hillen, *History of . . . King's Lynn*, Vol. 2 (Norwich, 1907), pp.615, 616.

190 *B.*, Vol. 17 (1859), p.351.

191 Ibid.

192 P.O. *Directory* (1861).

193 Leader, op. cit., p.32.

194 24 Vic., c.14.

195 26 & 27 Vic., c.87.

196 Horne, op. cit., p.217.

197 Lewins, op. cit., pp.246–50; Horne, op. cit., Chapter Ten.

198 Lewins, op. cit., p.247.

199 Lewins, loc. cit.

200 22 & 23 Vic., c.53.

Chapter Four

1 M. Girouard, *The Victorian Country House* (2nd ed., 1979; New Haven and London) lists some 28 houses out of a total of 203 discussed, which were for bankers or financiers.

2 Ibid., in respect of Robert Kerr's Ford Manor for Joseph Spender-Clay.

3 Ibid., in respect of George Devey's Godlings for Robert Abel Smith.

4 *B.N.*, Vol. 7 (1861), p.359.

5 *B.*, Vol. 23 (1865), p.901.

6 Ibid., Vol. 18 (1860), pp.268, 804.

7 Ibid., Vol. 20 (1862), pp.604, 605.

8 *B.N.*, loc. cit.

9 Ibid.

10 *B.*, Vol. 22 (1864), p.770.

11 Ibid., p.769.

12 J. Summerson, *The Architecture of Victorian London* (Charlottesville, 1976), pp.17, 18.

13 *B.N.*, Vol. 7 (1861), p.359, and Vol. 11 (1864), p.660; ibid., Vol. 11 (1864), p.660; *B.*, Vol. 22 (1864), pp.758.

14 *B.N.*, Vol. 12 (1865), p.613; *B.*, Vol. 22 (1864), p.770.

15 *B.N.*, Vol. 7 (1861), pp.359, 360.

16 Ibid., p.359; *B.*, loc. cit.

17 *B.*, Vol. 35 (1877), p.5.

18 The most expensive bank was probably the National Provincial Bank's head office, reckoned to cost £50000 exclusive of site (*B.*, Vol. 23 (1865), p.384).

19 Hardwick succeeded C.R. Cockerell in 1855. There was little rebuilding to be done at Threadneedle Street, so Hardwick was relatively free (cf. Marston Acres, op. cit., Vol. 2, p.586).

20 Porter also worked for the rival London & Westminster Bank as late as 1885 (*B.*, Vol. 49 (1885), pp.716, 718, 719).

21 Two different designs were published: *B.*, Vol. 23 (1865), pp.607, 609; *B.N.*, Vol. 15 (1868), p.46.

22 *B.*, Vol. 23 (1865), pp.834, 835, 901–3, 908, 909; *I.L.N.*, Vol. 48 (1866), pp.57, 60–2; Graves, op. cit., Vol. 3 (1905), p.230; A.E. Richardson, *Monumental Classic Architecture* ... (London, 1914), pp.100, 101, plate 60; G. Stamp & C. Avery, *Victorian Buildings of London 1837–1887* (London, 1980), p.75.

23 Fullest explanation of the symbolism is in *B.*, op. cit., p.902.

24 *B.*, Vol. 20 (1862), p.604.

25 Ibid., Vol. 22 (1864), p.770.

26 Gothic details were published in *B.N.*, Vol. 12 (1865), p.613, with suitably Gothic lettering for the caption, but no remarks passed in relation to banking.

27 *G.M.*, Vol. 103 (1833, Part 1), p.543; Hitchcock, op. cit., p.369.

28 *G.M.*, loc. cit.

29 Especially as there was contemporary criticism of Shaw's building as 'bad Italian architecture with some of the characteristics of the pointed style' (Hitchcock, loc. cit.).

30 Nat. West. Bank Archives, Manchester & Liverpool District Bank minute book.

31 J. Ward, *The Borough of Stoke-upon-Trent* (London, 1843), pp.381, 382.

32 Pevsner & Harris, *Lincolnshire*, p.471: 'The Gothic theme is continued by the adjacent County Hall of 1925–7 and by Barclays Bank with a face S. towards the Market Place. This is of 1835 and was designed by Lockwood & Mawson of Bradford'; Dora Ware, *A Short Dictionary of British Architects* (London, 1967), p.152, *sub* H.F. Lockwood: 'Built Barclays Bank, Market Place, Boston, Lincs. (1835)'; Ministry List also dates it to 1835.

33 *B.*, Vol. 34 (1876), p.1175; *B.N.*, Vol. 31 (1876, Part 2), p.533.

34 S.N. Davis, *Banking in Boston* (Boston, 1976), p.28.

35 Nat. West. Bank Archives, Nat. Prov. Bank minute book.

36 Wood's extraordinary character, and stories of his wealth, are recounted in W.J. Lawson, *The History of Banking* (London, 1850), pp.262, 263.

37 Nat. West. Bank Archives, loc. cit.

38 *D.N.B.*

39 Verey, *Gloucestershire. The Vale and the Forest of Dean* (London, 1970), pp.297, 298.

40 *B.N.*, Vol. 3 (1857), p.582.

41 *Punch*, 10 Sept. 1864.

42 *B.*, Vol. 22 (1864), p.769.

43 Hilton Price, op. cit., and P.O. *Directories*.

44 *I.L.N.*, Vol. 46 (1865), p.233; ibid., Vol. 52 (1868), p.29.

45 G.G. Scott, *Remarks on Secular and Domestic Architecture* (London, 2nd ed., 1858), p.203.

46 Vol. 1 was published in 1851 and Vols. 2 and 3 in 1853. Also influential was Ruskin's *The Seven Lamps of Architecture* (1849).

47 By 21 & 22 Vic., c.91.

48 Scott, op. cit., p.204. He was referring to public buildings, in a list headed by banks.

49 Ibid.

50 Ibid.

51 Pevsner & Hubbard, *Cheshire*, p.252.

52 Pevsner, *Cornwall*, p.165; R. Dixon & S. Muthesius, *Victorian Architecture* (London, 1978), p.131; I. Rabey, *The Book of St. Columb & St. Mawgan* Buckingham, 1979), pp.47, 77, 80, 133.

53 *Western Gazette*, 14/3/1958, in feature from its files of 1858.

54 *B.*, Vol. 27 (1869), p.407.

55 Ibid., Vol. 29 (1871), p.509; *A.*, Vol. 10 (1873), p.174.

56 *B.*, Vol. 22 (1864), p.497, and Vol. 25 (1867), p.449; D. Linstrum, *West Yorkshire Architects and Architecture* (London, 1978), pp.37, 40, 364, 383, plate 296, who calls demolition of the 'Gothic palazzo' in 1964 'the greatest single loss in Leeds' (p.37); Pevsner, *Yorkshire. The West Riding* pp.317, 318, 634; D. Cole, *The Work of Sir Gilbert Scott* (London 1980), pp.124, 217.

57 J. Hall, *A History of the Town and Parish of Nantwich* (Nantwich, 1883), p.248; Pevsner & Hubbard, *Cheshire*, p.287. For the Lombard Street bank, see refs given earlier. *B.N.*, Vol. 13 (1866), pp.848, 850, 851; Pevsner, *Bedfordshire, Huntingdon and Peterborough*, pp.110, 111. *B.M.*, Vol. 76 (1903, Part 2), pp.457, 461; *B.*, Vol. 89 (1905), p.238.

58 *B.*, Vol. 25 (1867), p.449.

59 C.J. Billson, *Leicester Memories* (Leicester, 1924), p.33.

60 There is an excellent coloured, contemporary perspective of the banking-hall reproduced as plate 3.7 in A.R. Holmes & E. Green, *Midland. 150 Years of Banking Business* (London, 1986).

61 Sherwood & Pevsner, *Oxfordshire*, p.308; *B.*, Vol. 24 (1866), pp.426, 427, and Pevsner, *Cambridgeshire*, p.241.

62 In New Bridge Street, designed by Deane & Woodward.

63 Design reproduced in *B.*, Vol. 24 (1866), pp.326, 327.

64 Design reproduced in ibid., Vol. 27 (1869), p.307.

65 *B.N.*, Vol. 4 (1858), pp.76, 425; W.J. Knox, *Decades of the Ulster Bank 1836–1964* (Belfast, 1965), pp.65–70.

66 Knox, loc. cit.

67 N. Simpson, *The Belfast Bank 1827–1970* (Belfast, 1965), pp.65–70.

68 The bank was built on 'running sand', requiring deep piling and little accommodation below ground level.

69 These, and the other facts of decorative detail in this paragraph, are taken from Knox, loc. cit., who quotes contemporary descriptions 'compiled from various sources'.

70 Knox, op. cit., p.70.

71 *B.*, Vol. 27 (1869), pp.444, 447.

72 Graves, op. cit., Vol. 3 (1905), p.50 (1862 Exhibition).

73 I.e. the National Provincial Bank branch, 1863, also from the Elmslie partnership (Pevsner).

74 *B.N.*, Vol. 9 (1862, Part 2), pp.218, 219; *B.*, Vol. 110 (1916, Part 1) p.236; Grindon, op. cit., p.282; W.A. Shaw, *Manchester Old and New*, Vol. 2 (London, 1896), p.64.

75 Walters's obit. in *B.*, Vol. 30 (1872), pp.199–201.

76 *B.N.*, loc. cit.

77 *B.*, Vol. 25 (1867), p.593, and Vol. 27 (1869), pp.40, 47; *A.*, Vol. 1 (1869), pp.39, 40; R.K. Dent, *Old and New Birmingham* (Birmingham, 1880), pp.615, 616; *B.M.*, Vol. 76 (1903, Part 2), pp.7–14; Holmes & Green, op. cit., p.55.

78 *B.*, Vol. 16 (1858), p.127.

79 Ibid., Vol. 27 (1869), p.40.

80 *A.*, loc. cit.; Dent, loc. cit.

81 *D.N.B.*; A.E. Richardson, op. cit., pp.100, 101; article 'John Gibson of Westminster, 1817–1892' in *A.J.*, Vol. 54 (1921, Part 2), pp.523–7.

82 This figure appears to have been first mentioned by Alfred Waterhouse ('upwards of forty branches') in *B.*, Vol. 58 (1890), p.449.

83 *A.*, Vol. 1 (1869), pp.39, 40; *B.*, Vol. 32 (1874), p.358.

84 *B.*, Vol. 24 (1866), p.179; *A.*, Vol. 13 (1875), p.52; Pevsner *Suffolk*, p.149.

85 *B.*, Vol. 30 (1872), p.786, and *I.L.N.*, Vol. 60 (1872), p.120; *B.*, Vol. 32 (1874), pp.154, 155, 157; Pevsner, *County Durham*, p.131; *B.*, Vol. 28 (1870), p.503 and Vol. 29 (1871), p.651; ibid., Vol. 34 (1876), p.250 and Vol. 35 (1877), p.661; ibid., Vol. 37 (1879), pp.1379, 1381 and *B.N.*, Vol. 36 (1879, Part 1), p.170; Littlebury's *Worcestershire Directory* (1873), p.806; *B.*, Vol. 33 (1875), p.307; *A.*, Vol. 16 (1876), p.268.

86 Pevsner, *Cambridgeshire* p.499.

87 Pevsner & Harris, *Lincolnshire*, p.160.

88 E.g. Gingell at Bristol and Elmslie at Hereford.

89 E.g. Perkin & Bulmer at Whitby (*B.*, Vol. 45 (1883, Part 1), p.62).

90 Richardson, op. cit., p.101.

91 *A.*, Vol. 13 (1875), p.52.

92 This building, in Gosditch Street, Cirencester, was for some years used as District Council offices, with all the badges remaining.

93 Goodhart-Rendel, p.113.

94 A. Saint, *Richard Norman Shaw* (New Haven and London, 1976), pp.86, 87; N. Temple, *Farnham Buildings and People* (London & Chichester, 1973), p.58, plate 38; E. Smith, *Victorian Farnham* (London & Chichester, 1971), p.69; *Dark Horse*, Jan. 1962, pp.93, 94. Plans, elevations and details are in RIBA Drawings Collection.

95 Shaw's similar fireplace at Farnham was removed to the Lloyds Bank branch built on the site.

96 For Truefitt's friendship with (Sir) William Cunliffe Brooks, MP, see his obit. in *J.R.I.B.A.*, Third Series, Vol. 9 (1902), p.461.

97 *B.*, Vol. 28 (1870), p.886.

98 *Ibid.*, Vol. 33 (1875), pp.436, 439; Graves, op. cit., Vol. 8 (1906), p.24 (1870 Exhibition); Pevsner & Hubbard, *Cheshire*, p.61.

99 *B.N.*, Vol. 39 (1880), p.152; cf. *A.R.*, Vol. 2 (1897), p.93: 'Mr. Nesfield showed, in his bank at Saffron Walden and elsewhere the adaptability of Gothic.'

100 *B.*, Vol. 43 (1882, Part 2), p.289; Pevsner, *Wiltshire*, p.401.

101 Pevsner, loc. cit.

102 *Wiltshire County Mirror & Express*, 2/7/1897.

103 *B.*, Vol. 37 (1879), p.1061.

104 *Wiltshire County Mirror & Express*, loc. cit.

105 Ibid.

106 In the context of banking, this term seems to have been used first by *B.N.* (Vol. 39 (1880, Part 2), p.111) to describe a bank at Wakefield.

107 *B.*, Vol. 43 (1882, Part 2), pp.460, 464; cf. *B.N.*, Vol. 45 (1883, Part 2), p.709; Pevsner, *Staffordshire*, p.171.

108 For the history of the movement, see M. Girouard, *Sweetness and Light. The 'Queen Anne' Movement 1860–1900* (Oxford, 1977).

109 Ibid., pp.88, 89.

110 R.S. Sayers, *Lloyds Bank in the History of English Banking* (Oxford, 1957), p.236.

111 Lloyds Bank Archives, HO/D/Boa. 2,5.

112 E.A. Bailey, *A History of Southport* (Southport, 1955), p.140, quoting newspaper of 1857.

113 E.L.S. Horsburgh, *Bromley, Kent* . . . (London, 1929), p.63.

114 Lloyds Bank Archives HO/D/Boa. 7.

115 These were wound up in 1866 and 1867 respectively.

116 Lloyds Bank Archives, HO/D/Boa. 5.

117 Ibid.

118 Ibid.

119 Holmes & Green, op. cit., pp.69, 70.

120 Of these, Hardwick was the first to be paid a fixed salary (£300).

121 *C.E. & A.J.*, Vol. 3 (1840), p.183.

122 Nat. West. Bank Archives, Nat. Prov. Bank minute book (No. 675), p.272.

123 *B.*, Vol. 58 (1890), p.449. A.E. Richardson, writing in 1914 (op. cit., pp.100, 101), was less specific, suggesting that he 'designed the head office and nearly all the important branches . . .'.

124 *I.L.N.*, Vol. 61 (1872), p.517.

125 *A.*, Vol. 14 (1875), p.146, and Graves, op. cit., Vol. 3 (1905), p.230; *B.*, Vol. 39 (1880, Part 2), pp.279, 310, 642, 646, and Graves, loc. cit.

126 Although Gibson was probably not salaried.

127 Lloyds Bank Archives, HO/D/Boa. 2,3.

128 Lloyds Bank Archives, Board minute books. Ironbridge branch was mentioned in *B.*, Vol. 34 (1876), p.935.

129 Lloyds Bank Archives, HO/D/Boa. 3.

130 Ibid., HO/D/Boa. 7.

131 For instance, premises at Derby for Messrs Crompton & Evans's Union Bank (*B.N.*, Vol. 38 (1880, Part 1), p.85), and the Hemel Hempstead branch of the Bucks & Oxon Union Bank, completed in 1885 (Lloyds Bank Archives, A40b/7).

132 For the branches built by Henry Hall for this bank, see his obit. in *J.R.I.B.A.*, Vol. 17 (1910), p.122, 123.

133 Their architects in the 1870s were Barker & Ellis.

134 *B.*, Vol. 29 (1871), p.509.

135 Nor vice versa. At Carlisle, for example, Hetherington & Oliver designed premises for the Clydesdale Bank (*B.*, Vol. 37 (1879), p.759).

136 All refs in following paragraphs are from Lloyds Bank Archives, Board minute books, unless otherwise stated.

137 Lloyds Bank Archives, HO/D/Pre. 1.

138 *B.*, Vol. 22 (1864), p.769.

139 Ibid.

140 W.F. Crick & J.E. Wadsworth, *A Hundred Years of Joint Stock Banking* (London, 1936), p.78.

141 It is interesting that Waterhouse's Gothic bank for Messrs Alexanders in Lombard Street was reckoned to cost about £11 000, less than a third of the cost of some contemporary banks nearby.

142 *A.*, Vol. 3 (1870), p.229.

143 Cumbria Record Office, Ca/E4, Nos 400, 711, 1079, 2631, etc. Cf. *B.*, Vol. 32 (1874), p.510 referring to plans of a Carlisle bank 'passed by the local Health Committee'.

144 *B.N.*, Vol. 18/19 (1870), p.293.

145 Ibid.

146 Ibid.

147 Ibid.

148 *B.*, Vol. 23 (1865), pp.572, 573.

149 Ibid., Vol. 41 (1881, Part 2), pp.764, 765. Cf. Pevsner, *Lancashire. The Rival North*, p.72: 'the architecturally best building of Blackpool'.

150 *B.*, Vol. 49 (1885, Part 2), p.621.

151 Ibid.

152 Ibid., p.701.

Chapter Five

1 *Q.R.*, Vol. 162 (1886), p.133.

2 *B.M.*, Vol. 47 (1887), p.125.

3 *B.N.*, Vol. 40 (1881, Part 1), pp.404, 437, 468, 469, 500, from which all refs in this paragraph are taken. See also, A. Saint, *Richard Norman Shaw* (New Haven & London, 1976), pp.150, 238.

4 J. Orbell, *Baring Brothers . . . A History to 1939* (London, 1985), p.56.

5 *B.N.*, op. cit., p.500.

6 The judges' own description of the competitions in ibid., Vol. 70 (1896, Part 1), p.816.

7 Ibid., Vol. 37 (1879, Part 2), pp.810, 811.

8 Ibid., Vol. 52 (1887, Part 1), p.474.

9 Ibid., Vol. 58 (1890, Part 1), pp.832, 850.

10 Ibid., Vol. 70 (1897, Part 1), p.816, plate after p.817.

11 Ibid., Vol. 77 (1899, Part 2), pp.756, 757, plates after p.765.

12 Ibid., Vol. 83 (1902, Part 2), p.425, plate after p.435.

13 Ibid., Vol. 92 (1907, Part 1), pp.302, 303, plates after pp.308, 309.

14 Ibid., Vol. 74 (1898, Part 1), p.218.

15 Ibid., Vol. 71 (1896, Part 2), p.896, and Vol. 83 (1902, Part 2), pp.8, 9, plates after p.46: *A.*, Vol. 67 (1902, Part 1), plate after p.208, and Vol. 70 (1903, Part 2), plate after p.328.

16 By J. Macvicar Anderson (*B.*, Vol. 85 (1903, Part 2), pp.206, 338; *A.*, Vol. 70 (1903, Part 2), plates after pp.8, 40, 88, 104, 152, 312, 392).

17 *B.M.*, Vol. 47 (1887), p.1180; *A.*, Vol. 37 (1887, Part 1), p.291.

18 *B.N.*, Vol. 56 (1889, Part 1), p.87.

19 *B.*, Vol. 77 (1899, Part 2), p.357; ibid., Vol. 80 (1901, Part 1), p.589; *B.N.*, Vol. 77 (1899, Part 2), p.438; ibid., Vol. 79 (1900, Part 2), p.251, plate after p.270; *A.R.*, Vol. 10 (1901, Part 2), pp.146–55; Graves, op. cit., Vol. 7 (1906), p.96; ibid., Vol. 8 (1906), p.299.

20 C.H. Reilly, *Some Liverpool Streets and Buildings in 1921* (Liverpool, 1921), p.34, 35.

21 *A.R.*, loc. cit.

22 Ibid., Vol. 7 (1900, Part 1), p.163, in article 'Modern Architecture: Messrs. Barclay's New Bank in Fleet Street'.

23 Littlebury's *Directory and Gazetteer of the County of Worcester* (1873), pp.102, 103.

24 Ibid.

25 Ibid.

26 *B.*, Vol. 42 (1882, Part 1), p.702.

27 Ibid.

28 Lloyds Bank Archives, A16b/1.

29 The architects were Harris, Martin & Harris and the sculptor Barfield of Leicester (Pevsner & Wedgwood, *Warwickshire*, p.164).

30 The site had been taken 20 years earlier and possibly this was the second Gothic branch there.

31 *B.*, Vol. 52 (1887, Part 1), p.190; *B.N.*, Vol. 53 (1887, Part 2), p.454.

32 *B.N.*, Vol. 93 (1907, Part 2), p.285, plate after p.304.

33 Ibid., Vol. 101 (1911, Part 2), p.763, plate after p.778.

34 The plate is still in place, the building now being owned by Lloyds Bank.

35 *B.*, Vol. 80 (1901, Part 1), p.119.

36 *A.*, Vol. 76 (1906, Part 2), plate after p.148. By George E. Clay.

37 *B.N.*, Vol. 81 (1901, Part 2), p.519, plate after p.538.

38 Ibid., Vol. 82 (1902, Part 1), p.5.

39 Ibid., Vol. 89 (1905, Part 2), p.865.

40 *B.*, Vol. 106 (1914, Part 1), p.44.

41 *B.N.*, Vol. 53 (1887, Part 2), p.611.

42 I.e. at Great Harwood (ibid., Vol. 72 (1897, Part 1), p.485) and Loughton (*A.R.*, Vol. 9 (1901, Part 1), p.263).

43 *A.*, Vol. 60 (1898, Part 2), p.169.

44 *B.M.*, Vol. 53 (1892, Part 1), p.292.

45 *A.*, Vol. 56 (1896, Part 2), plate after p.362.

46 By Maxwell & Tuke for the Lancashire & Yorkshire Bank (*B.N.*, Vol. 60 (1891, Part 1), p.328).

47 *B.*, Vol. 106 (1914, Part 1), p.703.

48 Lloyds Bank Archives, A50b/85. The architects made a total of 36 journeys to Sleaford for various matters in connection with the new bank.

49 *B.N.*, Vol. 80 (1901, Part 1), p.263.

50 *B.N.*, Vol. 49 (1889), p.347.

51 Ibid., Vol. 64 (1897, Part 2), p.114.

52 Ibid., Vol. 48 (1888), p.30.

53 Ibid., Vol. 65 (1898, Part 1), p.452.

54 Ibid., Vol. 48 (1888), p.132.

55 Ibid., Vol. 57 (1894, Part 1), p.178.

56 *B.N.*, Vol. 83 (1902, Part 2), p.541.

57 Illus. in *B.N.*, Vol. 83 (1902, Part 2), after p.542. See also Graves, op. cit., Vol. 6 (1906), p.12.

58 *B.*, Vol. 71 (1896, Part 2), pp.511, 519, and Vol. 75 (1898, Part 2), p.490; *B.N.*, Vol. 70 (1896, Part 1), p.857; plate after p.858; ibid., Vol. 75 (1898, Part 2), p.714; Graves, op. cit., Vol. 8 (1906), p.160. Interior illustrated in Burmantofts Catalogue, 1902.

59 *B.M.*, Vol. 45 (1885), p.587.

60 G. Rae, *The Country Banker* ... (London, 1885), p.288; cf. *B.M.*, op. cit., p.118: 'opening a new office is rather a convenience to the customer than an advantage to the bank: an unavoidable incident in the business ...'.

61 *B.M.*, Vol. 48 (1888), p.132.

62 Ibid.

63 Ibid., Vol. 57 (1894, Part 1), p.178.

64 *B.*, Vol. 37 (1879), pp.254, 543, 545, and Vol. 38 (1880, Part 1), p.326.

65 *B.M.*, Vol. 60 (1895, Part 2), p.259, reporting Chairman of London Joint Stock Bank: '... his own experience was that it took ten years in London to make a branch pay.'

66 Ibid., Vol. 44 (1884), p.1023.

67 Ibid., Vol. 50 (1890), pp.461, 1568.

68 *B.N.*, Vol. 62 (1892, Part 1), p.369.

69 Ibid., Vol. 75 (1898, Part 2), p.751.

70 In fact, Truefitt & Watson were also called architects to the bank in 1893.

71 I.e. West Ealing branch (*A.*, Vol. 66 (1901, Part 2), p.248).

72 *B.N.*, Vol. 68 (1895, Part 1), p.371; *A.*, Vol. 56 (1896, Part 2), plate after p.378.

73 Cf. *B.M.*, Vol. 47 (1887). p.88, referring to a new branch of Martin's Bank: 'This is the first extension of business made to private banks in London, in the way of opening branch offices, which we have ever had occasion to record.'

74 Aggregate of figures in annual volumes of ibid. between Vol. 47 (1887), p.88, and Vol. 61 (1896, Part 1), p.171.

75 Ibid., Vol. 59 (1895, Part 1), p.289.

76 *B.*, Vol. 61 (1891, Part 2), p.265; *B.N.*, Vol. 61 (1891, Part 2), p.485.

77 Wooler was by F.W. Rich; Forest Hall was by White & Stephenson.

78 *B.M.*, Vol. 55 (1894, Part 1), p.99.

79 Ibid., Vol. 57 (1894, Part 1), p.218.

80 Ibid., Vol. 59 (1895, Part 1), pp.702–4.

81 *B.N.*, Vol. 44 (1883, Part 1), p.526; Vol. 47 (1884, Part 2), p.362; and Vol. 48 (1885, Part 1), p.128. For the difficulties, see C. Donald Hebden, *The Trustee Savings Banks of Yorkshire & Lincoln* (1981), p.135.

82 *B.N.*, Vol. 78 (1900, Part 1), p.195.

83 *A.*, Vol. 66 (1901, Part 2), p.72.

84 Ibid., Vol. 24 (1880, Part 2), p.197.

85 *B.N.*, Vol. 56 (1889, Part 1), p.332.

86 Ibid., Vol. 62 (1892, Part 1), p.697. For Wigan, see ibid., Vol. 60 (1891, Part 1), p.621.

87 Ibid., Vol. 68 (1895, Part 1), p.439.

88 Ibid., Vol. 81 (1901, Part 2), p.10, plate after p.12.

89 Ibid., Vol. 96 (1909, Part 1), p.69.

90 *B.M.*, Vol. 55 (1893, Part 1), p.491.

91 Cf. *D.N.B.*, which mentions he appears to have retired from practice around 1883.

92 *B.*, Vol. 60 (1891, Part 1), p.216 (Cardiff); ibid., Vol. 63 (1892, Part 2), p.267, and *B.N.*, Vol. 63 (1892, Part 2), p.476 (Hereford); ibid., Vol. 64 (1893, Part 1), pp.4, 82, and *B.*, Vol. 66 (1894, Part 1), p.257 (York).

93 *B.N.*, York reference above where he had been called W.J. Gribble. In the same commission, *B.* called him G.H. Gribble.

94 *B.N.*, Vol. 60 (1891, Part 1), p.625. For Piccadilly, see *B.*, Vol. 66 (1894, Part 1), pp.698, 733, and other refs in *B.N.* and *A.*

95 *B.N.*, Vol. 74 (1898, Part 1), p.218 (Leeds); *B.*, Vol. 63 (1892, Part 2), p.460 (Liverpool); Pevsner, *Cambridgeshire*, p.239.

96 Lloyds Bank Archives, HO/D/Pre. 1.

97 Ibid.

98 *B.N.*, Vol. 61 (1891, Part 2), p.414; Graves, op. cit., Vol. 7 (1906), p.247.

99 Lloyds Bank Archives, HO/D/Pre. 4.

100 *B.N.*, Vol. 102 (1912, Part 1), p.811, and Vol. 109 (1915, Part 2), p.380; *B.*, Vol. 106 (1914, Part 1), pp.703, 705.

101 Lloyds Bank Archives, HO/D/Boa. 11, 12, 14.

102 *B.N.*, Vol. 64 (1893, Part 1), p.421.

103 Ibid., Vol. 59 (1890, Part 2), p.876.

104 E. Green, *The Making of a Modern Banking Group* . . . (London, 1979), p.6.

105 *B.*, Vol. 59 (1890, Part 2), pp.43, 349 (Leeds); ibid., Vol. 64 (1893, Part 1), p.268 (Bradford); ibid., Vol. 67 (1894, Part 2), p.248 (Coventry).

106 Pevsner, *Northumberland*, p.182.

107 *B.N.*, Vol. 79 (1900, Part 2), p.464. For date of opening, see *B.N.* Vol. 63 (1897, Part 1), p.295, and Vol. 64 (1897, Part 2), p.233.

108 See Whinney's obit, by H. Austen Hall, in *J.R.I.B.A.*, Vol. 33 (1926), p.491.

109 Graves, op. cit., Vol. 3 (1905), p.279.

110 Midland Bank Group Archives, Accession 123.

111 Sir Arthur Blomfield had been appointed architect to the Bank of England in 1883; he died in 1899 and was succeeded by his son, Arthur Conran Blomfield, who held the post for 20 years (W. Marston Acres, op. cit., Vol. 2 (1931), p.588).

112 The various sources, as follows, suggest that the building was designed by Sir Arthur Blomfield but completed, and certainly publicised by A.C. Blomfield (*B.*, Vol. 74 (1898, Part 1), p.387; *B.N.*, Vol. 74 (1898, Part 1), p.635, plate after p.654; *A.R.*, Vol. 7 (1900, Part 1), pp.163–7; Graves, op. cit., Vol. 1 (1905), p.212).

113 *B.*, Vol. 88 (1905, Part 1), p.494; *R.A. Exhibitors*, Vol. 1 (1973), p.155.

114 Holmes & Green, op. cit., p.103.

115 Ibid.

116 *B.N.*, Vol. 101 (1911, Part 2), p.763.

117 *R.A. Exhibitors*, Vol. 6 (1982), p.325.

118 Midland Bank Group Archives, diaries of Sir Edward Holden (26/9), 9 September 1913.

119 Lloyds Bank Archives, HO/D/Pre. 3.

120 Ibid., HO/D/Boa. 12.

121 Ibid., HO/D/Boa. 13.

122 The earliest was probably the building (still standing) in Threadneedle Street, London, erected 'to suit the requirements of banks and insurance offices' by the

freeholder, Mr W. Bass (*B.N.*, Vol. 58 (1890, Part 1), p.652, plate after p.653). A later, West End, design for banking premises and chambers, initiated by the freeholders, the Norwich Union, was published in *A.*, Vol. 75 (1906, Part 1), p.288.

123 Gwyther's death was noted in *J.R.I.B.A.*, Vol. 11 (1903–4), p.116, without comment or detail.

124 *A.*, Vol. 59 (1898, Part 1), plate after p.320 (Bishopsgate); *B.N.*, Vol. 72 (1897, Part 1), p.110 (Hull); and *B.*, Vol. 77 (1899, Part 2), pp.429, 491.

125 *B.N.*, Vol. 86 (1904, Part 1), p.375.

126 Ibid.

127 *B.N.*, Vol. 56 (1889, Part 1), p.888; *A.R.*, Vol. 16 (1904), pp.263, 271–4. For refs to another major bank by Anderson (for the British Linen Company), see note 16 above.

128 *A.R.*, Vol. 21 (1907, Part 1), pp.323–32.

129 *B.*, Vol. 76 (1899, Part 1), p.98; *B.N.*, Vol. 89 (1905, Part 2), p.757.

130 *B.*, Vol. 107 (1914, Part 2), pp.429, 430.

131 His obit. (*J.R.I.B.A.*, Vol. 59 (1952), p.229) mentions that he was responsible for some 50 branches in London and the Home Counties for the Westminster Bank: many of these were probably, strictly speaking for the London & County and the London, County & Westminster Banks.

132 There is a useful appreciation of Wheeler's Sussex banks in Nairn & Pevsner, *Sussex*, pp.245, 297, 310.

133 *B.N.*, Vol. 77 (1899, Part 2), p.513, and Vol. 79 (1900, Part 2), p.109, plate after p.128.

134 *B.*, Vol. 100 (1911, Part 1), p.780.

135 *B.N.*, Vol. 59 (1890, Part 2), p.714.

136 *B.*, Vol. 39 (1880, Part 2), p.489.

137 *B.N.*, Vol. 100 (1911, Part 1), p.490.

138 P. Nuttgens, *York* (London, 1971), p.74.

139 *B.N.*, Vol. 55 (1888, Part 2), p.570; *A.*, Vol. 50 (1893, Part 2), p.25; Graves, op. cit., Vol. 4 (1906), p.60.

140 Premises combined with those of the Economic Assurance Society: *B.*, Vol. 82 (1902, Part 1), p.592; ibid., Vol. 85 (1903, Part 2), p.587; *B.N.*, Vol. 82 (1902, Part 1), p.307.

141 *B.*, Vol. 106 (1914, Part 1), p.511, and Vol. 109 (1915, Part 2), p.458; *B.N.*, Vol. 109 (1915, Part 2), pp.738, 776.

142 *B.*, Vol. 91 (1906, Part 2), p.602.

143 Cf. articles on W.H. Brierley in *C.L.*, 23/9/1982 and 30/9/1982.

144 Occasionally rising to around £10000 for branches in important areas of cities like Birmingham and Coventry.

145 *Q.R.*, Vol. 176 (1893), pp.54, 55.

146 Ibid. Cf. article 'Bank & Insurance buildings' in *A. & B.J.*, Vol. 39 (1914, Part 1), p.259, typical of continuing criticism: 'Unfortunately it is of the nature of the case that wealthy corporations should build pompously and lavishly as an expression of their prosperity rather than of their taste.'

147 Chairman of London & County Bank (*B.M.*, Vol. 53 (1892, Part 1), p.466).

148 Rae, op. cit., p.172.

149 Ibid.

150 Cf. *B.M.*, Vol. 44 (1884), p.1017, and Vol. 48 (1888), p.229.

151 Ibid., Vol. 50 (1890), p.1359.

152 Ibid., Vol. 51 (1891, Part 1), p.65.

153 Ibid., Vol. 52 (1891, Part 2), p.498.

154 E.g. ibid., Vol. 55 (1893, Part 1), p.491, in respect of branches at Ashby, Wellingborough and Grantham, and ibid., Vol. 57 (1894, Part 1), p.461, in respect of Loughborough.

155 Ibid., p.478.

156 Lloyds Bank Ltd, *Annual Report* (1896).

157 Ibid., (1897).

158 *B.M.*, Vol. 67 (1899, Part 1), pp.238, 240.

159 Ibid.

160 *Annual Report* (1896).

161 *B.M.*, Vol. 48 (1888), p.441.

162 Ibid.

163 Ibid., Vol. 61 (1896, Part 1), p.473.

164 *B.*, Vol. 37 (1879), pp.596, 641.

165 *B.M.*, Vol. 47 (1887), p.1180.

166 Ibid.

167 Ibid., Vol. 48 (1888), pp.868–77; cf. *B.N.*, Vol. 54 (1888, Part 1), p.871.

168 Lloyds Bank Archives, A26c/1.

169 Ibid., HO/D/Pre. 3, 4

170 Ibid., HO/D/Pre. 3.

171 Ibid., HO/D/Pre. 1.

172 Ibid.

173 Ibid., HO/D/Pre. 3.

174 Ibid.

175 Ibid., HO/D/Pre. 7.

176 *B.M.*, Vol. 45 (1885), pp.47, 48; ibid., Vol. 50 (1890), p.762.

177 Ex inf. Mr E. Green, Group Archivist, Midland Bank.

178 Ex. inf. Mr G. Miles, Archivist, Barclays Bank.

179 Lloyds Bank Archives, HO/D/Pre. 4.

180 *B.*, Vol. 68 (1895, Part 1), pp.282, 361; ibid., Vol. 69 (1895, Part 2), pp.48, 314; ibid., Vol. 70 (1896, Part 1), p.470; *B.N.*, Vol. 68 (1895, Part 1), p.178; ibid., Vol. 69 (1895, Part 2), p.115; *A.*, Vol. 54 (1895, Part 2), plate after p.200; Graves op. cit., Vol. 4 (1906, p.158.

181 *B.N.*, Vol. 76 (1899, Part 1), pp.266, 441, 442; ibid., Vol. 82 (1902, Part 1), p.842; *B.*, Vol. 76 (1899, Part 1), p.170; ibid., Vol. 82 (1902, Part 1), p.596. The architect was A. Marshall Mackenzie.

182 *B.N.*, Vol. 26 (1881, Part 2), p.287.

183 Ibid., Vol. 70 (1896, Part 1), p.167.

184 Ibid., which also mentions that spending was restrained 'in deference to the desire of the National Debt Commissioners'.

185 *B.*, Vol. 64 (1893, Part 1), p.495; *B.N.*, Vol. 64 (1893, Part 1), p.92.

186 *B.N.*, Vol. 82 (1902, Part 1), p.917.

187 Ibid., Vol. 99 (1910, Part 2), p.295.

188 W.G. Newton, *The Work of Ernest Newton, R.A.* (London, 1925), p.210 and plates 42–4; *A.R.*, Vol. 26 (1909, Part 2), p.32; *R.A. Exhibitors*, Vol. 5 (1981), p.318.

189 *B.N.*, Vol. 101 (1911, Part 2), plate after p.778.

190 *A.J.*, Vol. 53 (1921, Part 1), p.273, suggests the design was influenced by St Alban's Town Hall, a neo-classical building nearby.

191 *B.M.*, Vol. 58 (1894, Part 2), p.508.

192 *B.*, Vol. 54 (1888, Part 1), p.91 (Sheffield); *B.N.*, Vol. 51 (1886, Part 2), p.895 (Halifax); *B.*, Vol. 62 (1892, Part 1), p.486, and *B.N.*, Vol. 67 (1894, Part 2), p.271 (Leeds).

193 Figures vary between £30000 (*B.*, loc. cit.) and £60000 (*B.N.*, Vol. 89 (1905, Part 2), p.183, with more evidence towards the higher total.

194 Chosen as representative of work of twentieth century [*sic*] in Berlin publication, *Architektur des XX. Jahrhunderts* (*B.N.*, Vol. 89, loc. cit.).

Chapter Six

1 *B.*, Vol. 128 (1925, Part 1), p.596.

2 I.e. Lloyds Bank, in Tudor style, built 1924.

3 Among many sources for this well-known bank are: *B.*, Vol. 124 (1923, Part 1), plates after p.26, 770; *B.N.*, Vol. 124 (1923, Part 1), pp.459, 473; E. Green, *Buildings for Bankers* (London, 1980), *passim*.

4 *A. & B.N.*, Vol. 122 (1929, Part 2), p.617.

5 *A.R.*, Vol. 66 (1929, Part 2), pp.197, 198.

6 *B.M.*, Vol. 123 (1927, Part 1), p.490 (quoting Bank's *Annual Report*).

7 *B.*, Vol. 112 (1917, Part 1), p.368.

8 Ibid., Vol. 127 (1924, Part 2), p.394.

9 I.e. Lloyds Bank at Rye.

10 *B.*, Vol. 121 (1931, Part 2), p.653.

11 Ibid., Vol. 128 (1925, Part 1), p.112.

12 Ibid., Vol. 140 (1931, Part 1), p.999.

13 *A.J.*, Vol. 53 (1921, Part 1), p.272.

14 Green, op. cit., p.19.

15 *B.*, Vol. 136 (1929, Part 1), p.372.

16 Ibid.

17 *A.J.*, Vol. 64 (1926, Part 2), pp.45–52; *Ba.*, Vol. 1 (1926, Part 1), pp.182–4.

18 *Ba.*, Vols 37, 38 (1936, Part 1), pp.291–300.

19 *A. & B.N.*, Vol. 117 (1927, Part 1), p.1088; *A.J.*, Vol. 66 (1927, Part 2), p.417; *A.R.*, Vol. 61 (1927, Part 1), pp.222, 223.

20 *Ba.*, Vols 27, 28, (1933, Part 2), pp.73, 74.

21 *B.*, Vol. 119 (1920, Part 2), p.604.

22 *Ba.*, Vols 33, 34 (1935, Part 1), pp.236–48.

23 The architect was T. Arnold Ashworth: *B.N.*, Vol. 120 (1921, Part 1), p.343; *A.J.*, Vol. 53 (1921), Part 1), pp.641, 659, and Vol. 58 (1923, Part 2), pp.282–93.

24 P. Sawyer, 'Planning the Modern Bank', and editorial and other comments in *Architecture*, Vol. 43 (No. 3, 1921), pp.65–87.

25 A phrase coined by Eric L. Bird in *A.J.*, Vol. 68 (1928, Part 2), pp.498–505.

26 *Architecture*, loc. cit.

27 *A.J.*, Vol. 53 (1921, Part 1), pp.233–76.

28 Ibid., p.239.

29 Sawyer, op. cit., p.70.

30 Ibid., p.66.
31 Illustrated in *B.*, Vol. 125 (1923, Part 2), after p.643.
32 Sawyer, op. cit., p.74.
33 See, for instance, illustration of branch in Philadelphia of the Germantown Trust Company in Sawyer, op. cit., p.84.
34 Sawyer, op. cit., p.80.
35 Ibid.
36 *A.J.*, Vol. 66 (1927, Part 2), p.511.
37 Ibid., p.512; ibid., Vol. 68 (1928, Part 2), pp.498–505; *A.R.*, Vol. 64 (1928, Part 2), pp.106–11; *Ba.*, Vols 31, 32 (1934, Part 2), pp.258–70; *R.A. Exhibitors* Vol. 5 (1981), p.156.
38 *B.M.*, Vol. 126 (1928, Part 2), pp.373–87.
39 Ibid., p.381. When the bank was nearing completion it was visited by the Prince of Wales who is reported to have said 'that many of the features of the building reminded him of some of the structures he had seen in the United States of America' (ibid., p.386).
40 Sawyer, op. cit., plate XLI.
41 *B.*, Vol. 121 (1921, Part 2), p.783.
42 Barclays did not rebuild their head office until 1959; the style was influenced by the 1940 design of the Bankers' Clearing House. The building was demolished in 1991.
43 *B.*, Vol. 120 (1921, Part 1), pp.437 ff.; *B.N.*, Vol. 122 (1922, Part 1), p.130, and plates after; *A.*, Vol. 105 (1921, Part 1), pp.296, 316; *A.J.*, Vol. 53 (1921, Part 1), pp.440–5.
44 *B.*, Vol. 132 (1927, Part 1), opp. p.54, p.722; Vol. 134 (1928, Part 1), pp.63, 410, 413, 496, 497; Vol. 145 (1933, Part 2), p.857; *A. & B.N.*, Vol. 117 (1927, Part 1), pp.45, 771, 778; J.R. Winton, *Lloyds Bank 1918–1969* (Oxford, 1982), pp.51–7.
45 *A.*, Vol. 113 (1925, Part 1), p.321, plate after p.330; *A. & B.N.*, Vol. 118 (1927, Part 2), pp.570, 571, 600, 654, 655; *A.J.*, Vol. 61 (1925, Part 1), pp.692, 693, and Vol. 68 (1928, Part 2), pp.124, 355, 356, etc.; Green, op. cit., pp.1, 10–6.
46 *B.*, Vol. 141 (1931, Part 2), p.913; *B.N.*, Vol. 128 (1925, Part 1), p.12; *A. & B.N.*, Vols 125, 126, (1931, Part 2), pp.67, 68.
47 *B.*, Vol. 142 (1932, Part 1), pp.760 ff; *A.J.*, Vol. 73 (1931, Part 1), p.647; *A.R.*, Vol. 71 (1932, Part 1), pp.135–48.
48 For the full extent of Lutyens's involvement with the Midland, see Green, op. cit. Also, Holmes & Green, op. cit., p.171.
49 Ibid.
50 J. Ruskin, *The Stones of Venice*, Vol. 1 (1851), chap. 26, para. 2.
51 Goodhart-Rendel, op. cit., p.237.
52 Ibid.
53 Green, op. cit., p.17.
54 *B.M.*, Vol. 121 (1926, Part 1), p.741.
55 *B.*, Vol. 130 (1926, Part 1), pp.349, 352; *A. & B.N.*, Vol. 117 (1927, Part 1), pp.55–7; *A.R.*, Vol. 60 (1926, Part 2), pp.14–7.
56 *B.*, loc. cit.
57 *A.J.*, Vol. 63 (1926, Part 1), pp.451–5; *A.R.*, Vol. 60 (1926, Part 2), pp.20–3.
58 *B.*, Vol. 143 (1930, Part 2), after p.16; *A. & B.N.*, Vol. 124 (1930, Part 2), p.8; *A.J.*, Vol. 73 (1931, Part 1), pp.373–7, and Vol. 79 (1934, Part 1), pp.81–6.

59 Goodhart-Rendel, op. cit., p.238.

60 J. Summerson, *Georgian London* (Pelican Books, London, 1962), p.158.

61 *A.J.*, Vol. 54 (1921, Part 2), p.649.

62 E.g. *A.*, Vol. 108 (1922, Part 2), pp.55–7; Baker's plan 'shows the most careful consideration of the means by which the chief features of the work of Soane can be preserved and amalgamated ... The official statement regarding the scheme ... leaves little ground for criticism, except that the authorities have shown themselves, if anything, over-cautious in their desire to retain Sir John Soane's work unaltered.'

63 *A.R.*, Vol. 49 (1921, Part 1), pp.43–5.

64 Ibid., p.43.

65 *A.J.*, Vol. 53 (1921, Part 1), pp.233–76.

66 Ibid., Vol. 60 (1924, Part 2), pp.485, 486.

67 *B.*, Vol. 125 (1923, Part 2), p.633.

68 Ibid., pp.653–55.

69 Ibid., Vol. 133 (1927, Part 2), pp.768–70.

70 Ibid., Vol. 125 (1923, Part 2), p.651.

71 Ibid.

72 *B.*, Vol. 136 (1929, Part 1), p.372.

73 Ibid., p.373.

74 Ibid.

75 Ibid.

76 *A. & B.N.*, Vol. 120 (1928, Part 2), pp.137–41.

77 Ibid.

78 *B.M.*, Vol. 120 (1925, Part 2), pp.321–6.

79 Ibid., p.325, made the novel and important point that 'the manager would far rather live elsewhere'.

80 Very rarely (Vols 5, 6 (1928, Part 1), pp.166–73; and Vols 21, 22 (1932, Part 1), pp.177–94) the *Ba.* published instead articles by Professor A.E. Richardson of the University of London.

81 In the case of Lloyds, for instance, he was not certain whether half-timbered Hereford branch was original or fake, and he accepted the interior of Corn Street, Bristol, branch (c. 1854–7), albeit with some surprise, as contemporary.

82 *Ba.*, Vol. 1 (1926, Part 1), pp.292, 294.

83 Ibid., p.85.

84 Ibid., pp.292, 293.

85 Later Sir Edward Maufe (architect of Guildford Cathedral). Reilly wrote an article in 1928 (*Ba.*, Vols 7, 8 (1928, Part 2), pp.175–80) on branch banks by W. Edmund Maufe [*sic*].

86 *Ba.*, Vol. 1 (1926, Part 1), p.289.

87 Biographical notes from Archivist, National Westminster Bank.

88 Cf. Reilly's admission of 'prejudice against the official salaried architect' in *Ba.*, Vols 23, 24 (1932, Part 2), pp.74–82.

89 *Ba.*, Vols 23, 24 (1932, Part 2), p.75.

90 *B.*, Vol. 128 (1925, Part 1), p.596.

91 Ibid., Vol. 134 (1928, Part 1), p.136.

92 *A. & B.N.*, Vol. 120 (1928, Part 2), p.137.

93 *Ba.*, Vols 33, 34 (1935, Part 1), pp.288–98.

94 *A. & B.N.*, Vol. 148 (1936), pp.230, 231; Vols 41, 42 (1937, Part 1), p.255; ibid., Vols 45, 46 (1938, Part 1), pp.172–82.

95 *B.*, Vol. 125 (1923, Part 2), p.653.

96 According to Arthur J. Davis (in *B.*, Vol. 136 (1929, Part 1), p.373) rubber was too quiet; 'when people were writing out a cheque they objected to others creeping up silently behind them.'

97 *A. & B.N.*, loc. cit.

98 *Ba.*, Vols 51, 52 (1939, Part 2), pp.76–90.

99 Ibid., Vols 37, 38 (1936, Part 1), pp.291–300. First mention of a bank which gives 'literally hundreds of branches to one architect' had been in ibid., Vol. 1 (1926, Part 1), p.291.

100 Ibid., Vol. 1 (1926, Part 1), p.87.

101 Ibid., Vols 41, 42 (1937, Part 1), pp.297, 298.

102 Some building inspectors, like F.H. Shann, were qualified architects.

103 *Ba.*, Vol. 1 (1926, Part 1), p.289.

104 Drawings of five of his branches were exhibited (*R.A. Exhibitors*, Vol. 6 (1982), p.223).

105 This was Reilly's own paraphrase (*Ba.*, Vol. 3 (1927, Part 1), pp.258–63) of Holland Martin's address at the Annual Meeting in January 1927 of the Bank of Liverpool & Martins. The official report of the speech is a little different: '. . . it is our intention, whenever we build a branch, to put up a dignified building worthy of the Bank and one that will add to the artistic amenities of the town in which it is built.' (*B.M.*, Vol. 123 (1927, Part 1), p.490).

106 *A. & B.N.*, Vol. 120 (1928, Part 2), p.283; *A.J.*, Vol. 72 (1930, Part 2), pp.187–9; *A.R.*, Vol. 64 (1928, Part 2), p.193, and Vol. 65 (1929, Part 1), pp.182, 183.

107 *Ba.*, Vol. 1 (1926, Part 1), p.292.

108 Lloyds Bank Archives, HO/D/Pre. 20.

109 I.e. H. Chalton Bradshaw, who returned in 1920. Bradshaw had held the first Rome scholarship in architecture in 1913, and he completed his studies there when the war was over.

110 *Ba.*, Vol. 1 (1926, Part 2), p.450.

111 *A. & B.N.*, Vol. 120 (1928, Part 2), p.546.

112 Ibid., Vol. 119 (1928, Part 1), pp.724, 726, and Vol. 122 (1929, Part 2), pp.467–9; *A.J.*, Vol. 70 (1929, Part 2), pp.632–7.

113 *B.*, Vol. 141 (1931, Part 2), pp.963, 964, and Vol. 143 (1932, Part 2), p.47.

114 *A. & B.N.*, Vol. 123 (1930, Part 1), p.851.

115 *B.*, Vol. 140 (1931, Part 1), pp.103, 104: *A. & B.N.*, Vols 125, 126 (1931, Part 1), pp.52–4.

116 *A. & B.N.*, loc. cit.

117 Ibid.

118 *Ba.*, Vols 9, 10 (1929, Part 1), pp.272–8; ibid., Vols 17, 18 (1931, Part 1), pp.358–66.

119 *A. & B.N.*, Vols 127, 128 (1931, Part 2), pp.108, 109.

120 *Ba.*, Vols 19, 20 (1931, Part 2), pp.180–92.

121 Ibid., Vols 17, 18 (1931, Part 1), p.361.

122 Ibid., Vols 21, 22 (1932, Part 1), pp.260–78.

123 Ibid., Vols 13, 14 (1930, Part 1), pp.486–96.

124 *Ba.*, Vols 33, 34 (1935, Part 1), p.147: 'I hope the Directors of Lloyds Bank have not forgotten their scheme . . .'

125 *A. & B.N.*, Vol. 148 (1936), p.230.

126 *Ba.*, Vols 37, 38 (1936, Part 1), pp.186–202; cf. *A.R.*, Vol. 73 (1933, Part 1), pp.101–6.

127 *Ba.*, Vols 27, 28 (1933, Part 2), pp.244–54: *A.R.*, Vol. 77 (1935, Part 1), p.161.

128 All six designs were reproduced in *A. & B.N.*, Vol. 116 (1926, Part 2), pp.47–50.

129 *Ba.*, Vols 25, 26 (1933, Part 1), pp.176–84.

130 *B.*, Vol. 140 (1931, Part 1), pp.266, 1089, 1092–7; *A. & B.N.*, Vol. 136 (1933), pp.271, 275; *A.J.*, Vol. 73 (1931, Part 1), pp.891–3.

131 *B.*, Vol. 149 (1935, Part 2), pp.361, 371, etc.; *A. & B.N.*, Vol. 143 (1935), pp.241–4; *A.J.*, Vol. 82 (1935, Part 2), pp.444–8.

132 *A. & B.N.*, Vol. 136 (1933), pp.271, 275.

133 Ibid., Vol. 143 (1935), p.241.

134 *Ba.*, Vols 37, 38 (1936, Part 1), pp.270–84; *A. & B.N.*, Vol. 145 (1936), pp.302–4.

135 *Ba.*, loc. cit.

136 Ibid., Vols 71, 72 (1944, Part 2), pp.135–7.

137 After the Historic Buildings and Ancient Monuments Act, 1953.

138 *B.*, Vol. 195 (1958, Part 2), p.491, and ibid., Vol. 199 (1960, Part 2), pp.21, 197.

139 Ibid.

140 Ibid., Vol. 191 (1956, Part 2), pp.657–79.

141 Lord Esher, 'What's in a Facade?' in *B.M.*, Vol. 221 (1977), pp.8–11.

142 *A.R.*, Vol. 145 (1969, Part 1), pp.42, 43, 62.

143 See P. Galvin, 'The Banks and their Properties' in *Ba.*, Vol. 114 (1964), pp.640–5.

144 Tuke and Gillman, p.52.

145 *A.R.*, Vol. 131 (1962, Part 1), pp.130, 131.

146 Ibid., Vol. 128 (1960, Part 2), p.208.

147 Ibid., Vol. 130 (1961, Part 2), p.335.

148 Ibid., Vol. 144 (1968, Part 2), p.347.

149 Holmes & Green, op. cit., p.223.

150 *A.R.*, Vol. 144 (1968, Part 2), p.347.

151 *A.J.*, Vol. 150 (1969, Part 2), pp.724–6.

152 Ibid.

153 Ibid.

154 It is sad to record, as this book goes to press, that Standard Chartered Bank has just removed to smaller premises in Aldermanbury Square, and 38 Bishopsgate has lost its greenery.

Appendix One

Savings Banks purpose-built by the end of 1852

This is not claimed as a comprehensive list but is believed to be a reasonable reconstruction of the position, based mainly on published returns to the House of Commons, enhanced by a variety of other historical and visual evidence.

The abbreviation S.F. in the headings means Surplus Fund. Parliamentary returns at 1838, 1843 and 1848 established what money was then in the fund for each bank, and how much had been withdrawn by November 1843. The fact that construction of premises was usually financed by withdrawals from the fund, points to the importance of these figures for establishing or confirming building dates. For example, as Bridport savings bank had not touched its surplus fund by 1843 but had reduced the balance of £830 to nil in 1848, it is reasonable to suppose that building took place between those years. In that instance a building lease helps to date construction more closely but for some banks such corroborating evidence has been more difficult to find. It has been impossible to list in detail the wide-ranging sources which have been used, but a full discussion of these, and particularly of the significance of the 1852 return and of the fund itself, is given in Chapter Three.

The column 'Remarks' attempts to give no more than a summary of the style of a building and, whenever possible, its fate or modern use. This use was accurate to 1984–5 and although it is still believed to reflect the general position, obviously changes can occur at any time. When no architectural description is given, it can be assumed that the bank has no special features beyond modest respectability. 'Classical' means some recognised motif of the Italian Renaissance, such as rustication, an Order (usually with pilasters) and/or a pediment, not necessarily over the whole frontage. 'Italianate' means in the style of Barry. Other characterisations (e.g. Tudor, Jacobean) are self-explanatory, but none should be regarded as conveying anything more than the broadest indication of a bank's appearance.

References quoted in brackets, except directories, are explained in the Bibliography. For initials of periodicals, see introduction to References in main text.

Bank name/ location	Date of estab.	Bldg date	S.F. at 1838	S.F. drawn by 11/1843	S.F. at 1843	S.F. at 1848	Known cost	Architect	Description in 1852 return to parliament	Remarks
1 Alnwick 11 Narrowgate	1816	1835	£98	£1511	£210	£280	c.£1300 (Tate)	William Smith	Describes other premises 'recently purchased'	Gothic. Sold in 1851 for £270 (Tate)
2 Arundel 10 Tarrant St	1818	c.1848-9	£501	Nil	£719	£616			'The newly-erected savings bank'	Now Victoria Institute
3 Ashbourne Church St	1818	c.1840-3	£1558	£2000	£140	£131	c.£2000 (Bagshaw's Directory)		'Savings Bank Buildings'	Italianate. Now TSB
4 Bakewell Bath St	1818	Dated 1848	£809	£1113	£245	£88	c.£500 (White's Directory)		'The bank'	Perhaps second bank, in view of large S.F. withdrawal by 11/1843. One storey. Now TSB
5 Bath Charlotte St	1815	1842	£7843	£3818	£6339	£6726		George Alexander	'A building specially erected for the purposes of a bank, in 1842'	Italianate. Described in *C.E. & A.J.* Now Register Office
6 Bedford Harpur St	1816	1836	Nil	£1000	£1301	£470		T.G. Elger	'Buildings erected for the sole use of the savings bank'	Part of Assembly Rooms. Perhaps later bank at 10 St Paul's Square (after 1845) now demolished
7 Beverley Lairgate	1818	c.1842	£1207	£1800	£320	£865			'East Riding Savings Bank, Lavigate [*sic*], Beverley'	Classical
8 Biggleswade Town Hall	1816	1844	£464	£120	£515	£10		J.T. Wing	'In a building erected for the purpose, by the trustees . . .'	Probably annex to Town Hall. Now no trace
9 Birmingham 31 Cannon St	1827	1849-50	£900	Nil	£2100	£3500		Charles Edge	'Cannon-street in a building erected for the purpose'	Classical. Demolished. Drawings in Birmingham ref. lib.
10 Bolton 10-12 Wood St	1818	c.1849	£1000	Nil	£1100	£2100	c.£2700 (Whittle)		'In a newly-erected bank'	Classical. Whittle wrote 'built in 1817'

Bank name/ location	Date of estab.	Bldg date	S.F. at 1838	S.F. drawn by 11/1843	S.F. at 1843	S.F. at 1848	Known cost	Architect	Description in 1852 return to parliament	Remarks
11 Bradford 33 Kirkgate	1818	c.1837	Nil	£1162	Nil	£100			'No. 33, Kirkgate'	No details known. Sold in 1852 for £3060 (Hebden)
12 Bridgnorth Bank St	1818	c.1837	£600	£1750	£800	£1100			'In a building erected expressly for the purpose'	Rebuilt 1859. Now TSB
13 Bridport 36 East St	1817	c.1848	£500	Nil	£830	Nil	£900 (B.P.P.)		'Savings bank house'	Borough building lease of 1847
14 Bristol St Stephen's Ave	1813	1831	£3741	£5200	£7855	£10549	£3500 with site (Latimer)	Charles Dyer	'In a house erected in 1831, paid for out of the separate surplus fund'	No illus. known. Closed 1888
15 Bury, Lancs Silver St	1822	1850	£487	Nil	£655	£855			'New building, erected 1850'	Demolished. Modern TSB on site
16 Bury St Edmunds 1-2 Crown St	1816	Dated 1846	£1600	Nil	£2260	£695	£2300 (White's Directory)	L.N. & N.J. Cottingham	'In the savings bank'	Tudor-style. Alterations 1857-8. Now offices
17 Cainscross, Glos. Westward Rd	1817	c.1842	£500	£625	£25	£200			'Office erected for the purpose'	No illus. known. Garage on site
18 Cambridge 62 Sidney St	1817	1848	£1429	£190	£1917	£119	£3185 (B.P.P.)		'A brick and stone building'	Rebuilt 1900
19 Carlisle 38 Fisher St	1818	1842	£1120	£924	£800	£1000			'The Savings Bank'	Taken over by building soc. 1894. Demolished 1978
20 Cheadle, Staffs. Bank St	1819	c.1842	£950	£1150	£60	£359			'The Savings Bank'	Jacobean-style. Altered. Now club
21 Chelmsford 75 High St	1817	c.1843	£1930	£2372	£300	£200	£950 bldg tender (Essex Standard)	? James Fenton	'Savings Bank offices'	No illus. known. Demolished

Place	Date	Date					Cost (other source)	Architect	Quotation	Notes
22 Chelsea 142 Kings Rd	1819	c.1840	Nil	£447	£100	£100			'In the bank, King's-road. Leasehold, for 81 years. from 29 Sept. 1840 . . .'	Cadogan Estate lease. One storey. Became branch of Barclays Bank. Demolished
23 Chester Grosvenor St	1817	1852	£2700	Nil	£3600	£3970	£3000 (White's Directory)	James Harrison	[Footnote to 1852 return]: 'There is a new bank-building in course of erection, which will be the property of the trustees'	Tudor-style. Clock tower. Now TSB
24 Clitheroe Church St	1845	—	—	—		[Not returned]			'In a room erected for the purpose'	No other information. Bank closed 1890
25 Cockermouth 4 Main St	1818	1846	£720	Nil	£1220	£50			'Bank office, connected with the secretary's dwelling-house'	Classical. Central clock turret. Now offices
26 Colchester 3 Church St	1817	c.1842	£1667	£1760	£794	£1402			'A building erected for the purposes of the bank'	Now offices
27 Derby Friar Gate	1818	1840	£2240	£2800	£1000	£1780	£2800 (Bagshaw's Directory)	H.J. Stevens	'In the bank built by the trustees'	Demolished
28 Devizes 15 High St	1817	1848	£875	Nil	£1525	£900			'In the "Savings Bank"'	Jacobean-style. Now offices
29 Devonport 65 Chapel St	1818	By 1830	£3800	£500	£4800	£6000			'In a house, comprising bank offices, board-room, and private apartments; built expressly for the purpose out of the surplus funds of the bank'	No illus. known. Believed blitzed
30 Doncaster 16 High St	1817	1843	£1455	£2000	£1107	£1493	£1400 (Sheardown)	W. Hurst & Moffatt	'In a building appropriated for the savings bank'	Papers of William Sheardown, antiquary, refer to 'Rotunda' form. Demolished
31 Eccleston, Lancs. 119 Towngate	1818	Dated 1849	£90	Nil	£146	£215			'In a bank built for the purpose'	Tudor–Gothic features. Influenced by nearby school of 1819

Bank name/ location	Date of estab.	Bldg date	S.F. at 1838	S.F. drawn by 11/1843	S.F. at 1843	S.F. at 1848	Known cost	Architect	Description in 1852 return to parliament	Remarks
32 Ellesmere Scotland St	1817	1830	£450	Nil	£700	£340	£360 (Harrison) £550 (Bagshaw's Directory)		'At the Savings bank. Held by the trustees under a building lease from the trustees under the will of . . . Earl of Bridgewater . . . for 99 years, commencing 25th March 1830'	Classical. Now TSB.
33 Exeter Bedford Circus	1815	1836–9	Nil	£5100	£1000	£3024			'A building erected for the purpose, in Bedford Circus, Exeter'	End-of-terrace. Blitzed
34 Finsbury 18½, Seckford St	1816	Dated 1840	£2350	£3050	Nil	Nil	£2850 (C.E. & A.J.)	Alfred Bartholomew	'In a building in Sekforde-street, St. John-street, built specially for the trustees' purposes'	Classical. Long, dated inscription. Now offices.
35 Gloucester 1–2 Commercial Rd	1818	1850	£1181	Nil	£1330	£1430	c.£1350 (Builder)	Hamilton & Medland	'In the house erected for that purpose in 1850'	Awkward triangular site attracted article in *B*. Now offices
36 Grantham 14 Finkin St	1818	Dated 1841	£700	£2087	Nil	£200		Anthony Salvin	'In a building erected for the purpose'	Jacobean-style. Now TSB
37 Hexham Priest Popple	1818	1838	£48	£1000	£570	£1056		John Dobson	'The Savings Bank'	'Mr. Dobson's Statement' copied in bank's archives. Now TSB
38 Horncastle Union St	1817	1840s	£198	£2	£248	£319			'In an office built expressly for the purpose'	Bldg not positively identified
39 Howden 9 Church Yd	1818	1850–1	£126	£264	£300	£432			'In the new savings bank'	Tudor-style. Built with mechanics' institute, etc., nearby. Now offices/rooms

	Est.	Built					Source	Architect	Description	Remarks
40 Huddersfield 23 Buxton Rd	1818	1837	No return	£362	£117	£556	£940 (Hebden)	George Jackson	'In a separate building, No. 14, Buxton-road'	Street number varied between 14, 16 and 23. Rebuilt 1887–8
41 Hull Posterngate	1818	1830	Nil	£500	£2700	£3450	£1196 (Hebden)		'Bank for savings, Posterngate, Hull'	Classical. Altered in 1863. Now demolished
42 Kirkby Lonsdale Market Place	1818	1848	£381	£305	£800	Nil		George Webster	'In a house lately erected'	Classical. Bell turret and clock. Now TSB
43 Knutsford Princess St	1818	1840	£400	£500	£180	£315	£500 (Bagshaw's Directory)	Robert Gregson	'The Savings Bank'	One storey. Now TSB
44 Lambeth 86 Hercules Rd	1818	Dated 1849	£1034	Nil	£1077	£1449	c.£1500 (Scantlin)	W.R. Nixon, Jr	'The Savings Bank office, Hercules-buildings ... upon a building lease of 99 years'	Tudor-style. Demolished
45 Lancaster 23 New Street	1823	c.1848	£596	Nil	£1186	£20			'No. 23, New-street'	Street renumbered. Now museum store
46 Leeds 30 Bond St	1818	1834	£1847	£3700	£4897	£6779		John Clark	'In a building built on purpose'	Classical. Demolished 1971–2
47 Leek 16 Derby St	1823	c.1852	£193	Nil	£386	£65			'The Town Hall'	Described as 'intended' in 1851 directories. Now building society
48 Lichfield Bore St	1818	Dated 1849	£906	Nil	£1414	£1685	£1346 (White's Directory)	Thomas Johnson	'In a messuage lately erected for the purposes of the bank'	Built with corn exchange, etc. Tudor-style. Now shops
49 Lincoln 11–12 Bank St	1816	1836	Nil	£792	£200	£413	£848 (Hebden)		'Offices erected for the purpose'	Believed altered c.1858 by 'Mr. Goddard'. Further altered 1923
50 Macclesfield 10 Park Green	1818	c.1842	£3819	£4350	£599	£1213	£2583 (Bagshaw's Directory)		'In a building erected expressly for the purpose'	Neo-Greek. Now Barclays Bank
51 Malton 30 Yorkersgate	1827	c.1848	£200	Nil	£700	Nil	£1015 (Hebden)		'The Savings Bank'	Classical. Now TSB

Bank name/ location	Date of estab.	Bldg date	S.F. at 1838	S.F. drawn by 11/1843	S.F. at 1843	S.F. at 1848	Known cost	Architect	Description in 1852 return to parliament	Remarks
52 Manchester 84 King St	1818	1839–42	£5097	£6916	Nil	£5286	Nearly £11000	Richard Lane	'In a building specially erected for the purpose, situated 84, King-street'	Well documented. Neo-Greek. No Illus. traced. Demolished
53 Mansfield Market Place	1818	1843	£758	£1133	£61	£290	Over £1400 (White's Directory)		'The Savings Bank'	Neo-Greek. Now County Court
54 Market Drayton 15 High St	1818	c.1848	£288	Nil	£798	Nil			'In a building erected for the purpose'	Now shops
55 Montague St (Bloomsbury, London) 30 Montague St	1817	1838	Nil	£3100	Nil	£600		? Thomas Stead	'In the "Bank" building'	Bedford Estate building lease. Entrance canopy survives, with perhaps part of bank, in B.L. complex
56 Morpeth 13A King St	1816	1829	£726	£428	£1290	£1787			'The Savings Bank'	No illus. traced. Demolished
57 Nantwich 39 Welsh Row	1817	Dated 1846	£370	Nil	£700	Nil	£970 (Bagshaw's Directory)		'A building erected for that purpose only'	One storey. Disused, but renovation intended
58 Newark-upon-Trent 21 Lombard Street	1817	1831–2	£400	£1887	£970	£1292			'A building erected for the purpose'	Dated foundation plaques. Now health clinic
59 Newbury 134 Bartholomew St	1817	c.1849	£758	Nil	£1189	£1437		George Truefitt	'The Savings Bank'	Tudor-style. Demolished
60 Newcastle-upon-Tyne 1 The Arcade	1818	1833	£2956	£2563	£5706	£8107	c.£7000 incl. £2000 for site	John Dobson	'No. 1, Arcade'	No illus. traced. Demolished. New premises taken in 1862

Place	Date	Date					Cost	Architect	Description	Remarks
61 Newcastle-under-Lyme, 93 High St	1845	1852	—	—	—	—			'In the Savings Bank built by the trustees'	Formerly called 25, Penkhull St. Now offices
62 Northwich, Winnington Hill	1818	1840	£1234	£1180	£381	£811	£1188 (Bagshaw's Directory)		'In a building erected for the purpose'	No illus. traced. Demolished
63 Norwich, Haymarket	1816	1843	£1356	£2200	£702	£500	£3000 incl. Joseph Stannard £1500 for site (White's Directory)		'In a building erected by the trustees and managers in 1843'	Classical. Demolished. New premises taken in 1901
64 Nottingham, 11 Low Pavement	1818	1837-8	£1279	£2300	£3208	£4626			'A building erected for the savings bank, with a dwelling-house over it, Low Pavement'	Classical. Now TSB
65 Ormskirk, 9 Derby St	1822	c.1850	£450	Nil	£950	£1050			'The New Bank, in Derby-street'	Classical. Adjoins Sessions House. Now TSB
66 Oswestry, Arthur St	1818	1830	£340	£845	£441	£675	£511 (Harrison)		'Savings Bank'	'Domestic' elevation
67 Portsmouth, 88 St Thomas's St	1816	1837	£389	£950	£1430	£2200		T.E. Owen	'The office'	One large storey. Now private house
68 Poulton-le-Fylde, Bank St	1822	Dated 1839	£199	£212	Nil	£19			'In the bank, built for the purpose'	'Domestic' elevation. Disused as bank since 1862. Now offices. Street renamed Chapel St
69 Preston, 7 Lune St	1816	1842	£1330	£1300	£1050	£1850	£1300 (Hardwick)	John Latham	'The Savings Bank'	Classical. Disused as bank since 1872. Now Wesleyan Lecture Hall
70 Reading, 35 (now 72) London St	1817	1849	£1810	Nil	£2494	£1273	£2500 (B.P.P.)	John Billing	'A house, 35 London-street'	Classical. Now offices
71 Richmond, Yorks, 2 Frenchgate	1817	Dated 1851	£1762	Nil	£2424	£3044			'In a small tenement in a yard, known by the name of the Bank-yard'	Classical. Curious discrepancy between date and info. in return. Now TSB

Bank name/ location	Date of estab.	Bldg date	S.F. at 1838	S.F. drawn by 11/1843	S.F. at 1843	S.F. at 1848	Known cost	Architect	Description in 1852 return to parliament	Remarks
72 Romford Market Place	1817	c.1850	£955	Nil	£1342	£1571	£1000 (White's *Directory*)		'In their own freehold, recently erected'	No illus. traced. Demolished
73 Rotherham Howard St	1846	1851	—	—	—	Nil	c.£700 (Kelly's *Directory*)		'In a house and offices built on land leased by the Earl of Effingham to trustees for 99 years at a ground rent'	No illus. traced. Demolished
74 Rugeley Town Hall	1817	1844	£1292	Nil	£1791	£1386			'In a building erected for the purpose, the cost of which was defrayed out of the surplus fund of the bank'	Tudor-style extension to classical Town Hall. Demolished 1878–9
75 Saffron Walden 4 King St	1817	c.1848	£686	Nil	£1153	£92			'Premises built by the trustees with the surplus fund'	Now shop
76 St Martin's Place (Westminster, London) 5 St Martin's Place	1816	1830	£3000	Nil	£6500	£8500			'Leasehold house, No. 5, St Martin's-place'	Crown lease from 1830. Demolished
77 Scarborough King St	1818	Before 1832	£388	£250	£682	£863			'A building belonging to the savings bank'	Mentioned in town history, 1832. No illus. traced. Demolished
78 Settle Market Place	1818	1832	£876	Nil	£1383	£1639		George Webster	'The Savings Bank'	Part of neo-Tudor market house, etc. New bank, c.1860s
79 Sevenoaks 49 London Rd	1816	c.1841	£615	£920	£163	£471			'Savings Bank'	Classical. Now newspaper offices
80 Sheffield Surrey St	1819	1832	£1705	£3835	£504	£182	£898 and £215 for site	Robert Potter	'Bank, erected by the trustees'	Conflicting evidence as to identity and fate of original bldg. Moved to new premises

81 Sherborne 72 Cheap St	1818	c.1835	£176	£1392	£192	£251		'Stone-built and tiled, situate in Cheap-street'	Perhaps classical bldg with bowed upper storey on 4 Ionics cols., now showroom
82 Shields, South 24 Barrington St	1817	1841	£892	£1000	£126	£231		'No. 24, Borrington [*sic*] street'	Italianate. Demolished 1961
83 Shrewsbury College Hill	1818	1838	£3315	£2163	£5860	£7100	£2000 incl. £660 for site (Bagshaw's *Directory*) Edward Haycock	'A building situated on College-hill'	Pediment with 4 Doric pilasters. Now offices
84 Stockport 43 Lower Hillgate	1824	1843	£830	£1419	Nil	£283	£1500 (Bagshaw's *Directory*) Samuel Howard	'The Savings Bank'	No illus. traced. Extended in 1849. Demolished 1911
85 Stone High St	1818	1830	£200	Nil	£850	£1379	c.£700 (White's *Directory*)	'The Savings Bank'	No illus. traced. Demolished
86 Swindon Victoria St	1818	1852	£178	£37	£386	£600	£628 (minute book) 'Mr' Sage	'In the savings bank'	Classical. Now known as 99–100 Victoria Rd. Newspaper offices
87 Tamworth Lady Bank	1823	Dated 1845	£440	Nil	£795	£15	£900 (White's *Directory*)	'House built for the use of the bank'	Now known as 9 Hollow Way. Tudor-style
88 Taunton 1 Upper High St	1817	c.1830	£4783	£800	£5177	£5250	?Richard Carver	'In the High-street'	Classical. Now TSB
89 Tewkesbury 4 Church St	1818	1852	£170	Nil	£300	£400	£642 (minute book) Thomas Collins	'In a room of a dwelling-house, Church-street. A savings bank, built for the purpose, will be entered upon on the 24th May 1852'	Tudor-style. Now shop
90 Thirsk Castlegate	1819	1849	£1248	£50	£1664	£2036		'In the savings bank'	Classical. Puzzlingly massive. Now store
91 Tonbridge Bank St	1845	c.1850	—	—	—	Nil		'In the savings bank ... built by private subscriptions'	Flint-built cottage. Now shop

Bank name/ location	Date of estab.	Bldg date	S.F. at 1838	S.F. drawn by 11/1843	S.F. at 1843	S.F. at 1848	Known cost	Architect	Description in 1852 return to parliament	Remarks
92 Truro Frances St	1818	1847	£2160	Nil	£3279	£446		Philip Sambell	'In a separate building, erected by the trustees in 1847'	Classical. Now the Royal Institution of Cornwall
93 Ulverston Union St	1816	1837–8	£164	£1760	£484	£260	c.£1300 (Taylor)	George Webster	'In the savings bank'	Classical. Clock tower added 1845. Now TSB
94 Wakefield 1 Burton St	1817	1835	£154	£1946	£124	£798		Charles Mountain II	'In a house in Burton-street, erected by the trustees and managers out of the surplus fund of this bank'	Classical
95 Warminster 71 Market Pl	1823	1852	£870	Nil	£1510	£1895	£2000 (P.O. Directory)		'Dwelling-house'	Jacobean-style. Clock in gable. Post office since 1933
96 Wenlock, Much Bull Ring	1817	Dated 1829	£1220	Nil	£2070	£2200			'At Much Wenlock'	Inscribed sill. Now house
97 Whitchurch, Shrops. 1st Bank 'the coal recepticle ground'	1818	1823	—	—	—	—	£152 (Harrison)		—	Harrison refers to erection of first bank, comprising office and ante-room
98 2nd Bank St Mary's St	1818	Dated 1846	£578	Nil	£1200	£500	£668, and £260 for lease (Harrison)		'Building erected for the purpose'	Classical. Long, dated inscription. Now house
99 Whitehaven 59 Lowther St	1818	1833	£459	£2700	£1029	£1279		Thomas Rickman	'Savings Bank'	Classical. Royal Arms on cornice. Now TSB
100 Wigan Standishgate	1821	Before 1843	£305	£1200	£1050	£1939			'In the savings bank building, Standishgate'	No illus. traced. Demolished
101 Windsor Victoria St	1816	1834	£443	£1410	£605	£814			'A building in Victoria-street, erected for the express purpose'	Closed 1868. Present attribution doubtful

								Architect	Quote	Remarks
102	Wirksworth 6 St John's St	1818	1843	£375	£861	Nil	£76	£1200 (Bagshaw's *Directory*)		'Savings bank'	Classical. Now offices
103	Witham 19 Guithavon St	1817	c.1850	£560	Nil	£710	£790			'In the savings bank'	Tudor-style. Now offices
104	Worcester (St) Nicholas St	1818	Before 1825	£7347	Nil	£10829	£13247			'Office built purposely'	Newspapers confirm early date. No illus. traced. New bank erected in Shaw St., 1853
105	Workington Pow St	1827	1844	£140	£382	Nil	£23			'In a building erected for that purpose in Pow-St.'	No illus. traced. Believed demolished
106	Worksop 65–7, Bridge St	1817	1843	£1353	£1300	£350	£350	£300 [sic] (White's *Directory*)		'In a large room forming part of the savings bank. House built from funds drawn on the commissioners by the trustees' draft, 1 March 1843'	Classical. Now TSB
107	Wycombe, High 15 Church St	1818	1842	£340	£570	Nil	£100	£623, incl. £120 for site (records)	Henry Crook	'The savings bank'	Classical. Refronted as shop
108	Yeovil Princes St	1818	1839	£639	£1601	£70	£161			'In a house erected for the purpose'	Site believed occupied by shoe shop
109	York St Helen's Sq	1816	1829–30	£2735	£300	£4742	£5234	£4691 (Hebden)	James Pigott Pritchett (with Charles Watson)	'In the building erected for that purpose'	Classical. Now TSB

Appendix Two

Catalogue of Significant Banks,
1731–1939

Banks included in this catalogue are significant for a number of reasons. Some are stylistically important, or the work of a noteworthy architect; others are head offices, qualifying for inclusion by size or position. In places where banking enclaves developed of considerable interest (e.g. London, Lombard Street; Bristol, Corn Street; Leeds, Park Row; Southport, Lord Street) as many banks as possible have been listed.

The decision to include or omit a bank was often difficult to take, and obviously the list as it is presented may disappoint some people in respect of any given building. In particular, it has been impossible to cover smaller towns to the extent they deserve.

No savings banks erected before 1852 are listed here, as they form Appendix One.

When two dates are given (e.g. 1731–4) these indicate the beginning and end of building work, as far as it is known. One date signifies completion (opening) only. A dagger (†) shows that the work involved refronting or altering existing premises rather than building anew.

It should not be assumed that the banks listed necessarily still exist, or that those which do exist have not been significantly altered in some way over the course of time.

Date	Location	Bank	Architect(s)
1731–4	London Threadneedle St	Bank of England	George Sampson
1750–4	Edinburgh Old Bank Close	Royal Bank of Scotland[1]	S. Neilson
1757	London Birchin Lane	Glyn's Bank	
c. 1757	London Lombard St	Asgill's Bank	Sir Robert Taylor
1758–60	London Charing Cross	Drummond's Bank	
1766	Halifax	Royds's Bank[2]	John Carr
1769	Exeter	Exeter Bank	

---

[1] Plans had originally been prepared in 1744 by William Adam.
[2] The banking side of Royds's work might have begun later than 1766 (see p.22).

Date	Location	Bank	Architect(s)
1770–1	London Strand	Coutts' Bank[3]	James Paine
1776	Bristol Clare St	Bristol Old Bank	
1776	Sheffield Bank St	Shore's Bank	
1777–8	London Charing Cross	Drummond's Bank†	Robert Adam
1785	Margate King St	Cobb's Bank	
1785–6	Ipswich Tavern St	Crickitt, Truelove & Kerridge's Bank	
1787	Liverpool Castle St	Heywood's Bank	
1790–1	Perth	Perth Banking Company	
1791	London Pall Mall	Ransom, Morland & Hammersley's Bank†	Sir John Soane
c. 1791	Tavistock Market St	Tavistock Bank	
c. 1792	Kendal Highgate	Maude, Wilson & Crewdson's Bank	
1793–5	London Lombard St	Martin's Bank	George Dance, jun.
1794	Bristol Corn St	Bristol Old Bank	
1796	London Lombard St	Robarts & Curtis's Bank	Thomas Leverton
1798–9	Liverpool Brunswick St	Heywood's Bank	
1799	Kendal	Wakefield's Bank	
1801	London Fleet St	Praed's Bank	Sir John Soane
1802–6	Edinburgh The Mound	Bank of Scotland[4]	Crichton & Reid
c. 1803	Chester Foregate St	Williams, Hughes's Bank	Benjamin Wyatt
1805–6	Leith	Leith Bank	John Paterson
1808	London 60 West Smithfield	Lacy, Hartland & Woodbridge's Bank	

[3]Further alterations by Paine, 1780–3.
[4]Remodelled c. 1870.

Date	Location	Bank	Architect(s)
c. 1810	Leicester Gallowtree Gate	Mansfield's Bank	
1811	Liverpool Dale St	Moss, Dale & Rogers's Bank	
1812–3	Leeds Commercial St	Union Bank	Thomas Taylor
1813	Bradford Bank St	Bradford Old Bank	
pre-1814	Reading King St	Simonds's Bank	
1814	Boston	Skirbeck Quarter Bank	
pre-1816	Hull Silver St	Moxon's Bank	
pre-1817	London Lothbury	Jones, Loyd's Bank	George Maddox
pre-1817	London Pall Mall	Hammersley's Bank	George Maddox
1817	London Regent St	Hopkinson's Bank	G.S. Repton
1818	London Threadneedle St	Grote, Prescott & Grote's Bank†	Sir John Soane
c. 1820	London Lombard St	Whitmore's Bank	Sir Robert Smirke
c. 1821	London Craig's Court	Greenwood, Cox & Hammersley's Bank	
1821	Manchester Norfolk St	Daintry & Ryle	
1823	Dundee Murrygate	Union Bank	William Burn
1823	London Pall Mall East	Ransom's Bank	William Atkinson
1824	Manchester Market St	Crewdson's Bank	
1825	Stirling Spittal St	Commercial Bank	? J.G. Graham
1826	Aberdeen Union St	Town & Country Bank	Archibald Simpson
1827	Edinburgh Parliament Sq	Sir William Forbes's Bank	William Burn
1827	Glasgow Royal Exchange Sq	Royal Bank of Scotland	Archibald Elliot

Date	Location	Bank	Architect(s)
1827	Manchester Market St	Brooks's Bank	Royle & Unwin
1828	Glasgow Ingram St	Bank of Scotland	William Burn
1829–30	London Fleet St	Hoare's Bank	Charles Parker
1830	Birmingham Bennett's Hill	Birmingham Banking Company	T. Rickman & H. Hutchinson
1830	Caernarvon Bank Quay	Roberts's Bank	John Lloyd
1830	Devizes St John's St	Devizes & Wiltshire Bank	
1830	Hull Whitefriargate	Smith's Bank	Charles Mountain, Jr
1832	Bewdley Severn Side	Nichols & Baker's Bank	
c. 1832	Birmingham Bennett's Hill	Bank of Birmingham[5]	Charles Edge
1833	Hanley Market Sq	Manchester & Liverpool District Bank	T.W. Atkinson
1833	Kirkcaldy High St	Bank of Scotland	William Burn
1833	Stirling King St	Bank of Scotland	William Burn
1834	Manchester Spring Gardens	Manchester & Liverpool District Bank	T.W. Atkinson
1834	Stroud High St	Gloucestershire Joint-Stock Bank	
1834–5	Kendal Highgate	Bank of Westmorland	George Webster
1835	Peterhead Broad St	North of Scotland Bank	Archibald Simpson
1836	Aberdeen King St	Commercial Bank of Scotland	J.G. Graham
1836	Birmingham Union St	Birmingham & Midland Bank	Charles Edge
1836	Burslem Market Place	Commercial Bank of England	
1836	Leeds	Yorkshire District Bank	John Clark
1836	London 1 Lombard St	Smith, Payne & Smith's Bank	

[5]Later used by Bank of England.

Date	Location	Bank	Architect(s)
1836	Newcastle Mosley St	Northumberland and Durham District Bank	Richard Grainger
1837	Banff Low St	North of Scotland Bank	Archibald Simpson
1837	Greenock	Bank of Scotland	William Burn
1837	York Parliament St	City & County Bank	Robinson & Andrews
1837–8	Birmingham	Lichfield & Tamworth Bank	Bateman & Drury
1837–8	Liverpool Dale St	Royal Bank	Samuel Rowland
1837–8	London Lothbury	London & Westminster Bank	C.R. Cockerell & W. Tite
1837–8	Manchester Mosley St	Manchester & Salford Bank	R. Tattersall
1837–8	Newcastle Grey St	Bank of England	? Richard Grainger
1837–8	Norwich Old Haymarket	East of England Bank	
1837–8	Sheffield Church St	Sheffield & Hallamshire Bank	Samuel Worth
1837–9	Derby	Derby & Derbyshire Bank[6]	Robert Wallace
1837–9	Gloucester	Gloucestershire Banking Co.	S.W. Daukes
1838	Glasgow Virginia St	Glasgow Union Bank[7]	
1838	London 62 Lombard St	Barnett, Hoares's Bank	Samuel Kempthorne
1838	Whitehaven Queen St	Whitehaven Joint-Stock Bank	
1838–9	London Strand	Coutts' Bank†	Thomas Hopper
1838–9	Reading King St	Simonds's Bank	H. & N. Briant
1838–41	Liverpool Brunswick St	Liverpool Union Bank	John Cunningham
1839	Montrose	Bank of Scotland	William Burn
1839	Portsmouth	Bank of England	C.R. Cockerell

[6]Part of development of athenaeum, hotel, post office, etc.
[7]Occupied almost immediately by City of Glasgow Bank.

Date	Location	Bank	Architect(s)
1839–40	Leicester Granby St	Leicestershire Bank	
c. 1840	Birmingham Bennett's Hill	National Provincial Bank	Charles Edge
1840	Glasgow Miller St	Western Bank[8]	David Hamilton
1840	Glasgow Queen St	Clydesdale Bank	David Hamilton
1840	London Argyle Place	Union Bank of London	W.H. Newnham & G.B. Webb
1840	Rochdale	Manchester & Liverpool District Bank	Harrison of Rochdale
1840–1	Glasgow Queen St	British Linen Bank	David Hamilton
1840–1	Liverpool Derby Sq	North & South Wales Bank	Edward Corbett
1840–1	Whitby	Yorkshire Agricultural & Commercial Bank	J.B. & W. Atkinson
1840–1	York High Ousegate	Yorkshire Agricultural & Commercial Bank	J.B. & W. Atkinson
1840–2	Aberdeen Castle St	North of Scotland Bank	Archibald Simpson
1840–2	Glasgow Ingram St	Glasgow & Ship Bank[9]	David Hamilton
1841	Northampton Drapery	Northamptonshire Union Bank	E.F. Law
1842	Dundee Reform St	Bank of Scotland	William Burn
1842–4	Plymouth Courtney St	Bank of England	C.R. Cockerell
1843–4	Gloucester Westgate Rd	National Provincial Bank	S.W. Daukes
1844–7	Bristol Broad St	Bank of England	C.R. Cockerell
1844–7	Edinburgh George St	Commercial Bank	David Rhind
1844–7	Manchester King St	Bank of England	C.R. Cockerell
1846	Belfast	Belfast Banking Company	Charles Lanyon
1846	Lerwick	Union Bank of Scotland	Archibald Simpson

[8]Enlarged by Burn & Bryce, 1845.
[9]Occupied by Union Bank of Scotland from 1843.

Date	Location	Bank	Architect(s)
1846–7	Liverpool Castle St	Liverpool Commercial Bank	John Cunningham
1846–8	Liverpool Castle St	Bank of England	C.R. Cockerell
1846–51	Edinburgh	British Linen Bank	W. Burn & D. Bryce
c. 1847	London Lombard St	Overend, Gurney's Bank	G. Briand
1847	Warrington Sankey St	Manchester & Liverpool District Bank	Edward Walters
1848–9	Glasgow Queen St	National Bank of Scotland	John Gibson
1848–9	Manchester St Ann's Sq	Heywood's Bank	J.E. Gregan
1850	Darlington High Row	National Provincial Bank	John Middleton
1850	Northampton By Corn Exchange	Northamptonshire Banking Company	E.F. Law
1851	Edinburgh St Andrew Sq	British Linen Bank	W. Burn & D. Bryce
c. 1851	Norwich Bank Plain	Gurney's Bank	Anthony Salvin
1851–4	Bristol Corn St	Stuckey's Banking Company	R.S. Pope
c. 1853	London Holborn	London & Westminster Bank	Henry Baker
c. 1854	Yarmouth, Gt	Gurney's Bank	Anthony Salvin
1854–5	London Threadneedle St	Bank of Australasia	P.C. Hardwick
1854–7	Bristol Corn St	West of England & South Wales District Bank	W.B. Gingell & T.R. Lysaght
1856	Hull Whitefriargate	Bank of England	P.C. Hardwick
1856	London Threadneedle St	City Bank	W. & A. Moseley
1856	Preston Fishergate	Preston Banking Company	J.H. Park
1856–7	Glasgow Gordon St	Commercial Bank of Scotland	David Rhind
c. 1857	London Leicester Sq	Seale, Low's Bank	John Billing
c. 1857	London Lothbury	Jones, Loyd's Bank	P.C. Hardwick

Date	Location	Bank	Architect(s)
c. 1857	London Temple Bar	Union Bank of London	G. Aitchison
1857	St Columb Major (Cornwall)	St Columb Bank	William White
1857–8	Bradford Kirkgate	Bradford Banking Company	Andrews & Delauney
1857–8	Preston Fishergate	Lancaster Banking Company	J.H. Park
1858	Aberdare	West of England & South District Bank	W.B. Gingell
1858	Wells High St	Stuckey's Banking Company	
1858–9	Nottingham Carlton St	Wright's Bank	C.H. Edwards
1858–9	Belfast Waring St	Ulster Banking Company	James Hamilton
1859	Kings Lynn St James's St	Savings Bank	Medland & Maberley
1860	Louth Eastgate	Savings Bank	James Fowler
1860–1	London 73 Cornhill	London, Scottish & Australian Bank	Henry Baker
1860–2	Manchester Mosley St	Manchester & Salford Bank	Edward Walters
1860–2	Newcastle-upon-Tyne Grainger St	Savings Bank	J.E. Watson
1860–2	Sheffield Norfolk St	Savings Bank	T.J. Flockton
1861–2	London Lombard St	London & County Bank	C.O. Parnell
1861–4	London Lombard St	Robarts, Lubbock's Bank	P.C. Hardwick
c. 1862	Worcester The Cross	City & County Bank	E.W. Elmslie
1862–5	Leeds South Parade	Bank of England	P.C. Hardwick
1863	Leeds Park Row	Leeds & County Bank	Lockwood & Mawson
1863–7	Leeds Park Row	Beckett's Bank	Sir G.G. Scott
1864	Bristol Corn St	National Provincial Bank	W.B. Gingell

Date	Location	Bank	Architect(s)
1864	London Lombard St	Barclay & Bevan's Bank	P.C. Hardwick
1864–5	London Bishopsgate	National Provincial Bank	John Gibson
1864–5	London Lombard St	Alexander & Cunliffe's Bank	Alfred Waterhouse
1864–6	Nantwich	Manchester & Liverpool District Bank	Alfred Waterhouse
1864–6	Tamworth	National Provincial Bank	John Gibson
1864–7	Huddersfield Westgate	Halifax & Huddersfield Union Bank	Paull & Ayliffe
1865–6	Birmingham Temple Row	Birmingham Joint-Stock Bank	J.A. Chatwin
1865–6	London Chancery Lane	Union Bank of London	F.W. Porter
1865–6	Norwich	Harvey's & Hudson's Bank[10]	P.C. Hardwick
1865–8	London opp. Mansion Ho.	Union Bank of London	P.C. Hardwick
1865–9	Glasgow George Sq	Bank of Scotland	J.T. Rochead
1866	Darlington High Row	Backhouse's Bank	Alfred Waterhouse
1866	Leighton Buzzard Market Sq	Bassett's Bank	Alfred Waterhouse
1866	Oxford High St	London & Westminster Bank	F. & H. Francis
1866	Southampton High St	Hampshire Banking Company	R. Critchlow
1866–7	Cambridge Trumpington St	London & County Bank	F. & H. Francis
1866–7	Sheffield Church St	Williams Deacon's Bank	Flockton & Abbott
1866–8	Farnham Castle St	Knight's Bank	Norman Shaw
1867	Bradford Cheapside/Market Sq	Bradford Old Bank	Alfred Waterhouse
1867	Southampton High St	National Provincial Bank	John Gibson
1867	Stafford	District Bank	Robert Griffiths

[10]Later the main Post Office and now H.Q. of Anglia TV.

Date	Location	Bank	Architect(s)
1867–8	Bradford Bank St	Bradford Commercial Bank	Andrew, Son & Pepper
1867–8	Bury, Lancs.	Bury Banking Company	Blackwell, Son & Booth
1867–9	Birmingham New St	Birmingham & Midland Bank	Edward Holmes
1868–9	Birmingham Ann St	Birmingham Town & District Bank	Yeoville Thomason
1868–70	Manchester Chancery Lane	Brooks's Bank	George Truefitt
1869	Birmingham Bennett's Hill	National Provincial Bank	John Gibson (studio of)
1869	Kidderminster High St	Worcester City & County Bank	H. & E.A. Day
1869	Leicester 1 Granby St	National Provincial Bank	Millican & Smith
1869	Salisbury Market Sq	Wilts & Dorset Bank[11]	Henry Hall
1869–70	Birmingham Ann St	Lloyds Bank	J.A. Chatwin
c. 1870	Altrincham	Brooks's Bank	George Truefitt
c. 1870	Blackburn Darwen St	Brooks's Bank	? George Truefitt
1870	Leicester Granby St	Leicestershire Bank	Joseph Goddard
1870–1	Manchester Dean St/Mosley St	National Provincial Bank	John Gibson
1870–2	London Charing Cross	Union Bank of London	F.W. Porter
1870–3	Glasgow St Vincent Place	Clydesdale Bank	John Burnet
1871	Bishop Auckland Market Place	Backhouse's Bank	G.G. Hoskins
1871	Burslem Market Place	Manchester & Liverpool District Bank	Barker & Ellis
1871	Huddersfield	Yorkshire Banking Company	William Cocking
1871	London Throgmorton St	Imperial Ottoman Bank	William Burnet
1872	Manchester Booth St	Savings Bank	E. Salomons

[11]Greatly extended 1882.

Date	Location	Bank	Architect(s)
1872	Newcastle-upon-Tyne Mosley St	National Provincial Bank	John Gibson
1873	Jersey St Helier	Jersey Banking Company	John Hayward
1873	London 212 Piccadilly	National Provincial Bank	John Gibson
1873–4	Nottingham Victoria St	Nottingham Joint-Stock Bank	Evans & Jolley
1873–6	Birmingham New St	Birmingham Joint-Stock Bank	F.B. Osborn
1874	Carlisle English St	Carlisle & Cumberland Banking Company	Crosby & Hetherington
1874	Hanley	National Provincial Bank	John Gibson
1874	London Charing Cross	Cocks Biddulph's Bank	Richard Coad
1874	London Temple Bar	London & Westminster Bank†	Edward Barry
1874	Middlesbrough	National Provincial Bank	John Gibson
1875	London Ludgate Hill	City Bank	John Tarring & Sons
1875	Portsmouth Portsea	National Provincial Bank	John Gibson
1875–7	Exeter	City Bank	John Gibson
1876	London West Smithfield	Lacy, Son & Hartland's Bank	Robert Walker
1876	Norwich Gentleman's Walk	Lacon's Bank	W.O. Chambers
1876–7	Stockton-on-Tees	National Provincial Bank	John Gibson
1876–7	Wakefield	Wakefield & Barnsley Union Banking Company	Lockwood & Mawson
1877	London Bishopsgate	Royal Bank of Scotland	T.C. Clarke
1877–9	London Charing Cross	Drummond's Bank	P.C. Hardwick
1878	Dorchester	Eliot, Pearce & Eliot's Bank	G.R. Crickmay
1878	Saffron Walden	Gibson's Bank	W.E. Nesfield
1878	Salisbury Market Place	Pinckney's Bank	Henry Hall
1878–9	Carlisle Bank St	Clydesdale Bank	Hetherington & Oliver

Date	Location	Bank	Architect(s)
1878–9	London Temple Bar	Child's Bank	John Gibson
1878–9	Wellingborough	Northamptonshire Banking Company	Edward Sharman
1878–9	Wellingborough	Northamptonshire Union Bank	Edward Sharman
1878–80	Bristol Corn St	London & South Western Bank	J. Weir
1878–80	Manchester King St	Manchester & County Bank	Mills & Murgatroyd
1879	Colchester	Round, Green's Bank	E.C. Lee
1879	Halifax Silver St	Halifax Commercial Bank	W. & R. Mawson
1879	Sunderland	National Provincial Bank	John Gibson
1879	Wakefield Westgate	Wakefield & Barnsley Bank	W. & R. Mawson
1880	Birmingham Ann St (Colmore Row)	Worcester City & County Bank	Osborn & Reading
1880	Bristol Corn St	Wilts & Dorset Bank	G. Silley
1880	Derby Irongate	Crompton & Evans's Union Bank	J.A. Chatwin
1880	Southport Lord St	Southport & West Lancashire Bank	Mellor & Sutton
1880–1	London 8 Bishopsgate	Baring's Bank†	R. Norman Shaw
1881	Blackpool	Manchester & County Bank	Mills & Murgatroyd
1881	Dundee	Clydesdale Bank	Spence & Son
1882	Leek	Manchester & Liverpool District Bank	W. Sugden & Son
1882–4	Hull George St	Savings Bank	R. Clamp
c. 1883	Lincoln Stonebow	National Provincial Bank	John Gibson
1883	Stratford-upon-Avon Chapel St	Birmingham Banking Company	Harris, Martin & Harris
1883–4	Bristol Clare St	Capital & Counties Bank	F. Mew
1883–4	Weymouth Bond St	Stuckey's Bank	Paull & Bonella

Date	Location	Bank	Architect(s)
1884–7	London Lombard St	Lloyds, Barnetts & Bosanquet's Bank	J.A. Chatwin
1885	London West Smithfield	Hill & Sons' Bank	Scott & Cawthorn
c. 1886	Birmingham Temple Row	Staffordshire Bank	W. Doubleday
1886	London Kensington Court	London & County Bank	Alfred Williams
1886–8	Halifax Waterhouse St	Yorkshire Penny Bank	Perkin & Bulmer
1886–8	London Temple Bar	Bank of England	Arthur Blomfield
1886–8	Sheffield	Yorkshire Penny Black	Perkin & Bulmer
1887	Canterbury High St	Hammond's Bank	J.G. Hall
1887–8	London Fenchurch St	London & South Western Bank	J.S. Edmeston
1882	Retford	Beckett's Bank	Chorley & Connon
1888–9	Manchester King St	Lancashire & Yorkshire Bank	Heathcote & Rawle
1888–9	Southport Lord St	Preston Bank	E.W. Johnson
1889	Aberdeen Union St	Commercial Bank of Scotland	Sydney Mitchell
1889	London Lombard St	Commercial Bank of Scotland	J. Macvicar Anderson
1889	London Pall Mall	London Joint-Stock Bank	R.C. Harrison
1889	Preston	Preston Union Bank	Garlick & Sykes
1889–90	Ipswich Cornhill	Bacon, Cobbold & Tollemache's Bank	T.W. Cotman
1890	Llanelli	South Wales Union Bank	J.B. Wilson & G. Moxham
1890–1	Hull Lowgate	York Union Bank	Smith & Brodrick
1890–2	Leeds Kirkgate	London & Midland Bank	William Bakewell
1890–2	Leeds Park Row	York City & County Bank	Smith & Tweedale
1891	London Ludgate Hill	City Bank	T.E. Collcutt

Date	Location	Bank	Architect(s)
1891	Manchester York St	National Provincial Bank	A. Waterhouse & C.R. Gribble
1891	Newcastle-upon-Tyne Collingwood St	Hodgkin, Barnett, Pease & Spence's Bank	R.J. Johnson
1891	Wigan	Parr's Bank	William Owen
1891–2	Bradford	Yorkshire Penny Bank	James Ledingham
1891–2	Oldham	Oldham Joint-Stock Bank	Thomas Taylor
1891–3	Cambridge Sidney St	Foster's Bank	A. & P. Waterhouse
1892	Liverpool Castle St	Adelphi Bank	W.D. Caröe
1892	London 50 Cornhill	Prescott, Dimsdale, Tugwell & Cave's Bank	H.C. Boyes
1892	Newport (Gwent) High St	National Provincial Bank	C.R. Gribble
1892	Southport Lord St	Parr's Bank	William Owen
1892–4	Leeds Infirmary St	Yorkshire Penny Bank	Perkin & Bulmer
1893	Bradford Market St	London & Midland Bank	James Ledingham
1893	Felixstowe	Bacon, Cobbold & Tollemache's Bank	T.W. Cotman
1893	London Pall Mall	Williams Deacon and Manchester & Salford Bank	W.W. Gwyther
1893	London Piccadilly	National Provincial Bank	A. & P. Waterhouse
1893	London 39 Threadneedle St	Capital & Counties Bank	Kidner & Berry
1893	Oxford	Metropolitan, Birmingham & South Wales Bank	H.G.W. Drinkwater
1894	Glasgow Ingram St	Savings Bank	J.J. Burnet
1894	Neath	London & Provincial Bank	W. Wilson & G. Moxham
1894–5	Coventry High St	London & Midland Bank	F.B. Osborn
1894–5	Southport	Bank of Bolton	Bradshaw & Gass
1895	Bolton	Bank of Bolton	Bradshaw & Gass
1895	Sheffield	London & Midland Bank	Holmes & Watson

Date	Location	Bank	Architect(s)
1895–6	London Chancery Lane	Birkbeck Bank	T.E. Knightley
1895–8	Halifax Commercial St	Halifax & Huddersfield Union Bank	Horsfall & Williams
1896	Brighton	Brighton Union Bank	Arthur Keen
1896	Doncaster	York City & County Bank	Demaine & Brierley
1896	Hexham	London & Midland Bank	G.D. Oliver
1896	London Bishopsgate	Bank of Scotland	W.W. Gwyther
1896	Wimbledon	London & County Bank	Cheston & Perkin
1896–8	Bromley, Kent	Martin's Bank	Ernest Newton
1896–8	Leeds Park Row	W. Williams Brown's Bank	A. & P. Waterhouse
1897	Hull Silver St	Pease's Bank	W.W. Gwyther
1898	Gloucester Eastgate St	Lloyds Bank	Waller & Son
1898–9	London Fleet St	Gosling's Bank	A.C. Blomfield
1898–9	Stratford-on-Avon Bridge St	Lloyds Bank	J.A. Chatwin
1899	Leeds City Square	Yorkshire Banking Co.	W.W. Gwyther
1899–1900	Bedworth	Leicestershire Bank	H.L. Goddard
1899–1900	Birmingham Edgbaston	Birmingham District & Counties Bank	Bateman & Bateman
1899–1901	Liverpool Castle St	Parr's Bank	R. Norman Shaw and Willink & Thicknesse
1899–1901	Norwich Red Lion St	Savings Bank	G.J. & F.W. Skipper
1899–1902	Douglas Athol St	Isle of Man Banking Company	A. Marshall Mackenzie
1900	Cheltenham	Lloyds Bank	Waller & Son
1900	Liverpool Aintree	Bank of Liverpool	Willink & Thicknesse
1901	Birkenhead Charing Cross	Bank of Liverpool	Douglas & Minshull
1901	Manchester West Didsbury	Mercantile Bank of Lancashire	J. Swarbrick
1901	Petworth	London & County Bank	Frederick Wheeler

Date	Location	Bank	Architect(s)
1901–2	Leicester St Martin's	Pare's Bank	Everard & Pick
1902	Kilmarnock	National Bank of Scotland	T.P. Marwick
1902	Leeds Park Row	West Riding Union Bank	Oliver & Dodgshun
1902–3	Manchester York St	Parr's Bank	Charles Heathcote & Sons
1902–3	Sunderland	York City & County Bank	W.H. Brierley
1903	London Threadneedle St	British Linen Co.	J. Macvicar Anderson
1904	Darlington High Row	North Eastern Bank	Clark & Moscrop
1904	Kettering	London, City & Midland Bank	Gotch & Saunders
1904	London Lothbury	London & Provincial Bank	A. Blomfield
1904	London Strand	Coutts & Co.	J. Macvicar Anderson
1904	York Parliament St	Barclays Bank	Edmund Kirby
1904–5	Gravesend	Capital & Counties Bank	George E. Clay
1905	Chelmsford	Barclays Bank	A.C. Blomfield
1905	Maidstone	London & Provincial Bank	G.E. Bond
1905	Sheffield	York City & County Bank	W.H. Brierley
1906	Dover	Lloyds Bank	F.W. Waller
1906	Worcester	National Provincial Bank	Charles Heathcote & Sons
1907	London Lombard St	London & County Bank	W. Campbell Jones
1907	London Nicholas Lane	National Bank of Scotland	J. Macvicar Anderson
1907	Ludlow	North & South Wales Bank	Woolfall & Eccles
1908	Taunton Market Place	Stuckey's Bank	Oatley & Lawrence
1908–9	Birmingham Edgbaston	Lloyds Bank	P.B. Chatwin
1909	London Bishopsgate	Chartered Bank of India, Australia & China	Gordon & Gunton

Date	Location	Bank	Architect(s)
1909	London Chelsea	London & County Bank	R. Blomfield
1909	Manchester Brown St	Palatine Bank	Briggs, Wolstenholme & Thorneley
1910	Glasgow	National Bank of Scotland	A.N. Paterson
1911	Birkenhead Laird St	North & South Wales Bank	Edmund Kirby
1911	London Gracechurch St	London & South Western Bank	Edward Gabriel
1911	Norwich	London & Provincial Bank	G.J. Skipper
1911–4	London St James's St	Lloyds Bank	Waller & Son
1912–5	Manchester King St	Lloyds Bank	Charles Heathcote & Sons
1914	Guildford	Barclays Bank	Arthur Blomfield
1914	London Gracechurch St	Hong Kong & Shanghai Bank	W. Campbell Jones
1915	Luton	Barclays Bank	Arthur Blomfield
1915	Wolverhampton	Metropolitan Bank	Cossins, Peacock & Bewlay
1918–21	London Pall Mall East	Barclays Bank	Arthur Blomfield
1920	Liverpool Water St	Bank of British West Africa	Briggs & Thorneley
1921–2	London Pall Mall	Cox's Bank	E. Keynes Purchase & Durward Brown
1921–3	Liverpool James St	National Bank	T. Arnold Ashworth
1922–5	London Piccadilly	Midland Bank	Sir Edwin Lutyens and Whinney, Son & Austen Hall
c. 1923	Southport	Manchester & Liverpool District Bank	F. Jones & H.A. Dalrymple
c. 1923	Stockport	Manchester & Liverpool District Bank	F. Jones & H. A. Dalrymple
1923–5	London Threadneedle St	Westminster Bank[12]	Mewès & Davis
1923–31	London Threadneedle St	Bank of England[13]	Sir Herbert Baker & A.T. Scott
c. 1924	London Leadenhall St	Schroder's Bank	Messrs Joseph

[12]Much enlarged 1930.
[13]Further reconstruction till 1942.

Date	Location	Bank	Architect(s)
1924–30	London Poultry	Midland Bank[14]	Sir Edwin Lutyens & Gotch & Saunders
1925	London Cornhill	District Bank	Francis Jones
1925	Ludlow	National Provincial Bank	Holden & Palmer
1925	Ware	Westminster Bank	Septimus Warwick
1925–30	London Lothbury	Westminster Bank	Mewès & Davis
1926	Chelmsford	National Provincial Bank	Palmer & Holden
1926	London Bishopsgate	Hambro's Bank	Niven & Wigglesworth
1926	London Gt. Winchester St	Morgan, Grenfell's Bank	Mewès & Davis
1926	London Old Broad St	Lazard's Bank	A.V. Heal
1926	London Pall Mall	Midland Bank	T.B. Whinney
1926	London Tokenhouse Yard	Bank of London & South America	Messrs Joseph
1926–8	Glasgow St Vincent St	Union Bank of Scotland	James Miller
1926–8	London Piccadilly	Westminster Bank	W. Curtis Green
1926–30	London Lombard St	Lloyds Bank	Sir John Burnet & Partners and Campbell Jones Sons & Smithers
c. 1927	Glasgow Renfield St	Bank of Scotland	Andrew Balfour & Stewart
1927	London Muswell Hill	Lloyds Bank	Edward Maufe
1927	London Piccadilly	Barclays Bank	W. Curtis Green
1927	Richmond	Lloyds Bank	Horace Field
1927–8	Manchester Piccadilly	Manchester & County Bank	Mills & Murgatroyd
1927–32	Liverpool Water St	Bank of Liverpool & Martin's Bank	H.J. Rowse
1928	Caversham	Lloyds Bank	H. Chalton Bradshaw
1928	Coventry Hertford St	Westminster Bank	E. Guy Dawber

[14]Extension to Princes St built 1930–9.

Date	Location	Bank	Architect(s)
1928	London Edgware	National Provincial Bank	Palmer & Holden
1928	London Southwark	Lloyds Bank	P.D. Hepworth
1928	Maidstone	Martin's Bank	Braddell & Deane
1929	Birmingham Moseley	Barclays Bank	Peacock & Bewlay
1929–31	Coventry High St	National Provincial Bank	F.C.R. Palmer
1929–31	London Leadenhall St	Midland Bank	Sir Edwin Lutyens and Whinney, Son & Austen Hall
1930	Staines	Lloyds Bank	S. Rowland Pierce
1930–2	London Lombard St	Glyn Mills, and Martin's Banks	Sir Herbert Baker & A.T. Scott
1930–2	London Poultry/Princes St	National Provincial Bank	Sir Edwin Cooper
1931	Glasgow Sauchiehall St	Bank of Scotland	Keppie & Henderson
1931	Orpington	Lloyds Bank	Edwin Williams
1931	Teddington	Lloyds Bank	A. Randall Wells
1931	Welwyn Garden City	Lloyds Bank	Marshall Sissons
1931–3	Birmingham Civic Centre	Municipal Bank	T. Cecil Howitt
1932	Liverpool Church St	Lloyds Bank	H.J. Rowse
1933	Horley	Barclays Bank	Mitchell & Bridgwater
1933–5	Mancheter King St	Midland Bank	Sir Edwin Lutyens and Whinney, Son & Austen Hall
1936	Edinburgh George St	National Bank of Scotland	T.P. Marwick & Son
1936	Osterley	National Provincial Bank	W.F.C. Holden
1937	Derby Market Place	Martin's Bank	Bromley, Cartwright & Waumsley
1938–42	Edinburgh St Andrew Sq	National Bank of Scotland	A.J. Davis and L. Grahame-Thomson
1939–40	Edinburgh Hanover St	Savings Bank	William Patterson and T. Cecil Howitt
1953	Exeter Bedford St	Devon & Exeter Savings Bank	R.M. Challice & Sons

Date	Location	Bank	Architect(s)
1953	Exeter High St	Lloyds Bank	Charles E. Ware & Son
1953–5	Portsmouth Commercial Rd	Lloyds Bank	Sir John Burnet, Tait & Partners
1953–7	London Queen Victoria St	Bank of London & South America	Victor Heal
1955–60	London Old Broad St	Barclays Bank D.C.O.	Ley, Colbeck & Partners
1956	Canterbury St George's St	National Provincial Bank	B.C. Sherren
1956	Cardiff Queen St	Barclays Bank	W. Curtis Green, Son & Lloyd
1958–60	Plymouth St Andrew's Cross	National Provincial Bank	B.C. Sherren
1958–62	London Gracechurch St	Midland Bank Overseas Branch	Whinney, Son & Austen Hall
1959	Winchester Jewry St	Barclays Bank	W. Curtis Green, Son & Lloyd
1959–71	London Lombard Street	Barclays Bank	Sir Herbert Baker, A.T. Scott, and V. Helbing
1961–7	Birmingham Colmore Row	Lloyds Bank	Sir Howard Robertson
1962–6	Manchester York St	Barclays Bank	Green, Lloyd & Son
1963	Bristol Wine St	Bank of England	Sir Howard Robertson
1963–5	London St Swithin's Lane	Rothschild's Bank	Fitzroy Robinson Partnership
1963–5	Manchester Mosley St	Williams Deacon's Bank	Harry S. Fairhurst & Son
1964–6	Leeds Park Row	Westminster Bank	Green, Lloyd & Son
1964–8	London Gracechurch St	Guinness Mahon's Bank	R. Seifert & Partners
1965–7	London Upper Thames St	Barclays Bank Foreign Exchange Centre	Campbell Jones & Sons
1965–70	Manchester King St	District Bank[15]	Casson, Conder & Partners
1967	Shrewsbury Pride Hill	Lloyds Bank	Percy Thomas Partnership

[15] Completed for National Westminster Bank.

Date	Location	Bank	Architect(s)
1967–9	Birmingham Colmore Row	Westminster Bank	Madin Group
1968	Lowestoft London Rd	Barclays Bank	Taylor & Green
1968–70	Birmingham Temple Row	Bank of England	Fitzroy Robinson Partnership
1968–70	Huddersfield Cloth Hall St	Midland Bank	P. Womersley, and Kitson & Partners
1968–70	Leeds Park Row	National Provincial Bank	Boreham F., Son & Wallace
1969–71	Leeds King St	Bank of England	Building Design Partnership
1969–71	Manchester Faulkner St	Bank of England	Fitzroy Robinson Partnership
1969–71	Newcastle-upon-Tyne Pilgrim St	Bank of England	Fitzroy Robinson Partnership
1970–6	London Bishopsgate	Hongkong & Shanghai Banking Group	Ley, Colbeck & Partners and R. Seifert & Partners
1970–81	London Old Broad St	National Westminster Bank Tower	R. Seifert & Partners
1971–6	Belfast Donegall Sq	Northern Bank	Building Design Partnership
1972–6	Poole Wimborne Rd	Barclays House	Wilson, Mason & Partners
1973–6	Leeds Park Row	Lloyds Bank	Abbey and Hanson Rowe & Partners
1974–6	London Queen Victoria St	Credit Lyonnais	Whinney Mackay–Lewis Partnership
1974–8	London Strand	Coutts' Bank	Frederick Gibberd & Partners
1975	Kilmarnock John Finnie St	Royal Bank of Scotland	Henry Dawes & Sons
1975–80	Glasgow Buchanan St	Clydesdale Bank	G.D. Lodge & Partners
1976–9	London King William St	Banque Nationale de Paris	Fitzroy Robinson Partnership
1976–81	London Bishopsgate	Baring's Bank, and Banque Belge	GMW Partnership
1977–80	Leeds Merrion Way	Yorkshire Bank	Abbey and Hanson Rowe & Partners

Date	Location	Bank	Architect(s)
1978–81	Edinburgh Fettes Row	Royal Bank of Scotland, Admin. and Computer Centre	Michael Laird & Partners
1979	Banbury Bridge St	National Westminster Bank	IDC Group
1982–6	London Bishopsgate	Standard Chartered Bank	Fitzroy Robinson Partnership
1984	Glasgow Sauchiehall St	National Bank of Pakistan	Elder & Cannon
1987–90	London King William St	Westpac Banking Corporation	Thomas Saunders Partnership
1988–91	Bristol Canons Marsh	Lloyds Bank	Arup Associates

Bibliography

1. Primary Sources: Documentary

(a) *Bank of England and Commercial Banks*
Records of the Bank of England (access via the bank's historian).
    In particular: 'Court' Books and Ancillary Papers.

Records of the clearing banks and their defunct constituent banks (access via archivist to each clearing bank).
    In particular: board minute books; premises (building) committee minute books; letter books (files); photographs, drawings, etc.

Note: (1) Every modern edition of the *Bankers' Almanac and Yearbook* carries an appendix tracing the closure or descent of every British bank from the earliest days of private banking.
(2) The archives of all British commercial banks, defunct or otherwise, are summarised in L.S. Pressnell & J. Orbell, *An Historical Guide to the Records of British Banking* (Aldershot, 1985).

(b) *Savings Banks*
Records of defunct savings banks (access traditionally via local TSB manager, but see Note 3 below).
    In particular: trustees' minute books.

Records of National Debt Office (access via Public Record Office, Kew).
    In particular: Commissioners' minute books (ref: NDO/9).

Note: (1) An appendix to H.O. Horne, *A History of Savings Banks* (Oxford, 1947) traces the closure or descent of all nineteenth century savings banks.
(2) Records of some defunct savings banks have survived in local record offices (e.g. Gloucestershire R.O.; the Minet Library, Lambeth, etc.) and in the custody of the Big Four clearing banks.
(3) The policy of the TSB is to deposit records of defunct banks still in their own custody with local record offices, whose existing holdings will thereby be supplemented.

2. Primary Sources: Printed

(a) *Bank of England and Commercial Banks*
Acts of Parliament
    In particular: 7 Geo. IV, c. 46 (1826) and 3 & 4 Will. IV, c. 98 (1833), breaking monopoly of B. of E. in joint-stock banking.

334

Parliamentary Papers
In particular: *B.P.P.*, 1831–2 (vi), pp. 3–486, 'Report from the Committee of
Secrecy on the Bank of England Charter'; *B.P.P.*, 1833 (xxiii), pp. 315–25,
'Accounts of Places where Joint-Stock Banks are established' and 'Memorials of
Country Bankers to Government, 1828–33', *B.P.P.*, 1836 (ix–2), pp. 1–252
(411–669), 'Report from the Secret Committee on Joint-Stock Banks together
with the Minutes of Evidence'.

Deeds of Settlement of banking companies
Invariably published: certain clauses govern buildings. Most deeds are in the
British Library, catalogued under the bank's name.

Annual Reports of banking companies
Chairman's address to shareholders was published *in extenso* in *Bankers'
Magazine* until c. 1914; indexed in each vol. by name of bank, under general
heading 'Reports'.

(b) *Savings Banks*
Acts of Parliament
In particular: 57 Geo. III, c. 130 (1817), 5 Geo. IV, c. 62 (1824); 9 Geo. IV, c. 92
(1828); all regulating management and practice.

Parliamentary Papers
In particular: *B.P.P.*, 1837–8 (xxxvi), pp. 493–5; *B.P.P.*, 1844 (xxxii), pp. 801–4;
B.P.P., 1849 (xxx), pp. 403–25; all giving surplus fund statistics; *B.P.P.*, 1852
(xxviii), pp. 757–817 (of which one page is reproduced opposite page 95), the
basis for Appendix One to this book.

Newspapers
Bank trustees often caused to be published their annual accounts (with surplus
fund figures); sometimes, also, trustees issued public notices, invitations to
tender, etc.

Directories
Addresses can be useful to confirm deductions as to premises made from other
evidence. Descriptive preamble is also useful, but is more properly a secondary
source and can be unreliable.

Periodicals
Although secondary in the field of articles and descriptive reporting, periodicals
may also have primary status, for instance when publishing a letter, a verbatim
account of a meeting, or a ground plan. All periodicals are listed alphabetically
among the secondary sources which follow.

3. Secondary Sources

Acres, W. Marston, *The Bank of England from Within*, 2 vols (London, 1931).

'Aero', 'The Design of Banking Premises' in *Architects' Journal*, Vol. 53 (1921, Part 1),
pp. 233–76.

Anderson, R., *Examples of the Municipal, Commercial and Street Architecture of France and
Italy from the 12th to the 15th Century* (London, 1870–5).

Anderson, W.J. (Stratton, A., ed.), *The Architecture of the Renaissance in Italy (5th ed.,
London, 1927)*.

An Historical Catalogue of Engravings, Drawings and Paintings in the Bank of England
(London, 1928).

Annual Register (1758–   ).
Architect (1869–1980).
Architect & Building News (1926–71).
Architects' & Builders' Journal (1910–9).
Architects' Journal (1919–   ).
Architectural Magazine & Journal (1834–9).
Architectural Publication Society Dictionary, 8 vols (London, 1853–92).
Architectural Review (1896–   ).
Ashton, T.S., *An Economic History of England: the 18th Century* (London, 1966).
Audsley, G.A., *The Stranger's Handbook to Chester* . . . (Chester, 1891).
Avery Obituary Index of Architects (2nd ed., Boston, 1980).
Axon, W.E.A., *The Annals of Manchester* (Manchester & London, 1886).
Bailey, E.A., *A History of Southport* (Southport, 1955).
Baines, T., *History of the Commerce and Town of Liverpool* . . . (London and Liverpool, 1852), p. 470.
Banker (1926–   ).
'Bank Façades and their Influence' in *Builder*, Vol. 125 (1923, Part 2), p. 633.
Bankers' Almanac (1845–   ).
Bankers' Magazine (1844–1983).
Barnard, E., *One Hundred and Fifty Years. 1817–1967. The Somerset & Wilts Trustee Savings Bank* (Taunton, 1967).
Billson, C.J., *Leicester Memories* (Leicester, 1924).
Binney, M. 'Sir Robert Taylor's Bank of England' in *Country Life*, 13 Nov. 1969, pp. 1244–8.
Bland, E., *Annals of Southport* . . . (Southport, 1903).
Blyth, T.A., *History of Bedford* (London & Bedford, 1873).
Bolitho, H. and Peel, D., *The Drummonds of Charing Cross* (London, 1967).
Bolton, A.T., *The Architecture of Robert and James Adam*, 2 vols (London, 1922).
Booker, J., *The Face of Banking* (London, 1979).
British Parliamentary Papers.
Broster, J., *A Walk around the Walls and City of Chester* (Chester, 1821).
Brown, C., *The Annals of Newark-upon-Trent* . . . (London, 1879).
Builder (1843–1966).
Building News (1857–1926).
Burrough, T.H.B., *Bristol* (Studio Vista Series, London, 1970).
Butler, A.S.G., *The Architecture of Sir Edwin Lutyens*, 3 vols (London & New York, 1950).
Cave, C.H., *A History of Banking in Bristol* (Bristol, 1899).
A Century of Thrift. An Historical Sketch of the Stockport Savings Bank 1824–1924 (Stockport, 1925).
Chandler, G., *Four Centuries of Banking* [Martin's], 2 vols (London, 1964).
Checkland, S.G., *Scottish Banking. A History 1695–1973* (Glasgow & London, 1975).
Civil Engineer & Architects' Journal (1837–67).
Clapham, Sir J., *A Concise Economic History of Britain* (Cambridge, 1949).
Clapham, Sir J., *The Bank of England. A History*, 2 vols Cambridge, 1944).
Clark, K., *The Gothic Revival* (London, 1964).
Clarke, G.R., *The History & Description of* . . . *Ipswich* (Ipswich, 1830).
Clarke, P., *The First House in the City* (London, 1973).

Clarkson, H., *Memories of Merry Wakefield* (Wakefield, 1887).

Cole, D., *The Work of Sir Gilbert Scott* (London, 1980).

Coleridge, E.H., *The Life of Thomas Coutts Banker*, 2 vols (London, 1920).

Collins, P., *Changing Ideals in Modern Architecture* (London, 1964).

Colvin, H.M., *A Biographical Dictionary of British Architects 1600–1840* (London, 1978).

'Corner Sites and Banks' in *Architects' Journal*, Vol. 60 (1924, Part 2), pp. 485, 486.

Country Life (1897–   ).

Crick, W.F. and Wadsworth, I.E., *A Hundred Years of Joint Stock Banking* [Midland] (London, 1936).

Crook, J.M., *Victorian Architecture. A Visual Anthology* (London, 1971).

Crook, J.M., *The Greek Revival* (London, 1972).

Cunningham, P., *Hand-Book of London Past and Present* (London, 1850).

Curwen, J.F., *Kirkbie–Kendall* (Kendal, 1900).

Davis, S.N., *Banking in Boston* (Boston, 1976).

Dent, R.K., *Old and New Birmingham* (Birmingham, 1880).

Dictionary of National Biography.

Dixon, R. and Muthesius, S., *Victorian Architecture* (London, 1978).

Eastlake, C.L. (Crook, J.M., ed.), *A History of the Gothic Revival* (Leicester, 1970).

Easton, H.T., *The History of a Banking House* [Smith, Payne & Smith's] (London, 1903).

Esher, Lord, 'What's in a Façade' in *Bankers' Magazine*, Vol. 221 (1977), pp. 8–11.

Fisher, P.H., *Notes and Recollections of Stroud, Gloucestershire* (London & Stroud, 1871).

Fitzmaurice, R.M., *British Banks and Banking* (Truro, 1975).

Froom, F.J., *A Site in Poultry* (London, 1950).

Fulford, R., *Glyn's 1753–1953* (London, 1953).

Galty, A., *Sheffield Past and Present* (Sheffield & London, 1873).

Galvin, P., 'The Banks and their Properties' in *Banker*, Vol. 114 (1964), pp. 640–5.

Gentleman's Magazine (1731–1868).

Gilbart, J.W., *A Practical Treatise on Banking*, 2 vols (London, 1849).

Gilbart, J.W., *The History and Principles of Banking* (London, 1834).

Girouard, M., *Sweetness and Light. The 'Queen Anne' Movement 1860–1900* (Oxford, 1977).

Girouard, M., *The Victorian Country House* (2nd ed., New Haven & London, 1979).

'Glasguensis', *Banking in Glasgow During the Olden Times* (Glasgow, 1884).

Gomme, A., Jenner, K. and Little, B., *Bristol. An Architectural History* (London, 1979).

Goodhart-Rendel, H.S., *English Architecture since the Regency* (London, 1953).

Graves, A., *The Royal Academy of Arts. A Complete Dictionary of Contributors . . . 1769–1904*, 8 vols (London, 1905–6).

Green, E., *Buildings for Bankers* [Midland] (London, 1980).

Green, E., *Debtors to their Profession* (London, 1979).

Green, E., *The Making of a Modern Banking Group* [Midland] (London, 1979).

Gregory, T.E., *The Westminster Bank Through a Century*, 2 vols (London, 1936).

Grindon, L.H., *Manchester Banks and Bankers . . .* (Manchester & London, 1877).

Gunnis, R., *Directory of British Sculptors 1660–1851* (London, 1951).

Hall, I. and S., *Georgian Hull* (York, 1978–9).

Hardcastle, D., Jr, *Banks and Bankers* (2nd ed., London, 1843).

Hardwick, C., *History of the Borough of Preston . . .* (Preston, 1857).

Hargrove, W. and J., *The New Guide . . . [to] The City of York* (York, 1838).

Harrison, A., *West Midland Trustee Savings Bank 1816–1966* (Shrewsbury, 1966).

Hebden, C. Donald, *The Trustee Savings Banks of Yorkshire & Lincoln* (1981).

Heginbotham, H., *Stockport Ancient and Modern*, 2 vols (London, 1892).

Hembrow, J., 'The Design and Planning of Banks' in *Builder*, Vol. 125 (1923, Part 2), pp. 653–5.

Hembrow, J., 'The Windowless Bank' in *Builder*, Vol. 133 (1927, Part 2), pp. 768–70.

Hickman, D., *Birmingham* (Studio Vista Series, London, 1970).

Hickman, D., *Warwickshire* (Shell Guide, 1979).

Hillen, H.J., *History of... King's Lynn*, 2 vols (Norwich, 1907).

Historical Catalogue of Engravings, Drawings and Paintings in the Bank of England (London, 1928).

Hitchcock, H.-R., *Early Victorian Architecture in Britain* (London & New Haven, 1954).

Hoare, C. & Co, *Hoare's Bank. A Record. 1673–1932* (London, 1932).

Holmes, A.R. and Green, E., *Midland. 150 Years of Banking Business* (London, 1986).

Horne, H.O., *A History of Savings Banks* (Oxford, 1947).

Horsburgh, E.L.S., *Bromley, Kent...* (London, 1929).

Howard, D., *The Architectural History of Venice* (London, 1980).

Hughes, J., *Liverpool Banks & Bankers 1760–1837* (Liverpool & London, 1906).

Hughes, J. Quentin, *Liverpool* (City Buildings Series, London, 1969).

Hughes, T., *The Stranger's Handbook to Chester...* (Chester, 1856).

Hughson, D., *Walks through London...* (London, 1817).

Hussey, C., 'Hoare's Bank, Fleet Street, E.C.4' in *Country Life*, 6 March 1958 pp. 450–3.

Illustrated London News (1842–   ).

James, J., *Continuations and Additions to the History of Bradford...* (London, 1866).

Jones, A.G.E., 'Early Banking in Ipswich' in *Notes and Queries*, Vol. 196, No. 19 (1951), p. 403.

Joslin, D.M. 'London Private Bankers, 1720–1785', in *Economic History Review* (Second Series, Vol. 7), pp. 167–86.

Journal of the House of Commons.

Journal of the Institute of Bankers (1879–   ).

Journal of the Royal Institute of British Architects, 3rd Series (1893–   ).

Keith, A., *The North of Scotland Bank Limited 1836–1936.*

Kirshner, J. (ed.), *Business, Banking, and Economic Thought in Late Medieval and Early Modern Europe. Selected Studies of Raymond de Roover* (Chicago & London, 1974).

Knight, C.B., *A History of the City of York* (2nd ed., York, 1944).

Knox, W.J., *Decades of the Ulster Bank 1836–1964* (Belfast, 1965).

Lane, F.C. and Mueller, R.C., *Money and Banking in Medieval and Renaissance Venice*, Vol. 1 (Baltimore & London, 1985).

Latimer, J., *The Annals of Bristol in the Nineteenth Century* (Bristol, 1887).

Lawson, W.J., *The History of Banking* (London, 1850).

Leader, R.E., *Sheffield in the Eighteenth Century* (Sheffield, 1901).

Leader, R.E., *Sheffield Savings Bank — A Century of Thrift 1819–1919* (Sheffield, 1920).

Leader, R.E., 'The Early Sheffield Banks' in *Journal of the Institute of Bankers*, Vol. 38 (1917), pp. 230–43.

Leighton-Boyce, J.A.S.L., *Smiths the Bankers 1658–1958* (London, 1958).

Lewins, W., *A History of Banks for Savings...* (London, 1866).

Linstrum, D., *West Yorkshire Architects and Architecture* (London, 1978).

Little, B., *Birmingham Buildings* . . . (Newton Abbot, 1971).

Liverpool Heritage Bureau, *Buildings of Liverpool* (Liverpool, 1978), p. 30.

Mace, A., *The Royal Institute of British Architects. A Guide to its Archives and History* (London, 1986).

Mackie, C., *Norfolk Annals, 1801–1900*, 2 vols (Norwich, 1901).

Macleod, H.D., *The Theory and Practice of Banking*, 2 vols (London, 1866).

Malcolm, C.A., *The Bank of Scotland 1695–1945* (Edinburgh, 1948).

Malcolm, C.A. *The History of the British Linen Bank* (Edinburgh, 1950).

Malton, T., *A Picturesque Tour through the Cities of London and Westminster* . . . (London, 1742).

Martin, J.B., *'The Grasshopper' in Lombard Street* (London, 1892).

Mathias, P., *The First Industrial Nation. An Economic History of Britain, 1700–1914* (London, 1969).

Matthews, P.W. and Tuke, A.W., *History of Barclays Bank Limited* (London, 1926).

'Modern Banks' in *Builder*, Vol. 136 (1929, Part 1), pp. 372, 373.

Monthly Magazine (1796–1843).

Munn, C.W., *The Scottish Provincial Banking Companies 1747–1864* (Edinburgh, 1981).

Murray, P., *The Architecture of the Italian Renaissance* (2nd ed., London, 1969).

Nevin, E. and Davis, E.W., *The London Clearing Banks* (London, 1970).

Newton, W.G., *The Work of Ernest Newton, R.A.* (London, 1925).

Nicholson, C., *The Annals of Kendal* (2nd ed., London & Kendal, 1861).

Nuttgens, P., *York* (Studio Vista Series, London, 1971).

Orbell, J., *Baring Brothers & Co. Limited. A History to 1939* (London, 1985).

Outline of the 150 Years History of the London T.S.B., 1816–1966 (London, 1966).

Pevsner, N., *A History of Building Types* (London, 1976).

Pevsner, N., *et al.* (eds), *Buildings of England* series; *Buildings of Scotland* series.

Phillips, M., *A History of Banks, Bankers & Banking in Northumberland, Durham, and North Yorkshire* (London, 1894).

Pratt, J.T., *The History of Savings Banks* . . . (London, 1830).

Pressnell, L.S., *Country Banking in the Industrial Revolution* (Oxford, 1956).

Pressnell, L.S. and Orbell, J., *A Guide to the Historical Records of British Banking* (Aldershot, 1985).

Preston Savings Bank, 1816–1907 (Preston, 1907).

Price, F.G. Hilton, *A Handbook of London Bankers* (London, 1890–1).

Price, F.G. Hilton, 'Some Account of Lombard Street . . .' in *Journal of the Institute of Bankers*, Vol. 7 (1886), pp. 321–54.

Pugin, A.C. and Britton, J., *Public Buildings of London* (2nd ed., London, 1838).

Punch (10 Sept. 1864).

Quarterly Review (1809–1967).

Rae, G., *The Country Banker* (London, 1885).

Rait, R.S., *The History of the Union Bank of Scotland* (Glasgow, 1930).

Reilly, C.H., *Some Liverpool Streets and Buildings in 1921* (Liverpool, 1921).

Reilly, C.H., *Some Manchester Streets and their Buildings* (Liverpool & London, 1924).

Richardson, A.E., *Monumental Classic Architecture* . . . (London, 1914).

Roth, H. Ling, *The Genesis of Banking in Halifax* . . . (Halifax, 1914).

Royal Academy Exhibitors 1905–1970, 6 vols (Wakefield, 1973–82).

Royal Bank of Scotland 1727–1977 (Edinburgh, 1977).

Ruskin, J., *The Seven Lamps of Architecture* (London, 1849).

Ruskin, J., *The Stones of Venice*, 3 vols (London, 1851–3).

Russell, Frank (ed.), *Art Nouveau Architecture* (London, 1979).

Ryton, J., *Banks and Banknotes of Exeter 1769–1906* (Exeter, 1984).

'S', *British Losses by Bank Failures 1820–57* (London, 1858).

Saint, A., *Richard Norman Shaw* (New Haven & London, 1976).

Sawyer, P., *et al.*, 'Planning the Modern Bank' in *Architecture* [New York], Vol. 43, No. 3 (1921), pp. 65–87.

Sayers, R.S., *Lloyds Bank in the History of English Banking* (Oxford, 1957).

Scantlin, H. Morton, *Pennies into Pounds. The Story of the Lambeth Savings Bank* (London, 1950).

Scott, G.G., *Remarks on Secular and Domestic Architecture* (London, 1857).

Service, A., *Edwardian Architecture* (London, 1977).

Service, A. (ed.), *Edwardian Architecture and its Origins* (London, 1975).

Shann, F.H., 'Current Architecture: Modern Bank Premises', in *Architectural Review*, Vol. 49 (1921, Part 1), pp. 43–5.

Sharp, D., *Manchester* (Studio Vista Series, London, 1969).

Shaw, W.A., *Manchester Old and New*, 3 vols (London, 1896).

Sheahan, J.J., *History of . . . Kingston-upon-Hull* (London, 1846).

Simpson, N., *The Belfast Bank 1827–1970* (Belfast, 1975).

Stamp, G. and Amery, C., *Victorian Buildings of London 1837–1887* (London, 1980).

Steele, H.R. and Yebury, F.R., *The Old Bank of England* (London, 1930).

Stokes, M.V., *A Bank in Four Centuries* [Coutts] (London, 1978).

Stroud, D., *George Dance Architect 1741–1825* (London, 1971).

Stroud, D., *The Architecture of Sir John Soane* (London, 1961).

Strype, J., *A Survey of the Cities of London and Westminster . . . written at first . . . by John Stow . . .* (London, 1720).

Summerson, Sir J., *Georgian London* (London, 1962).

Summerson, Sir J., *The Architecture of Victorian London* (Charlottesville, 1976).

Survey of London, 42 vols (London, 1900–86).

Tallis, J., *London Street Views . . .* (London, 1838–40).

Tate, G., *The History of Alnwick*, 2 vols (Alnwick, 1868/69).

Taylor, A., 'A Bank and its Building: Ulverston Trustee Savings Bank' in *Transactions of the Cumberland & Westmorland Antiquarian & Archaeological Society*, Vol. LXXIV, New Series (1974), pp. 147–58.

Taylor, N., *Monuments of Commerce* (RIBA Drawings Series, London, 1968).

Teggin, H., *et al.*, *Glasgow Revealed* (London, 1989).

Townsend, G.F., *The Town and Borough of Leominster* (Leominster, 1863).

Tuke, A.W., and Gillman, R.J.H., *Barclays Bank Limited 1926–1969* (London, 1972).

Twining, S.H., *Two Hundred and Twenty-Five Years in the Strand . . .* (London, 1931).

Verdier, A. and Cattois, F., *Architecture Civile et Domestique au Moyen Age et à la Renaissance*, 2 vols (Paris, 1858).

Walker, D., 'Era of Banks and Churches' in *Country Life*, 28 August 1969, pp. 502–4.

Ward, J., *The Borough of Stoke-upon-Trent* (London, 1843).

Ware, D., *A Short Dictionary of British Architects* (London, 1967).

Watkin, D., *The Life and Work of C.R. Cockerell* (London, 1974).

Weale, J., *The Pictorial Handbook of London . . .* (London, 1854).

Westall, W. and Moule, T., *Great Britain Illustrated* (1830).

Westminster Review (1824–1914).

Wheatley, H.B., *London Past and Present* (London, 1891).

Whittle, P.A., *Borough of Bolton* (Bolton, 1855).

Wilkes, L., *John Dobson. Architect & Landscape Gardener* (Stocksfield, 1980).

Wilkes, L. and Dodds, G., *Tyneside Classical* (London, 1964).

Wilson, J., 'Banks: A Current Account' in *Architects' Journal*, Vol. 156 (1972, Part 2), pp. 589–95.

Winton, J.R., *Lloyds Bank 1918–1969* (Oxford, 1982).

Withers, H., *National Provincial Bank 1833–1933* (London, 1933).

Woodcroft, B., *Alphabetical Index of Patentees of Inventions* (London, 1854).

Worsdell, F., *Victorian City* (Glasgow, 1982).

Ziegler, P. *The Sixth Great Power. Barings 1762–1929* (London, 1988).

Index